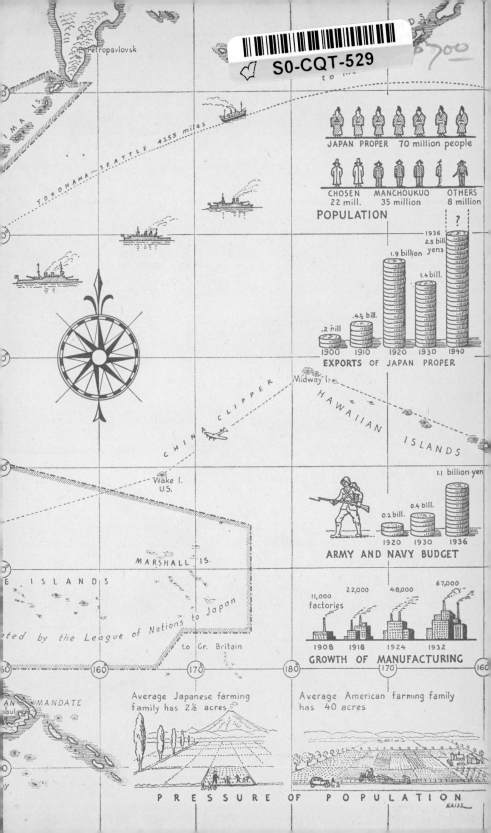

JAPAN OVER ASIA

Acme

EMPEROR HIROHITO

JAPAN OVER ASIA

BY

WILLIAM HENRY CHAMBERLIN

With Illustrations

REVISED AND ENLARGED EDITION

BOSTON
LITTLE, BROWN AND COMPANY
1939

GATHERING OYSTERS IN A JAPANESE OYSTER PARK

Prior to the spawning season, each oyster grower sets out an immense number of prepared bamboo stalks; these are thrust deeply into the soft bottom, and are arranged in definite lines or groups so as to intercept the floating spat. After remaining attached to the bamboo brush for one to two years, the oysters are planted on prepared bottoms, where growth and fattening are completed. The oysters are marketed when two to three years old.

PREFACE

THE original edition of *Japan over Asia* appeared shortly after the Japanese expansionist trend reached its climactic expression: the present war in China. War accelerates history. It compresses into years processes which might otherwise require decades for completion.

So there is an abundance of supplementary material for the book. Certain passages have also become outdated by the swift advance of events, although the original edition endeavored to set forth the fundamental causes of Japan's dynamic drive for Eastern empire.

I have followed two methods in revising the book. Anachronisms have been deleted and necessary links in bringing the narrative up to date have been inserted. One chapter has been dropped and three new ones have been added, dealing with the war, with the changes which war has brought about in Japan's internal political, economic, and social structure, and with Japan's chances of achieving its imperial dream.

The revised edition was prepared after the conclusion of four years of residence in Tokyo as Chief Far Eastern Correspondent of the *Christian Science Monitor*. During this period I visited China every year, my last and longest trip, early in 1939, taking me as far as Kunming, the capital of remote Yunnan Province. In the course of my work I also visited such Oriental countries as the Philippine Islands, Siam, French Indo-China, and Malaya.

The purpose of the revised, as of the original, edition of *Japan over Asia* is informative, not polemical. I have endeavored to write neither an indictment nor a vindication of Japan's expansion, but to set forth as objectively as possible the main events and causes of the Island Empire's forward drive in Asia, the factors which have prompted and opposed it, the favorable and unfavorable auguries for the future. In the same spirit I have tried to weigh China's prospects of prolonged resistance and of successful internal reconstruction without prejudice and without wishful thinking.

While the full significance of the events in the Far East is obscured at the present moment by the more spectacular and threatening developments in Europe, there is, I am convinced, a very intimate connection between these two centres of international ferment and crisis. Whatever may occur in Europe is certain to be reflected in the Orient. So an effort to analyze Japan's national balance sheet of strength and weakness is not without relation to the prospective shape of European events.

I am grateful to the Editorial Board of the *Christian Science Monitor* for their kind permission to incorporate in the book some material which I have published in the *Monitor*. A similar acknowledgment is due to the editors of *Asia*, the *Yale Review*, *Foreign Affairs*, and *Current History*, for authorization to make use of excerpts from articles which I have contributed to these publications.

WILLIAM HENRY CHAMBERLIN

BOSTON, *April* 15, 1939

CONTENTS

ILLUSTRATIONS

JAPAN OVER ASIA

I

THE SWEEP TOWARD EMPIRE

I<small>F</small> one may paraphrase a famous saying of Karl Marx, a spectre is haunting East Asia: the spectre of Japan. From icy Komsomolsk, eastern terminus of Russia's new strategic railway in Eastern Siberia, to humidly tropical Singapore, where Great Britain has built up a Far Eastern Gibraltar in the shape of a powerful naval and air base, on what was formerly a jungle swamp, Japan is the primary object of political, military, and naval apprehensions and calculations.

Japan's drive for expansion on the Asiatic mainland began when a mysterious bomb exploded on the line of the South Manchuria Railway outside of Mukden on the night of September 18, 1931. The bomb did very little damage, but its reverberations were heard around the world. For, using this incident as a pretext, the Japanese Army, flouting the feeble remonstrances of civilian officials at home and the equally impotent protests of the League of Nations, carried out a complete occupation of Manchuria. This brought under Japan's effective control an area more than three times as great as that of Japan proper and thrust forward the military frontier to the Soviet boundary on the Amur River.

Since that time incidents of forward movement have alternated with periods of relative calm. But the drive shows no signs of coming to a definite end, even though it may slacken in momentum from time to time in response to a stiffening of actual or potential obstacles. It would be a bold observer who would venture to predict how the Japanese Empire may appear on a map published in 1945 or 1950.

Every recent year has had its milestone on Japan's road to empire. In 1933 it was the slicing off of Jehol, with its old Chinese imperial palaces, its coal, and its strategic mountain passes, from the main body of China and its incorporation in Manchoukuo. In 1934 there was the Amau Statement, with its warning that Japan was assuming a veto power in regard to foreign "political" loans to China.

The year 1935 witnessed the elimination of the last vestige of the traditional Russian influence in North Manchuria through the transfer by purchase of the Soviet share of ownership of the Chinese Eastern Railway to Manchoukuo. It was also marked by a series of manœuvres, on the part of the Japanese military authorities in China, calculated to undermine the authority of the central government at Nanking over the seventy-five million inhabitants of the five provinces of North China. The culmination of these manœuvres was the setting up, with very obvious Japanese military connivance and sympathy, of a puppet régime headed by Yin Ju-keng in the eastern districts of North China.

Early in 1936 irregular forces, emerging from Manchoukuo, drove out the Chinese troops and militia and established a pro-Japanese régime in the large, sparsely populated province of Chahar, which is believed to be rich in undeveloped iron resources. Mr. Koki Hirota, in his capacity as Foreign Minister, put forward three points as essential prerequisites of Sino-Japanese understanding. These points were coöperation between China and Japan in suppressing Communism; recognition of Manchoukuo by China, and the cessation by China of all unfriendly actions in relation to Japan and of the policy of "playing off a third power against Japan." The first and third of these points were capable of elastic interpretation; they might be stretched to the point of asserting for Japan the right to supervise China's foreign relations and to send Japanese troops into any part of China where Communist forces might be operating.

Two other important events in the establishment of an informal Japanese hegemony in North China were the substantial increase of the Japanese garrison in the Peiping-Tientsin area and the inflow of smuggled goods, largely of Japanese origin, as a result of the paralysis of the authority of the Chinese customs inspectors and the free hand which was given to Japanese and Korean smugglers.

These developments proved only the prelude to Japan's biggest venture in imperialism, the war with China which started at the Lukowkiao Bridge on July 7, 1937. The origins and course of this war form the subject of another chapter. Its objective, clear if not always specifically stated, is to create for a large part of China a status of Japanese tutelage not very different from that which prevails in Manchoukuo. Its result so far has been to give Japan control of China's main ports and largest cities, together with over 80 per cent of the Chinese railway network. The Japanese Army claims the occupation of about 600,000 square miles of Chinese territory, inhabited by about 170,000,000 people. However, the Japanese have not, as a rule, been able to establish effective control far from their main lines of communications. What they had achieved up to the spring of 1939 was rather strategic penetration than absolute conquest.

Quite in line with the policy of expansion on land was the denunciation by the Japanese Government of the Washington Naval Treaty and the refusal to conclude any new naval agreement except on a basis of parity with the United States and Great Britain. The 5–5–3 ratio which had been considered adequate for Japan's security in 1922 was regarded as no longer satisfactory by the growing Empire of 1936.

Anyone who has been attending the press conferences at the Tokyo Ministry of Foreign Affairs and who has been in contact with representative Japanese officials and publicists could not fail to notice the intense unwillingness to assume any restraining obligations regarding future Japanese actions, especially in China. Japan has withdrawn from the League of Nations, and the Japanese press makes no secret of its belief that the Nine-Power Treaty concluded at Washington, which stipulates "respect for the sovereignty, the independence and the territorial and administrative integrity of China," and provides for communication between the nine powers with major interests in the Pacific in the event of any situation which may involve the application of this treaty, is a dead letter.

Questioned on one occasion as to the Japanese attitude in the event that the Nine-Power Treaty should be invoked in connection with some disputed point between Japan and China, Mr. Eiji Amau, the well-known spokesman of the Japanese Foreign Office, significantly replied: "The world is moving and the treaties are standing still." He added that China, anyway, had never carried out its obligations under that treaty.

Soon after my arrival in Japan I had an interesting talk with a professor in one of the leading Tokyo universities.

He remarked that, as the people of North China are of the same racial stock as the majority of the inhabitants of Manchoukuo, it would only be natural if, in time, these two territories should come under the same sovereignty.

Then, he suggested, would come the turn of vast, sparsely populated Outer Mongolia. Finally, the Japanese Empire might be rounded out by the addition of the maritime provinces of Siberia. After outlining this substantial programme of national aggrandizement, the professor, with a very amiable smile, concluded: —

"Some people say I am an imperialist. But I think I am only a sane liberal."

The professor, of course, was a private individual, with no official responsibilities. But similar expansionist voices are not infrequently raised in the Japanese newspaper and periodical press. So Mr. Chonosuke Yada, director of the Japan-Siam Society, offered the following suggestions in regard to Japanese southward expansion in the course of a recent lecture: —

The world situation is constantly changing. It is highly questionable how long the Netherlands can retain her territories in the East Indies, which are more than sixty times as large as her homeland, and continue to exploit them to her advantage. It is also uncertain how long India will remain a British possession. When we take account of these facts we are convinced that Japan must make her way southward. She must make her way southward immediately, for there is no time to be lost.

Other suggestions for a peaceful enlargement of Japan's possessions were the intimation by Foreign Minister Hirota, in the spring of 1935, that Japan would be glad to consider purchasing the Soviet northern part of the island of Sakhalin and the more recent proposal in the Japanese Diet that Japan should lease the huge, undeveloped Dutch portion of the island of New Guinea. The Soviet reaction to Hirota's suggestion was freezingly negative, and it is doubtful whether the Dutch Government would ever, except under duress, open up any part of its East Indian possessions to large-scale Japanese colonization and economic development. The fear is too great that any such concession would be only the prelude to the bringing of the whole rich East Indian archipelago under the Rising Sun flag.

Behind Japan's urge to expansion are a number of impelling forces. There is the explosive pressure of rapidly increasing population in a land that is already overcrowded. There is the feeling of being unfairly treated in the world distribution of territory and raw materials. There is the exceptionally strong position of the fighting services vis-à-vis the civil authorities. There is the high-flown sense of nationalism, which for many Japanese has all the force of religious conviction. There is the mystical idea of Japan's Pan-Asian mission, very popular with retired army officers and nationalist theoreticians, which envisages Japan as the leader of an Asia from which "white imperialism" has been banished. Finally, there is the great difficulty, not to say impossibility, of turning back from the imperial road on which the country has started, no matter how great may be the difficulties and obstacles which may be encountered.

This last consideration may be clarified through an illustration. If Japan had not seized Manchuria, the Soviet Union might not have considered it necessary to send a powerful army, with a large complement of tanks and airplanes, to the Far East and to create a flotilla of submarines in Far Eastern waters. But now that the Soviet troops and airplanes and tanks and submarines are there, the Japanese military leaders feel that it is an elementary requirement of national security to scale up their own military and air forces to meet the threat. This is only one of several instances in which the costs of imperialism grow because of the opposition and counter-pressure which it excites.

Japan may be regarded, along with Germany and Italy, as one of the three major dissatisfied "have-not" powers of the world. It was in Italian Fascist intellectual circles that the idea first found expression that there could just as logically be a "class struggle" between rich and poor nations as between the "bourgeoisie" and the "proletariat" in a single nation. German National Socialist leaders have displayed an increasing tendency to attribute their country's economic difficulties largely to the lack of colonial sources of essential raw materials. Japan sees itself confronted with a similar problem, despite the acquisition of Manchoukuo. So the spokesman of the Foreign Ministry, Mr. Amau, recently remarked: —

Unfortunately the territories which now feed Japan's population are too small. We are advised to practise birth control, but this advice comes too late, since the population of the Japanese Empire is already about 100,000,000. Japanese work harder and longer than people in Western countries; their opportunities in life are more restricted. Why? We need more territory and must cultivate more resources if we are to nourish our population.

A succinct statement of Japan's case as a "have-not" power is to be found in the following excerpt from a widely read Japanese economic textbook, which has been translated into English under the title *Nippon: A Charted Survey:* —

The territory of Japan represents one half per cent of the world's total, while her population makes up five per cent of the world's total. In other words, Japan's population density is approximately ten times

greater than the average population density of the world. Moreover, Japan is for the most part mountainous, favored with comparatively few stretches of open level land. Dearth of sown acreage
and overpopulation are two distinct fundamental factors of Japan's
national life. It will be no exaggeration to say that this particular
condition of the country underlies all the difficulties which its people
find in their way.

The belief that overpopulation (in relation to available
natural resources) is the root cause of Japan's difficulties runs
like a red thread through almost all Japanese publications
on social and economic subjects. Even liberal and radical
professors and publicists who are outspokenly or cautiously
critical of the high-handed methods of the country's military
leaders are quick to point out that the world-wide restrictions
on Japanese immigrants and Japanese goods greatly accentu-
ate the strains within the Japanese social order and play into
the hands of the advocates of violent courses.

There is abundant statistical proof that Japan's position is
that of a proletarian nation. It depends entirely, or almost
entirely, on foreign sources for such vitally necessary raw
materials as cotton, wool, rubber, and oil, which are the life-
blood of some of its most important industries. There is no
mineral of any consequence which Japan possesses in surplus
quantities; and there is an absolute lack or a grave deficiency
of such valuable industrial ores as iron, lead, zinc, and nickel.
Its consistent bad fortune in finding natural resources within
its own frontiers is exemplified in the northern island of
Sakhalin, which is divided between Japan and the Soviet
Union. Diligent prospecting has revealed no oil in the
southern Japanese part of the island, while there is an
abundant supply of this liquid fuel on the Russian side of
the border.

There is a school of thought, persuasively represented in England by Sir Norman Angell, among others, which contends that the national ownership of raw materials is unimportant and that the alleged grievances of the so-called "have-not" powers are largely, if not entirely, spurious. Members of this school of economic thinking declare that the expense of conquering and administering colonies is out of all proportion to the trade, investment, and migration benefits which accrue from colonial imperialism. Since producers of essential raw materials are only too eager to find buyers, there is nothing, according to this line of argument, to prevent a nation which is poor in raw materials from buying what it needs in the cheapest market and building up its industries on imported raw materials.

There is indubitable weight in these arguments. The horse of poverty in raw materials has been ridden too hard. Yet it is significant that it is usually economists and publicists who are citizens of states which are richest in colonies who are most eager to demonstrate the unimportance of colonial possessions. Spokesmen for the "have-not" peoples have often been guilty of exaggeration in their claims. But in a world of rampant economic nationalism and protectionism the proletarian nation is at a disadvantage compared with its well-to-do brother.

Two concrete illustrations will help to show how Japan is handicapped in the economic race with countries which, like Great Britain and France, possess large colonial empires, or which, like America and the Soviet Union, are notably rich in internal resources.

Japan needs rubber. The natives of Malaya need cheap textiles. But the process of normal exchange is upset when the British Government, quite naturally concerned by the plight of the Lancashire textile industry, imposes a quota which sharply reduces Japanese sales of textiles in Malaya.

The remarkable growth of the paper and rayon industries is making heavy inroads on Japan's reserves of timber. A time may come in the not very distant future when timber imports from Eastern Siberia will be desired. But the Soviet Union, with its tightly closed economic system and its state monopoly of foreign trade, will quite possibly refuse to sell this timber to Japan, if it wishes to pay off some political grudges, or may refuse to accept the exports which Japan can offer in exchange.

Of course it is theoretically possible for Japan to pay for Malayan rubber, or Siberian timber, or any other commodity which it may need, out of the receipts of its sales in other markets. But with trade restrictions established and multiplying all over the world, it is not easy to convince the Japanese that physical possession of essential raw materials is a matter of indifference. There is a strong temptation to cast the samurai sword into the mercantile scales that seem unfairly weighted against Japan.

The restless Japanese feeling of a need for expansion, for outlets, is intensified by the necessity of providing work and food for the half million people of working age who come on the labor market every year. Among the larger countries of the world Japan is second only to the Soviet Union in the rate of growth of its population. Between 1930 and 1935 the number of inhabitants of Japan proper [2] increased from 64,450,005 to 69,254,148. Births exceeded deaths in 1935 by more than 1,000,000.

[2] Japan proper consists of the four islands, Honshu, Kyushu, Shikoku, and Hokkaido, with a number of smaller islands scattered along their coasts. The Japanese Empire also includes Formosa, Korea, and Southern Sakhalin. The population of the empire is approximately 97,000,000.

With an area slightly less than that of California, Japan proper must support about twelve times the population of California.   Japan's problem is made more difficult by the mountainous character of the country.   Only 15.6 per cent of the area of Japan proper is rated as arable land.   While the density of population in relation to total area is greater in Great Britain, Germany, Belgium, and the Netherlands, density in relation to arable land works out much less favorably to Japan, as the percentage of cultivated area is 43.7 in Germany, 40.2 in Belgium, 24.2 in Great Britain, and 27.8 in the Netherlands.

A train journey or a cross-country walking trip gives abundant visual evidence that the rural districts of Japan are crowded to the saturation point.   Every available inch of land is cultivated; the carefully terraced, irrigated rice fields on the steep hillsides are a monument of patient toil and ingenuity.   Between 1920 and 1930, when the whole population increased by about eight and a half millions, the number of persons employed in agriculture slightly declined.

Three possible peaceful remedies for Japan's population problem are birth control, emigration, and industrialization. Birth control is frowned on by the authorities and runs counter to the strong impulse among the Japanese and other Oriental peoples to conceive many male children in order to ensure the continuity of the family line.   Its practice is spreading among the more Westernized and sophisticated Japanese of the larger towns, but it is not yet appreciably slowing up the number of births.   The middle-class family with five or six children is far more frequently found in Japan than in America or Great Britain.

There is still room for settlers in the northern parts of

the Island Empire, in Hokkaido and in Southern Sakhalin. But the absorption capacity of both these regions, so far as I could learn during a recent visit, is definitely limited. Hokkaido has reached its present population of about 3,000,000 over a period of sixty years. There is a twenty-year plan for the development of Hokkaido which calls for the doubling of this figure by 1956.

But experienced residents of Hokkaido, both Japanese and foreigners, expressed doubt whether this plan could be realized. The best land is already settled; Japanese coming from warmer parts of the empire find the climate of Hokkaido too cold and foggy; the percentage of assisted colonists who fail to stick out the rigors of pioneering in this northern island is already fairly high. The prospects in Sakhalin are still less promising. The Japanese part of this island now reckons about 336,000 inhabitants. It is questionable whether room can be found for more than 200,000 new settlers — a mere drop in the stream of population increase.

Manchoukuo is the uncertain element in Japanese emigration policy. The army dreams of solving two problems, relieving agrarian congestion in Japan and building up a solid human wall against the Russian threat, by settling millions of sturdy Japanese peasants in the northern provinces of Manchoukuo, where there is a considerable amount of untenanted land. But so far this is only a dream. Only a handful of Japanese agriculturists have settled in Manchoukuo, although there has been an influx of merchants, traders, artisans, employees, and other urban dwellers into the new state. It remains to be seen whether such unfavorable factors as a severely cold climate, chronic banditism, the lower living standards of the native Manchurian peasants with whom the Japanese settlers must compete, can be overcome or sufficiently alleviated to make possible a large-scale emigration movement.

The only other foreign country to which Japanese emigrants have been going or could go in any considerable number is Brazil. About 128,000 Japanese have settled there, the record figure of migration for any single year being 12,000. But a large immigration of Japanese settlers, like an inflow of Japanese goods, is apt to provoke restrictive measures. Japanese emigration to Brazil has now been placed on a quota basis, which seems likely to reduce it to small dimensions.

So emigration, like birth control, seems likely to make only a minor contribution to the solution of Japan's population problem. There remains industrialization; and here Japan has made remarkable strides during the last few years, as will be shown in detail in later chapters.

There are two considerations, however, which prevent industrialization from serving as a panacea, smoothly and automatically absorbing the steady increment of the working population. In the first place, machines have been replacing men and women very perceptibly in the larger and better equipped Japanese factories. More output with fewer workers has been especially characteristic of the textile industry, which gives more employment than any other form of factory production.

Moreover, Japan's striking progress in export trade has encountered more and more barriers in the form of tariffs, quotas, and self-limitation agreements, concluded by Japanese businessmen as a means of forestalling these restrictions. Industry, trade, and the traditional family system have thus far absorbed, after a fashion, Japan's annual contingent of

new mouths to be fed. Japan is a nation of shopkeepers;
a stroll through the streets of Tokyo, Osaka, or any Japanese
provincial town reveals an amazing number of people who
depend for their living on the proceeds of some very small
store. The family system is Japan's substitute for the dole;
it is taken for granted that the successful and prosperous
members of a family will look after their less capable or less
fortunate relatives.

But the sense of strain and tension is never absent. With
its unusual combination of an Oriental birth rate and an
Occidental death rate, Japan sees itself confronted with the
alternative of expanding or exploding. So there is a direct
line of connection between the numerous slant-eyed children
whom one finds in every Tokyo side street, playing battledore and shuttlecock, or flying kites, or playing soldiers with
sticks for guns and swords, and the patrols of real Japanese
soldiers who are hunting down guerrilla "bandits" in Manchoukuo or parading along the Bund of Shanghai. Japan
sees in empire a possible way out of its population impasse.

I have discussed at some length Japan's pressure of population, not only because, along with the closely related problem
of poverty in essential raw materials, it is a main driving
force in the sweep toward expansion, but also because it affects
very intimately many other phases of Japanese life. Many
peculiar features of industry and agriculture are attributable
in large measure to the fact that there are more people in
Japan than the country can comfortably support. Population pressure is a dynamic and explosive force internally as
well as externally. It feeds the ferment of dissatisfaction
that occasionally finds expression in spectacular plots and
assassinations.

Professor Teijiro Uyeda, one of Japan's leading economists

and a specialist on the population question, is convinced that Japan, like other countries which have gone through the process of industrialization and urbanization, will experience a gradual tapering off of the present sharp rate of increase in the number of its inhabitants. He points out that the birth rate has shown a tendency to decline (from 36.2 in 1920 to 31.6 in 1935) and foresees that in time this downward curve will be more significant than the simultaneous decline in the death rate. However, Professor Uyeda anticipates that for some time there will be no diminution in the annual number of young Japanese who come of working age, since a large child population has already been born. So the pressure of a rapidly growing population seems bound to influence Japan's development for the next two decades at least.

The extremely strong position of the fighting services in the Japanese constitutional scheme of things has also unmistakably promoted the vigorous forward move on the Asiatic continent. Soldiers are sometimes willing to take risks of international antagonism from which diplomats might shrink. And the army has exerted a powerful influence on the shaping of foreign policy during the last six years.

Japanese army and navy officers have never taken kindly to the idea that the Diet should control the activities of their services. Japan perhaps came nearest to civilian control over the fighting services in 1930 when Premier Hamaguchi, an unusually forceful personality for a Japanese civilian, pushed through the ratification of the London Naval Treaty [3] against the recommendations of some high naval officers.

But this proved a Pyrrhic victory. Hamaguchi was shot

[3] This was concluded as a supplement to the Washington Naval Treaty of 1922.

by an enthusiastic nationalist and died of his wound. The agitation against the London Treaty hardened navy sentiment against any new ratio agreement which would bind Japan to maintain a position of inferiority to America and Great Britain in naval strength. There were echoes of the London Naval Treaty and of the supposed "usurpation of the imperial prerogative" by a civilian Premier in every nationalist terrorist enterprise of succeeding years, including the spectacular rebellion of February 26, 1936.

The army also reacted sensitively to the conclusion of the London Naval Treaty. The War Minister, General Jiro Minami, openly encouraged army officers to take part in political activity when he said, in the course of an address before divisional commanders of the army, in August 1931: —

"Some people hastily advocate limitation of armaments, and engage in propaganda unfavorable to the nation and the army, while others take advantage of the present psychology of the people with a view to reducing the army for domestic reasons. I hope you will coöperate with the War Ministry authorities in correcting such mistakes."

If one looks back to the files of the Japanese press on the eve of the Mukden affair, he finds no lack of indication that the army was anticipating some striking developments in Manchuria. So *Asahi*, a leading Tokyo newspaper, on September 9, 1931, quoted Colonel (later General) Kenji Doihara, a very active officer in the Japanese forces stationed in Manchuria, as stating that "there was no telling what might happen in Manchuria." The Tokyo press of September 15 reported an important conference in which War Minister Minami and several other high military officials participated. According to the press it was decided to seek satisfaction by force for the murder of Captain Nakamura, a Japanese officer who had been killed while on a trip in the interior of China, if diplomacy failed to obtain the same result by peaceful means.

It would be oversimplification to suggest that the army "staged" the seizure of Manchuria simply as a means of restoring its shaken prestige at home and driving liberalism and pacifism into the background. Other considerations were involved: the many unsettled economic disputes with the Chinese authorities; the disposition of Chang Hsueh-liang, ruler of Manchuria, to establish closer relations with the nationalist régime in China; the desire to push back the reviving Russian influence in the Far East. But that the army took full advantage of the strengthened position which it acquired as a result of the outbreak of hostilities in Manchuria is unmistakable.   As a Japanese scholar writes: —

The actual authority for directing the nation's foreign policy was gradually shifting from Kasumigaseki (the Ministry of Foreign Affairs) to Miyakezaka (the Ministry of War) by the middle of August, 1931, and this tendency toward dual diplomacy became more pronounced during the first phase of the League procedure in September.   Towards the beginning of October, however, even this last vestige of dual diplomacy appeared to be waning, with the Miyakezaka in firm control of the government, directing the nation's policy toward the League as well as the Manchurian developments.[4]

The requirement that the posts of War and Navy Minister may be held only by a general and an admiral in active service makes it possible for either the army or the navy to frustrate the formation of any cabinet of which they disapprove.   So strong is the corporate spirit in the higher ranks

[4] Cf. Tatsuji Takeuchi, *War and Diplomacy in the Japanese Empire*, p. 357.

of the army and navy that no officer would accept an appointment in a cabinet against the advice of his colleagues.

Japan's sweep toward empire cannot be explained merely in terms of population pressure, desire for economic self-sufficiency, and the strong predominance of military and naval leaders in the councils of the empire. There are psychological elements in the Japanese character, in the Japanese cast of thought, that fit in readily with a programme of aggrandizement and expansion. Intense patriotism, red-hot nationalism, are deeply implanted in the Japanese masses. The divine origin that is attributed to the Emperor imparts an element of religious sanction to the most exalted conceptions of Japan's destiny. Take, for example, the grandiose conception of Japan's national mission (nothing less than world pacification), as set forth in Professor Chikao Fujisawa's book, *Japanese and Oriental Political Philosophy:* —

The [Japanese] Emperor as the Sage-King would think it his sacred duty to love and protect not only the people of this land, but also those alien peoples who are suffering from misgovernment and privations. It must be recalled that the Sage-King is answerable in person for the pacification of the entire Under-Heaven, which is the ancient name for the whole world: consequently his moral and political influence ought to make itself strongly felt through the length and breadth of the earth. Should any unlawful elements dare to obstruct in one way or another the noble activities of the Sage-King, he would be permitted to appeal to force; but this may be justified only when he acts strictly on behalf of Heaven. . . . This firm belief in our holy state mission moved Japan to assist Mr. Henry Pu Yi to found the new state of Manchoukuo, which will faithfully follow the way of the Sage-King. . . . Nippon's national flag is an ensign of "red heart," or fiery sincerity. It alludes to the heavenly mission of Japan to tranquillize the whole world.

The ease with which "the will of heaven" may be invoked to justify Japan's military and naval aspirations is reflected in the following excerpt from a pamphlet which was issued in the summer of 1935 by the Japanese Navy Ministry: —

In view of Japan's geographical position the powers should leave the maintenance of peace in the Orient in the hands of Japan, which is now powerful enough to perform this duty. If the other powers fail to recognize the mission of Japan they may well be said to disobey the will of Heaven.

Pan-Asianism is one of the potentially explosive ideas that have contributed to Japan's drive for expansion. It has become increasingly popular, especially among high military officers, both active and retired. Typical of the spirit of Japanese Pan-Asianism is an article by the publicist Rin Kaito, who, after recalling the religions, arts, and sciences which originated in Asia and repudiating the Occidental assumption of superiority to Orientals, ends on the following note: —

For over a century and a half the Asiatics have been pressed down by the Whites and subjected to Western tyranny. But Japan, after defeating Russia, has aroused the sleeping Asiatics to shake off the Western tyranny and torture.

It is significant that Major General Kenji Doihara, who had the reputation of being one of Japan's most astute military diplomats and experts on the mainland of Asia,[5] is an avowed believer in Pan-Asianism. "The doctrine of 'Asia for the Asiatics,'" Doihara wrote in an issue of *Dai Asia Shugi*, a magazine devoted to expounding Pan-Asian ideas,

[5] General Doihara, after long service with the Kwantung Army (the Japanese forces stationed in Manchoukuo), in the course of which he often visited China and Mongolia on mysterious missions, has been transferred to a command in Japan.

"is based on the supreme principle that Asia must be safe-guarded and maintained by Asiatics."

In other words, the Occidental should go, from China first of all, then from the Dutch East Indies, the Philippines, India, and other parts of Asia which should be "safeguarded and maintained by Asiatics." Under present conditions "Asia for the Asiatics" in practice would be synonymous with "Japan over Asia." The Japanese superiority over other Oriental peoples in such factors of national strength as military and naval power, general literacy, industrial development, and military organization is so great that there would be almost no limit to Japanese expectations of supremacy in Asia if the influence of the West were with-drawn.

I recently discussed the ideals of the Pan-Asian move-ment with General Iwane Matsui, former commander of the Japanese forces at Shanghai and a leading figure in the Dai Asia Kyokai (Great Asia Association) of Japan. Spare in build and alert in bearing, General Matsui, like many other Japanese high officers, gave the impression of keeping himself in an excellent state of physical fitness through rigorous exercise and simple living. He described as one of the ideals of his organization "an Asiatic League of Nations, based on the slogan 'Asia for the Asiatics,' " and declared that Pan-Asianism had won followers in China, India, French Indo-China, the Philippines, and Afghanistan. He gave me with approval a pamphlet in the English lan-guage entitled *Asiatic Asia: What Does It Mean?* by Pro-fessor Takeyo Nakatani, secretary of the association. The idea of Japanese hegemony in the Pan-Asian order was clearly put forward by Professor Nakatani in the following terms: —

To bring order and reconstruction to the present chaotic condition of Asia is a duty that rests mostly on the shoulders of Japan. . . . She has been asked to put to work all her forces, cultural, political, economic, and, if need be, military, in order to bring about unity and wholesale reconstruction in Asia.

The appeal of the Pan-Asian idea outside of Japan does not seem to be very wide or very great. Now and then a roving nationalist revolutionary from India or the Philippines may find shelter in Japan. But there is no evidence that Oriental nationalists, however much they may dislike British, French, or Dutch rule, would care to substitute Japanese. Japan's aggressive policy toward China has certainly not been calculated to win support for plans of cooperating on a Pan-Asian or any other basis.

But while Pan-Asianism is a negligible force outside of Japan, the propulsive force of the idea in Japan should not be underrated. General Matsui is not the only Japanese military leader who cherishes an almost mystical faith in Japan's mission as the driving force in an "Asia for the Asiatics" movement. If the Japanese Empire is to expand further, Pan-Asianism, to a certain type of Japanese mind, may become a slogan as inspiring as Kipling's phrase about the "white man's burden" was to the believer in the blessings of British imperial rule.

So behind the Japanese sweep toward empire one finds a whole complex of impelling forces. Some of these stem from Japan's romantic feudal past, with its cult of the sword; others are derived rather from the more prosaic counting-house considerations of the present.

The average Japanese does not possess a speculative mind. But those who try to draw lessons from their country's history must sometimes regret the two and a half centuries of self-imposed seclusion from which Japan emerged into the modern world with the Meiji Restoration of 1868. For while Japan was leading its static, shut-in life under the Tokugawa Shogunate, the rich colonial prizes were being staked out. Japan was handicapped in the race for colonial spoils by her superisolation, much as Germany and Italy were handicapped by the late achievement of national unity.

Two centuries ago, before Russia, Great Britain, France, and other foreign powers had struck firm roots in the Far East, it would have been far simpler and easier for Japan to carve out a vast Asiatic empire than it is at the present time. To-day Japanese pressure evokes counter-pressure. As a direct result of Japan's drive for expansion, East Asia is arming on a scale which recalls the military establishments of its great mediæval conquerors, Genghis Khan and Kublai Khan.

The more spectacular armament race in Europe should not obscure the fact that the Far East is also arming to the limit of its resources. From Vladivostok, Russia's main window on the Pacific, to Singapore, at the tip of the Malay Peninsula, every country, with variations dictated by size, population, and resources, is investing an ever-larger share of its income in troops and ships and airplanes and cannon.

Take a brief imaginary tour of the Far East from north to south. The long Soviet-Manchoukuo frontier, slightly defended a few years ago, now bristles on the Russian side with forts and blockhouses, gas- and bomb-proof hangars for a fleet of several hundred airplanes, cantonments and storehouses for an army that is generally estimated at between 200,000 and 300,000 men. Vladivostok, from which Japanese residents are being crowded out by none too gentle methods, is a large garrison town and submarine base.

On the other side of the frontier the Japanese army of occupation in Manchoukuo, while inferior to the Soviet forces in Siberia as regards size and equipment, is much the largest force that Japan has ever maintained on the Asiatic continent in time of peace. And Japan itself is passing through one political and economic crisis after another because of the effort to increase armaments at a pace which affects adversely both the financial stability of the country and the living standards of the people.

China in 1936 was America's best customer in the field of airplanes and aeronautical equipment. Chinese purchases amounted to $6,872,000, as against $2,293,000 in 1935. And military airplanes represent only one part of China's preparedness programme, which lays heavy burdens on the country's chronically straitened finances.

The Commonwealth Government of the Philippines has launched a universal-service army scheme which will train 400,000 men by the time full independence is realized in 1946. The annual military appropriation of 16,000,000 pesos ($8,000,000) is a substantial item in the limited Philippine budget, but is small in relation to the country's defense needs. It must be increased if the Philippine Army is to possess adequate air and naval auxiliary units.

Siam is spending money abroad for arms so fast that its British financial adviser has felt obliged to sound a gentle note of warning that financial equilibrium is under a strain as a consequence of the large outlay of foreign currency. Military appropriations have increased in the Dutch East Indies and in French Indo-China.

In the Dutch East Indies, where apprehension in regard to Japan's ultimate acquisitive designs, whether justified or unjustified, is very pronounced, a hundred and fifty fighting planes are held in readiness at the air base near Surabaya. Great Britain has been holding large-scale manœuvres, with units drawn from places as far apart as Hong Kong and Iraq, to test the effectiveness of the great naval and air base at Singapore.

Japan's sweep toward empire has by no means been purely military and territorial in character. Goods with the "Made in Japan" label have won their victories and made their enemies, just as the Japanese soldiers on the battlefields of Manchuria and Jehol. Japan's advance to a commanding position on the Asiatic continent may be graphically represented by three arrows, pointing in different directions. The first points north, to Manchoukuo and the troubled frontier with Russia. The second points west, to China, where the destiny of Japan as an imperial power may well be settled. The third points south, to the rich tropical lands where Japan's activities have thus far been purely commercial in character.

II

THE ADVANCE TO THE NORTH:
MANCHOUKUO

MANCHOUKUO is far and away Japan's most significant venture in imperialism. Its area is more than three times that of Japan proper and almost double that of the entire Japanese Empire.[1] In population and resources it well exceeds the older Japanese colonies, Korea and Formosa. Along with increased opportunities for trade, investment, and development, Manchoukuo has brought to Japan a heavy bill in the shape of much-increased administrative expenses and vastly greater military responsibilities.

Technically, of course, Manchoukuo is an independent empire, connected with Japan only by ties of friendship and alliance. But this transparent fiction deceives few Japanese and no one outside of Japan. The most powerful figure in Manchoukuo to-day is not the amiable young Emperor, descendant of the last Chinese dynasty, who has exchanged his former incongruous name of Henry Pu Yi for the more sonorous and dignified imperial appellation of Kang Te. It is not the Premier, the former Chinese Military chieftain, Chang Ching-hui, or any other member of the cabinet, with its decorative Chinese ministers and its potent

[1] The area of Japan proper is 382,314 square kilometres. Korea, Formosa, and Southern Sakhalin together comprise 292,675. Manchoukuo brought the huge augmentation of 1,306,894 square kilometres.

Japanese vice ministers. It is General Kenkichi Ueda, who, in his double capacity as Commander in Chief of the Kwantung Army — the Japanese force in occupation of Manchoukuo — and Japanese Ambassador to Manchoukuo, holds in his hands the threads of administration.

The Japanese Army, more than any other force, created Manchoukuo. And it is quite natural that the army should possess an even more authoritative voice in governing Manchoukuo than it enjoys in Japan itself. There is a strong military stamp on the whole development of the new state.

The industries which are being most energetically built up, iron and steel, chemicals, cement, machine building, possess clear strategic significance. The railways which have been constructed, while many of them will doubtless prove profitable from the economic standpoint, are calculated to serve two military objectives: to facilitate quick transportation of troops from Japan to Manchoukuo and to make the country's far-flung frontiers, many of which run through desolate, sparsely settled stretches of country, more accessible.

Moreover, Manchoukuo is now serving as a training ground for a considerable part of the Japanese Army and air force. Its rolling prairies and long distances afford a better stage for flying and for manœuvres with tanks and other mechanized weapons than the paddy fields and steep hillsides of Japan proper. Operations against the bandits who are still active in the more hilly and wooded section of the country impart an element of grim reality to military exercises. Ships periodically return bearing a number of little urns containing the cremated remains of Japanese soldiers who have lost their lives in some obscure brush somewhere along Japan's farthest frontier of empire.

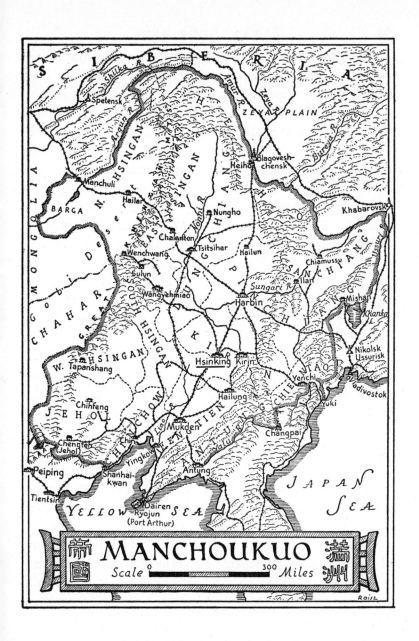

MANCHOUKUO

Scale 0 ▬▬▬▬ 300 Miles

More than five years have now passed since Japan extended its economic grip on South Manchuria, which dates back to the victorious conclusion of the Russo-Japanese War in 1905, into political domination of the whole country. What has been the balance sheet of Japan's sweeping advance to the north? It may be cast up from two standpoints, from the standpoint of Japan and from that of the people of Manchoukuo.

Japan has acquired a large and rich territory for economic exploitation and development. While Japanese industrial and commercial interests were predominant in Manchuria even before 1931, it is now possible to push through projects with no fear of the obstruction and passive resistance that were sometimes shown by the former ruler of Manchuria, Chang Tso-lin, and his son and successor, Chang Hsueh-liang.

Manchoukuo has been a big factor in Japan's trade and industrial boom of the last few years. Next to the United States it has become Japan's best market. Japanese sales to Manchoukuo in 1936 were three times greater than the Japanese exports to all China.[2] Both the absolute value of Japan's exports to Manchoukuo and its share in Manchoukuo's import trade have been steadily increasing. Goods with the "Made in Japan" label were 58.4 per cent of Manchoukuo's imports in 1932, 65.8 per cent in 1933, 75.4 per cent in 1935, and 78 per cent in 1938.

Particularly impressive has been the growth in the export of such products of Japan's heavy industries as machinery

[2] Japanese exports to Manchoukuo and the Kwantung Leased Territory reached the record figure of 598,000,000 yen in 1936, when exports to China were valued at 159,691,000 yen. While some of the exports to the Kwantung Leased Territory were doubtless smuggled into North China, much the greater part went to Manchoukuo.

and tools, automobile parts, vehicles, industrial appliances and materials, iron and steel products. Expansive municipal construction, combined with the building of many factories, railways, and roads, has brought a rich harvest of profits to Japanese firms and contractors. Expenditure on the upbuilding of Hsinking, the new capital, has been estimated at 100,000,000 yuan, or Manchoukuo dollars.[8]

So Manchoukuo has made an unmistakable contribution to the solution of Japan's eternal problem: to provide food and work for its increasing population. Manchoukuo also represents an addition to Japan's reserves of raw materials, an important consideration in an age which thinks in nationalist economic terms, especially where military necessities are concerned.

To be sure, its contribution in this field has been limited. It has no tropical products and the climate seems to be too cold for the effective cultivation of cotton and tobacco. Its main product is the versatile soya bean, which can be used for almost everything from soap to salad oil and is a staple item of Japanese diet. It has also given Japan large assured supplies of coal, timber, wheat, and low-grade iron, the value of which depends largely on the successful working of certain German patented processes which Japan has acquired.

Japan is better supplied with coal than with most other minerals; much of the interest in Manchuria's coal lies in the possibility that it may be turned into oil. Shale oil has been obtained in the past on a small scale from the large open-cut coal mines at Fushun. This is to be increased; and coal liquefaction plants are to be established in Fushun and in Supingkai. Up to the present time the extraction of oil

[8] The yuan has the same value as the Japanese yen, about 28.5 cents.

from coal has not proved economically profitable. But the army has a decisive influence on Manchoukuo economy, and is anxious to have a dependable supply of liquid fuel at almost any price.

While large sections of northern and eastern Manchoukuo are heavily wooded, difficulties of access have prevented large timber-cutting operations up to the present time. Rumors of large deposits of gold in the remote northwestern section of the country have not yet been verified or disproved by the test of large-scale scientific prospecting. There is a marked difference between South Manchuria, where Japan had invested over 2,000,000,000 yen in railways and industrial and commercial enterprises before the 1931 incident, and North Manchuria, which before the War was regarded as a Russian sphere of influence. Russian influence lapsed after the Revolution. Although the Soviet Government regained the pre-War Russian share of operating control of the Chinese Eastern Railway, main artery of communication across North Manchuria, in 1924, there was no effort to push a programme of economic expansion and development until Japan took over this section of the country. Consequently the resources of North Manchuria are less accurately known and the possibilities of future discoveries and of new exploitation there are greater than is the case in the southern provinces of the country.

West of the Hsingan Mountains, in Northwestern Manchoukuo, is a vast expanse of arid rolling steppe land on which nomad Mongols pasture their flocks and herds very much in the fashion of their forefathers as far back as the days of Genghis Khan. This cattle country gives Manchoukuo a larger supply of meat than Japan enjoys, and Japanese believers in nationalist economics hope to reduce their country's dependence on imported wool by increasing the numbers and improving the breed of the sheep. A good deal of education, persuasion, and experimentation will be required before any tangible results can be expected in this connection, however. The Mongols have been accustomed to raising sheep which yield a very coarse type of wool, unsuited to industrial use.

Japan's construction achievements in Manchoukuo have been impressive; the price has also been impressive. The drain on Japan's finances has been very heavy. Japanese investments during the five years after the occupation of Manchoukuo have been estimated at about 1,180,000,000 yen. During the same time military expenditures amounted to 1,067,528,000 yen. So every yen of invested capital has been almost matched by a yen of extra military and administrative expenditure. Manchoukuo has been a main cause of Japan's succession of unbalanced budgets since 1931.

The rapid inflow of Japanese capital, with its accompaniment of Japanese executive ability and engineering skill, has appreciably changed the outward aspect of Manchoukuo. Hsinking, the new capital, is itself a striking symbol of the material progress that is being achieved. When I visited this city in the autumn of 1935, I could scarcely realize that this was the sleepy little railway junction (then known as Changchun) where I had changed trains in 1927.

Hsinking to-day is as active as a Soviet industrial centre during the first Five-Year Plan. The sound of the axe and hammer is heard everywhere. A central boulevard runs to the so-called Tatung Square (Tatung being the name of the era inaugurated by the Emperor Kang Te), which is partially surrounded by three imposing buildings housing the Ministries of Foreign Affairs, Justice, and Education.

A new Hsinking, with wide asphalt roads, many parks, large public edifices, is rapidly assuming shape and form. The population has grown from 122,000 in 1932 to over 300,000 in 1937. Of all the cities of Manchoukuo, Hsinking is the most devoid of Western influences. There are almost no foreigners — Japanese of course excepted — in the city. There were no important business interests or consulates here before the change of régime, and so far only Salvador has associated itself with Japan in recognizing Manchoukuo's diplomatic existence. (The consuls of America, Great Britain, Germany, and other powers, stationed in Mukden, Harbin, and Dairen, carry on under the increasingly transparent fiction of being accredited to the Nanking Government in China. When a consul is replaced it is assumed that he has merely gone home on leave.)

While the outlay on public buildings and civic improvements is naturally greatest in the capital, the three other large cities of Manchoukuo, Dairen, Mukden, and Harbin, all give an impression of bustling activity. Dairen, the main gateway to Japan's new Asiatic empire, has prospered as the main point of import and transshipment for the vast quantities of Japanese goods which have been pouring into Manchoukuo.

Across the bay from Dairen, at Kanseishi, a whole new industrial town has grown up on what was formerly a stretch of desolate shore line. There are the factories of three large, recently established corporations, the Manchuria Chemical Company, the Manchuria Petroleum Company, and the Manchuria Soda Manufacturing Company. The largest of these three enterprises is the chemical plant,

GENERAL JIRO MINAMI (RIGHT) DISCUSSING ADMINISTRATIVE
PROBLEMS WITH GENERAL KENKICHI UEDA

IMPERIAL HOUSEHOLD MINISTER MATSUDAIRA AND HIS FAMILY

which is equipped to produce over 160,000 tons of ammonium sulphate, together with lesser quantities of ammonium nitrate, nitric and sulphuric acids, tar, creosote, pitch, and coke.

The large near-by oil refinery is a tangible sign that the day of the foreign oil company in Manchoukuo is over. Despite repeated protests from the American and British Governments, Manchoukuo has established an oil-monopoly system which left the foreign firms little alternative except to liquidate their holdings and withdraw. All three plants, producing chemicals, soda, and various kinds of refined oil, are calculated to promote the realization of the army's desire to make Japan and its satellite, Manchoukuo, as independent as possible of foreign imports.

Dairen itself is a good introduction to Japan's achievements in colonial upbuilding. When the present city, then known as Dalny, was taken over from Russia at the end of the Russo-Japanese War, it was a small town of some 20,000 inhabitants. Its annual foreign trade was valued at about 60,000,000 Chinese dollars. To-day the population is 362,000; the value of the trade over 1,000,000,000 Chinese dollars.

Dairen is a city with excellent port facilities, several broad boulevards and spacious parks, large modern buildings, and good motor roads running out into the country. Apart from its commercial significance, it is an industrial centre, as the large repair shops of the South Manchuria Railway, bean mills, and pottery and glass works are located there. It is more Western in appearance than the large cities of Japan itself; the colder climate has encouraged the building of more solid houses. One could understand the feeling of the Japanese girl, brought up in an American West Coast city, who acted as my interpreter at the Fushun coal mines. She said she liked Dairen more than the typical Japanese city; there seemed to be more space and elbow-room.

Mukden, former seat of the Manchurian Government, shares in the general growth of commercial and industrial activity, even though the capital has been transferred to Hsinking. Many small factories and workshops have sprung up during the last few years. Moreover, Mukden is in the centre of Manchoukuo's heavy industries, being located within a short distance of Anshan, site of the largest steel plant in the Japanese Empire, and of Fushun, the most productive coal field of East Asia. The Showa Iron Works at Anshan turned out 650,000 tons of pig iron and 350,000 tons of steel during its first year of operation; its capacity has been greatly enlarged at the present time with the aid of new German technical processes. Another consideration that marks out Mukden as a centre of military and semi-military industries is its location far away from the frontier. This makes it reasonably secure against attack except from the air.

Harbin, the other main city of Manchoukuo and the most important railway and industrial centre of the northern part of the country, is a relic of Old Russia. Just as the less modern quarters of Mukden are indisputably Chinese, just as Dairen bears the impress of modern-style Japan, so the business streets and residential districts of Harbin are saturated with Russian atmosphere.

One sees reflections of Russia everywhere: in the surging, tumultuous throngs which crowd up the city's inadequate railway station; in the signs on the streets and shops; in the lines of bearded *izvoschiks*, or cabmen, who hold their own against the cheaper rickshas and the swifter taxicabs and buses. There is something indefinably but unmistakably Russian in the spacious, sprawling layout of the town, which is bisected by the Sungari River.

Two persons whom I noticed talking on a street corner, a bearded middle-aged Russian in an engineer's uniform and an animated fair-haired woman, might have walked out of a Turgenev novel or a Chekhov play. One caught another glimpse of pre-War Russia when large numbers of worshipers filed out of the bulbous-domed Orthodox Cathedral after the special service called Pokrovsk, which commemorates a religious legend that originated in the early days of the Byzantine Empire. One instinctively felt that many of the little one- and two-story houses in the residential quarters of the city were old-fashioned Russian homes, with ikon corners and bubbling samovars for tea, with its accompaniment of cakes and *varenye*, or jam, for the casual or invited guest.

The Russians in Harbin fall into three main categories. In the first are a considerable number of Russians who have lived here all their lives, since the city was the main centre of Russian penetration into North Manchuria before the War. In Harbin is the large office building of the administration of the Chinese Eastern Railway, which Russia laid across the Manchurian plains in order to provide a more direct connection with Vladivostok. When I visited Harbin in the autumn of 1935, a Japanese, Mr. K. Sahara, had just taken over the reins of management of this railway from the last Soviet manager, Ivan Rudy. A second element consists of White émigrés who fled here before the onrush of the Bolshevik forces in Siberia. Finally, there are "Red" Russians, Soviet citizens.

The number of the latter has dwindled to a very small

figure because of the sale of the Chinese Eastern Railway, which formerly employed some 6000 Russians. Over 20,000 Russians, mostly Soviet railway employees and their families, left Harbin in 1935, after the sale of the road. About 40,000, mostly Whites or old-time residents, still remain.

Ironically enough, this wholesale exodus of the Reds has been a severe blow to the struggling White Russian community in Harbin. The places of the Soviet railway employees are being taken by Japanese and, to a lesser extent, by Manchurians. And whereas the Soviet Russians did not boycott the shops and restaurants of their White compatriots, the incoming Japanese buy, as a rule, only in Japanese stores. The economic underpinning of the Russian Whites, always precarious, has become desperately shaky. Japanese are coming into North Manchuria in ever greater numbers and Russian business enterprises are being pushed to the wall.

So it is not surprising that the faces of most of the Russians whom one sees in Harbin look worried and harassed. Apart from economic distress, political difficulties have arisen since the Japanese occupation. As everywhere, Russian émigrés in Harbin are divided into several hostile groups. The Japanese military authorities have given support to an ultra-conservative group headed by Ataman Semyenov, former Siberian Cossack leader. To be known as an opponent or critic of Semyenov or of the local Harbin leader of the Russians who are organized along Fascist lines, Rozdaevsky, is to invite persecution, arrest, and expulsion.

The Russian influence in Harbin dies hard. It will be many years before the Russian color of this North Man-

churian city has worn off.   But a process of steady unyield-
ing Japanese penetration has set in.   There seems little
doubt that within a few years the Japanese will have replaced the Russians as the main foreign element in the
former Russian zone of influence.   The samisen will re-
place the balalaika; tales of Japanese mediæval heroes will
supplant Russian operas and plays in the theatres; Russian
cabbage soup and meat will give way to Japanese fish and
rice and vegetables.

While its Russian inhabitants are being gradually squeezed
out, Harbin as a whole is growing in population and in significance as a centre of industry and transportation.   If
heavy industry is more characteristic of the Mukden region,
Harbin has developed more as a manufacturer of consumers' goods: soya beans and wheat flour, textiles and woolens,
soap, candles, and such.   Railway lines, old and new, radiate from Harbin like spokes from the hub of a wheel.   The
city is also a central point of air and river transportation.
With a population of about half a million, it is the largest
city in Japan's new Asiatic empire.

The most striking development in Manchoukuo since the
Japanese occupation has been the rapid extension of the network of railways.   Over two thousand miles of new lines
have been built since 1931, supplementing the four thousand miles which had been constructed before that time.
Three new lines of unmistakable strategic significance lead
directly to various points on or near the Soviet frontier.
The longest of these runs northward from Harbin to Heiho,
which is opposite the Soviet town of Blagoveshchensk, on
the northern bank of the Amur River.   A line which
branches off to the northeast from the eastern stretch of the
Chinese Eastern Railway touches the Soviet frontier at Hulin.

Still a third line has been pushed westward to Halunarshan, within easy striking distance of the frontier of Soviet-dominated Outer Mongolia. Jehol has also been made accessible by rail.

Most important, both from an economic and from a strategic standpoint, has been the intensive railway construction in the eastern part of Manchoukuo. This links up Harbin and Hsinking with the prospective large port of Rashin, in North Korea, which is one of the largest single construction enterprises Japan has undertaken on the mainland.

A few years ago Rashin was an obscure fishing village on the craggy coast of North Korea, unnoticed on most maps. Now it has some 50,000 inhabitants and is well on the way to becoming a major economic link between Japan and Manchoukuo. By the time it strikes its full stride of development it will number its dwellers in hundreds of thousands. It owes its spectacular rise to an admirable strategic and commercial location and to a naturally deep harbor, which will accommodate vessels of 10,000 tonnage after necessary improvements have been carried out.

Yosuke Matsuoka, who announced Japan's withdrawal from the League of Nations in 1933, is now finding a full outlet for his abundant energy in the responsible and exacting post of president of the South Manchuria Railway, the spearhead of Japanese economic penetration on the continent. This railway is in charge of city, port, and harbor construction at Rashin. Mr. Matsuoka, whom I caught for a brief interview in a moment of rest during an airplane inspection tour of the Manchurian railway system, is full of enthusiasm over the prospects of the new Korean port.

"Rashin is one of our largest new construction enterprises," he told me. "It is an ideal outlet for a hinterland that possesses a great future. The timber, soya beans, coal, and other mineral and agricultural products of Northern and Northeastern Manchoukuo will naturally proceed to Japan by way of Rashin. This route is shorter and cheaper than the present method of transportation through Dairen, which requires a long railway haul. The opening of Rashin is a great convenience for communication with Niigata and Tsuruga, the ports of Japan's west coast. But I imagine most of the commercial exchange will be with our great industrial centre, Osaka. The ships that leave Rashin loaded with Manchoukuo soya beans, timber, coal, and wheat will return with cargoes of Japanese textiles, sugar, and manufactured goods. Within ten years Rashin, with its subsidiary neighboring ports, Seishin and Yuki, will be able to handle ten million tons of freight a year."

Rashin to-day gives the impression of a mushroom boom town in the making. Twenty thousand laborers, mostly Koreans, are employed on the triple task of town building, pier construction, and harbor improvement. The engineering and executive staff is Japanese, and Rashin appears to be a Japanese, rather than a Korean, town. The one-story dwellings and offices, mostly constructed in Japanese style, with loose sliding doors and paper windows, are not adapted to the bitterly cold winds which sweep over the North Korean coast in winter. When the city is completed, the more solid type of architecture, characteristic of Dairen, will probably prevail.

Anyone who is acquainted with Dairen and with the Japanese quarter of Mukden can envisage Rashin as it will be after five or ten years. There will be a central square or circle on which one will find a comfortable and inexpensive

Yamato Hotel, several banks, and the most important government offices and business firms. From this centre will radiate the neat streets of a sanitary, well-policed, hard-working city.

The strategic significance of the new port cannot be overlooked. In the event of war with Russia, troops could be rushed via Niigata and Tsuruga to Rashin and thence to Harbin and to the centres of Northern and Northeastern Manchoukuo much more rapidly than they could be transported by the more familiar route from Kobe to Dairen. A saving of two or three days would be possible; and in modern warfare even two or three hours might be decisive.

Moreover, Rashin may become an excellent naval base. The appearance of a Soviet submarine force in Far Eastern waters, with its base at Vladivostok, has aroused apprehension in Japanese naval circles. Warships as well as commercial vessels can be accommodated in the capacious harbor of the new port. While no visible steps have yet been taken to fortify Rashin, it is unlikely that such an important future port, located so close to the Soviet frontier, will be left permanently undefended.

Japan's work of development in Manchoukuo is by no means completed. A five-year plan of industrial development was drawn up in the latter part of 1936; its cost was originally estimated at 1,500,000,000 or 2,500,000,000 yen. This figure was increased to about 6,000,000,000 yen in 1938, because the Manchoukuo Five-Year Plan, like its Soviet predecessor, was greatly enlarged in conception while it was being put into operation, despite increasing shortages of materials. Special emphasis was laid on mining, metallurgical, and chemical industries because of their direct connection with war needs. Faced with a shortage of labor and of technical skill, the Manchoukuo Government has issued several edicts providing for the conscription of both, in case of necessity.

Railways and heavy industries continue to play a prominent rôle among the enterprises which are projected under the five-year plan. Much of the new railway construction will take place in the rich and slightly developed regions of Eastern and Northeastern Manchoukuo. The output of coal is to be more than doubled, with the production of an additional 15,000,000 tons, and the plan calls for 3,000,000 tons of increased iron and steel production. The hydroelectric power resources of the Sungari River are to be tapped. Agriculture, which has hitherto been somewhat neglected in the rapid development of industry and transportation, is to receive more attention under the plan, which provides appropriations for encouragement of better stock breeding and for improvement in the yield of such staple crops as soya beans and wheat.

Japan, like Soviet Russia, has a fondness for long-term plans, with an accompaniment of precise figures. The Hirota Cabinet in 1936 authorized a plan for settling 1,000,000 Japanese families, or roughly about 5,000,000 persons, in Manchoukuo over a period of twenty years. This scheme, which has the hearty approval of the army, was endorsed by the Hayashi Cabinet, and an appropriation to cover the estimated expenses of settling 6000 families was included in the budget for the fiscal year 1937–1938.[4] It is estimated that the total cost of placing these 5,000,000 settlers will be 2,000,000,000 yen, of which 800,000,000 yen will be supplied by the government. The remainder is supposed to come from the settlers themselves and from railway and shipping companies and

---

[4] The Japanese fiscal year runs from April 1 to March 31.

other organizations which are interested in promoting migration into Manchoukuo.

The suggested figure of 5,000,000 settlers in twenty years is not large by comparison with the numbers of Chinese immigrants who were pouring into Manchuria before the Japanese occupation. The total net immigration of Chinese into Manchuria during the years 1927, 1928, and 1929 amounted to about 2,000,000 settlers.[5] Most of these came from Shantung Province, which was then suffering very much from gross misgovernment and chronic famines. The door to Chinese immigration was very nearly closed in 1935, when the excess of arrivals over departures was only about 25,000.

On the other hand, Japanese agricultural settlement in Manchoukuo made surprisingly little progress during the first five years after the overthrow of the régime of Chang Hsueh-liang. The number of settlers on the land during this period was less than 3000 and many attempts at colonization ended in complete failure. One of the most successful of the new settlements is inhabited entirely by members of the Tenrikyo, a Shinto sect. Most of the Japanese immigrants have received land north of the eastern branch of the Chinese Eastern Railway. There is more unoccupied land in North Manchuria than in the southern part of the country; and the potential military value of the colonies is greater if they are placed near the Soviet frontier.

There are several explanations for the slow progress of

[5] There is an annual large influx of seasonal laborers from Shantung into Manchoukuo. These men return to their homes after working for a few months. For detailed figures of Chinese immigration into Manchuria, 1926–1935, cf. *Fifth Report on Progress in Manchuria to 1936*, a South Manchuria Railway publication, p. 121.

Japanese agricultural settlement. The soil of North Manchuria is quite different from the irrigated rice fields to
which most Japanese farmers are accustomed. The prevalence of banditism, the difficulty of underliving the Manchurian peasants, the isolation from all the things that help
to make up the Japanese way of life, such as the ancestral
home, the village shrine, the little plot in the graveyard
which is haunted by the spirits of the departed ancestors —
all these things have militated against large-scale immigration up to the present time.

On the other hand two considerations speak strongly for a
positive, vigorous colonization policy. These are the constant pressure of population and the desirability, from the
military standpoint, of building up a human wall of Japanese
colonists, mostly ex-service men, as a reserve for the Kwantung Army, which must hold a far-flung frontier and carry
on protracted campaigns against elusive bandits. In this
matter of state-sponsored migration, a race, largely inspired
by military considerations, is in progress between the Soviet
Union and Japan. The former country is eager to fill up
the relatively empty spaces east of Lake Baikal with Russian
settlers, just as Japan wishes to tighten its grip on Manchoukuo through colonization.

The main agency of Japanese economic penetration and
exploitation of Manchoukuo is the South Manchuria Railway,
which deserves to rank with the East India Company and
the Hudson's Bay Company as one of the great semi-
governmental economic organizations of history. Founded
after the Russo-Japanese War with a modest capital of
200,000,000 yen, part of which consisted of the damaged
and depreciated properties which had been taken over from
the Russians, it has grown on a truly imperial scale and is

to-day far and away the largest corporation functioning in East Asia.

Receipts of 12,500,000 yen in the first year of its operation had increased to 302,000,000 yen in 1935–1936. Besides operating what is probably the most efficient railway system in Asia, the South Manchuria Railway is a heavy investor in almost all the major industrial enterprises of Manchoukuo, in Fushun coal, Anshan steel, the new chemical company, and many other mines, mills, and factories.

This industrial function of the railway received recognition in the reorganization of the institution which took place on October 1, 1936. An Industry Department has been set up which will act as a "brain trust" for Manchurian economic development. At the same time unified management of all the railways, old and new, of Manchuria and North Korea, has been established under the direction of the South Manchuria Railway. This potent corporation will also have charge of the projected Japanese economic development of North China, if the state of Sino-Japanese political relations and of Japanese finances makes this development feasible.

There are other colonial lands that would fit better into the Japanese economic scheme of things than Manchoukuo. Formosa, although much smaller in size and population, is a more convenient appendage inasmuch as its sugar, bananas, pineapples, camphor, and other products fill Japan's needs without competing with Japanese industry and agriculture. Mr. Katsuji Debuchi, former Japanese Ambassador in Washington, recently published an impressive list of Manchoukuo's economic deficiencies, emphasizing the lack of cotton, oil, and rubber, the poor quality of the iron, the difficulty of exploiting the timber resources. Pessimistic critics see in

Manchoukuo coal, chemicals, aluminum, and other products harmful competition for Japan's own industries.

Yet it cannot be doubted that Japan has, with few exceptions, made the most of its economic opportunities in Manchoukuo and developed the country with characteristic energy, resourcefulness, and thoroughness. According to the nationalist conception of economics which is now prevalent in other countries besides Japan, poor resources under one's own control are preferable to better foreign supplies of raw material which may be limited by exchange difficulties in peace and cut off altogether in war. And the enlarged military programme to which Japan is committed would seem to assure, at least for the next few years, a ready market for the coal, steel, chemicals, aluminum, and other products of heavy industry which Manchoukuo is turning out.

So far Manchoukuo has been considered primarily from the standpoint of Japan's interests and activities. What of the results of the establishment of the new state for the 35,000,000 people who live in it?[6] Japan's record of benefits conferred and grievances inflicted does not deviate very widely from the customary pattern of imperialist rule.

The whole economic development of Manchuria — the construction of new railways and roads, the building up of new industries and the expansion of old ones — has been unmistakably speeded up under Japanese direction. Equally

[6] The population of Manchoukuo, without the South Manchuria Railway Zone and the Kwantung Leased Territory, was 32,896,054 at the end of 1934. The population of the Railway Zone (a narrow right of way possessed by the railway, which includes large sections of Mukden and Hsinking) was 1,119,870 at the end of 1935; that of the Kwantung Leased Territory at the same time was 501,396. The Leased Territory, where Japanese authority was absolute before 1931, consists of the port of Dairen and a small hinterland.

typical of the Japanese capacity for practical organization has been the straightening out of the muddled financial situation which prevailed when Manchuria was occupied. At that time many kinds of currency, some of them greatly depreciated in value, were in circulation throughout the country. Now there is a uniform currency unit, the yuan, which since the latter part of 1935 has been held at a stable value precisely corresponding with that of the Japanese yen.

More modern methods of administration and tax collection have been introduced. The old-fashioned Manchurian feudalism, under which the general in control of a province treated it more or less as a private estate and squeeze and graft permeated the administration, has given way to a new form of centralized bureaucratic government. Fourteen provinces have replaced the three old subdivisions, Fengtien, Kirin, and Heilungkiang.

There is no evidence to show that the new régime has won any enthusiastic loyalty in any part of the Manchoukuo population. The rule by Japanese soldiers and bureaucrats has been harsh and alien in character. Manchoukuo is, after all, an overwhelmingly Chinese country as regards population, language, and culture, even though it always maintained a status of virtual independence in relation to China proper. Differences of language, habits, and psychology, combined with the naturally arbitrary methods of the military leaders who wield so much influence in the government of the country, have not made for cordial relations between rulers and ruled.

Another Manchoukuo grievance, which is recognized and deplored by Japanese administrators of the better type, is the influx into the new state of Japanese adventurers and undesirable characters, the men who are always attracted to a new frontier of empire. They engage in drug peddling and financial swindles. Their activities, combined with the arrogance which Japanese (and not only Japanese) often develop in a colonial country, have helped to make the new régime unpopular.

With the passing of time, the establishment of law and order and the development of a more settled type of government, some of these abuses, which are apt to be characteristic of an early phase of colonial administration, will quite probably be removed or mitigated. But there is one fundamental grievance of the Manchoukuo educated and middle class which does not seem likely to disappear in any near future.

Just as in Formosa and Korea, Japan in Manchoukuo, while unmistakably promoting material progress, has reserved the most desirable fruits of this progress for Japanese. Not only is all real political power in Japanese hands, the higher economic opportunities are also an almost exclusive Japanese preserve. If one visits a mine, a factory, or a railway in Manchoukuo the picture is always the same. The engineers, the executives, the overwhelming majority of the white-collar workers, are Japanese; the mass of the unskilled labor is Chinese. The South Manchuria Railway, for instance, after operating in Manchuria since 1905, did not report a single Chinese among its 180 higher officials and its 134 engineers in 1933–1934; there were only 71 Chinese among its 5608 clerical workers. In the chief repair shops of this corporation the average wages of the Japanese worker amounted to thirty sen an hour, as against seven sen an hour for the Chinese.[7]

To the Japanese this division of labor seems natural and logical. It is quite understandable that Japan, with its

[7] Cf. article by A. J. Grajdanzev, "Profit and Loss in Manchuria," in *Pacific Affairs* for June 1935. The author cites South Manchuria Railway publications as sources for his statements.

pressure of population, should try to find as many posts as possible for Japanese in its colonies and in a country, like Manchoukuo, which it controls. But it is equally understandable that this policy of favoritism for Japanese should excite resentment and a feeling of frustrated opportunity among those Manchurians whose education and training would have qualified them for political or economic advancement under a different régime.

Tens of thousands of Manchurians of the former official, military, and well-to-do classes fled into China with Chang Hsueh-liang. Their property, in most cases, was confiscated, and they have been left in the position of impoverished émigrés, naturally embittered against Japan. The spectacular detention of Chiang Kai-shek in Sianfu in December 1936 was attributable in large degree to the discontent of these Manchurian exiles, to their desire for a stronger anti-Japanese policy which might make it possible for them to return to their homes.

Another expression of the Japanese tendency to regard the natives of colonial and protected countries as hewers of wood and drawers of water is the slight attention which has thus far been devoted to education in Manchoukuo. The Department of Education received only 5,090,000 yuan (about $1,400,000) in the 1936 budget, which totaled 219,405,000 yuan. The former Northeastern University at Mukden was closed at the time of the Japanese occupation and is now carrying on as a "university in exile" in Peiping. It seems quite probable that in the future the Manchoukuo students will be obliged to seek higher education in the universities of Japan, from which they may be expected to absorb Japanese culture and world outlook.

The surest indication that a certain amount of political discontent prevails in Manchoukuo is the protracted bandit movement. Banditism, to be sure, is nothing novel in a wild, rough frontier country like Manchoukuo. But there is a specifically political and anti-Japanese tinge in such bandit activities as are reflected in the following two news items, reported by the chief Japanese news agency, *Domei Tsushin Sha:* —

Harbin, June 24 [1936] — Seventeen Japanese soldiers are believed to have been killed and three others seriously wounded when the twenty Japanese soldiers from the Iwamatsu punitive unit, riding in an ambulance car, were suddenly attacked by a horde of 300 bandits under Hsi Yun-kai at 11.30 A.M. last Monday near Fulungtung, in western Sankiang Province.

Hsinking, February 27 [1937] — Thirteen Japanese soldiers and three civilian officials attached to the Japanese garrison forces were killed in action when an investigation party of the Japanese Army encountered a band of some 300 bandits Wednesday afternoon near Laomaho, to the southwest of Tangyuan, Sankiang Province.

Ordinary highway robbers would not attack detachments of Japanese soldiers, where the risk would be considerable and the prospect of booty slight. A report of the Kwantung Army on the results of a "bandit-suppression campaign" during the last three months of 1935 states the losses of the Japanese-Manchoukuo forces as 263 killed and 570 wounded. These figures again suggest small guerrilla warfare rather than the suppression of ordinary criminality. The report notes that, "spiritually speaking, the ideas of many Manchoukuo inhabitants are not very different from those of the bandits."

The main centres of banditism are the northeastern corner of Manchoukuo, which is separated from the Soviet Union by the Amur and Ussuri Rivers, the wooded and hilly eastern districts near the Korean border and Jehol. A Japanese Army statement published in March 1937 estimates the total number of bandits in Manchoukuo at 9600, distributed as follows: 5000 in Sinkiang and Pinkiang (the northeastern provinces of the country); 3000 in Mukden and Antung; 1000 in Jehol and Chinchow; 500 in Kirin and Chientao. A census of bandits is obviously apt to be imperfect. Moreover, banditism is a seasonal occupation, rising to its peak when the kaoliang, one of the chief Manchurian grain crops, grows to such height as to offer concealment to bandits who are lurking in the fields.

While they are an annoyance, the bandits do not constitute a serious menace to the new régime. As more Japanese troops are poured into Manchoukuo, as the newly formed Manchoukuo Army becomes more trained and reliable,[8] as the network of railways stretches out over the wilder parts of the country, banditism, both of the political and of the nonpolitical variety, will probably diminish.

But, six years after the occupation, Manchoukuo cannot be regarded as an unqualified political asset to the Japanese Empire. It has, indeed, as one of the last frontiers of empire, one of the few undeveloped regions in the world, provided an outlet for Japanese capital and economic de-

---

[8] A Manchoukuo Army, with a strength of somewhat over 100,000 men, has been built up with the aid of Japanese instructors. Its reliability is not beyond question; there have been cases of desertions and sales of rifles to insurgent "bandits." Its fighting quality is vastly lower than that of the Japanese troops and it has not been provided with such modern weapons as airplanes, tanks, and heavy artillery. It has, however, a useful subsidiary rôle as a supplementary police force and is used for patrolling the quieter sections of the frontier.

velopment. It has been turned into a large training ground and arsenal for the Japanese Army. But the attitude of the people remains at best passive, in some cases obviously disaffected.

Before the new régime can feel sure of a broader basis than the bayonets of the Kwantung Army, one, or both, of two new developments must occur. Either the sparsely settled northern regions must be filled up with loyal and patriotic Japanese colonists or there must be a wider opening of the doors of political and economic opportunity and advancement to the natives.

Japan's advance in Manchoukuo has left little room for the commercial activities of other powers. The creation of an oil monopoly eliminated the British and American oil companies. The non-Japanese foreign business communities in the towns of Manchoukuo, especially in Mukden, have been rapidly dwindling. Agencies which were formerly held by foreigners have been more and more taken over by Japanese.

A serious fall in the world price of Manchoukuo's staple commodity, the soya bean, in 1933, sharply cut down the value of its exports. The three years 1933, 1934, and 1935 revealed increasingly unfavorable trade balances, the excess of imports in 1935 amounting to 183,071,606 yuan. However, a more favorable situation developed in 1936, when Manchoukuo's exports rose to 598,675,000 yuan, as against 421,077,000 in the preceding year, imports increasing in smaller measure from 604,149,000 yuan to 690,693,000. A trade agreement with Germany, under which that country engaged to purchase Manchoukuo goods to a value of 100,000,000 yuan annually, in consideration of Manchoukuo purchases of German goods to the amount of 25,000,000 yuan,[9] together with the upward trend in commodity prices, helped to improve the trade balance.

Manchoukuo was primarily the creation of the Japanese Army; and it is from a military, rather than from a purely economic, standpoint that its significance must be judged. Possessing a freer hand there, the army has created an economy with some of the features of the military state socialism which some of its leaders would also like to see in Japan. Russia, the hereditary enemy, has been ousted from its former zone of influence in North Manchuria and pushed beyond the Amur. But by making Japan's military frontier march for thousands of miles with that of Russia, by eliminating the former no man's land of Chinese buffer sovereignty, the army has assumed liabilities, besides gaining advantages. It has helped to bring an element of strain and tension into the relations between Japan and the Soviet Union — a subject that is inextricably connected with the present status and future prospects of Manchoukuo.

[9] This agreement granted favorable terms to Manchoukuo, because Germany enjoys a very favorable balance of trade with Japan proper. The agreement, therefore, represents an effort to balance trade between the three countries on a triangular basis.

III

FACE TO FACE WITH SOVIET RUSSIA

ONE cannot talk half an hour with any typical Japanese general without realizing that to him the Soviet Union is Public Enemy Number One. And among Japanese of all classes, if one excepts a small and submerged group of radicals and Communist sympathizers, Russia is an object of more suspicion and antipathy than any other country.

For this attitude there are many reasons, historical and contemporary, sentimental and practical. It was with Russia that Japan fought its greatest war, a war in which the issue, to the Japanese mind, was one of national life or death. Every middle-aged Japanese has a vivid recollection of the stirring days of 1904 and 1905; many Japanese families cherish the memory of members who fell during the costly siege of Port Arthur.

The Russo-Japanese War is commemorated every year on Army Day, which is celebrated on the anniversary of the Battle of Mukden. Then the Emperor himself, surrounded by the highest military leaders, proceeds in state to the Yasukuni Shrine, sacred to the spirits of Japanese who have given their lives for their country, and pays homage to the souls of the fallen soldiers.

Japan has no friendly ties with Russia which might soften and offset the memories of conflict. Russia made no contribution to Japan's process of reconstruction along Western lines comparable with that of America and Great Britain, or even with that of France and Germany. It is not unusual to meet a Japanese businessman or engineer who is an alumnus of Harvard or of Massachusetts Institute of Technology, an army officer who has studied in Germany, a naval expert who has received his training in Great Britain. Friendships formed and ideas received during impressionable years of study abroad play an important part in shaping Japanese policy toward foreign countries, especially as it is from the more influential classes that men have been selected for foreign training. The few Japanese who have studied in Russia since the Revolution were almost all Communists, who were put in prison by a watchful police as soon as they returned to their native country.

The few Soviet Russians in Japan, just as the Japanese in Russia, are closely watched; and Japanese who associate with them are likely to be questioned at length by the police. There are consequently very few contacts with individual Russians which might counteract the impression of Russia as a vast impersonal menace.

Especially since the establishment of Manchoukuo, geography makes it inevitable that suspicion and apprehension should prevail between the Soviet Union and Japan, unless the two nations can find some basis of stable understanding. Manchoukuo projects itself into Siberia like a huge wedge. It is encircled on three sides by Soviet territory. To the east, between the Ussuri River and the sea, is the Soviet Maritime Province, with its main centre in the port of Vladivostok. To the north are the boundless stretches of Siberia. To the west is more Siberian land, together with the Soviet-protected state of Outer Mongolia.

It is a little over seven hundred miles from Vladivostok

SOLDIERS RETURNING FROM WORSHIP AT THE YASUKUNI SHRINE

to Tokyo; a fleet of fast Soviet bombers could make the trip in three or four hours. Japanese military propaganda makes the most of this Sword of Damocles which is suspended over Japan, the danger of bombing from the air. A chart, punctuated with little red electric bulbs, showing the various points from which Japan was vulnerable to air attack, was a feature of an exhibition which I saw in a little town in Southern Sakhalin, northernmost part of the Japanese Empire. Several points in China are also within striking distance of the shores of Japan; but Russia is obviously a far greater potential threat than China.

The Soviet Far Eastern Army is the sole land force in East Asia which can meet Japan on equal, perhaps on superior, terms, from the technical standpoint. This is an added cause of irritation to those Japanese who believe that their country's destiny points in the direction of domination of the adjacent mainland of Asia.

The replacement of the Tsarist Empire by the Union of Soviet Socialist Republics has not made for improvement in Russo-Japanese relations. For the Japanese general or conservative official looks on Communism as an insidious and dangerous form of poison gas, a new weapon in the hands of an old enemy. Every Japanese military leader with whom I talked during a trip in Manchoukuo and North China emphasized the alleged menace of Communist propaganda, not so much in Japan proper as in Korea and Manchoukuo, where suppressed nationalism provides fertile soil for Communist agitation. Communism is a blatant challenge to everything that is held sacred in the traditional Japanese morality: reverence for the Emperor, filial piety, paternal relationship in industry, emphasis on a spiritual, rather than a materialistic, interpretation of life.

Japan's distrust and dislike of the Soviet Union are fully reciprocated in the latter country. The Soviet press never wearies of accusing Japan of designs on the Soviet Far East, or of assuring its readers that all such designs will be victoriously repulsed by the Red Army. Soviet propaganda, in Russia and abroad, holds up Japan as the ally of Germany and the enemy of the Soviet Union. Confessions in Soviet treason and sabotage trials formerly endeavored to implicate French and British agents in sinister plots for sabotage and intervention. The rôle of supplementary villains in recent trials of this kind has been reserved for unnamed German and Japanese agents.

With this background of mutual suspicion and antipathy it is not surprising that relations along the boundary between the Soviet Union and Manchoukuo (which is almost as long, incidentally, as the frontier between Canada and the United States) should have been chronically tense and strained. Premier Hayashi recently stated in the Japanese Diet that there had been 2400 border disputes, most of which remain unsettled, since 1931. This represents an average of more than one "incident" a day. Many of these disputes were of a trivial character; but there has been no lack of clashes, involving loss of life on both sides, as the following excerpts from a chronicle of current events in the magazine *Contemporary Japan* indicates: —

March 26 [1936] — The War Office announces that several casualties were suffered when nine Japanese soldiers, making a topographical survey near Changlingtzu, on the eastern Manchoukuo-Soviet border, were fired on yesterday by Soviet troops. With the arrival of Japanese reënforcements the fighting continued.

Ambassador Ohta is instructed to protest against the Changlingtzu clash and Premier-Foreign Minister Hirota makes an oral protest to Ambassador Yurenev when the latter presents a protest from Moscow.

March 27 — Moscow circulates Ulan Bator messages, saying further border clashes are anticipated because of a concentration of Japanese-Manchoukuo troops near Lake Buir. [Ulan Bator is the capital of Outer Mongolia; Lake Buir is on the frontier between Manchoukuo and Outer Mongolia.]

March 30 — The Kwantung Army announces that two Outer Mongolian airplanes bombed and machine-gunned a Japanese-Manchoukuo patrol party yesterday twenty kilometres north of Taulan, killing one soldier and wounding four. Manchoukuo and the Kwantung Army protest to Ulan Bator.

March 31 — Manchoukuo receives from Outer Mongolia a protest alleging that the border clash of March 29th was caused by Japanese-Manchoukuo attacks inside Outer Mongolia, fifty kilometres from the frontier, and urges a conference to discuss the situation as soon as possible.

April 3 — A Soviet bomber flies over Manchoukuo northwest of Heiho, and a scouting plane appears over Suifenho. [Heiho is on the northern, Suifenho on the eastern, border of Manchoukuo.]

April 8 — The Kwangtung Army headquarters, announcing more details of the clash of March 31 on the Manchoukuo-Outer Mongolian border, reveals that four Japanese soldiers were killed. Three Mongolian planes were forced down and two armored cars captured.

April 9 — A Japanese officer and two soldiers are killed in a clash with the Soviets near Suifenho.

Two points are worth noting in this chronicle of border skirmishes, which might be extended indefinitely. First, each side invariably accuses the other of being the aggressor. I know of no case where either the Japanese or the Soviet Government admitted that its troops had been at fault. Inasmuch as neither the Japanese nor the Soviet Army tolerates foreign observers in its exposed frontier sectors, it is difficult to assess with certainty the precise course of events and the degree of responsibility in each of these numerous frontier brushes.

Secondly, the most serious fighting has taken place at the extreme eastern and western ends of the long border. This is by no means accidental. The greater part of the frontier is plainly marked by the course of three large rivers, the Argun, the Amur, and the Ussuri, although there is dispute as to the proper ownership of some islands in the Amur River, especially of one strategically important island which lies in the delta formed where the Ussuri empties into the Amur near Khabarovsk. Possession of this island, now occupied by the Russians, would bring the Japanese within shell range of Khabarovsk, the headquarters of the Soviet Far Eastern Army.

Between Lake Khanka and the point where Siberia, Manchoukuo, and Korea come together the frontier runs through thickly wooded country. Many of the frontier demarcation posts have rotted away or disappeared. The combination of an indefinite frontier with mutual ill will has naturally led to many clashes between border guards and patrols in this part of the frontier.

Still more serious conflicts have taken place along the remote western frontier of Manchoukuo, in the neighborhood of Lake Buir. Here an important political question is involved, the ultimate mastery of the vast, sparsely populated, arid tablelands which are now inhabited by clans of nomadic Mongols, who move from place to place with the flocks and herds that furnish them with almost all they need for their primitive, self-contained existence.

The Mongols to-day, who are estimated to number about

five millions, are divided between four sovereignties. Approximately two million live in the western provinces of Manchoukuo. About a million and a half are in China, mostly in the three provinces of Chahar, Suiyuan, and Ningsia. Three quarters of a million make up the population of Outer Mongolia, which bears to the Soviet Union much the same relation that Manchoukuo bears to Japan. The majority of the remainder are to be found in the Buryat Mongol Republic, one of the many national republics included in the Soviet Federation. Buryat Mongolia adjoins Outer Mongolia on the northeast.

Mongolia is a pivotal problem of Japanese and Soviet strategy. It lies athwart the pathways which seem marked out for Japanese and for Soviet expansion. It is probably inevitable that the more ambitious spirits both on the Japanese and on the Soviet side of the dimly demarcated boundaries should try to exploit their own Mongols as a nucleus for propaganda and perhaps eventual advance into the Mongolian territory held by the other power.

A number of officers of the Kwantung Army, notably Lieutenant Colonel Terada, have become specialists in the Mongolian question, learning the language, becoming familiar with the religion and customs of the Mongols. There can be little doubt that some of these officers cherish dreams of a Pan-Mongolian state, protected by Japan, purged of all Bolshevik influence, based on the ancestral customs and the Lamaism (a corrupted form of Buddhism) which has long been the dominant religion in Mongolia. Outer Mongolia would be an integral part of such a state, and it is quite conceivable that the Japanese military authorities would be willing to consent to the detachment from Manchoukuo of the Mongolian provinces lying west of the Hsingan

Mountains, provided, of course, that Japanese influence on the new state was assured and unchallenged.

The Soviet Union, however, regards Outer Mongolia, where a puppet state under Soviet influence was set up with the aid of the Red Army in 1921, as a valuable outpost in the Far East which it does not propose to abandon. This was made very clear in a statement which Stalin made to an American newspaper published in March 1936, to the effect that the Soviet Union would be obliged to take positive action in the event of any attack on Outer Mongolia.

So long as it preserves its Soviet orientation, Outer Mongolia is a potentially useful corridor, through which Soviet cavalry and motorized units could strike into the western part of Manchoukuo, threatening the communications of the Japanese forces stationed in the northern part of the country. The loss of Outer Mongolia would lay bare a thousand miles of Siberian frontier. A Japanese air base in Ulan Bator, the capital of Outer Mongolia, would be a menace to the large new iron, steel, and machine-building works which have been constructed at Novosibirsk and at Kuznetsk, in Central Siberia. These plants would certainly be turned to military uses in the event of war.

Japanese agents have been active among the Mongols of China. An incursion of Mongols from Manchoukuo, obviously sponsored by the Japanese military authorities, led to the establishment of a pro-Japanese régime in Chahar in the winter of 1935–1936. An attempt to repeat the process in Suiyuan in the latter part of 1936 failed because the Chinese offered unexpectedly strong resistance and the Japanese did not wish to bring their own troops into action.

Outer Mongolia, which is, from a political and military standpoint, virtually a part of the Soviet Union, has thus far proved too hard a nut for the Kwantung Army to crack. Two prolonged conferences which were held at the Manchoukuo border town of Manchouli in 1935 failed to bring about any agreement between Manchoukuo and Outer Mongolia on such questions as exchange of diplomatic representatives and frontier delimitation.

I was present for a short time during one of these conferences and carried away the impression of a diplomatic puppet show, with Tokyo and Moscow vigorously pulling the strings that controlled the Manchoukuo and Outer Mongolian delegates. The latter lived in railway cars, surrounded by watchful Russian "advisers" and as inaccessible and uncommunicative as the Grand Lama of Tibet. A Japanese diplomat attached to the Manchoukuo Foreign Office was the moving spirit in the Manchoukuo delegation.

The conference broke down because the Mongols refused to admit a Manchoukuo mission to their capital, Ulan Bator. Trouble was freely predicted in Hsinking as a result of the breakdown of the conference; and trouble, during the first months of 1936, there was, in the form of vigorous skirmishes at various points along the frozen boundary. Since Stalin has made it plain that serious aggression against Outer Mongolia will mean war with the Soviet Union there have been fewer bellicose statements from the headquarters of the Kwantung Army. As will be shown in more detail later, war with Russia does not figure in Japan's immediate military calculations.

Two economic problems which have created friction between the Soviet Union and Japan at times are the regulation of Japanese fishing rights in Siberian waters and the operation of the oil concession which Japanese companies hold in the Russian northern half of the island of Sakhalin.

At the time of Allied intervention in Russia, Japan occupied Northern Sakhalin, Vladivostok, and a considerable
section of Eastern Siberia. Partly because of American
diplomatic pressure, partly because the interventionist enterprise was expensive and unpopular in Japan itself, where
the army was not entrenched in power as it has been since
1931, Japan gradually withdrew from Siberia, abandoning
Vladivostok late in 1922. Northern Sakhalin was restored
to Soviet sovereignty later, in 1925, as part of the general
agreement for restoration of normal diplomatic relations between the two countries. Japanese firms were granted long-
term concessions for exploiting part of the oil and coal deposits of this territory. The disputes which usually occur
when foreign business organizations endeavor to operate on
Soviet territory have not been absent in the Sakhalin oil concession. But in the summer of 1936 an agreement extending
the prospecting rights of the Japanese firm until 1941 and
clearing up various points of disagreement was signed in
Moscow. The Japanese hope that they may realize half a
million tons of oil from the concession by 1941. This would
be considerably in excess of the entire meagre output of oil
in the Japanese Empire, although it would only cover about
one eighth of Japan's present oil requirements.

Japan leads the world in its annual fish catch. Not only
is fish the substitute for meat for the masses of the Japanese
people; but canned salmon, crab, tuna, and other fish
figure as an increasingly important item in Japan's export
trade. Japanese fishing in Soviet waters began long before
the Revolution, and Japanese fishing rights were acknowl-
edged in the Treaty of Portsmouth, concluded after the
termination of the Russo-Japanese War.

Disputes over the terms on which Japanese fishing could

THE BOUNDARY POST BETWEEN RUSSIA AND JAPAN ON THE
ISLAND OF SAKHALIN

be carried on have been frequent during the last decade. Some of the chief causes of disagreement were removed by the pact concluded in 1933 between the Soviet Assistant Foreign Commissar, Leo Karakhan, and the Japanese Ambassador in Moscow, Mr. Koki Hirota. A fixed value of 32.5 sen was assigned to the Soviet ruble and the system of bidding at auction was abolished for the majority of the fishing grounds. This system, reasonable enough in pre-War years when there was commercial competition between private Russian and Japanese companies, had become meaningless and dis-advantageous to Japan because of the concentration of the Soviet fishing industry in the hands of the state.

The Hirota-Karakhan agreement was for a period of three years. A new convention, framed along similar lines and supposed to be effective for eight years, was left unsigned by the Soviet Government as a reprisal for the conclusion of the Japanese-German pact against Communism in November 1936. A provisional agreement for one year was sub-stituted.

Refusal to sign the fisheries convention was not the only sign of displeasure which the Soviet Government gave after the publication of the anti-Communism pact, which was inter-preted in Moscow as almost equivalent to a German-Japanese military alliance against the Soviet Union. Soviet deliveries of pig iron to Japan were abruptly stopped. New difficulties were created for the few remaining Japanese residents of Vladivostok and for Japanese ships which touched at that port.

In view of the many factors which make for discord in Soviet-Japanese relations it is not surprising that the few efforts to bring about an improvement have been half-hearted and have led to no positive results. The Soviet

Union proposed a nonaggression pact to Japan in the winter of 1931–1932. The Japanese Government, while officially repudiating any aggressive designs against Russia, has steadily refused to conclude this pact. Japanese spokesmen argue either that such a pact would be superfluous, in view of the existence of the Kellogg Pact, or that it would be advisable first to clear up pending questions which are in dispute. Another familiar Japanese counterproposal is that the Soviet Union should demonstrate its peaceful intentions by reducing its formidable armed forces in Eastern Siberia. Soviet comment, however, has been all in favor of strengthening, not diminishing, these armaments.

Proposals to establish commissions for settling border disputes on the spot and for redemarcating the frontier in doubtful places have been discussed in Tokyo and in Moscow; but the anti-Communism pact helped to postpone indefinitely their realization.

Despite the long record of pinpricks on both sides, despite the frequent predictions of impending war which emanate from Moscow and the bellicose outbursts of some Japanese publicists,[1] the omens of 1937 do not seem to indicate that a second Russo-Japanese war is imminent or even that it is sooner or later inevitable. A state of uneasy truce, of equilibrium precariously resting on tanks and bayonets, has been established on the Amur and Ussuri frontier.

Experience has shown that border incidents, even when they involve loss of life, are not a probable *casus belli*. If

---

[1] Reiji Kuroda, Japanese newspaper correspondent in Berlin, published an article in the magazine *Diamond* late in 1936 asserting that "the only way to deal with the Soviet Union, which is humanity's common enemy, is to drive it into the ice-bound regions of the North."

There is no country in the world where statesmen so frequently (and thus far so incorrectly) predict the coming of war as in the Soviet Union.

2400 registered disputes could occur since 1931 without any outbreak of hostilities, there is no reason why a few hundred more may not develop during future years without leading to anything more explosive than the exchange of irate and contradictory notes.

If it were a cardinal point of Japanese policy to seize Eastern Siberia and drive Russia behind Lake Baikal, the best opportunity to achieve this objective at comparatively small cost and risk has been missed.   Japan's time to strike would have been soon after the occupation of Manchoukuo, in 1932, or, at the latest, in 1933.   At that time the defenses of the Soviet Far East were weak and internal morale was at a low ebb, as a result of the severe privations, including actual famine in the winter of 1932–1933, which were the result of the merciless drive for high-speed industrialization.

Now the Soviet position, military and economic, is much stronger.   A Far Eastern Army of picked troops, with a strength estimated at 250,000 or 300,000 men, is stationed along the frontier.   This is at least double the Japanese armed force in Manchoukuo; [2] and the Soviet superiority is even more marked in tanks and armored cars.   The Soviet side of the Siberia-Manchoukuo frontier is dotted with forts and blockhouses, more elaborate steel and concrete fortifications being erected at those places where the character of the country makes invasion easier.   The double tracking of the Trans-Siberian Railway has been completed, so that the flow of troops, munitions, and supplies to the Far East in the event of war could be greatly accelerated.   Moreover, internal conditions have improved to a point where the collapse

---

[2] No official statement as to the numbers of the Kwantung Army is available.   Competent foreign observers believe that it has been increasing in recent years and is now probably in excess of 100,000.

of morale and outbreaks of mutiny and revolt among mobilized peasant soldiers, which would have been not improbable if Russia had been exposed to the strain of a large-
scale war in 1931 or 1932, could not be anticipated at the
present time, at least not in the early stages of the war.

Japanese military men are able to appreciate and respect
the military efficiency of a prospective enemy. The former
Japanese Military Attaché in Moscow, Colonel Hikosaburo
Hata, after returning to Tokyo, published a series of articles in the Japanese newspaper *Asahi,* giving a high appraisal of the striking power of the Red Army. Colonel
Hata emphasized especially the fast bombing planes which
could reach Tokyo in three and a half hours and the many
types of tanks.

I once had the opportunity of talking at length with General Senjuro Hayashi, the former Premier and War Minister,
at a time when he was not occupying any public office. General Hayashi frankly admitted the technical inferiority of
the Japanese Army to the Soviet at the present time, although
he expressed confidence that the superior Japanese morale
and fighting spirit would enable Japan successfully to resist
attack. It is scarcely conceivable that he or any other
Japanese military leader would sanction the kind of light-
hearted, unprovoked attack of Japan on Russia which Soviet
spokesmen in Russia and Communist sympathizers elsewhere
like to represent as an imminent probability.[3]

[3] According to an estimate of the Foreign Policy Association, of New
York, the Soviet Union led the world in armament appropriations in
1936, with an expenditure of $3,000,000,000. Japan's expenditures
in the same year were approximately $300,000,000. Even if one allows
for some exaggeration of the Soviet expenditure, because of the uncertain
purchasing power of the Soviet ruble, there can be little doubt that the
real defense outlay of the Soviet Union, in view of its greater natural
wealth, was considerably in excess of Japan's. This fact should certainly
be considered in estimating the probability of a Japanese attack on Russia.

What of the reverse possibility, that the Soviet Union, intoxicated with its rapid strides in the armament field, should take the offensive against Japan? This may also be dismissed as highly improbable, at least for the predictable future. The Soviet Union has been stiffening its diplomatic attitude in proportion as its military preparations in the Far East have become more extensive and complete. It is now quite willing to give blow for blow in frontier brushes and to do its full share of pinpricking in the way of diplomatic and commercial reprisals for manifestations of Japanese ill will. But it is a long step from this attitude to one of outright aggression.

The following considerations speak loudly against any Soviet action which would be calculated to precipitate hostilities. There is no adequate motive; the Soviet Union has an abundance of land and natural resources. Moreover, any Soviet military adventure in the East would greatly increase the possibility of that conflict with Germany in the West which Soviet statesmen apprehend. Finally, there could be no assurance of a certain or easy victory.

So a kind of deadlock has been reached on Japan's northern frontier of empire, which is only likely to be broken as a result of the injection of some radically new factor into the situation. As remote possibilities in this connection one might mention the emergence of a Bonapartist military dictator in the Soviet Union or the seizure of power by young military extremists in Tokyo. Soviet and Japanese trends of expansion may also clash in China. While Japan has been occupying Manchoukuo and encroaching on North China, the Soviet Union has established predominant influence in vast, although scantily populated areas which still figure on most maps as parts of China, in Outer Mongolia and in Sinkiang, or Chinese Turkestan. Another Soviet outpost in China is represented by the Chinese Red Armies, which occupy an indeterminate and shifting region in the northern parts of Shensi and Kansu provinces and in Ningsia, the western part of Chinese Inner Mongolia. The chances of conflict in this connection cannot be altogether ruled out. But China is a country with plenty of elbowroom. Assuming, as is probable, that neither government desires war, the spheres of influence which they have carved out on Chinese territory may be kept from too close contact.

The most serious threat to equilibrium in the Far East would be the outbreak of a general European war. Such a war, by diminishing, if not nullifying, Russian land power and British sea power in the Far East, would give Japan tempting opportunities for expansion which probably would not be overlooked. But, barring such a European war, the Soviet-Manchoukuo frontier, troubled though it may be at times, does not seem likely to be the point of ignition for a second Russo-Japanese conflict.

Supposing that war should come between Japan and the Soviet Union, what would be the probable issue? The Russo-Japanese War of 1904–1905 casts little light on the answer to this question. Both Russia and Japan have altered materially as a result of industrial development and the progress of science. Moreover, the weapons and strategy of the World War were quite different from those of the Russo-Japanese War; a new war will bring still greater surprises in these fields.

One element, that of geographical nearness to the scene of conflict, remains in Japan's favor. Despite the double-tracking of the Trans-Siberian Railway, Japan can send re-enforcements and supplies where they may be needed much more rapidly than the Soviet Union can send out its necessary replacements of men and materials from its main centres of industry and population in European Russia.

Moreover, Manchoukuo, as regards supplies and communications, is more favorably situated than Eastern Siberia. The Soviet Government, for reasons which are at least as much military as economic, is making strenuous efforts to develop the latter region, to make its rich resources in coal, iron, gold, and timber the basis for new towns and industries. But this effort has only been initiated during the last few years; Eastern Siberia is still far behind Manchoukuo in its agricultural and industrial production. The Japanese Armies possess the further advantage of being able to fight on interior lines; the Soviet troops are necessarily distributed over the outer rim of the rough semicircle that represents the boundary of Manchoukuo to the north, east, and west.

On the other hand, the new weapons which were unknown when Nogi stormed the defenses of Port Arthur and Kuroki hammered away at the Russian lines at Mukden generally operate to Russia's prospective advantage. This is especially true of the airplane. The Russians are better natural fliers than the Japanese; the Soviet aviation industry is more advanced; and the crowded inflammable cities of Japan are far more vulnerable and important targets for air attack than the towns of Eastern Siberia. The Soviet superiority in tanks and mechanized weapons has already been mentioned. This is in part the reflection of natural Russian economic advantages. Nature, niggardly in its treatment of Japan, has provided the Soviet Union with vast reserves of coal, iron, manganese, and other valuable ores; Russian agriculture can absorb hundreds of thousands of tractors, which would be wasted on Japan's little plots of rice land. And ability to produce tractors connotes ability to produce tanks. Russia's annual output of iron, steel, and motor vehicles is about four times that of Japan; and the discrepancy tends to widen in Russia's favor with the passing of time.

To be sure, the coefficients of quality and efficiency are still in favor of Japan. Japan's railways function with clockwork regularity and punctuality that contrast favorably with the frequent delays and numerous wrecks on the Soviet transportation system.[4] Japan's industries are less subject than Russia's to sudden interruptions of full production schedule, attributable to failures of supply of raw materials or technical defects.[5] But the Soviet ability to surpass Japan in the manufacture of many modern weapons and kinds of munitions is scarcely open to question.

Another disadvantage to Japan would be the necessity of protection at the rear. Whatever may be the case as regards Soviet aid to bandits in Manchoukuo now,[6] this aid would certainly be forthcoming in the fullest possible measure from the moment war was declared. The Japanese High Command would have to expend much effort in guarding bridges,

[4] One of the many curious features of the second trial of Trotzkyists, held in Moscow in January 1936, was the confession of some of the defendants that they had caused thousands of wrecks on the Soviet railway lines. Such a confession reflects little credit on the vigilance or competence of the higher Soviet railway authorities.

[5] Among many illustrations of this tendency one may note an Associated Press dispatch from Moscow of February 17, 1937, reporting a stoppage of Russia's largest automobile factory which had lasted for several days because of failure to receive steering rods from another factory where the power plant was inadequate.

[6] Japanese officers with whom I talked in Manchoukuo expressed positive conviction that the bandits in Northeastern Manchoukuo were receiving aid from the Soviet Union; a Soviet official denied the charge with the remark: "If we were really helping the bandits, there would be a much bigger insurgent movement than there actually is."

THE THREE "HUMAN BOMBS" STATUE

Erected in memory of the three Japanese soldiers who rushed forward to certain death with explosives tied around their bodies at Shanghai in 1932

EMIGRANTS FROM JAPAN TO MANCHOUKUO VISITING THE MEIJI SHRINE BEFORE DEPARTURE

exposed stretches of railway, ammunition and supply depots, against raids of guerrilla insurgents. On the Soviet side of the frontier there are considerable numbers of kulaks (former well-to-do peasants) and other "criminals" who have been employed at forced labor on railways and other construction enterprises in the Far East and whose attitude toward the Soviet régime, to put it mildly, is not enthusiastic. But their capacity to disorganize the Soviet rear, at least in the beginning of the war, would be less than that of the armed bands which are already operating in Manchoukuo to inflict damage on the Japanese stores and communications. War against the Soviet Union would necessitate considerable contraction of Japan's operations in China, and the Chinese would try to take advantage of this relaxation of pressure.

Another modern weapon that would probably benefit Russia is the submarine. The Soviet Union would scarcely repeat the Tsarist folly of sending a fleet halfway around the world to fight the Japanese in their home waters. A number of submarines have been transported overland to Vladivostok and would undoubtedly try to raid Japanese lines of communication with the mainland in the event of war.

Morale on both sides could be rated as high at the outbreak of hostilities. Communism, like Fascism, generates fanatical enthusiasm among its devotees. An additional stimulus, on the Russian side, would be the visibly reviving Russian nationalism. The Russian Army would have a far better propaganda service than it possessed in 1904. The fighting quality of the Japanese is proverbial. It is a tradition that no Japanese officer ever surrenders. Two who were captured during the fighting at Shanghai in 1932 committed hara-kiri in expiation. The Japanese soldier, who is usually recruited from among the peasantry, has always shown himself courageous, obedient, capable of great endurance. It should not be forgotten that the Japanese soldiers are just as well schooled in their propaganda of nationalism as the Russians are in theirs of Communism.

If Russia and Japan confronted each other in war, with no foreign intervention in favor of either side, the odds would appear fairly evenly balanced. Neither side could count on certain or overwhelming victory; and this is the main factor which is preserving peace along the armed and tense Siberia-Manchoukuo frontier. The issue of the war might well be determined by the attitude of other powers. If the Soviet Union, without an ally, were obliged to fight Japan in the East and Germany and Poland in the West, the struggle might end in a defeat for Russia which would not only give Japan the frontier on Lake Baikal which is coveted by some extreme nationalists, but would mean the end of Stalin's dictatorship, if not of the entire Soviet régime. If, on the other hand, Japan not only had to face the full military power of the Soviet Union, but also became embroiled with America or Great Britain, or both, and was attacked by a resurgent China, the outlook would be dark for the Island Empire.

IV

THE ADVANCE TO THE WEST: CHINA

WHAT does Japan want in China? Markets and raw materials? Military strategic advantages? Complete political domination? Mere assurance of orderly peaceful development? These questions concern the statesmen and merchants of all countries with commercial interests in China. They must rise to-day in the minds of millions of people all over the world.

For the long struggle between these two nations, united by geographical proximity and cultural ties, divided by profound differences of temperament and historical experience, has now entered the dramatic phase of open warfare. The threat of armed conflict, which from 1931 to 1937 periodically appeared on and receded from the horizon of Sino-Japanese relations, has become a fact. And just as it was impossible to find a formula to avert the war, so it is extremely difficult to work out a basis on which it can be brought to an end, destructive and impoverishing as it is to both nations.

Japanese and Chinese have much in common that distinguishes both peoples from Europeans and Americans. Japan's cultural debt to China is enormous. From its neighbor Japan, that great borrower and assimilator of foreign cultural achievements, absorbed the Buddhist conceptions of religion and the Confucian ethical precepts which

are foundation stones of Japanese civilization. From China
came the thousands of complicated hieroglyphs which make
the Japanese written language the despair of all but the
most gifted or persistent students.[1] Japan's old capital,
Kyoto, strangely enough is the easiest Japanese city in which
to find one's way about. Its streets, laid out in straight
regular parallels, are not the result of modern town planning, but of a mediæval imitation of the plan of one of
China's ancient capitals, Sianfu.

With so much of Japan's civilization stemming from
Chinese sources it is natural that there should be much
similarity in the everyday habits, prejudices, preferences, of
the two peoples. In both Chinese and Japanese one finds a
dislike for blunt, clear-cut decisions, a fondness for convey-
ing ideas by indirection. To the Westerner this trait of
Oriental mentality seems annoyingly devious and tortuous;
to the Chinese or Japanese the Westerner seems regrettably
lacking in manners and finesse.

Probably the outstanding single distinction between Eastern and Western civilizations is that the latter is centred
around the individual, whereas the former subordinates the
individual to the family. It is a rare and forceful personality
either in Japan or in China who can emancipate himself from
the clinging ties of the family system, which offers security
at the expense of individuality and creates a kind of small-
scale collectivist life.

Yet if there is much that unites Japan and China, culturally
and psychologically, there is perhaps still more that divides
them. Within the framework of Eastern civilization these

[1] Although Japan borrowed the hieroglyphic method and most of the
hieroglyphs from China, there is no similarity between the spoken languages of the two countries.

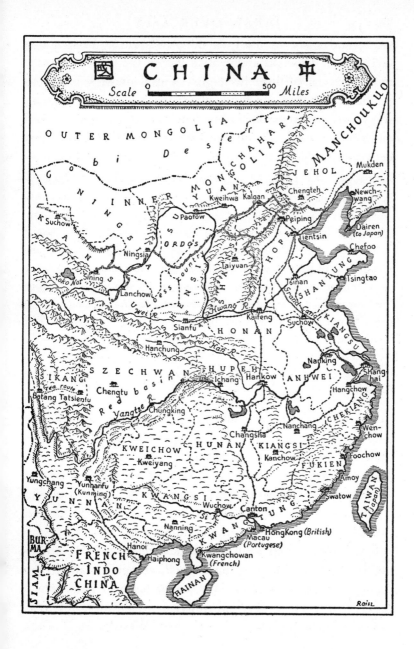

CHINA 中
Scale 0 |———————| 500 Miles

OUTER MONGOLIA

Gobi Desert

MANCHOUKUO

INNER MONGOLIA

CHAHAR'

JEHOL

Mukden

Kweihwa Kalgan

Chengteh

Newch-
wang

Paotow

Peiping

Suchow

ORDOS

Tientsin

Dairen
(to Japan)

Ningsia

Taiyuan

Chefoo

Sining

Lanchow

HOPE

Tsinan

SHANTUNG

Tsingtao

Koko Nor

Hwang R.

Kaifeng

Sianfu

HONAN

Sychow

KIANGSU

Hanchung

Han R.

Nanking

Shang-
hai

SIKANG

SZECHWAN

HUPEH

Hankow

ANHWEI

Hangchow

Batang Tatsienfu

Chengtu basin

Ichang

Red

Yangtze Chungking

Changsha

Nanchang

CHEKIANG

Wen-
chow

KWEICHOW

HUNAN

KIANGSI

Kweiyang

Kanchow

FUKIEN

Foochow

Yungchang

Yunnanfu
(Kunming)

YUNNAN

KWANGSI

Wuchow

Si R.

Canton

Amoy

Swatow

TAIWAN (Japan)

Nanning

KWANGTUNG

Hong Kong (British)
Macau (Portugese)
Kwangchowan
(French)

BURMA

FRENCH
INDO
CHINA

Hanoi

Haiphong

SIAM

HAINAN

Roisl

two peoples are at least as differentiated as French and Germans or Russians and British within the orbit of a common Western cultural heritage. The Chinese scholar and publicist, Dr. Lin Yu-tang, whose book *My Country and My People* is a remarkably brilliant piece of national cultural and psychological self-analysis, draws the following contrast between Japanese and Chinese national temperaments: —

> Compare the Japanese, busy and bustling, reading a newspaper in the tram or in the train, with a dogged face and determined chin and a cloud of imminent national disaster hanging over his brow, determined that Japan must either smash the world or be smashed in the next great conflict, and preparing for its coming — and the Chinese in his long gown, as placid, as contented, as happy-go-lucky as if nothing could ever shake him out of his dreams. . . . The "yellow peril" can come from Japan but not from China. Deep down in our instincts we want to die for our family, but we do not want to die for our state. The propaganda of the Japanese militarist clique that says a nation should aggrandize itself in order to bring "peace and harmony" to Asia, or even to the world, can have no appeal to the Chinese.

Dr. Lin is a Chinese; and the most mellow and tolerant Chinese to-day is very naturally apt to weight the scales a trifle on the negative side when he is discussing Japan. A Japanese might retort that certain unmistakable material advantages which Japan enjoys over China to-day — freedom from banditism, relatively less suffering from flood and drought and political corruption, higher standards of hygiene and sanitation, complete national independence — are attributable in large degree to the dogged, energetic traits in the Japanese character and to the sense of national unity which is only beginning to develop, slowly and painfully, in China.

Both Japan and China have had Western civilization

thrust on them, partly through the forceful arguments of the navies and landing parties which follow in the wake of adventurous traders, partly through the irresistible progress of invention and communication. But the reaction of the two Oriental countries to a similar challenge was profoundly different, revealing marked differences of tastes and aptitudes.

Japan has been most successful in assimilating the material gifts of the West, China the intellectual. By a feat of adaptation which has no parallel in history, requiring a high degree of discipline, efficiency, and coördination, Japan, within two generations after it had emerged from its three centuries of self-imposed isolation from the outside world, placed itself in a position to talk to the West on equal terms in everything from battleships to bills of exchange.

Several factors helped to promote Japan's rapid modernization. The Island Empire was small, compact, well adapted to centralized government. The impact of the West, embodied in Perry's "black ships," coincided with an internal ferment, with a strong tendency to break away from the bonds of a régime that had become stagnant, even retrogressive. Around the young Emperor Meiji, whose restoration to sovereignty was the symbol of the modernist revolution, was a group of strong, fresh-minded advisers, who were not afraid to dare, to experiment, to make drastic changes in the customs and economic life of feudal Japan. At the same time the cult of Emperor worship, impressed on every Japanese from his earliest schooldays, was a stabilizing force, a bond of unity which enabled the country to pass through a swift transition from old to new ways of life with a minimum of social disturbance and civil strife.

China came into large-scale contact with the West under vastly less favorable circumstances. The imperial régime had become decadent; but there was no one to bury it. The enormous size of the country (China in the nineteenth century represented the largest land unit in the world except Russia) and the absence of rail communication hindered the development of national spirit and the execution of measures designed on a nation-wide scale.

When the empire collapsed in 1911 the republican régime, based on Western models, which took its place proved quite unworkable. Ninety or 95 per cent of the people were illiterate; only a handful of Western-educated Chinese had any conception of parliamentary institutions; the immemorial Chinese tradition was against popular participation in the business of government, which was supposed to be reserved for a special class of magistrates and officials.

The sequel to the fall of the empire was a period of senseless and destructive civil conflicts, not unlike the feuds of rival underworld gangs, between the various "war lords," or military governors of provinces and groups of provinces. Dr. Sun Yat-sen, the pioneer leader and theorist of Chinese nationalism, maintained a precarious hold on the city of Canton, in the South, which was always most hospitable to innovations and radical ideas.

But it was only in 1925 that the Kuomintang (National People's Party), the political organization of which Dr. Sun was the leader, began to win nation-wide support as a result of the upsurge of a nationalist movement, especially among the students. The action of foreign-controlled police in Shanghai and Canton in firing on Chinese crowds in 1925 fanned the nationalist flame to a white heat.

Russian Communist advisers whom Dr. Sun Yat-sen invited to Canton gave the Chinese their first lessons in mass propaganda and organization. The outstanding figure among these advisers was the astute Michael Borodin, while the Soviet General Bluecher, now commander of the Far Eastern Army, serving under the pseudonym of Galen, guided the military councils of the nationalists.

During the latter part of 1926 and the first months of 1927 the nationalist armies, led by the rising young general, Chiang Kai-shek, swept northward to the Yangtze Valley, their advance culminating in the capture of Shanghai, China's commercial and industrial metropolis, and the mediæval capital, Nanking, which was subsequently made the capital of nationalist China.   At the same time a schism developed between the moderate and extremist elements in the nationalist movement.

The labor and peasant unions which were organized as the nationalist armies advanced put forward the extreme demands which are customary when masses which have been completely unused to any kind of collective bargaining suddenly feel an intoxicating sense of new-found power.   A massacre of landlords broke out in Hunan Province and the life of the employer was made difficult in all the large cities. Exploiting the growing dissatisfaction of the moderate elements in the nationalist movement, Chiang Kai-shek in the spring of 1927 broke with the Russian advisers, outlawed the Communists, and established a government under his own leadership at Nanking.   Some of the more Left-Wing Kuomintang leaders created a rival régime at Hankow; but this evaporated after a few months.   With the capture of the old capital, Peking, by the nationalist troops in 1928, China was nominally united under the rule of the Kuomintang, the sole legal party in the country.   This organization was purged of its more radical members, some of whom joined the Communists, who raised the standard of revolt in some districts of Kiangsi and Fukien Provinces, in the south central part of the country.

The time lag in China's unification under a party which, whatever its faults and weaknesses, represented a great advance over the feudal war lords, in so far as it gave the educated classes more opportunity to participate in the government and upheld modern and progressive ideas of social reform and economic development, is of the utmost importance. China's unity was reached sixty years after Japan had definitely turned its face toward the West. It was realized twenty-three years after Japan fought itself into the ranks of the great powers by defeating Russia.

This long start which Japan enjoyed, combined with the fact that the Japanese have shown greater keenness and aptitude, as a rule, in learning the tricks of Western industrial and commercial technique, helps to account for the fact that practically every material comparison between Japan and China works out in favor of the former country. Although Japan has only about one sixth of China's population, it is far ahead of its neighbor in the annual value of industrial production and foreign trade.

China has no transoceanic shipping lines, and a considerable part even of its coastal and river shipping is in the hands of British, Japanese, and other foreign firms. Japan's passenger liners and fast freighters sail the seven seas and compete successfully with those of America and Europe. The ricksha in Japan to-day is already a rarity; it has given way to the taxicab. In China the incredibly cheap human labor performs a vast amount of the work which is left to machines and beasts of burden in most other countries.

Japan is a major naval power; the Chinese Navy is barely able to cope with smugglers. At Shanghai, both in 1932 and in 1937, and in several other battles during the recent hostilities, the Chinese soldier has proved himself capable of stubborn resistance.[2] But usually the Japanese have advanced successfully, even against superior numbers. In single combat a Chinese might not be inferior to a Japanese. But Japan's superiority in discipline, organization, and military equipment has been overwhelming.

While Japan has thus been more successful in imitating the material achievements of the more advanced Western countries, a comparison of Japan and China in the intellectual field would yield quite different results. The Japanese take fairly well to Western clothes and Western machines, but they are apt to become fuzzy and muddled in handling Western ideas. Chinese intellectuals, on the other hand, are not only usually better natural linguists than the Japanese; they are also far more at home in discussing Occidental political, economic, social, and philosophical ideas. This is why, as the Japanese themselves admit, they usually come off second best in debates with Chinese before Western audiences.

No Japanese has ever written about his country a book remotely comparable with Lin Yu-tang's study of the Chinese national character and culture, at once mellow, tolerant, humorous, critical, and at the same time profoundly sympathetic. To the Japanese the gift of self-expression, of self-analysis, seems to have been denied. The Chinese

[2] There were several reasons for the stiff resistance which the Chinese Nineteenth Route Army maintained against the Japanese attacks on the outskirts of Shanghai. This army was one of the best Chinese fighting units. It was strongly entrenched, so that the Japanese superiority in field manœuvring was of little advantage. Finally, the Japanese themselves sacrificed strategy to prestige by hammering away in frontal attacks for weeks before they finally dislodged the Chinese by a flanking movement.

intellectual also has a quicker and surer gift of insight into the spirit and mentality of other countries. Japanese discussions of Fascism, Socialism, Communism, and other foreign ideas in magazines and newspapers are likely to be either superficial or confused, or both.

Tens of centuries of respect for learning have inevitably influenced the making of the modern Chinese intellectual. Moreover, the Chinese professor is still relatively free from regimentation; his Japanese colleague is very much of a scholar in uniform. The family system, with its emphasis on collective rather than individual decisions, its implied obligation to take counsel with others, tends to make the Oriental personality more repressed and reserved than the Occidental. Superimposed on this family system the Japanese has a rigidly bureaucratic state. The resultant discipline and coördinated effort have helped Japan, the nation, in its struggle for a place in the military and industrial sun. But Japanese individuality has paid the price of being in many ways subdued, fettered, and cramped.

China's weakness was a stimulus to Japan's expansionist urge, which began to be felt as the population increased rapidly after the abandonment of the policy of self-isolation. All Japan's important accessions of territory have been entirely or partially at the expense of China. The Sino-Japanese War of 1894–1895 led to the acquisition of the rich semi-tropical island of Formosa, which is now Japan's sugar bowl. Another result of the war was the disappearance of the vague protectorate which China had hitherto exercised over Korea. This was replaced by a Japanese protectorate which ended in outright annexation. Manchuria, which had always been geographically reckoned as a part of China, had become racially Chinese as a result of the rapid influx of colonists from the neighboring Chinese provinces of Shantung and Hopei.

There is an element of continuity in Japan's efforts to establish itself as the predominant power in East Asia. Professor W. W. McLaren ends a history of Japan in the Meiji Era, published over two decades ago, with the following sentences, which might have been lifted from a contemporary book or magazine article: —

> There is no political party at present, nor has there been one during the last decade, opposed to militarism and to an indefinite expansion of the Japanese power in China. . . . Japan's predominance in eastern Asia has become the foundation of the national policy. "Nibbling at China" is no longer the propaganda of the military party alone; that policy has come to be universally accepted as leading directly to the realization of the national destiny. . . . In the event of China's inability to defend herself, what Western power will intervene to save her?

At the same time Japan has gone about the realization of its objectives in China in a zigzag course, rather than in a straight line. One can distinguish four separate phases of Japanese policy toward China during the last generation. The first was inaugurated by the presentation to China of Japan's famous Twenty-one Demands, supported by an ultimatum, in May 1915.

At this time the preoccupation of the European powers with the World War seemed to Japanese statesmen to afford an excellent opportunity of advancing their country's interests in China with small risk of effective opposition from other countries. Until recently these demands were regarded as a landmark of the extreme high point of Japanese aggression. China still commemorates them by observing a national Day of Humiliation on the anniversary of their presentation.

The Twenty-one Demands fell into five groups. The first was designed to ensure for Japan the predominant position which Germany had held in Shantung Province before the War. It specified, among other things, that China should assent to any agreements which might be reached between Japan and Germany regarding the disposition of the German rights and privileges in Shantung. (Japanese troops, shortly after the outbreak of the War, had occupied the German Leased Territory of Kiaochow, with its main seaport of Tsingtao.)

The second group of demands was concerned with the maintenance and extension of Japan's favored position in South Manchuria and East Inner Mongolia. It provided for the prolongation to ninety-nine years of the leases of Port Arthur, Dairen, and the South Manchuria Railway, for the right of Japanese subjects to own and lease land for agricultural, commercial, and industrial purposes in South Manchuria and East Inner Mongolia, and for the granting of various other rights and privileges to Japanese residents in these regions.

The third group was intended to secure mining and railway concessions in Central China and the fourth stipulated that China should not lease to a third power any harbor, bay, or island along the Chinese coast.

The fifth group was in a separate category and was not covered by the ultimatum which preceded China's acceptance of the other demands. Some of its points involved far-reaching abrogation of Chinese sovereignty, notably the suggestions that China should employ Japanese as political, military, and financial advisers and that a joint Sino-Japanese police force should be organized in cities where many Japanese live. The sole point of this fifth group of demands which figured in subsequent agreements was an assurance by China that she had given no permission to foreign military powers to establish military or naval bases in Fukien provinces and did not propose to borrow money for this purpose. The other demands were formally accepted; but some of them were subsequently relinquished, while others were never effectively realized.

For instance, the Washington Conference of 1922 led to the restoration of China's sovereignty in the former German Leased Territory around Tsingtao. The Washington Conference, incidentally, may be taken as the starting point of a new, much more conciliatory, phase of Sino-Japanese relations, which lasted until 1931. A leading figure in this new phase was Baron Kijuro Shidehara, who for years held the portfolio of Minister of Foreign Affairs in Japan.

Some time ago I had an opportunity to discuss with Baron Shidehara the principles of his policy toward China, which was violently denounced as "weak-kneed" by the militarists. The heavy guard which was posted around the approaches to the Baron's spacious villa, which is adjoined by one of the most beautiful gardens in Tokyo, was a symbol of the changed mood of the time, of the necessity for protecting Shidehara against the possibility of attack by nationalist extremists who still cherish resentful memories of his "weak-kneed" diplomacy.

"It is my belief," declared the former Foreign Minister, "that Japan would gain more than any other country from an honest application of the 'open-door' idea in China. Our geographical propinquity, our low production costs, assure us a dominant place in the Chinese market if our trade is not artificially restricted by boycotts."

It was on the basis of this belief that Shidehara conducted

his foreign policy, refraining from bullying and nagging tactics on minor disputed points in the conviction that he was advancing the larger interests of Japanese commerce.

A fundamental change came over Japan's continental policy in 1931, when Manchuria was seized and Shidehara was swept out of office. For the next five years the practice of "nibbling at China" was resumed with vigor; some of the nibbles assumed the proportions of fairly large bites. So Jehol Province was detached from China and added to Manchoukuo in 1933. More recently four million more Chinese were brought under a régime that is directly dependent on the Japanese Army through the creation of the East Hopei Government, headed by Yin Ju-keng, and a similar process has taken place in a large part of Chahar, the eastern part of Inner Mongolia.

Apart from direct territorial changes there have been substantial nibbles at Chinese administrative authority and economic integrity in the Peiping-Tientsin area. An inconspicuous news item which appeared in the press when I was visiting North China in the latter part of 1935 casts a good deal of light on the potent character of Japanese influence in that region: —

Colonel Yuan Liang, who during the last few days has been the subject of bitter attacks in the local Japanese press as well as by Japanese newspaper correspondents, left by this afternoon's through train for Nanking. . . . Colonel Yuan's resignation as Mayor of Peiping was accepted yesterday by the Nanking Government.

A nod from the Japanese garrison headquarters in Tientsin, an inspired campaign in local Japanese newspapers — and the mayor of China's ancient capital hastily boards a train for Nanking. Many similar instances of the tightening

Japanese grip on the Chinese administrative machinery in the provinces north of the Yellow River, and especially in the Peiping-Tientsin area, could be cited.

On one occasion the Japanese police swooped down on the Chinese censorship office in Tientsin and arrested several of the officials on the suspicion that they belonged to the Blue Jacket Society, a secret Chinese nationalist organization. The mayor of the Chinese city of Tientsin,[8] Mr. Cheng Ko, was served with demands by the Japanese authorities that all allegedly anti-Japanese passages should be eliminated from Chinese textbooks.   A Chinese editor in Tientsin remarked to me: —

"There is no reason why the Japanese should take any military action here.   They have already gained everything they could desire, so far as control of the Chinese local government is concerned."

The most striking example of the breakdown of Chinese authority in the northern provinces is the stream of goods, mostly of Japanese origin, which pours into the country through Tientsin and some of the neighboring smaller ports without paying duty.   This orgy of smuggling during 1936 became a matter of visible concern not only to the Chinese Government, which addressed several ineffectual protests to the Japanese Government, but also to foreign powers with commercial interests in China, especially to Great Britain.   British interests were suffering in two ways.   The smuggled Japanese goods could undersell British goods on which duty had been paid.   Moreover, the best security for foreign loans to China, most of which have been granted

---

[8] Side by side with the Chinese city of Tientsin are the foreign-administered British, Japanese, French, and Italian Municipal Areas, which have so far been unmolested.

by British financial interests, is a lien on the Chinese customs revenue, which is collected under foreign supervision. The loss of customs revenue through smuggling, if it went far enough, might, therefore, undermine the security for the loans.

The extent of smuggling in North China, as it had developed by the spring of 1936, was reflected in the comment of a businessman who had returned to Tientsin from the near-by port of Peitaiho: —

"I saw no smuggling. I only saw thirty-eight vessels of all sorts and sizes lying out in the bay and discharging cargo into dozens of sampans [Chinese rowboats], and the beach as busy as the Bund here in Tientsin in the height of the shipping season. You can't call that smuggling any more. That's free trade. It is not even a free port; it is a free coast nowadays."

The Chinese Government officially estimated the loss of customs revenue between August 1935 and April 1936 at 25,000,000 Chinese dollars (about $7,500,000 in American money) and reckoned an additional loss of 8,000,000 Chinese dollars in April alone.[4] To quote one of its notes to Tokyo: —

At Shanhaikwan and other places the audacity of armed Japanese and Korean smugglers has been amazing, numerous cases having occurred in which Customs officers were attacked with impunity and goods already seized by the Customs were recovered by force.

[4] The customs revenue figures published at the end of 1936 indicate that the Chinese Government may have somewhat exaggerated the loss of income through smuggling in North China. The decline in customs collections at the North China ports amounted to a little over $8,000,000, while the customs revenue for all China showed a gain of almost $9,000,000, as against the figure for 1935.

Japanese military pressure helped to paralyze the Chinese customs officials, who were forbidden to carry revolvers. The arming of revenue cutters was also prohibited by Japanese demand. The ostensible basis for these demands was the Tangku Truce, which put a stop to the fighting between Japanese and Chinese troops in North China in the spring of 1933. At this time the Japanese forces were at the gates of Peiping and Tientsin; and the Truce is a very one-sided document which Japanese officers in North China have liked to interpret as giving them a license to interfere in almost every phase of Chinese civil and military administration.

The setting up of a pro-Japanese régime headed by Yin Ju-keng in the former demilitarized zone south and west of the Great Wall also facilitated evasion of the Chinese customs collectors. Yin Ju-keng lowered the Chinese tariff rates by 75 per cent and Japanese military leaders contended that goods which had paid this lower duty should be permitted to circulate freely in China.

Rayon, sugar, piece goods, and oil figured prominently in the operations of the smugglers, among whom Koreans predominated. Their main commercial base of operation was Dairen. The Chinese Government, unable to check smuggling directly at the ports, took strong preventive measures against an influx of contraband goods into the interior of the country. The death penalty was prescribed for Chinese who participated in smuggling operations. A cordon was thrown around the relatively narrow area where Japanese authority was paramount; trains and buses were carefully searched. These measures unquestionably yielded some positive results and warded off the flooding of Shanghai and other Yangtze Valley cities with smuggled products.

However, the British Inspector General of the Chinese Maritime Customs, Sir Frederick Maze, in a statement which he issued in March 1937, emphasized the point that smuggling is still a serious problem in North China. He declared that in Tientsin the customhouse had recently been attacked by armed Koreans, who forcibly removed a considerable amount of smuggled goods stored there, while in Tsingtao, the main port of Shantung Province, a customs officer was attacked in the discharge of his duty and injured by a Japanese mob. Sir Frederick expressed the opinion that a radical solution of the smuggling problem would only be possible if Chinese sovereignty were restored in East Hopei.

This smuggling offensive may be regarded as in some measure a reprisal against the Chinese tariff, which Japan regarded as unduly high. It is only fair to say that this tariff has stimulated contraband trade in other parts of China where Japanese influence is not predominant.[5] But nowhere has the challenge to Chinese authority been so blatant as in the North China ports. This fact suggests a certain amount of political motivation in the obvious unwillingness of the Japanese military and political authorities to take any strong action against the practice. It is the dream of some of Japan's expansive military economists to create a triangular block, embracing Japan, Manchoukuo, and North China.

---

[5] The American Collector of Customs at Canton, with whom I talked during a recent trip in China, mentioned an increased volume of smuggling across the Chinese frontier from the three foreign territories of Hong Kong, Macao (under Portuguese rule), and Kwangchouan, a French leased territory. Moreover, before Canton was placed under the effective control of the central government, the local Chinese officials promoted a good deal of smuggling for the purpose of diverting revenue from central to local use.

The breaking down of the customs wall around North China would be a step toward the realization of this dream.

Japan during recent years has pursued a policy of penetrating and encroaching on North China without actually taking over the administration of this large region, which stretches over an area of almost 400,000 square miles and is inhabited by about 75,000,000 people.[6] This policy has been facilitated by the exploitation of certain privileges which Japan, along with America, Great Britain, France, Italy, and some of the smaller powers, enjoys in China.

Smuggling has been made much easier because Japanese and Koreans, as subjects of Japan, enjoying the right of extra-territoriality, are not amenable to trial and punishment by the Chinese courts.   When they are apprehended in smuggling or selling narcotics they may only be handed over to the Japanese consular authorities, who have displayed little zeal in checking these activities.

Under the Protocol which was signed after the Boxer antiforeign outbreak had been subdued by the dispatch of an international expeditionary force, the foreign signatory powers have the right to maintain unspecified numbers of troops in the Peiping-Tientsin area.   Some of these troops are stationed in the Legation quarter of Peiping; others in Tientsin.   The purpose of the authorization was to ward off any new antiforeign outbreak or attack on the embassies in Peiping and also to preserve access from Peiping to the sea.

There has been no serious antiforeign outbreak in North China during the last generation and it has never proved necessary for the foreign troops in that region to resort to armed force.   On March 1, 1936, the numbers of troops

[6] Cf. *China Year Book*, 1936, p. 1.

stationed in North China, by nationalities, were as follows: 2203 Japanese, 1789 French, 1377 Americans, 1003 British, 381 Italians. Later in the spring the Japanese force was substantially increased. Precise figures were not published; but it is generally believed that the Japanese garrison in North China then increased to eight or ten thousand men, outnumbering all the other foreign forces put together. There was nothing in the Boxer Protocol to forbid such an increase; its significance as a means of exerting pressure on the Chinese authorities is obvious. Still earlier, in the summer of 1935, all Chinese Central Government troops had been obliged to evacuate North China, as a result of the peremptory demands of the Japanese military leaders.

Japan's advance in North China has been motivated by two considerations, military and economic. Most Japanese Army leaders believe that war with the Soviet Union, if not inevitable, is very probable. In the event of such a conflict North China, which adjoins Manchoukuo, would be a region of high strategic significance. Japanese military opinion is, therefore, concerned with means of neutralizing in advance any hostile use of this region and of making it as serviceable as possible to Japan's ends.

The Japanese Army is pursuing two specific objectives in North China. It is endeavoring both to drive a wedge between China and Russia and to ensure control of the railways and natural resources of the region in the event of war. Closely associated with the aim of inserting a strip of Japanese-controlled territory between China and the Soviet Union is the effort to exploit the traditional antagonism between the nomadic Mongols and the Chinese, whose methods of settled agriculture spoil the wide grazing areas which the Mongols need for their flocks and herds.

The three northernmost provinces of China, Chahar, Suiyuan, and Ningsia, which border on the Soviet protectorate of Outer Mongolia, make up Inner Mongolia. This is a region vast in extent, thinly populated, much of its soil being arid and unsuited for cultivation, and is inhabited by a mixed population of Chinese and Mongols. The Mongols are the indigenous inhabitants; the Chinese have largely come in as immigrant colonists, following, in many cases, the line of the Peiping-Suiyuan Railway. Administrative authority has been divided, in that vague, indeterminate way which is possible only in China, between the Chinese governors of the provinces and a body known as the Mongolian Autonomous Political Council, which includes the representatives of various Mongolian "banners," or clans, and represents Mongolian interests. Japanese officers have been active in Inner Mongolia, endeavoring to persuade the Mongol princes that their interests would be served by throwing off Chinese rule and setting up an autonomous régime under Japanese protection.

A swift raid from Manchoukuo, carried out by Manchoukuo Mongols with Japanese "advisers," brought a large part of Chahar within the orbit of Japanese Army influence in the winter of 1935–1936. But similar tactics failed when they were tried in the neighboring province of Suiyuan in the autumn of 1936. Here again mysterious "irregular" Mongol forces appeared on the scene. Chinese allege that they were supported by Japanese airplanes. It is a matter of record that the Kwantung Army professed sympathy with this Mongol attack on Chinese rule in Suiyuan, although the Japanese Government disclaimed interest in the conflict. In Suiyuan, however, the Chinese military commander, General Fu Tso-yi, successfully resisted the invaders and drove them back into Chahar. This episode showed that the Chinese forces in Suiyuan are strong enough to cope with the limited Mongol forces which can be incited against them, although it is unlikely that they could withstand an invasion by regular Japanese troops. At the moment, however, the desire for a wedge between China and Russia is subordinated to other Japanese interests in China. The idea is therefore in abeyance; it has certainly not been abandoned.

The Japanese Army has been more successful in destroying Chinese military strength than in establishing its own positive control over North China. It has forced the Central Government troops to withdraw; but this has not caused the local Chinese rulers, Sung Che-yuan in Hopei, Yen Hsi-shan in Shansi, and Han Fu-chu in Shantung, to cast in their lot with Japan. On the contrary, every new aggressive step of Japan further solidified Chinese sentiment and made it more difficult for a Chinese leader to take any steps which might be interpreted as pro-Japanese.

On the economic as on the military side much remains to be done before Japan's ambitions may be regarded as satisfied. North China is relatively rich in mineral resources, containing about 55 per cent of China's coal and about 40 per cent of its iron reserves. About a quarter of China's cotton (a commodity in which Japan is especially interested) is grown in Hopei. North China also contains almost half of China's very limited railway mileage.

Japan's schemes for the economic development of North China, as canvassed in the press and in statements by politicians and economists, are far-reaching. It has been proposed to build several railway lines: one between Tsangchow and Shihchiachung, linking up China's two main north-south railway lines, the Tientsin-Pukow and the Peiping-Hankow; another from Tatung, coal centre in mountainous Shansi, to the coast; a third to link up Jehol with the Peiping-Suiyuan line.

Another favored plan is to develop such extensive cotton plantations in Hopei and Shantung that Japan's present dependence on America and British India for most of the cotton which feeds its busy mills would be lessened appreciably. River-conservancy projects and coal and iron mines also figure in Japan's economic calculations.

But there is a wide gulf between aspiration and realization. Although the South Manchuria Railway, the familiar agency of Japanese economic advance on the continent, opened a large branch office in Tientsin in 1935, the vigorous pace of development which is so noticeable in Manchoukuo has been altogether lacking in North China. Several Chinese textile mills in Tientsin have passed into Japanese hands, and Japanese capital is participating in the construction of a new electrical power station in Tientsin. But the larger proposed enterprises remain as yet mere paper projects.

There have been two main reasons for Japan's failure to follow up its military and administrative encroachments with large-scale economic development. Japan is not very rich in surplus capital. Two heavy drains on its spare funds are represented by Manchoukuo and by the big defense appropriations, which must be financed in large part by the purchase of annual new issues of government bonds. The Ministry of Finance, anxious to preserve the stability of the Japanese currency at its present lowered value, is reluctant to grant permission for large transfers of capital for investment in North China.

The second reason for the lag in economic development was the reluctance of the Chinese to coöperate in a process which, in the light of the past record, seemed likely to end in the detachment of the five northern provinces [7] from China. The Japanese policy of systematic aggression since 1931 makes the Chinese regard the most innocent-looking proposals for economic coöperation with grave suspicion. And no one is such a past master in the art of delay, sabotage, and obstruction as the Chinese, be he general, official, businessman, cook, or coolie.

With Japan balked in the immediate prewar period in its plans for outright alienation of Chinese territory and unable to invest large sums in industrial and mining development,[8] and with China thoroughly noncoöperative, economic stagnation prevailed in North China. The Nanking Government, which was pushing ahead economic reconstruction in other parts of China as rapidly as the limited resources of the country permitted, was naturally unwilling to sink money in a part of the country where its hold was so precarious, as subsequent events were destined to prove very convincingly.

[7] North China consists of five provinces: Hopei, Chahar, Suiyuan, Shantung, and Shansi. Chahar and Suiyuan are Mongolian territories and may be reckoned among the most primitive and backward regions in China. Hopei, the province in which Peiping and Tientsin are located, is a populous agricultural region, producing a good deal of wheat, millet, kaoliang, and other grains, besides cotton. Shansi, a poor and mountainous province, is rich in coal, which, like the iron of Chahar, is largely undeveloped, the mines being small and worked with very little equipment or engineering skill. Shantung, where Japan has large commercial interests, has suffered much from flood, drought, and maladministration in the past, although the present governor, Han Fu-chu, has a better record than his predecessor, Chang Tsung-chang.

[8] A good deal of capital would be required to develop effectively the Chahar iron and the Shansi coal, since there is virtually no modern equipment or machinery in the existing mines of these provinces.

And Japan at this time could not take over the country and force through a Manchoukuo programme of development.

Chinese sovereignty was swept from the northern provinces by the Japanese military onset in 1937, and a host of Japanese economic planners, businessmen big and small, descended on Peking and Tientsin in the wake of the army. Impressive paper plans were drawn up for the exploitation of the five provinces, which are inhabited by about 76,000,000 people and occupy an area of almost 400,000 square miles. A semi-government corporation, the North China Development Company, capitalized at 350,000,000 yen and authorized to float debentures to the amount of five times its capitalization, was set up for the avowed purpose of investing funds in "major traffic and transportation enterprises, major communications enterprises, major power-generation enterprises, major mining enterprises, salt and salt-utilization enterprises, and other enterprises recognized as especially necessary for the acceleration of the economic development of North China."

But a visit which I made to North China early in 1939 gave the impression that little economic progress had actually been made. The extraction of industrial salt deposits, which are conveniently located near the sea, was proceeding fairly rapidly. The construction of a new railway between Tungchow, east of Peking, and Kupeikow, on the border of Jehol, provided a strategically valuable shorter rail link between Peking and Mukden. A moderate amount of iron ore (about 600 tons a day) was being taken out of the Lungyen mines. A little coal was coming out of Shansi. But no really big economic enterprise was under way. While the Japanese obtained a fair amount of cotton which had been stored in towns along the railways, the prospects for the new crop were poor because the guerrillas, still very active in the hinterland, were forcing or persuading the peasants to plant food crops instead of cotton.   The guerrillas were one factor that was blocking Japanese economic development; another was lack of necessary machinery, equipment, and skilled labor because of the mortgaging of the entire Japanese industrial plant for the satisfaction of war needs.   The overhead costs of conquest were so high that its fruits, in North China, could not be harvested on any large scale.   Whether this situation will change in the future depends largely on the duration and intensity of the war.

The Japanese forward thrust in China that had been carried on with little interruption since the army kicked over the traces and seized Manchuria in 1931 received a definite check in the latter part of 1936.   For the first time China displayed ability to outface Japan, to stand its ground on both the diplomatic front in Nanking and the military front in Suiyuan.

Tangible evidence of the check which Japan had received in China was furnished by the course of events after several killings of Japanese in China by mobs and individuals during August and September, 1936.   The first of these incidents was a mob outbreak in Chengtu, the capital of remote Szechuen Province, where anti-Japanese feeling had been stirred up because of the Chinese opposition to the demand that the Japanese consulate there should be reopened.   A party of four Japanese visitors was set on; two of them, both journalists, were murdered and the others severely beaten.

Soon after this a Japanese druggist named Nakano was murdered in the town of Pakhoi, in Southwest China, by soldiers of the Chinese Nineteenth Route Army, which had borne the brunt of the fighting against the Japanese in Shanghai in 1932. Then Chinese gunmen assassinated a Japanese policeman in Hankow and a Japanese sailor in Shanghai. All these attacks on Japanese, taken together, represented a far more provocative challenge than the alleged minor act of sabotage which served as the excuse for the occupation of Manchuria.

But Japan's reaction, measured by previous precedents, was surprisingly mild. Warships and landing parties were dispatched to the scenes of the various killings. But no violent steps were taken. Foreign Minister Arita endeavored to turn the incidents to diplomatic account by insisting that negotiations for satisfaction should be linked up with a settlement of all the numerous points at issue between Japan and China. His attempt completely miscarried. Japan obtained nothing except an indemnity and an expression of regret for the Chengtu and Pakhoi killings. The Chinese refused to admit responsibility for the Hankow and Shanghai shootings because these occurred in foreign concessions, where Chinese jurisdiction does not prevail.

During the first half of 1937 there was a relatively peaceful interlude in Sino-Japanese relations. The practice of presenting one-sided demands to China was abandoned. Mr. Naotake Sato, the notably liberal Foreign Minister in the cabinet of the stiffly conservative Premier, General Senjuro Hayashi, publicly declared himself in favor of treating China on a basis of equality and endeavored to take up questions of economic collaboration with China, putting aside the more difficult and complicated political issues.

The Nanking Government, however, possibly overrating its new military and political strength, showed no disposition to respond to the new moderation in Japanese policy. Japanese efforts to obtain railway and other economic concessions in North China were blocked because of opposition from the Chinese Central Government, which insisted that the East Hopei and North Chahar régimes should be abolished before questions of economic coöperation could be discussed. Some of the more ardent Chinese nationalists began to talk of reasserting China's lost sovereignty in the north by force. A conviction began to gain ground among educated Chinese that Japan would not venture to fight.

Developments in the summer of 1937 quickly showed the fallacy of this assumption. The spark which ultimately set off a serious explosion was a conflict between Japanese troops who were carrying out night manœuvres and a Chinese military unit at Lukowkiao, west of Peiping, on the night of July 7. When a truce which had been patched up was followed by further firing on the night of the tenth, the Japanese Government decided to send reënforcements to its North China garrison. The Nanking Government dispatched some troops to Paoting-fu, about ninety miles southwest of Peiping.

Efforts to reach a local settlement with General Sung Che-yuan, head of the Hopei-Chahar Political Council, were unsuccessful, a short lull being followed by new clashes at Langfang, between Peiping and Tientsin, and at one of the gates of Peiping itself. On July 28 and 29 the phase of sporadic skirmishing gave way to outright, although undeclared, war. The Japanese troops, vastly superior in equipment and training, if not in numbers, drove the 29th Army, the Chinese force in the Peiping-Tientsin area, from its positions around Peiping and subjected the Chinese city of Tientsin, where Chinese forces had established themselves,

THE HAYASHI CABINET OF FEBRUARY 1937

Seated, left to right: Toyotoro Yuki, Finance Minister; Senjuro Hayashi, Premier and (at the time of this picture) also Minister of Education and Foreign Minister; Iatsunosuki Yamazaki, Agriculture and Forestry Minister. *Standing*, Takuo Godo, Industry and Commerce Minister; Mitsumasa Yonai, Navy Minister; Kotaro Nakamura, War Minister; Kakichi Kawarada, Home Minister; Suehiko Shiono, Justice Minister

to a severe air bombardment. By the morning of July 30 the Japanese military authorities claimed complete control of the environs of Peiping and Tientsin. The Japanese losses in killed and wounded amounted to several hundred; the Chinese casualties probably ran into thousands.

Who fired the first shots at Lukowkiao is a subject of acrimonious dispute between the Japanese and Chinese; and the versions of other skirmishes which preceded the larger conflicts are also flatly contradictory. More important than the question of which finger pressed a trigger first is the general background of ill will, suspicion, and absolutely opposed viewpoints about the status of North China which made a conflict there sooner or later, on some pretext, quite unavoidable.

Japan has more and more come to look on North China as a sphere of influence in which its will should be supreme and as an economic preserve which is valuable because of its rich stores of coal, iron, salt, and cotton. To the Chinese, the northern provinces, with the historic capital, Peiping, and the important port and industrial centre, Tientsin, are an integral part of China. Even the most innocent-looking Japanese scheme of economic development is profoundly suspect in Chinese eyes.

The Japanese officer or sentry in China is apt to be arrogant and overbearing; the typical provincial Chinese military unit is not well disciplined and is likely to open fire on slight provocation. In view of these circumstances it is easy to realize that combustible material for "incidents" was present in abundance.

There were probably two main reasons which impelled the Japanese to press the minor Lukowkiao clash to extremities. First, there was the intransigent attitude of the Nanking

Government toward the more or less clearly outlined Japanese suggestions for political appeasement and economic cooperation in North China. Second, there was an international situation which seemed to afford reasonable security against any foreign intervention in the affair.

America seemed committed to a policy of maximum isolation from foreign wars. Great Britain's hands were tied by preoccupations much closer home, especially in Spain. As for the Soviet Union, Japan had only recently obtained a decisive, if small, diplomatic and military victory in sinking with impunity a Soviet gunboat and inducing the Soviet troops to withdraw from two islets in the Amur River, the ownership of which is in dispute. The retreat of the Soviet Union in the Amur islands controversy, occurring only a few days before the outburst of fighting at Lukowkiao, helped to convince the Japanese military leaders that they could go ahead in North China without fear of Russian intervention.

So the moment seemed opportune to "teach China a lesson." Whether the newly aroused nationalism and the military preparations of the last years have placed China in a position to take its own part more effectively than on past occasions is being put to the test. Chiang Kai-shek has issued a statement to the effect that "unless China wins a final victory over Japan on the battlefield it will be impossible for her to make Japan respect China's rights and interests and it will be impossible to obtain honorable peace and justice." At the time of writing it is still impossible to predict with assurance whether the fighting around Peiping and Tientsin is merely an unusually severe local "incident" or whether it is ushering in a major trial of strength between Japan and China which may drag on to a protracted course and have incalculable international consequences. One thing may safely be foreseen. Except in the highly improbable event of a Chinese military victory, the strategically and economically important Peiping-Tientsin area seems destined to pass effectively under Japanese control. Whether Japanese expansion will go beyond this area and take in such neighboring provinces as Shantung and Shansi depends on the scope and the course of the conflict.

V

CHINA'S NATIONALIST REVIVAL

I VISITED Nanking, the new capital of nationalist China, twice, in November 1935 and November 1936. The two visits produced strikingly contrasted impressions. During the year there had been a great change in the official attitude. In 1935 any critical remark about Japanese policy was followed by an anxious "Hush," an appeal that it should not be cited in any form which would remotely suggest the source from which it originated. At the time of my second visit Nanking officialdom was franker, freer in conversation, more indifferent to the consequences of being quoted. The Foreign Minister at that time, General Chang Chun, was not regarded as one of the more uncompromisingly anti-Japanese members of the government. But, in the course of an interview which he granted me, he committed himself to a definite *non possumus* as regards three Japanese claims: that Japan is entitled to play a special rôle in East Asia, that North China should be treated as a region distinct from the rest of the country, and that China should accept Japanese coöperation against Communism. General Chang Chun's exact words were as follows: —

"North China is undoubtedly a part of China; its integrity is not to be violated. If Japan wishes to encroach on this integrity there is no hope of readjustment of relations. . . .

We cannot recognize the Japanese claim to a special rôle in East Asia or their right to decide what loans should and should not be granted to China by other powers. . . . As regards the question of coöperation against Communism, we need no outside aid in fighting the Chinese Communists. We have our own independent foreign policy and we don't think this question should be discussed."

There is also a significant change in the Chinese Government's attitude toward criticism of Japan in Chinese newspapers. During 1935 anything of this kind was strictly forbidden. A Chinese editor in Shanghai received a prison sentence for publishing an article which contained some uncomplimentary reflections about emperors and kings. The local Japanese representatives protested against the article as disrespectful to the Emperor of Japan, although there was nothing scurrilous or personal in it.

In 1936 a Nanking "mosquito newspaper," as small newspapers are called in China, displayed a cartoon purporting to show the three stages of Sino-Japanese relations. The first stage, captioned "The Past," showed Japan trampling on a prostrate China. The second stage, "The Present," depicted Japan and China as glaring at each other on equal terms. And the third stage, "The Future," was represented by a sketch of an aroused China vigorously hurling Japan out of its territory. No punitive measures were applied in this case, although there was a vigorous verbal remonstrance from a Japanese official.

The Chinese firmness toward Japan found practical expression in the successful resistance which was offered in Suiyuan when Mongolian irregulars attacked that province. I was in the office of one of the prominent Nanking political leaders, a well-known Chinese scientist named Oong

Wen-hao, when the news of the capture of the Mongol stronghold of Pailingmiao arrived. The effect was like a tonic; his whole tone in conversation became more animated and hopeful. The taking of Pailingmiao was a small enough military event, a skirmish in the cold wind-swept steppes of Inner Mongolia. But even little victories are immensely encouraging to a country which, like China, has had such a long record of national defeats and humiliations.

Behind the present Chinese attitude is a new feeling of national unity and self-confidence. This feeling itself is attributable to several causes. First of all, perhaps, one should mention the relentless pressure from Japan, which has distinctly acted as a unifying factor. Public opinion (and, despite the absence of any kind of political democracy in China, there is a definite public opinion of the educated classes) looks with disfavor on civil strife at a time when the existence of the Chinese nation may depend on the organization of firm resistance to foreign aggression. A leading Chinese editor in Shanghai summed up a general mood when he said to me: —

"Manchuria and Jehol were painful losses. But these regions were not so organically a part of China as the northern provinces, which seem to constitute the new objective of the Japanese militarists. The very cradle of our civilization is there. We can't give way. Even the most peaceful individual or nation will fight if pushed into a corner from which there is no escape."

Apart from the Japanese pressure, several factors, human and material, have been working in the direction of Chinese unity during the last few years. Take the human factors.

Prominent among these is the personality of China's national leader, Marshal Chiang Kai-shek. Chiang has unmistakably grown in political stature during the decade in which he has played a prominent rôle on the political stage. To-day he has supplied China with something that has been lacking since the fall of the empire: a visible centre of unity and loyalty. The best proof that he fills an indispensable place was furnished by the incident which at first seemed to threaten the fragile edifice of China's national unity — his detention at Sianfu in December 1936. There was widespread condemnation of this act, even by persons who had been critical of some of Marshal Chiang's policies; no pretender endeavored to take advantage of the fortnight of interregnum, and Chiang resumed his post after his release with undiminished prestige and influence.

Spare in figure and soldierly in bearing, Marshal Chiang doubtless owes his rise to power in large measure to a quality of energy that is scarcely a Chinese characteristic. He is constantly making trips of inspection throughout the country, usually traveling by air, studying local conditions and correcting abuses and grievances on the spot.

Chiang is one of the most elusive and reserved of modern dictators. He avoids the flamboyance of Mussolini, the mystical self-exaltation of Hitler, the hard dogmatic pronouncements of Stalin. His few talks with journalists have been vague and guarded in character. When the correspondent of *Asahi* tried to talk with him about Sino-Japanese relations, all he could elicit was the cryptic statement: "Sino-Japanese relations cannot be improved unless both China and Japan exert themselves for this purpose."

Chiang Kai-shek has kept a firm grip on the Central Government military machine, although, as his experience at Sianfu showed, his control over some of the armies in outlying parts of China is not so secure. Acting under Chinese conditions, leading a country that is just beginning to acquire the characteristics of an organized modern state, Chiang Kai-shek does not and cannot enjoy the sense of absolute mastery over his country, its policies and resources, that belongs to his fellow dictators in Germany, Italy, and the Soviet Union. He must know when to cajole as well as when to coerce, when to tread softly as well as when to strike. Much of his continued ascendancy is attributable to an astute political sense that has seldom failed him in dealing with the various semi-independent war lords with whom he must reckon and with the cliques that exist in the governing party, the Kuomintang.

Once, in a speculative mood, Chiang Kai-shek bluntly posed the question why the Kuomintang, unlike the rising political parties in Western countries, is "spiritless, a skeleton, not a true revolutionary party." On another occasion he endeavored to supply the answer to this question, declaring: —

"The members of the Kuomintang have failed to pay adequate attention to their individual moral training. We have, therefore, failed to win the implicit confidence of the people. This is not surprising when we remember that the greater proportion of our work consisted merely of posting bills, shouting slogans, and issuing manifestoes, not in getting down to actual work."

The Kuomintang certainly does not convey the impression of possessing the vitality or the measure of mass support which one finds in the case of the Soviet Communist Party, the German National Socialists, and the Italian Fascisti. The question as to who may succeed Chiang Kai-shek therefore acquires urgency, especially as there is no obvious

political heir apparent.   However, it would be overly pessimistic to assume that China would immediately lapse back
into its former dreary round of provincial satrapies and
provincial feuds if Chiang Kai-shek were eliminated from
the scene.   There are other forces, more permanent than
the life of any individual, that are working for a united
China.

The cumulative effects of a generation of growing Western cultural influence and of modern education are just beginning to be felt.   To cite only one among many similar
significant facts, China now has 43,519 university students,
as against 481 in 1911, the year of the fall of the empire.   The Central Military Academy at Nanking, to which
Chiang Kai-shek has devoted much attention, is turning out
a new type of young officer, men who feel themselves
Chinese patriots rather than the mercenaries of rival war
lords.

Experienced foreign residents of China spoke to me with
genuine surprise of the altered conception of government
which is making its way in the more advanced parts of China.
Formerly the Chinese magistrate, or local official, at his
worst simply milked the people under his rule for his
personal enrichment.   At his best he let them alone, meting
out justice according to Confucian precepts.   Now there
is a growing insistence from above that the official should
take positive interest in the welfare of the people.

The mayor of Nanking, for instance, makes almost daily
rounds of inspection to see how the new building projects
which have already completely changed the external appearance of the old Chinese city are advancing.   The mayor
of Canton, Mr. Tseng Yang-fu, as I found, was a young man
of dynamic energy.   Besides presiding over the municipal

administration he was driving through a score of economic development projects, such as the building of a railway to the projected port at Whampoa, the construction
of new roads radiating out from the city, and so on.

The mayor of Shanghai, General Wu Te-chen, recently
announced that within a year a quarter of a million illiterates had been given elementary training in reading and
writing, along with instruction in citizenship. General Wu
declared that this drive would be continued until illiteracy
in Shanghai was entirely eliminated.

Another unifying force which is found all over China
is the so-called New Life Movement, which is energetically
sponsored by Generalissimo Chiang Kai-shek himself and
by his wife, the former Meiling Soong, a Wellesley gradu-
ate, who is his very able and devoted co-worker. The aims
of the movement are numerous and range in importance
from laws combating nation-wide evils like opium addiction
and corruption in office to minor sumptuary regulations
such as forbidding smoking in the streets and fining individuals who appear with gowns or jackets unbuttoned. Enforcement varies a good deal according to locality. It is
most severe in Kiangsi Province, which has been a centre
of social and economic experimentation since a large part
of it was recovered from the Reds, and least observable in
a cosmopolitan city like Shanghai. There is an effort to
make Nanking a model capital, and such vices and diversions
as opium smoking, the employment of "singsong girls" in
restaurants, and dancing are frowned on.

There is a puritanical streak in the New Life Movement,
which is a curious compound of old Confucian moralities
and a modern Y.M.C.A. programme. Cleanliness — which,
it must be said, few Chinese have ever been disposed to place

next to godliness — and thrift are strongly emphasized. Desperately poor as the majority of Chinese are, the average family will indulge in great expense on such occasions as weddings and funerals. New Life is supposed to do away with this, to encourage simplicity and economy. One substitute for the old-fashioned wedding is the mass marriage, when a large number of couples are united simultaneously by the magistrate, without any of the customary extravagant feasting.

It should not be supposed that a miracle has been wrought in China or that age-old habits of self-centred family life, with the accompaniment of indifference to public welfare, of sloth and bribe taking on the part of officials, of absence of elementary hygiene among the masses, could be overcome in a few years. During short visits to China I encountered more than one concrete case of military officers selling protection to bandits, of local officials levying taxes which had supposedly been abolished.

The vast mass of China's abject poverty has scarcely even been scratched. Indeed there are occasions when the visitor to China feels that little matters except this stark appalling poverty in which the masses of the people live. Truculent statements by Japanese generals, international manœuvres and counter manœuvres in trade and finance, shifts of power and influence from one clique to another in Nanking, all seem of slight account when one passes through a tremendous flooded area, such as I once saw in Shantung, where the land as far as the eye could see from the raised railway embankment looked like an immense lake, with roofs of houses and tops of trees sticking grotesquely out of it. It is estimated that 140,000 people were drowned in the great Yangtze flood of 1931; and every inundation leaves large numbers of hapless destitute refugees who are an easy prey to famine and disease.

Behind the visible fact of China's poverty lie many causes, some of them natural, some of them the result of human actions. There is no scientific support for the popular belief, stimulated perhaps by vague memories of Marco Polo's wonderful tales of the riches of Kublai Khan and by the fascination of an exotic, little-known country, that China contains vast natural wealth. It is notably poor in mineral resources. China has neither oil nor gold in any appreciable quantity. Its known coal reserves are about twice those of France and about the same as Czechoslovakia's. Its position as regards iron is even less favorable: China's iron reserves are a little over two tons per capita, as against 37.9 tons in the United States.

There is thus no very favorable base for a large industrial development, even when and if China acquires the requisite capital, and the engineering and organizing skill. China bulks large on the map; and this obscures the fact that China's problem of population pressure is as acute as Japan's. The northern and western borderlands of China, huge in area but sparse in population, — with the exception of Manchoukuo, — are being or have been separated from Chinese sovereignty. In actual political practice Manchuria is part of the Japanese Empire and Outer Mongolia is another Soviet-affiliated republic. China exercises no authority in Tibet. Moreover, five of China's large northwestern provinces, Kansu, Kokonor, Shansi, Shensi, and Sinkiang,[1] which comprise 29 per cent of China's area, contain only 5 per cent

[1] Judging from the accounts of the few travelers who have been able to visit Sinkiang, Soviet influence is already predominant, reducing the authority of the Chinese Central Government to a mere shadow.

of its population. Any large migration from the overcrowded valleys of the Yangtze and Yellow Rivers and from
the still more densely populated area about Canton to these
"open spaces" of the northwest would only be feasible if
vast irrigation works were carried out. China must support
almost a quarter of the world's population on an area that
amounts to about one twenty-fifth of the earth's surface.

China to-day is paying the penalty for having lagged behind in industrial and economic efficiency in an era of rapid
technical change and intense competition. Its traditional
silk market has been lost to Japan. Chinese tea has been
ousted to a considerable extent by the products of India
and Ceylon. China's skill in the ceramics industry gave
the country its name. But now more chinaware is imported
than is exported.

Notwithstanding these formidable handicaps the Nanking Government during recent years has been driving
ahead with a programme of economic development, and a
number of material factors now reënforce the human forces
which make for national unity. The country is being made
more nationally-minded by the growth of air communication and by the expansion of the country's network of railways and roads. The airplane makes it possible to accomplish in a few hours trips which would have formerly
required weeks. The political establishment of the authority of the Central Government which took place in the
summer of 1936 had its economic complement. This was
the completion of the Canton-Hankow Railway, opening
the first rail connection between the populous Yangtze Valley
and the metropolis of South China. As soon as the Yangtze
at Hankow is spanned by a bridge, the City of Rams, as
Canton is called, will be the eastern terminus of the longest

continuous railway line in the world. It will be possible to travel overland from Canton to Paris within about two weeks.

The Lunghai Railway, China's main east-west line, is gradually creeping westward in spite of occasional interludes of banditism, civil war, and famine in the territory through which it passes. Szechuen, China's far-western province, with its fifty million inhabitants, will soon lose its distinction of not having a mile of railways. A French syndicate has advanced cash and materials for the construction of a railway between Chengtu, the capital of Szechuen, and Chungking, its largest city and main port on the Yangtze River. The hinterland of Shanghai and Nanking is better served with railways than ever before — a circumstance which will be of strategic advantage to China if open warfare breaks out with Japan.

Roads are cheaper to build than railways and China now possesses 58,000 miles of highways, as against 28,000 in 1930 and 600 in 1921. All the new means of communication, railways, roads, airlines, are weapons against the old Chinese provincial isolation and particularism.

Another centralizing tendency is the drastic change in the Chinese currency system which occurred in November 1935. A number of factors, among which the silver-buying policy of the United States Government was not the least,[2] had produced a grave economic and financial crisis. Silver was

[2] The American Silver Purchase Act, adopted on June 19, 1934, designed to raise the price of silver, had the same. deflationary effect on China's economy that a rise in the price of gold would have on a country which adhered to the gold standard. It seems to have played the rôle of the proverbial straw that broke the camel's back and induced China's statesmen and financiers to take the risk of cutting adrift from silver entirely.

rapidly flowing out of the country by contraband means because its value abroad as a metal was higher than its value
as currency in China.   The enhancement of the world market
value of silver, China's traditional standard of currency
value, was accompanied by a disastrous fall in internal commodity prices.   The prices which farmers received for their
products fell faster than prices of city goods, while such
fixed charges as debts and taxes remained unchanged.
Bank and business failures multiplied.   China's volume of
foreign trade diminished and exports fell off disastrously.

One advisedly uses the modifying phrase "in theory."

Faced with these conditions, China went off silver, much
as America and Great Britain went off gold.   A managed
paper currency was substituted, with the right of note issue
restricted to the three leading Chinese banks.   The Chinese
dollar was stabilized at a value of a little less than thirty
American cents.   With a managed currency came naturally
much greater national control over the finances.   The old
system under which almost every province had its own banknotes, which often differed considerably in value, gave way,
in theory, to a uniform national currency.

One advisedly uses the modifying phrase "in theory."
China is too vast and sluggish an organism to adopt a financial
change with the speed and completeness of a Western country.   One still finds in some provinces, such as Kwangtung
and Kwangsi, local currency of varying value, and silver
is sometimes used in transactions in remote parts of the
country.   But national banknotes of uniform value circulate
to a far greater extent than was formerly the case and represent a new link binding the country more closely together.

The Nanking Government's position is now much stronger
as regards administrative unity and internal order than it
was when the Japanese offensive began, in 1931.   At that

time there was a semi-independent political régime at Canton, and the two southwestern provinces, Kwangtung and Kwangsi, were only nominally under the authority of Nanking. The writ of the Central Government could scarcely be said to run in the large provinces of the West and Southwest. And in the territory under the more direct control of Nanking a Communist rebellion, accompanied by widespread guerrilla warfare, was in progress.

One writes with reserve of the Chinese Communists. There is no reliable or even approximately impartial record of their activities. Most of the information about them consists of extravagant and in some cases obviously false claims of their sympathizers and of the equally prejudiced accounts of the Nanking Government publicists, who try to represent them as mere bandits. Inasmuch as no foreigner was able to live and move about freely in Communist-controlled territory until 1936, when their movement had assumed a much milder form,[3] it is impossible to say with any great assurance how much of their paper programme was put into operation or what was the precise course of their many campaigns against the government forces.

However, Communism has been an important force in modern China and it is possible to sum up briefly the general trend of the long civil war which was waged between the Chinese Red armies and the government troops and to note the significant change which took place in Communist tactics in 1936.

The Chinese Communist movement was at its peak during the years 1930–1932. At this time a Soviet régime

[3] Mr. Edgar Snow, a sympathetic journalist, was permitted to make an extensive trip in the Communist-controlled area of northwestern China in 1936.

had been set up over a considerable area, inhabited perhaps by fifteen or twenty million people, in Northeastern Fukien and Southern Kiangsi. A much larger area, extending as far north as the Yangtze River and beyond, was exposed to raids by the mobile guerrilla bands of the Communists, and there were enclaves of territory in other provinces, such as Hunan and Hupeh, which were held more or less firmly by Red units of varying size. The original nucleus of the Communist forces consisted of nationalist troops under the command of two young generals, Chu Teh and Ho Lung, who were dissatisfied with the rightward political turn which Chiang Kai-shek had taken.[4] They first seized the town of Nanchang, in Kiangsi; but were soon driven out. After wandering through some of the neighboring provinces they established themselves in Kiangsi and Fukien, where corrupt local administration and oppressive conditions of land tenure were their best recruiting agents.

There were almost no industrial workers and no large towns in the region of Chinese Soviet rule. Chinese "Communism," therefore, manifested a strong agrarian tinge and in practice was not unlike the Taiping Rebellion in the middle of the nineteenth century and other peasant uprisings which have punctuated the long annals of Chinese history. The rich were systematically killed and despoiled; land title deeds were burned; boundary stones were obliterated. There seems to have been little effort at collective farming; but there was redivision of the land along lines favorable to the poorer peasants. Russian methods of organization were copied in many fields, in the make-up of the army, in the circulation of propaganda, in the formation of youth associations. A Red capital was created at the town

[4] Cf. p. 81.

of Juikhin in South Kiangsi, and the Soviet régime printed its own money. The Red Army was supported partly by booty taken from the well-to-do landowners, partly by requisitions.

The geographical location of the Chinese Soviets made it impossible for Russia to grant direct help in munitions and supplies. It seems, however, that a kind of liaison was established through Communist secret agents in Shanghai; systematic instructions were issued by the headquarters of the Communist International in Moscow; and money trans-ferred through Shanghai could readily be turned into arms, as a result of the looseness and corruption of Chinese official-dom. A missionary who was on the fringe of the Red area told me that there were a few Russian advisers with the Chinese Reds. He added that the local councils which were chosen immediately after the Reds occupied a town or village were generally democratically chosen, but that ap-pointed Communist agents were later set over the elected Soviet officials with power to supervise their conduct and supplant them if necessary.

For several years this Soviet area held out against re-peated drives of the government forces. The officers in command of these drives were often incompetent and will-ing to take bribes, and the morale of the troops was low. Desertions to the Reds were not uncommon. The Soviet troops in 1930 temporarily occupied the large city of Chang-sha, capital of Hunan Province; and Hankow, main city of the middle Yangtze region, was threatened more than once.

By 1933, however, a turn of the tide set in. Bit by bit the Red line was pushed back. Chiang Kai-shek began to realize that the problem of suppressing Communism was social and economic, as well as military. Better discipline was enforced among the government troops, who were obliged to pay for what they took from the population. A cordon of blockhouses was thrown around the Red area; supplies of salt and other essential commodities were cut off. In the latter part of 1934 Juikhin was taken and the Red region was completely overrun. People who have visited it after its reoccupation say that it presents a ghastly aspect of desolation and that it is one of the few parts of China where there are not enough working hands to till the soil adequately. The ruthless wholesale killings which characterized the warfare on both sides brought about a positive and noteworthy decline in the population.

The Red Armies were not destroyed. They slipped through the encircling forces of the government and moved in a generally westward direction. The guerrilla war continued; but the Communists were nowhere able to strike root as firmly as in their original strongholds of Kiangsi and Fukien. They were gradually pressed out of the rich and populous Szechuen Province and are now concentrated in a rather desolate region in the Chinese Northwest, in the northern parts of Kansu and Shensi and the adjoining section of Ningsia. The chances of their undertaking any significant social revolutionary experiments in this backward part of China, with its scanty population, which includes many conservative Mohammedans, would seem to be slight.

And the Communists themselves have voluntarily scrapped a large part of their original programme, which called for the setting up of a Soviet régime very similar to that in Russia. This was clearly indicated by a letter which Mao Tse-tung, outstanding political and military leader of the

Chinese Communists, addressed to four leaders of the National Salvation Association in the summer of 1936. (The National Salvation Association is a semi-legal body which sets as its goal anti-Japanese action by all means, including strikes, demonstrations, and boycotts of Japanese goods. It is a sort of informal link between the Kuomintang and the Communists, since its membership includes both Communists and Left-Wing members of the Kuomintang. The government accords it some toleration, although a number of its leaders were arrested in November 1936, when their activities were regarded as dangerous to peace and order.)

Mao's letter is couched in defensive, almost apologetic terms, very different from the tirades against landlords and capitalists which were formerly the stock in trade of Chinese Communists. He points out, for instance, that the Communist régime, in the territory under its control, has abolished laws for the control of industry and has "persuaded the workers not to press for extreme demands which the capitalists cannot grant." Quoting an earlier communication from the National Salvation Association which had advised the Communists "to adopt a tolerant attitude toward landlords, merchants and rich peasants and to attempt to curb all labor troubles in the towns," Mao comments: "We have acted in this way." He furthermore expresses willingness to drop all agitation against a special party or class, — that is, against the Kuomintang and the "bourgeoisie," — and suggests that the Communists take their place in an all-national, anti-Japanese front, with the government troops and the Red forces suspending all hostilities.

Another prominent Communist, Mr. Chou en-lai, told foreign newspapermen that the Communists are prepared to cease all opposition to the Nanking Government, to stop all confiscation of property, to change the name of their army from "Red" to "Revolutionary," and to place it under the direction of the Nanking military authorities, provided it received support on the same basis as other Chinese armies. In return for these concessions he proposed that the Nanking Government, on its part, should cease fighting the Communists, grant freedom of speech, press, and assembly, and unite all national forces for struggle against Japan.[5]

Several considerations impelled the Communists to renounce their original programme of outright class war and social revolution.   First of all, their rebellion, from a political and military standpoint, must be considered a failure. After almost a decade of destructive guerrilla warfare they were as far as ever from the goal of overthrowing the Central Government and setting up an all-China Soviet régime. Chiang Kai-shek had not annihilated their armies.   But he had forced them into a remote, barren part of the country, far away from the large cities and more fertile agricultural lands.[6]

From this failure, despite the relative weakness of the Nanking Government and the abundant material for Communist propaganda, provided by widespread oppression and poverty, one may draw the conclusion that Communism, in

[5] An amusing instance of the milder course which the Communists are now pursuing is a letter to a Shanghai newspaper from one of their most ardent foreign sympathizers, Miss Agnes Smedley, indignantly denying that there had been any looting or destruction of mission property in a town which the Communists occupied in Shensi.   In the earlier and wilder phase of the movement the looting and burning of mission property and the murder and kidnapping of missionaries were familiar Communist practices.

[6] Chiang Kai-shek skillfully made the Communists serve his own political ends by pushing them into provinces of doubtful allegiance, like Szechuen, and then sending in his own troops to combat them, establishing his authority in the process.

its Soviet form, is not suited to the Chinese character and
to present-day Chinese economic and social conditions.
"No idealistic system will ever succeed in China," said a
witty Chinese journalist in commenting on the various
failures of the Soviet régimes set up at various times in the
southern part of the country. And it is certainly true that
such strong Chinese traits as the family system and the instinct for private gain which characterize the smallest trader
in lichee nuts as well as the wealthiest Shanghai banker are
strong psychological obstacles to the nation-wide success of
a movement that repudiates the family, subordinates the individual to the dictates of a party machine, and proscribes
private trade.

Moreover, two circumstances that made for the success
of the Bolshevik Revolution are lacking in China. Large
landlordism is far less prevalent than it was in Tsarist Russia.
Consequently it is impossible for Chinese Communists to
mobilize the masses of the peasants against a small, clearly
defined, and alien class, whose spoliation can be represented
as directly beneficial to the masses of the peasants.

The backbone of the Communist Party in Russia consisted of industrial workers with an elementary idea of
Marxian principles and a burning hatred for the well-to-do
and educated classes. The proportion of industrial workers
to the general population is much smaller in China to-day
than it was in Russia in 1917. And while there are doubtless Communist sympathizers among the sweated workers
in the fetid factories and workshops of Shanghai and Tientsin
and Canton, the Communists were never strong enough to
take and hold for any length of time any large city.[7] Their

[7] The Chinese city of Shanghai was largely under the control of the
Communist-directed General Labor Union for a short time after the na-

movement therefore remained predominantly a peasant rebellion which was bound with the passing of time to drift
farther and farther away from the theoretical ideas of some
of its Moscow-trained leaders.

A second consideration that has influenced the Chinese
Communists is the new tactics of the Communist International. That organization during the last years has given
up its propaganda for direct overthrow of existing governments, at least in democratic states, and has been instructing
Communists in all countries to enter into "popular fronts,"
coalitions with moderate Socialists, and even with "bourgeois"
radicals and liberals, on the basis of opposition to Fascism
and advocacy of social reforms. The new methods of the
Chinese Communists are clearly designed to prepare the way
for a popular front in China. This tendency is all the more
understandable because the Soviet Government, in its present
nationalist stage of development, is far more interested in
building up a strong anti-Japanese front in China than in
promoting a probably unrealizable dream of turning China
into a Soviet state.

Finally, Communists in China do not cease to be Chinese.
"Face" is an important consideration with them. A graceful
way out of an unfavorable military and political situation is
to put aside social revolutionary objectives and profess a
violent antagonism to Japan, which is shared by many Chinese
who have no sympathy with Communism.

There is a close connection between the changed tactics

---

tionalist troops occupied it in March 1927. This state of affairs ended
when Chiang Kai-shek smashed the radical elements in the Kuomintang.
The Communist occupations of Nanchang, Swatow, and Changsha were
all brief; and the effort to set up a commune in Canton in December
1927 was crushed with much bloodshed.

of the Chinese Communists and the spectacular "kidnapping" of Chiang Kai-shek which focused international attention on China in December 1936. The demands broadcast by Chiang's temporary jailer, the "Young Marshal," Chang Hsueh-liang, as an explanation and a justification of his action were precisely those which the Communists had been urging as a basis for cessation of civil war and reconciliation with the Kuomintang. These demands included hostilities against Japan; a truce with the Chinese Communists; alliance with the Soviet Union; reorganization of the Kuomintang and admission of Communists into the party; replacement of the dictatorship by constitutional government, with liberation of political prisoners, freedom of speech, press, and assembly.[8]

It would be a gross oversimplification to suggest that the detention of Chiang Kai-shek occurred because Chang Hsueh-liang had been suddenly converted to the new Communist programme for China. Several factors must be taken into account in judging the background of this spectacular although ultimately quite abortive *coup*.

Many of the officers in Chang Hsueh-liang's army, which had been sent to the northwest for the purpose of fighting the Reds, were natives of Manchuria. They had, therefore, special personal reasons for hating Japan and hoping that the Nanking Government, by adopting a stronger policy, might make it possible for them to fight their way back to

---

[8] Chinese Communists, like Communists in other countries, have no sincere belief in the value of democratic liberties. The record of the Communist Party in Russia, the sole country where Communism has been in power, in "liquidating" opposition and regimenting thought is convincing proof in this connection. But the Communists in China, as an opposition group, would of course be able to spread their propaganda more freely if the present Kuomintang dictatorship were relaxed.

their homes again.   Chang Hsueh-liang was responsive to their pressure.

Moreover, Chiang Kai-shek, somewhat imprudently, as the result showed, had gone to Sianfu, capital of Shensi and headquarters of Chang Hsueh-liang, for the purpose of disciplining the latter and his army, which had been making a poor showing in the campaign against the Reds.   It was proposed to transfer the army to Fukien, an inhospitable province in a distant part of China.   Finally, funds for the support of the army had been arriving irregularly.   So there was abundant cause for mutiny and dissatisfaction.

An anxious two weeks followed Chiang's arrest.   Plans for a military expedition against Chang alternated with visits to the rebel headquarters of Chiang Kai-shek's wife, of his brother-in-law, T. V. Soong, and his Australian adviser, Mr. W. H. Donald.[9]   Ultimately the generalissimo was released and Chang Hsueh-liang, after issuing a public statement admitting that he was "rustic, surly and unpolished," and recommending severe punishment for himself, proceeded to Nanking.   Here he was duly sentenced to ten years of imprisonment, but promptly pardoned. This was doubtless all part of a prearranged comedy.   The attempt to push China into war with Japan or to bring about a radical reconstruction of the Nanking Government had failed.   During the period of suspense when Chiang Kai-shek's personal fate was unknown, no war lord came out in

---

[9] After Chiang's release there was an exchange of sharp recriminations between Mr. Donald and some Nanking officials, the former asserting that a clique of Nanking military and civil leaders carried out preparations for air bombing and other hostile operations against Sianfu which would have gravely endangered the generalissimo's life.   It was suggested that this clique was more interested in consolidating its own power than in ensuring the safety of Chiang Kai-shek.

support of the mutineers.   China's newly forged unity had stood the test of this shock.

For several weeks after the release of Chiang Kai-shek an uneasy atmosphere prevailed in Sianfu, some elements among the troops of Chang Hsueh-liang and Yang Hu-cheng, another general who had been implicated in the detention of the Generalissimo, displaying a tendency to continue resistance to the Central Government.   The crisis ended, however, in a typical Chinese compromise, which was probably assisted by the distribution of "silver bullets," in the shape of subsidies, where these would accomplish the most good.   The Central Government troops occupied Sianfu without bloodshed; the disaffected troops were shifted to other parts of Shensi Province.

The plenary session of the Kuomintang which was held in Nanking in February 1937 expressed itself as opposed to any dealing with the Communists, except on a basis of complete surrender and acceptance of Nanking's authority by the latter.   But here too the spirit of compromise seems to have been at work.   The sharp denunciations of the Communists at the plenary sessions were significantly not accompanied by any positive suggestion of further military action against them.   While it is doubtful whether any formal documentary agreement has been concluded between the Nanking Government and the Communists, there seems reason to believe that an informal understanding has been reached.

This informal understanding hastened the Japanese decision to strike at what was regarded as a fundamentally anti-Japanese bloc of Chinese nationalism and Communism.   The Chinese Communists adhered to their united-front promises and during the first two years of the war made no effort to promote social revolution in the provinces of northwestern China (northern Shensi, Shansi, parts of Hopei) where their mobile guerrilla units were most active.   All mistrust between the Communists and the Kuomintang was not banished; one sometimes heard complaints that the Communist units were not so well supplied as others.   But there was no open breach.

Many Chinese have believed for some time that war with Japan, in the long run, could not be avoided.   Dr. Hu Shih, one of China's most eminent scholars and publicists, once said to me: —

"Although during most of my life I have been a pacifist, I am afraid conflict with Japan is inevitable.   There is no limit to Japanese appetite.   There is a limit to Chinese patience."

Mme. Sun Yat-sen, widow of the leader of the Chinese national revolution, expressed a similar conviction in the course of a message to the plenary session of the Kuomintang: —

Humiliating negotiations with Japan must cease.   Japan cannot defeat China because (1) she is economically and financially too weak to withstand a long war, (2) because the Japanese people themselves are opposed to war, (3) because the military strength of Japan is numerically inferior and technically backward.   Lastly, because the Chinese people themselves have resolved to fight to the end.

Mme. Sun has lived in seclusion in the French Concession at Shanghai since 1927.   She is convinced that the breach with Russia and the suppression of the Communists were grave mistakes, inconsistent with her husband's teachings.

Marshal Feng Yu-hsiang, vice chairman of the Military Affairs Commission of the Nanking Government, told a correspondent of the *London Daily Herald* in the spring of 1936 that he considered armed resistance to Japan inevitable and favored a Sino-Soviet alliance, cessation of warfare against the Communists, and restoration of civil liberties throughout China.   The interview was afterward officially and partially repudiated; but there was a hollow note about the repudiation.   Marshal Feng, who rose from lowly origin to the command of one of China's largest armies, has been successively a Christian and a Communist sympathizer and is now regarded as one of the most anti-Japanese of the military figures in the Nanking Government.

Throughout the last pre-war years, 1935, 1936, 1937, Chinese public opinion was kept in a state of effervescent indignation by repeated new Japanese encroachments.   Chiang Kai-shek pursued a policy of iron self-control, the true significance of which was much misunderstood at that time by Left-Wing critics, both in China and abroad.   On the one hand he drove ardent Chinese nationalists almost to despair by retaining in office a number of defeatist and pro-Japanese officials, by suppressing anti-Japanese manifestations, by refusing to make any open gesture of defiance or resistance. All this, however, in the light of later events, may be interpreted as a play for time to build up China's sadly inadequate defenses.   A German military mission helped to train modern-minded officers for a nucleus of crack divisions, very different from the disorderly rabble that took the irregular pay and frequent pillage offered by old-fashioned war lords.   Heavy purchases of airplanes and aeronautical material were made in America.   The immensely important Canton-Hankow Railway, without which China's resistance would have been much less effective, was rushed to completion by the end of 1936.   New highways helped to open up and knit together the remote, neglected Chinese Far West and provided easier means of access to such towns as Chungking, Kunming, Kweiyang, then places which few foreigners or well-to-do Chinese ever visited, now key points in China's last line of defense. Arsenals were constructed in such towns of the interior as Sianfu and Chengtu, in Szechuen, Chungking and Nanning in Western Kwangsi.

Chiang Kai-shek did not keep his plans for resistance entirely secret. He delivered talks to selected groups of officials and officers. Some of these talks were reported to the active and efficient Japanese espionage service. As early as 1935, high Japanese officers in China with whom I talked were delivering diatribes against Chiang Kai-shek.

It was an ironical fact that the Japanese were swifter to apprehend Chiang's designs than were the majority of his own countrymen, who were seething with indignation over what looked like an unchecked process of Japanese aggression. Chiang Kai-shek's policy, a thoroughly reasonable one, since China fought far better in 1937 than it could have hoped to fight six years or even two years earlier, exposed him to grave internal political risks and almost cost him his life at Sianfu.

Another warning signal was the revolt of the Kwangsi generals, Pai Chung-hsi and Li Tsung-yen, who demanded immediate action against Japan in the summer of 1936. Some dross was mingled with the pure gold of patriotism in this revolt. Pai Chung-hsi, himself a forceful and ambitious man, had long been personally jealous of the Generalissimo. And Chiang Kai-shek had cut off some of the opium revenue from Kwangsi — a factor that is apt to be a fighting issue in Chinese internal squabbles. Still, the loyal coöperation of the Kwangsi generals with Chiang Kai-shek during the war with Japan proves that their display of nationalist feeling was not a mere pretense, as some of the more cynical "old China hands" were inclined to suggest.

In some respects educated Chinese foresaw the course of the impending war very accurately. I remember quite vividly a long talk with Dr. V. K. Ting, President of the Academia Sinica, in Nanking toward the end of 1935. Dr. Ting was not only a distinguished geologist, but also a man of keen judgment and broad information in politics and economics and a confidant of the Generalissimo.

We shall lose the coast, the North China plain, and the more accessible Yangtze River ports [he observed philosophically]. It was unfortunate that our Empress Dowager spent the money that might have started us toward a modern navy on the marble boat that you can see in the Peking Summer Palace. And we have no means of stopping the Japanese tanks on level ground. But we shall fall back into our deep interior, into Szechuen and other such provinces, and continue our resistance there.

I asked Dr. Ting what would happen if the Japanese refused to carry the war into the deep interior and merely held their acquisitions in the north and on the coast. He professed confidence that China could outlast Japan in any case.

So the idea of losing much of the territory which the Japanese have occupied, and of protracted resistance in the interior, considerably antedates the war. But while the Chinese have thus anticipated and to some extent discounted their territorial losses, I think they have been disappointed in some developments of the war. Their air force has made a much weaker showing than was generally expected. This is partly because the original system introduced by American instructors at the Hangchow flying school, of training pilots strictly according to merit, after the departure of the Americans [10] was considerably relaxed for the benefit of sons of influential and well-to-do families; partly because of the defective Chinese instinct for mechanics, which has probably cost them more airplanes through neglect and accident than the Japanese have shot down. The Chinese also, I think, underestimated Japan's economic staying power and overestimated the prospects of foreign help.

In discussing China with a Japanese, one not uncommonly detects a note of exasperated futility. This is partly attributable to the fact that the Japanese in China are pursuing ends which can scarcely be reconciled. The military leaders think in terms of conquest, physical domination, and strategic advantage. The businessmen and financiers prefer less aggressive methods of penetration.

Japan gives the impression of wanting a China, or Chinas (many Japanese, especially in military circles, believe it is advisable to break up the country and to encourage regional secessions from the authority of Nanking), strong enough to maintain internal order and yet too weak to challenge Japan. It would like to see China prosperous enough to buy Japanese goods and yet too backward industrially to compete with the products of Japanese mills and factories.

It is most improbable that all these contradictory aims can be realized. Japanese military power may smash the Nanking Government. But in its place will come not a régime more acceptable to Japan, but a chaos of unstable local governments, with large parts of the country passing under the control of the Reds.

Individual Japanese businessmen may make money by

[10] They were replaced by Italians, who quit at the very outbreak of the war, in line with Mussolini's pro-Japanese policy.

buying up existing plants or building new ones in China. But a sweeping extension of Japanese enterprise in China seems calculated only to make the solution of Japan's domestic population problem more difficult. For plants operated by cheaper Chinese labor, directed by Japanese organizing ability and technical skill, could soon undersell the present Japanese industrial establishments.

General Sadao Araki, an outstanding personality among the Japanese militarists, once remarked that the Japanese are a people of clay, the Chinese a people of sand. There is much truth in the characterizations, even though Chiang Kai-shek to-day is doing his best to give a more cohesive quality to the Chinese national personality. Yet just this sandlike quality of the Chinese, which makes it so impossible for any outsider, whether he be an American missionary, a Russian Communist propagandist, or a Japanese general, to make them over in the image of a foreign culture or doctrine, is China's last and perhaps surest line of national self-defense.

The foreign aid which China, with the old tradition of playing one alien barbarian against another, has hoped to receive may not materialize. China's recent spurt toward the objectives of national unity, industrial progress, and military power may have come too late to ward off the impact of the Japanese military machine.

There should be no reliance on the traditional Chinese capacity to absorb conquerors that is sometimes superficially and misleadingly invoked in connection with the present situation. China's triumphs of absorption were achieved with races like the Mongols and the Manchus, which were superior to the Chinese in martial vigor, but vastly inferior in culture and forms of social organization. The American and the British businessman or missionary, the Russian émigré, in Shanghai, is very seldom culturally absorbed; he retains his national traits and habits even if most of his life has been spent in China.

There is no prospect that the Japanese will ever expose themselves to absorption by overrunning China like the Mongol hordes of the Middle Ages. Very few Japanese, it may safely be predicted, will migrate to a land that is already overcrowded to the suffocation point. If the maximum programme of Japanese imperialism is ever realized, China will become a larger Manchoukuo, with Japanese "advisers" dictating all policies, with Japanese business and banking interests dominant, but with very few Japanese settling as immigrants and colonists.

The best assurance that China will never be Japanized, that it will retain its cultural integrity and individuality regardless of the political vicissitudes of decades and centuries, is just that sandlike quality, that ability to bend without breaking, which General Araki recognized in the Chinese people.

The fear that Japan may swallow China whole and swell to the greatest empire in the world in the process is based on a gross underestimate of Chinese subtlety and Chinese capacity for evasion, procrastination, sabotage, and passive resistance. The Japanese clay may break if there is too reckless an expenditure of men and money in pursuit of ambitious dreams of overlordship in China. But the Chinese sand will never run in Japanese moulds.

VI

ISSUES WITH THE OCCIDENT

JAPAN's drive for empire in the East has inevitably raised issues and sharpened friction with those Western powers which possess important trade and colonial interests in the Orient. Any survey of Japan's relations with America and Great Britain logically starts in China. For China is a focal point of international political and commercial rivalries and jealousies. If there were no China there would be much less tension in Japanese-American and Anglo-Japanese relations.

China's peculiar international status fosters a free play of antagonisms of foreign powers on its soil. China is the only large power which cannot prevent the stationing of alien troops on its soil and the maintenance of foreign residential settlements, independent of its jurisdiction. The consequence is that there are several places in China (Shanghai is the most noteworthy example) where troops of several nationalities are posted, where the powers of the governing authority are ambiguous and uncertain. In periods of severe international stress such places are apt to become powdermills, with highly explosive possibilities.

America and Japan were probably never so close to the danger of armed conflict as during the early period of fighting between the Japanese and Chinese at Shanghai in January and February, 1932.   While the Japanese were rushing in ships and men to overcome the unexpectedly stiff Chinese resistance, the entire American Asiatic Squadron, which is usually at Cavite, near Manila, was standing by in the harbor of Shanghai and a regiment of American troops had been brought to Shanghai from the Philippines.   The American fleet, which had arrived in Hawaii when the fighting at Shanghai was at its height, was deliberately left there after its regular manœuvres had been completed.   In the words of Mr. Henry L. Stimson, American Secretary of State at that time: —

It was a potent reminder of the ultimate military strength of peaceful America which could not be overlooked by anyone, however excited he might be.[1]

The sections in the International Settlement of Shanghai occupied by American and Japanese troops were adjacent, and this gave rise to a number of irritations and incidents during the early period of the fighting.   Given the mood of the time, it is difficult to exaggerate the grave consequences which might have ensued if a misdirected Japanese bomb or shell had caused loss of life among the American troops or American citizens.   To quote Mr. Stimson again: —

For nearly a week the situation had been like a tinder-box.[2]

Feeling between America and Japan ran high even before the conflict at Shanghai began because of the acrimonious interchange of notes between the two governments in regard to the Japanese occupation of Manchuria.   Mr.

[1] Cf. *The Far-Eastern Crisis*, p. 138.
[2] *Ibid.*, p. 144.

Stimson, in his note of January 7, 1932, committed America to the policy of refusing to recognize "any situation, treaty or agreement" which might be brought about by means contrary to the Kellogg Pact. This was a stronger stand than any other power was prepared to take at that time. The British Foreign Office did not associate itself with Mr. Stimson's position, with the result that America was placed in the position of being the power which was on record as most definitely opposed to Japan's continental expansion. This was not the only occasion when the British Foreign Minister, Sir John Simon, failed to see eye to eye with Mr. Stimson. In the end, however, Great Britain, together with all the other states which were members of the League of Nations, adopted the policy of not recognizing the new state of Manchoukuo.

During the crisis of 1931–1932 America gave the impression of being willing to go farther than Great Britain in opposition to breaches of the Nine-Power Treaty and the Kellogg Pact. During recent years, however, Great Britain has displayed much more activity in bolstering up China and endeavoring to counteract Japanese pressure on that country.

American Far Eastern policy since the first inauguration of Mr. Roosevelt has been essentially passive. The "Stimson Doctrine" of nonrecognition has been adhered to. But America was markedly cool in responding to tentative British suggestions for coöperative financial aid to China in 1935.

Great Britain, on the contrary, while avoiding any steps that might have involved risk of conflict with Japan, has taken several opportunities to assert its interest in the preservation of China's political integrity and financial stability.

A high British Treasury official, Sir Frederick Leith-Ross, paid a prolonged visit to the Orient in 1935 and 1936, spending most of his time in China, but also visiting Japan twice.

Sir Frederick endeavored to convince the Japanese officials and financiers whom he met that it would be to Japan's interest to join in an international scheme of financial rehabilitation for China. He may have found some receptivity in business circles; but the attitude of the army, always inclined to regard China as Japan's exclusive preserve, was uncompromisingly negative. During his stay in China Sir Frederick helped to shape the form of China's financial reform, substituting a managed paper currency for silver.

The British Ambassador in Tokyo more than once offered representations in connection with the wholesale smuggling which was taking place in North China with the connivance, if not with the direct encouragement, of the Japanese military authorities. A special representative of the Export Credits Guaranty Department was sent to China to facilitate the sales of British goods to sound Chinese firms. British financial advice was helpful in arranging composition settlements of several of the Chinese railway loans which had been in default. Early in 1937 there were reports, not altogether specific as to details, of British financial aid for railway construction in South China and for the development of Hainan, a large island off the southwest coast of China.

Much of this British activity was a direct challenge to the implied claim of the Amau Statement in 1934 that Japan should decide as to what loans should be granted to China. It was all the more welcome to China for this reason and at that time Great Britain probably enjoyed more prestige and influence than any other foreign power at Nanking.

There can be little doubt that, from a practical standpoint, Great Britain's systematic effort to give China diplomatic and economic support was more in line with permanent national interest than Mr. Stimson's zeal for the sanctity of treaties in 1931 and 1932. The British stake in China is almost six times that of the United States.[3] While America sells more goods to China than Great Britain, there are no American banking, shipping, real-estate, and other vested interests in China comparable with those of Great Britain. Moreover, and this is at least an equally important consideration, Great Britain has vast imperial interests in the Orient which would be adversely affected if there were a visible weakening of the British position in Central and South China before the impact of Japan's dynamic advance. America has only the Philippines to consider, and, barring some unforeseen development, will be rid of this responsibility within the next decade.

It would seem, therefore, that Mr. Stimson and Sir John Simon exchanged their proper rôles during the Manchurian crisis. Great Britain stands to lose far more than America from any sweeping expansion of Japanese political and economic power in China. There is scarcely any conceivable Japanese forward move that would not be calculated to injure British interests more than American. So, while there might be hypothetical circumstances under which coördinated British-American action might commend itself both

[3] Professor C. F. Remer, in his book *Foreign Investments in China*, estimates the value of American investment in that country in 1930 as $196,800,000, as against $1,189,200,000 for Great Britain. A Japanese economist, Mr. Hotsumi Ozaki, estimates that in 1934 British investments amounted to $1,202,000,000, American to $230,000,000.

to Washington and to London, there would seem to be no valid reason why America at any future time could go ahead of England in opposing Japan.

There is indeed a school of thought in America that believes the United States is being pushed toward conflict with Japan in China by potent, if not irresistible, economic forces. A summary of this viewpoint is to be found in the following excerpts from an article which appeared in the opening number of *Amerasia,* a magazine devoted to Far Eastern affairs: —

The stability of the economic welfare of the United States cannot long remain without free access to the markets of the Far East, particularly those of China. The trade potentialities of a free and developed China are limitless. . . . It is unreal to hope that the United States can carry on its legitimate trade with a China shackled by the Pan-Asiatic empire dream of Japan. . . . It can therefore be said with reasonable certainty that the United States cannot retreat from the Far East without weakening its economic stability.

The underlying conception here, that America's economic welfare is peculiarly bound up with the Chinese market and that America is therefore most interested in opposing Japanese encroachments in China, will not stand the test of critical analysis. The available facts and statistics would suggest that, if America should become involved in hostilities with Japan, it would be for sentimental rather than materialistic reasons. Not only does China account for a very small proportion of America's export trade (its purchases have ranged, as a rule, between 2.5 and 4 per cent of America's total volume of sales abroad), but its share has been consistently and substantially less than that of Japan.

In 1936, for instance, China's purchases of America's

goods were valued at 185,512,000 Chinese dollars, or about $55,000,000 in American money. During the same year Japan paid out 847,490,000 yen (about $242,000,000) for imports from America. Of the two Oriental countries, Japan, despite its smaller size and population, has regularly been the better customer. In 1933, China's purchases amounted to $51,941,000; Japan's to $143,434,000. In 1929, when world trade was better and prices were higher, China placed orders in America to a value of $124,163,000, as compared with Japanese orders valued at $259,127,000. If trade figures mean anything it would seem that, if America's "economic stability" is intimately bound up with the Chinese trade (a very questionable assumption), it is anywhere from two to four times more intimately bound up with the Japanese trade.

It may, of course, be contended that it is not so much the Chinese present as the Chinese future that is important for America. Here, however, one is dealing with a purely arbitrary hypothesis if it is assumed that China's capacity as a market will expand with any great or spectacular rapidity. It is worth noting, incidentally, that American sales to China decreased from about $145,000,000 in 1920 to about $55,000,000 in 1936. No doubt in 1920 there were optimists who talked of the "limitless" possibilities of the Chinese market of the next two decades.

If one puts aside the hypnotism of China's size and population and examines the economic and physical realities of the situation, there seems to be no valid reason for believing that China, within any predictable future, will represent a market of such vital importance for America's well-being that it could be a reasonable cause for a costly and protracted war with Japan. China to-day is an overwhelmingly agricultural land where the buying power of the enormous majority of the peasants is kept to an extremely low minimum by a variety of factors: excessive density of population, antiquated farming methods, double exploitation of a large part of the peasants by an oppressive land-lord system and by local officials with a long tradition of graft. While Chiang Kai-shek and his immediate associates are doubtless sincere in trying to banish corruption in office, the task, in view of the Chinese tradition and the size of the country, is an enormous one and is not likely to be successfully completed within any near future.

One reason why Americans often overlook the fact that sales to Japan far exceed those to China is that China is usually thought of a "market," while Japan is regarded more in the light of an exasperatingly efficient competitor. But if China ever should become a major market for American goods it will inevitably and simultaneously become a commercial competitor, perhaps no less formidable than Japan. For labor in China is pitifully cheap, even cheaper than in Japan. If China succeeds in overcoming the political disabilities and the lack of aptitude for large-scale economic organization which have hitherto made it a negligible competitive factor in the world's industrial markets, the result may very well be a deluge of "Made in China" goods that may even undersell the "Made in Japan" products. For the merciless pressure of the vast reserve mass of poverty-stricken peasants, seeking work on almost any terms, will keep China's labor cost of production low for as long a time as anyone can foresee.

There is no present or prospective American stake in China that warrants, on purely materialistic grounds, any presumption of an ultimately inevitable American-Japanese clash, assuming that the Japanese aggressive policy on the mainland of Asia continues. Considering the situation from a cold-blooded economic standpoint, nothing could be more absurd than the casting away of a better market, together with the assumption of the immense and incalculable costs of war, in order to maintain such a limited export trade as the United States carries on with China to-day. (Much of this limited trade, incidentally, is noncompetitive, so far as Japan is concerned, because it consists of sales of products like oil and tobacco, which Japan does not produce.) The relatively scant importance which America attaches to export markets is indicated by the fact that she is voluntarily withdrawing from the Philippines, surrendering a preferred trade position which had made the Islands almost as good a market as all China during recent years.

To say that there is no element of economic predestination about a future Japanese-American clash over China is not to suggest that no such clash may at some time occur. There is a dash of Don Quixote as well as a trace of Sancho Panza in the American national character. Don Quixote had the upper hand when large numbers of Americans were sincerely convinced that the results of America's intervention in the World War would be enduring peace and universal democracy. Sancho Panza prevailed when "cash and carry" neutrality was prescribed as an axiom of American foreign policy in the event of future wars. No one can foresee with certainty which trait will rise to the surface in a new Far Eastern crisis.

American policy in the Far East to-day gives the impression of being poised uncertainly midway between the two extreme courses of withdrawal from the Orient and a vigorous, assertive stand in that part of the world, carried

out in close understanding with Great Britain. Withdrawal, in the sense of a liquidation of American economic
interests in China, would be technically difficult, if not impossible to carry out. At the same time public sentiment
would seem to be strongly opposed to any binding alliances
or engagements with foreign powers that would imply an
element of war risk. It is easy to criticize the essentially
passive policy which America has pursued during the last
few years in the Orient as indecisive and irresolute. It is
not so easy to propose a workable and practicable alternative
policy.

In one field, at least, that of naval policy, there has been
nothing indecisive or irresolute in American procedure. The
principle of maintaining a margin of superiority over Japan
has been firmly adhered to.

Next to the problem of China, that of relative naval
strength with America and Great Britain has probably bulked
largest in Japan's relations with the Occident. The complete frustration of all efforts not only to preserve the essential framework of the Washington Naval Treaty but to
salvage some modest measure of agreed naval armament restriction is symbolic of the uncertain political outlook in the
Orient.

A threatened race in naval building was averted as a result of the agreements reached at the Washington Conference, attended in 1922 by all powers with interests in the
Pacific area except the Soviet Union.[4] The main naval results of this conference were the adoption of a 5–5–3 ratio
as to capital ships, by the three leading naval powers,
America, Great Britain, and Japan, and the adoption of a

[4] The Soviet Union at that time had not received diplomatic recognition from the majority of the powers.

self-denying ordinance as to constructing new bases and building new fortifications in certain Pacific possessions of these three powers. America renounced additional fortification rights for the Aleutian Islands, the Philippines, Guam, Wake, and Samoa; Great Britain for Hong Kong and the South Seas Islands; Japan for the Kuriles in the north, and in the south for Formosa, the Loochoo and Bonin Islands, and the widely scattered groups of the Caroline, Marshall, and Marianas Islands, former German colonies which Japan holds under a mandate from the League of Nations.

This whole scheme of naval limitation has now gone by the board. Toward the end of 1934 Japan gave the required two years' notice of denunciation of the Washington naval agreements. A naval conference which was held in London in December 1935 and January 1936 was doomed to failure in advance because of the immutable determination of the Japanese delegates, headed by Admiral Osami Nagano, to accept nothing less than parity with the strongest naval power and the equally uncompromising decision of America and Great Britain[5] to maintain the previous ratio. Such a deadlock could have only one result: Japan withdrew from the conference. All naval limitation in the Pacific area lapsed on December 31, 1936. The very minor point of naval limitation on which the other powers agreed after Japan's withdrawal from the London discussions, the establishment of a fourteen-inch maximum gun calibre, lost validity when Japan refused to accept it.

[5] British and American naval experts differed sharply at previous conferences. But the forward drive of Japan in China, together with the menacing developments in German and Italian foreign policy, has tended to obliterate British apprehension in regard to American naval strength.

Japanese naval officers with whom I have discussed the question have invariably cited the greatly changed conditions of naval warfare since 1922 in justification of their demand for parity with Great Britain and America. The 5–5–3 ratio, they argue, may have assured Japan a fair measure of security when the cruising range of submarines and the speed and range of aircraft were much smaller than is the case at the present time. Now the progress of science and communications has appreciably diminished the advantage which Japan formerly enjoyed in its home waters because of the vast distance which an American or British fleet would have to cover before it could come within striking distance of the Island Empire.

Japan's increased responsibilities on the continent as a result of the creation of Manchoukuo are sometimes mentioned as a reason for greater naval strength. I am inclined to believe, however, that considerations of a more intangible character have strongly motivated Japan's intransigence on the question of naval limitation.

In the first place, Japan's naval leaders have interpreted the lower ratio assigned to Japan at Washington as implying a stigma of national inferiority. Once the argument was put on this emotional plane there could be only one issue, for a people as proud and sensitive as the Japanese. No Navy Minister, no Premier, could have survived the storm of nationalist denunciation that would have been raised if a Japanese delegation had accepted any solution that fell short of full equality of naval strength.

China has also loomed large in Japan's calculations. It was felt in Tokyo that fixed inferiority in warships to America and Great Britain was not compatible with Japan's self-assumed rôle as "the main stabilizing force in East Asia."

Finally, the factor of secrecy is very highly prized by the Japanese Navy. A French naval officer once remarked to me that, when he paid a visit of courtesy to a Japanese warship, he was allowed to see just as little of the vessel as possible. No country is so nervous as Japan about the photographing of the most innocent objects within naval fortified zones. It was against the ingrained instinct of the Japanese admiral to be obliged to lay all his cards on the table, to be bound by rigid categories of tonnage in construction of warships of every type. The naval professional desire for secrecy and surprise played a very considerable part in arousing Japan's opposition to a continuation of the system of fixed limitations.

From more than one practical viewpoint it seems doubtful whether Japan will be the gainer from the lapse of naval building and fortification limitations. While the Japanese Navy now possesses the theoretical right to build itself up to parity with America and Great Britain, its actual ability to do this seems highly questionable. Great Britain, determined to maintain the security of its far-flung imperial possessions against any challenge by Japan in the Pacific and by Italy in the Mediterranean, and also to safeguard its home waters against the possible menace of the new German Navy, has announced a breath-taking rearmament programme. Of the billion and a half pounds which will be spent during the next five years for general rearmament, about 600,000,000 pounds, it is estimated, will be earmarked for the navy.

It is indicated that Great Britain, besides modernizing its present fifteen battleships, will build ten more of these capital ships during the next five years, that the tonnage of the British Navy will increase by approximately 50 per cent, and that its fighting efficiency will be doubled. America in the past has adhered to the formula of parity with Great Britain, and it seems probable that the British building programme, at least in capital ships, will be matched in the United States.

Japan also has drawn up a five-year plan of naval building, the so-called third replenishment programme, starting in 1937. New building expenditure under this plan is officially stated at the figure of 837,049,000 yen (about $240,000,000). Even when one takes into account the lower Japanese costs of production, this appropriation will not, according to the best available estimates, cover a building programme comparable with Great Britain's. Details of the third replenishment programme have not been published. But, on the basis of known costs, it has been calculated that Japan, with this sum, could build four battleships of 35,000 tons, mounting fourteen-inch guns, one 20,000- or two 10,000-ton aircraft carriers, two light cruisers, and a number of smaller auxiliary craft, such as destroyers, submarines, and torpedo boats.

There have been rumors, for which it is impossible to obtain official verification, that Japan's rejection of the fourteen-inch limit for gun calibre was motivated by a desire to construct battleships larger than any afloat, of 50,000 or 60,000 tons, carrying eighteen-inch guns.[6] Such vessels

---

[6] The former chief of the Japanese Naval Staff, Admiral Kanji Kato (now retired), was known as an advocate of the huge battleship. One strategic argument advanced for the construction of such warships is that America would find it difficult to bring vessels of such immense size through the Panama Canal. There would seem to be no reason, however, why America, if it decided to build such battleships, could not station them in the Pacific, as there is no serious threat to America's Atlantic Coast.

would of course be very expensive and there seems no reason
to believe that America and Great Britain, with their much
greater financial reserves and supplies of raw material, could
not outmatch Japan in a race here, as with other types of
fighting ships.

In the matter of balance Japan would seem to be a loser,
especially in relation to America, as a result of the lapse of
the limitation on new naval bases and fortifications. This
limitation represented a greater sacrifice for America than
for Japan. By forgoing the right to construct new bases and
fortifications west of Hawaii the American Navy greatly
limited, if it did not actually surrender, its striking power in
the Western Pacific. For bases are of equal value with
ships in modern naval warfare, especially when the potential
theatre of hostilities is as wide as the Pacific Ocean. The
strongest navy in the world is severely handicapped in offensive ability if it is obliged to sail many thousands of miles
to attack its opponent, with no base on the route at which
it can put in for refueling, repairs, and general overhaul-
ing.

Indeed bases are in some respects more important than
the actual number and tonnage of ships of the line. Japan
would probably view with more alarm and resentment the
construction of a powerful American naval base in the Philippines or at Guam, the lonely island which is now a way station on the trans-Pacific air route, than the laying of the
keels of several new battleships and heavy cruisers.

In view of the fact that America has certain footholds in
the Western Pacific, while Japan has none in the Eastern
Pacific, America rather than Japan stands to gain from any
alteration in the *status quo* as to naval bases and fortifications. A new Japanese naval base in Formosa would not

increase the likelihood, not very great in any case, of a Japanese attack on California or Hawaii. Bases in Formosa and in the Japanese Mandated Islands would indeed tighten the Japanese naval pincers about the Philippines. But, in any event, most American military and naval writers are inclined to write off the Philippines as a certain Japanese conquest in the early stages of a Japanese-American conflict.

On the other hand an American naval base, comparable in size with Pearl Harbor or Singapore, and located at Guam, within fifteen hundred miles of Yokohama, would not unnaturally be regarded in Japan as a direct menace to its security. One can imagine the corresponding reaction in America if Japan should begin to fortify some island off the coast of Mexico as close to Los Angeles as Guam is to Yokohama. The well-known British naval writer, Hector Bywater, has described Guam as the key to the Western Pacific, and its strategic importance is analyzed in the following terms in a recent book by two American authors who are discussing the probable course of a naval war between America and Japan: —

The nerve centre of the Japanese Empire and its life-lines to Asia and the South, our objectives, are well within reach from Guam, and we could ask nothing better than to see our fleet established there with its chain of communications running to Pearl Harbor and the United States by way of Wake Island-Midway or (better yet) by way of the Carolines, the Marshalls and Pearl Harbor.[7]

On the other hand, it is possible that the development of aviation, which is distinctly a threat to Japan's security in

[7] *War in the Pacific*, by Sutherland Denlinger and Charles B. Gary, Lieutenant Commander, U.S.N.R., p. 241.

some respects, may diminish the menace to the empire of a strongly fortified Guam. An American naval officer of long Far Eastern experience once expressed the opinion to me that the construction of a large base at Guam would be of doubtful expediency, because, as the island is almost surrounded by neighboring Japanese mandated islands, the base might be bombed out of existence soon after the war broke out.

America, under the Tydings-McDuffie Act, which is the charter of Philippine independence, reserves the right to negotiate for the maintenance of a naval base in the archipelago after the political ties between the two countries are severed. At the present time the navy yard at Cavite, regular station of the American Asiatic Squadron, is only equipped for handling small vessels; America possesses no facilities for docking large warships west of Pearl Harbor. In the Philippines, as at Guam, the creation of a powerful American naval base, assuming that it could be defended until the arrival of the main American fleet, would alter the balance of power in the Western Pacific to the advantage of America and to the disadvantage of Japan.

If one studies a map of the Northern Pacific one finds that the westernmost of the Aleutian Islands, Attu, is only 800 miles from the nearest Japanese possession and about 2000 miles from Yokohama. A heavily fortified, well-equipped naval and air base at Dutch Harbor or at some other point in the Aleutians would open up for the American Navy another line of advance against Japan through the cold and foggy seas of the North Pacific. Some observers believe that this line of attack would be more promising, because of the immense distances which must be traversed in approaching Japanese waters from the southern direction.[8]

America will ultimately be forced to choose between two alternative conceptions of naval strategy in the Pacific, which, in turn, reflect two different political policies in that region. One alternative would be to regard a line from Alaska to Hawaii as America's outer line of defense, to liquidate political obligations in the Philippines as rapidly as possible, to build no bases west of Pearl Harbor. Such a policy would be based on the assumption that America is under no more obligation to maintain the integrity of China, by forceful means, than it is obliged to go to the help of Czechoslovakia, Poland, or any other European country that might be the victim of attack.[9] It would be based on the further assumption that America's trade and investment interests in China, even if they should be injuriously affected by new aggressive Japanese steps, are not worth vindicating at the expense of a war that would most probably prove both expensive and long-drawn-out.

The other policy would start out from the proposition

[8] Pearl Harbor, the main American naval base in the Pacific, is about 4000 miles in a direct line from Yokohama. Guam is about equally distant from Pearl Harbor, while the Philippines are 1730 miles further west from Guam. This element of distance would be of great defensive value to Japan in the event of a conflict with America, especially as Japanese island possessions, scattered over the South Pacific, afford excellent natural submarine and air bases from which an advancing fleet could be harassed.

[9] Dr. Stanley K. Hornbeck, head of the Far Eastern Division of the American State Department, recently defined as follows the American attitude toward the principle of the integrity of China: "It has endeavored to show respect for that principle. It is committed by agreement with other powers to that course. It has not, however, as is frequently affirmed, at any time undertaken to guarantee or to enforce observance of that principle."

that America must, in case of necessity, be prepared to fight a war in the Western Pacific. Among the implications of this policy would be the closest possible understanding with Great Britain; retention, if possible, of a naval foothold in the Philippines; utilization of the opportunity offered by a non-treaty régime to establish naval bases and fortifications in advanced American possessions which could serve as starting points for an offensive against Japan in her own waters.

The choice between these alternatives for America in the Far East should be a matter of broad policy, to be decided, so far as possible, in response to popular will. It should not be left exclusively to the judgment of naval experts who are naturally inclined to place professional technical considerations above everything else. A strong navy is quite compatible with the decision to regard the Hawaii-Alaska line as America's Pacific frontier. On the other hand, the building of bases in remote American Pacific outposts which would be of little benefit for the defense of America but might be of advantage as starting points for attack against Japan would be an indication that the more aggressive policy in the Orient had been adopted.

Great Britain cannot afford the luxury of choice as to its Far Eastern policy. It must defend its position in Central and South China because, if this is lost, still larger British interests will be placed in jeopardy: Malaya, with its rich stores of tin and rubber; the sea and air routes to Australia; even India.

The plainest concrete symbol of Great Britain's intention to defend its Far Eastern interests is the impressive naval base which has been rushed to virtual completion at Singapore. A sum of £7,700,000 sterling has been appropri-

ated for these naval expenditures; if one reckons in the outlay for the land and air forces which are also supposed to
play their part in the defense of this very important link in
the chain of imperial defense, the investment in Singapore
has been much larger.

There are several geographical and economic features of
Singapore, which is located on an island at the southern tip
of the elongated Malay Peninsula, that mark it out as a
natural bulwark of British imperial defense in the Far East.
It is the outlet of the rich Malayan hinterland that produces
about 45 per cent of the world's rubber and about 30 per
cent of the world's tin.   It commands the main navigable
channel through the maze of islands and treacherous reefs
in the Malay Archipelago.   It is the crossroads of southeastern Asia, the place where the main trade route from Suez
and India diverges northward to China and Japan and southward to Australia and New Zealand.   Last, but by no means
least, it is the Eastern gateway to India.

In visiting the base I was most impressed by the enormous
graving dock, 1000 feet long and 130 feet wide, completely
surrounded by concrete walls and deep enough to handle
any ship afloat to-day.   Main work on the graving dock
had been completed at the time of my visit about the
end of 1936; but some additional excavation was necessary
before it would be ready for use.   Only less striking was
the huge floating dock, third largest of its kind in the world,
which was towed out to Singapore in several parts and is
able to lift a 50,000-ton battleship out of the water.

The defense plans for Singapore conceive coördinated
operations of the land, sea, and air forces.   Manœuvres
which were held on a large scale in February 1937, with the
participation of British warships and airplanes from places

as far distant as Hong Kong and Irak, are said to have yielded satisfactory results. British officers with whom I talked were confident that the base was in no danger from a sudden or surprise attack. Considerable air forces, including two squadrons of flying boats, which are regarded as especially useful for the defense of the island, are stationed at Singapore, where the civil airdrome is one of the largest in the Orient. There are formidable long-range guns at Changi, the garrison town which is at the entrance to the Strait of Johore, separating Singapore Island from the mainland, on which the base is located.

The primary significance of Singapore is that it provides Great Britain with what America lacks: a base sufficiently large and well equipped to take care of any fleet which the British Government might find it necessary to send out to Far Eastern waters. Now that the Pacific non-fortification agreement has lapsed, plans are under way to strengthen the defenses of Hong Kong, the picturesque rocky island which is Great Britain's outpost of empire off the southwestern coast of China. But Hong Kong, which is within bombing range of Formosa, is rather too exposed to be the main base of British seapower in the Orient. Singapore is much better qualified for that rôle.

Apart from China and the naval question, what are Japan's chief issues with the two Western powers with which she comes into closest contact, America and Great Britain? A standing grievance against America in Japan is the discriminatory exclusion act, applying to Japanese immigrants, which was adopted in 1924. The extreme sensitiveness and national pride of the Japanese have created around this issue an atmosphere of emotional bitterness that is out of proportion to the effect of the legislation on Japanese immigration into America, which had been pretty effectively checked by the "gentlemen's agreement" of 1907. Under this agreement the Japanese authorities consented to withhold passports from Japanese who proposed to go to America not for study or business but for permanent settlement. The effect of the exclusion act is described as follows by the late Dr. Inazo Nitobe, one of the most internationally-minded of Japan's scholars and publicists: —

Japan felt as if her best friend had, of a sudden and without provocation, slapped her on the cheek. She questioned the sanity of American legislators. At heart, however silent, she does not now and never will accede to this law. . . . Each year that passes without amendment or abrogation only strengthens and sharpens our sense of injury, which is destined to show itself, in one form or another, in personal and public intercourse.[10]

A more materialistic cause of misunderstandings and occasional recriminations between America and Japan is that of trade. It is not unusual for an American manufacturer or Congressman to paint a dire picture of America's economic welfare being gravely threatened by a deluge of cheap Japanese goods. Japanese businessmen and newspaper writers, in turn, not infrequently cite the fact that Japan buys in America much more than it sells there,[11] and denounce as unreasonable the clamor that is apt to be aroused in America by small shipments of Japanese textiles, canned fish, pencils, and other exports. America retorts that the

[10] Cf. his book *Japan*, p. 167.

[11] Japan's purchases from America in 1934, 1935, and 1936 amounted respectively to 769,359,000 yen, 809,645,000 yen, and 847,490,000 yen. Its sales to America in the same years were 398,928,000 yen, 535,389,000 yen, and 594,252,000 yen. (The yen has fluctuated moderately in exchange value during these years, averaging approximately 28.5 cents.)

largest item in Japan's imports from America is cotton, which Japan must obtain to feed its large textile industry and which is not produced in Japan. The Japanese exports to America, on the other hand, consist of competitive goods; and even small quantities of these goods, if sold at very low prices, may disorganize markets and reduce profits and wages.

In this matter of trade there is a fundamental difficulty in the fact that each country is largely right, looking at the question from its own standpoint, and naturally finds it hard to appreciate or make concessions to the standpoint of the other. The economic policies of America and Japan are as different as the lines of historical development and the physical characteristics of the two countries. America's energetic development of its rich natural resources has created a tradition of a relatively high material standard of living. During recent years an idea that has gained ground and found practical application is that the government itself, in case of necessity, should throw its vast influence into the scale in order to maintain satisfactory wage standards for labor and satisfactory price levels for farmers. Japan's economic coat has necessarily been cut to a much narrower pattern. The lesson which Japan has more or less consciously drawn from the exigencies of its position as an overcrowded country, poor in natural resources, is to keep factories operating, steamships running with full cargoes, and working hands employed — at the price of a low wage and salary standard and a low margin of profit.

So the impact of the cheaper Japanese goods on an American economic system based on higher wages and higher expectations of profit inevitably leads to difficulties. One way of solution was shown when a delegation representing America's textile manufacturers visited Japan early in 1937 and negotiated an agreement with Japanese textile industrialists under which the latter agreed to limit their exports to America to 155,000,000 yards in 1937 and to 100,000,000 yards in 1938. While the former figure, especially, is a considerable advance over Japan's textile sales to America in 1936,[12] the American textile industry obtains the advantage of knowing precisely what quantity of Japanese textiles will enter the country.

A new cause of friction that loomed up in 1937, the extension of Japanese deep-sea fishing to Alaskan waters, has been eliminated through Japan's agreement to suspend salmon fishing in this part of the world. American and Canadian fishing interests had raised angry protests, on the ground that the supplies of fish were being depleted. Japan's willingness to recede from technical rights in this case, like its moderation in protecting the claims of its nationals in the Philippines, is symbolic of the Japanese desire to avoid friction with the United States, except on issues where the army and navy in China have the decisive voice. Here America, like other foreign powers, has found much cause for complaint as regards bombing of mission and other American property, restrictions on travel and residence of Americans, and monopolistic economic practices. American notes have especially singled out for protest the enforced use of new Japanese-sponsored currency in North China, the establishment of semi-governmental monopolies for exploiting natural resources and other enterprises in North and Central China, and the closing of the Yangtze to foreign merchantmen.

[12] Starting from a low figure of 1,000,000 yards in 1933, Japanese textile exports to the United States have been increasing rapidly. They amounted to 7,000,000 yards in 1934, 36,000,000 yards in 1935, and 66,000,000 yards in the first eleven months of 1936. Even this last figure, however, represented only about 1 per cent of America's total domestic production of cotton textiles.

Before the war the main issue in Anglo-Japanese relations, apart from competing interests in China and naval rivalry, was perhaps Japan's access to the markets of the far-flung British Empire. This problem is complicated because of the varied systems of administration which prevail within the empire and which range from the complete political independence of Canada and Australia, through the halfway house of India under its new constitution, to the benevolent autocracy which prevails in some of the less advanced Crown Colonies. At the time when Sir Frederick Leith-Ross visited Japan in the hope of obtaining Japanese coöperation, or at least absence of obstruction, in the financial rehabilitation of China, the Japanese press was filled with apparently inspired suggestions that a reasonable price for Japanese collaboration with England in China would be trade concessions for Japan in British dependencies and possessions. Nothing came of this suggestion, and Japan's commercial relations with various parts of the British Empire have been left to go their way without any direct understanding between Tokyo and London.

The detention and alleged maltreatment of three British sailors in Keelung, the northern port of Formosa, by the Japanese police in the autumn of 1936 led to a marked coolness in Anglo-Japanese relations. The customary courtesy calls of British ships in Japanese ports were suspended. The Japanese authorities insisted that the police had acted within their rights. The British version of the incident was that the sailors had been arrested in the first place on an unjust charge of failing to pay a taxicab fare, and that they had then been tortured in order to make them sign confessions, one of them sustaining a broken jaw.

The incident, small in itself, dragged on for a long time without settlement because each country felt touched in a sensitive point. Great Britain, in protecting citizens who, it believed, had suffered unjust treatment, displayed that characteristic firmness which has more than once aroused the amazement of governments which attach less value to personal liberties.[13] The Japanese officials felt that the British attitude smacked of an assertion of extraterritorial rights and contempt for the Japanese authorities.

Japan's relations with most Western powers, apart from America and Great Britain, are of minor importance. One important exception to this observation is Germany. International attention was aroused when the Japanese and German Governments, on November 25, 1936, concluded a pact against the Communist International. Under the terms of this instrument the two governments are bound "to keep each other informed concerning the activities of the Communist International, to confer upon the necessary measures of defense and to carry out such measures in close coöperation." They also agree to take "stringent measures against those who at home or abroad work on direct or indirect duty for the Communist International or assist its disintegrating activities," and to invite other states to associate themselves with the agreement.

The Soviet Government denounced this pact as nothing but a veiled military alliance against the Soviet Union.[14]

---

[13] A similar instance occurred in Moscow in 1933, when the British Government took a very firm stand on behalf of six British engineers in the employment of the Metropolitan-Vickers Company, virtually suspending commercial relations with the Soviet Union until two of the engineers, who had been sentenced to prison on charges of espionage and sabotage, were released.

[14] The Soviet Ambassador in London, Mr. I. Maisky, in a public speech on March 13, 1937, referred to "the German-Japanese rapprochement, which, according to the most reliable information at our disposal, amounts practically to a German-Japanese military alliance against the U.S.S.R."

Comments in Great Britain and France were mostly critical and the Japanese press itself displayed little enthusiasm over the agreement. So the prominent Tokyo newspaper *Nichi Nichi* sounded a warning against "making lukewarm friends at the expense of red-hot enemies" and suggested that the conclusion of an agreement between two states against the Communist International was not unlike using a hatchet to kill a fly. The Japanese Foreign Minister at that time, Mr. Hachiro Arita, endeavored to counteract the unfavorable impression which the pact excited in England and other foreign countries by asserting several times that it was not directed against any foreign power. He even suggested, with a glint of humor, that the Soviet Government might associate itself with the pact, if it would only take decisive measures against the Communist International.

The German-Japanese pact is almost certainly more than an innocuous agreement to coördinate police measures against Communism. It is almost certainly less than the full-fledged military alliance which is envisaged in Moscow.

Both in Japan and in Germany Communism is an outlawed creed. Neither country requires any police or military assistance from the other in tracking down suspected agents of the Communist International. A mere understanding for exchange of information between the police of the two countries would scarcely require the fanfare of publicity which naturally accompanied the signature of the pact between two governments.

One may therefore reasonably interpret the pact as a demonstration of sympathy between the two states. There are several reasons, political, economic, and cultural, for this sympathy. Many Japanese officers have been sent abroad for training in Germany and have retained high respect for

German fighting spirit, discipline, and economic efficiency. The younger officers in Japan, who are impatient with bureaucrats and capitalists and dream of remaking the country along lines of military state socialism, see much to admire in Hitler and his régime. Germany and Japan have both turned their backs on the League of Nations; both are in revolt against the static conception of unchangeable frontiers which, as they believe, strangles their legitimate aspirations for expansion. The Soviet Union is a common object of antagonism.

But it is a long step from general sympathy to an outright military alliance, with all the responsibilities and risks which this would imply. There are strong reasons for doubting whether this step has been taken. Such an alliance, in order to possess binding validity, would have to receive the approval of the Privy Council, in which there is a predominance of relatively moderate senior statesmen. And there was a conspicuous absence of enthusiasm over the conclusion of the pact among Japan's moderates; the reaction of the press varied from lukewarm acceptance to downright hostility. Moreover, if a secret military alliance had been concluded it would scarcely have been in the interest of either country to call attention to such a possibility by concluding a public pact against Communism. Japan and Germany are geographically remote from each other. While their interests do not conflict anywhere, they also do not coincide, except in the matter of antagonism to the Soviet Union. It is inherently improbable that Japan would commit itself to support German plans of expansion in Europe or that Germany would underwrite Japan's aspirations in Asia.

It is still too soon to speak with categorical certainty of

the background and implications of the German-Japanese pact. But the balance of probability is that the signature of this instrument was a gesture of sympathy with Germany, made at the urging of the Japanese Army against the sober judgment of the diplomats and civilian statesmen. Whether Japan and Germany will ever find themselves on the same side of the front in an international war has not been predetermined by this pact. The answer to this question depends on two larger questions: whether the war-making or the peace-preserving forces prove stronger in Europe, and what is the balance of power as between extremists and moderates in Japan itself when and if the signal for war comes from Europe.

If one takes a broad survey of Japan's issues with the Occident, mainly exemplified in Anglo-Japanese and Japanese-American relations, one finds unmistakable elements of disturbing friction, best typified in the breakdown of all efforts to create any kind of new naval limitation agreement, but no urgent or immediate threat to peace. There is no such element of constant strain and irritation as one finds in Japan's relations with the Soviet Union, with the frequent border incidents and the almost fabulous amount of espionage to which Japanese in the Soviet Union and Russians in Japan are subjected. Important business interests in Japan stand to gain by maintaining a reasonable measure of good will with Great Britain and America; and there is no challenging irritant in the shape of Communism, so far as Japan's issues with the Occident are concerned.

Distance is a pacifying element in Japan's dealings with America and Great Britain. There is no long common frontier, as there now is with Russia, and no American or British possession represents such a constant potential threat to Japanese security as does the Soviet air base at Vladivostok. The vast breadth of the Pacific, which no scientific invention can altogether eliminate as an obstacle to offensive warfare, is the best permanent guaranty of peace between the United States and Japan.

The most important issue between Japan and the West is China; and here Great Britain, because of its greater immediate stake in China and its closely related imperial interests, seems more definitely predestined than America to stand athwart Japan's path of expansion. This fact, however, does not indicate that a clash between Great Britain and Japan is either inevitable or imminent, even if a retired Japanese naval officer [15] has written a book with the suggestive title, *Japan Must Fight Britain*, and a well-known politician, Mr. L. S. Amery, recently expressed the blunt opinion: "The most formidable potential menace to Britain is implied in the development of the Japanese Navy."

A Russian push toward the Far East which was distasteful to England was checked without active British intervention by the Russo-Japanese War of 1904–1905. It is not beyond the bounds of possibility that a distasteful Japanese forward thrust on the mainland of Asia might be stopped by a new Russo-Japanese war. This is only the most drastic of several means by which Great Britain's position in the Far East might be maintained without an open clash with Japan. Great Britain's naval power, which will be so considerably strengthened by the rearmament programme, and the immense economic power represented by the British Empire, are other factors which may deter Japan from any line of policy that would make a conflict with England unavoidable.

[15] Lieutenant Commander Tota Ishimaru.

VII

THE ADVANCE TO THE SOUTH

As we have seen, Japan's advance to the north has pushed its political and military frontier far into continental Asia, up to the Amur River, where it is faced by a formidable "Great Wall" in the shape of Soviet steel and concrete fortifications, tanks, and airplanes. The advance to the west has strengthened Japan's grip on North China, while simultaneously stimulating China's will to resist and accentuating the rivalries and jealousies between Japan and other powers with interests in China.

A third line of Japanese advance is to the south. The South Seas countries, British India, Ceylon, Dutch East Indies, Australia, New Zealand, the Philippines, Siam, and Malaya, represent at once an important and growing market for Japan's cheap manufactured goods and a storehouse of the minerals, raw materials, and tropical foodstuffs which Japan needs. Cotton and wool, iron and gold, rubber and tin, oil, hemp, and copra, are only the leading items in the long list of products which Japan imports from India and from the lands of the South Pacific. Some of these cannot be obtained at all in Manchoukuo and North China; the supply of others in Japan's continental domain is limited and uncertain.

With the exception of Australia and New Zealand, all these countries are poor. The sales appeal of Japan's low-priced textiles, bicycles, rubber goods, pottery, and miscellaneous wares has been irresistible. The total share of Japan's foreign trade carried on with the South Seas countries enumerated above increased from 18.7 per cent in 1929 to 28.4 per cent in 1934. It has been in this part of the world that the Japanese trade offensive which will be described in the next chapter has been carried out with the greatest energy and success. The most striking increase in the purchase of goods with the "Made in Japan" label was in the Dutch East Indies, where the proportion of imports from Japan grew from 10.9 per cent in 1929 to 31.6 per cent in 1934. But India and the Philippines, Siam and Malaya, registered noteworthy gains in imports of Japanese goods during the same period.

Just as the army is the patron of Manchoukuo, the consistent advocate of continental expansion, so the navy is the sponsor of Japan's southward advance. While army economists point to the timber, soya beans, coal, and gold of Manchoukuo, to the iron of Chahar, the coal of Shansi, the cotton of Hopei, navy spokesmen not infrequently call the attention of Japanese businessmen to the wealth of foodstuffs and raw materials in the South Pacific. Admiral Sankichi Takahashi, when he was Commander of the Japanese Combined Fleet in 1936, told a gathering of Osaka industrialists, according to the report of the leading Japanese news agency: —

Japan's economic advance must be directed southward, with either Formosa or the South Sea Island Mandates as a foothold. In this case the cruising radius of the Japanese Navy must be expanded suddenly as far as New Guinea, Borneo, and Celebes.

Another naval advocate of the southward line of expansion is Captain Gumpei Sekine, who was for a time head of the Press Bureau of the Navy Department. Writing in the August 1935 number of the magazine *Dai Asia Shugi,* Captain Sekine urged the Japanese nation not to forget the necessity for maritime advancement because of the expansion on the continent and set forth the following view of naval economics: —

I believe that the most economical policy for Japan is to import raw materials produced by Japanese enterprises abroad and to export goods produced in this country, employing our steamers in both cases, and to let our overseas traders distribute Japanese goods. . . . And for the purpose of protecting our nationals' overseas enterprises we should occasionally despatch our warships. It will encourage our emigrants and make them feel significant among the foreign peoples, with the result that they will exert all their energies in their professions. But the result produced by despatching our warships to encourage our nationals abroad depends upon the strength of our Navy in comparison with those of other powers.

Admiral Takahashi and Captain Sekine find a civilian sympathizer in Mr. Koichiro Ishihara, shipping magnate and prominent financial supporter of the Meirinkai, one of the more respectable and less violent nationalist associations, which has a large membership among retired military and naval officers. Ishihara, who operates a shipping line between Japan, the Straits Settlements, and the Dutch East Indies, and also holds an iron-ore concession in Malaya, published an article in the magazine *Diamond,* recommending that Japan conclude a treaty of alliance with Germany and the Soviet Union "in order to make the European Powers keep their hands off the Orient." He characterized as "unnatural" policies which prevent Japanese from settling in Australia and the Dutch East Indies, declared the Dutch administration in the latter country was pursuing a self-destructive policy in restricting imports of Japanese goods, and confidently predicted that "Japan's southward policy will solve the political, economic, and social problems confronting the country."

The term "southward advance" has become a byword and a slogan; it is constantly encountered in Japanese publications. As the Japanese themselves are beginning to realize, it is capable of more than one interpretation and is hence apt to create misunderstanding and suspicion in the countries to which it refers. Officially Japan has always adhered to the proposition that its sole interest in the Southern Pacific was normal, peaceful promotion of its commercial and shipping interests.

Articles deploring the plight of the natives under Dutch rule and suggesting by implication that they would be better off under Japanese sway, when the cheap products of Japanese factories could reach them without restriction, appear from time to time in the Japanese periodical press. Lieutenant Commander Tota Ishimaru, in his book *Japan Must Fight Britain,* motivates his thesis on the following grounds: —

England is already on the downgrade; Japan has started on the upgrade. The two come into collision because England is trying to hold on to what she has, while Japan must perforce expand. Territorial possessions and natural resources England has in abundance, she can afford to relinquish some. Japan has neither, and to her they are a matter of life and death.[1]

Lieutenant Commander Ishimaru foresees uprisings of the natives in the Dutch East Indies to facilitate a Japanese

[1] P. 319.

attack on British bases in that part of the world, the seizure
of Singapore and Hong Kong and the final acquisition of
Australia and New Zealand by the Japanese Empire.

Ishimaru's book has been officially repudiated by the Japanese Government and official responsibility for other
speeches and articles advocating an aggressive policy in the
South Pacific can also doubtless be disclaimed. But uneasiness as to the forms which Japan's much publicized
"southward advance" might assume at some future time
cannot be altogether eliminated. Three conspicuous concrete reflections of this uneasiness are the huge naval base at
Singapore which was described in the preceding chapter,
the new air base at Surabaya, in the Dutch East Indies, and
the creation of an army in the Philippines, based on universal liability to service.

Putting aside speculative guesses about the future, what
is the record, up to the present time, of Japanese expansion
in the tropical islands and countries that beckon invitingly
from the south?

The Japanese Empire has two southern outposts: the
island of Formosa, taken over after the war with China in
1894–1895, and the widely scattered South Seas Mandated
Islands, former German colonies which represented, for
Japan, the chief spoils of the World War. Of the two
Formosa is much the more important economically. After
forty years of Japanese rule this naturally rich semitropical
island represents a conspicuous object lesson in profitable imperialism.

In no colony that I have visited are the material benefits
to the ruling power so obvious and the costs of defense and
policing on the other side of the balance sheet so light.
Apart from the Singapore base Malaya might have sustained

a favorable comparison with Formosa in this respect; but the past and prospective expenditures on Singapore raise the cost of safeguarding Malay's tin and rubber to the British taxpayer. Moreover, Formosa makes the impression of being more intensively developed than Malaya in many ways, from providing the last available job for deserving Japanese to extracting the maximum agricultural wealth from its fertile soil. Japan's pressure of population and scanty colonial possessions doubtless help to explain this difference.

I saw Formosa after visiting Fukien, the Chinese south-eastern coastal province from which the majority of the Formosans originally came. In such matters as municipal cleanliness and sanitation, communication facilities, hygienic measures calculated to root out infectious diseases, freedom from banditism and piracy, the contrasts were striking and were overwhelmingly in favor of Japan.

Japanese rule in Formosa has been unmistakably imperialistic. The interests of Japan have been systematically preferred to those of the five million Chinese who make up the majority of the Formosan population whenever the two have come into conflict. The educated and articulate Formosans have many legitimate causes of complaint, from discrimination as to educational opportunity[2] to systematic preference for Japanese in the higher and even middle grades of the administrative services. Japanese workmen and

[2] Universal elementary education is the rule for Japanese children in Formosa, as elsewhere. The proportion of Formosan children of school age in school is about 40 per cent. The sole university in the island is mainly attended by Japanese students, and the professors are practically all Japanese. Admission to high schools is much easier for Japanese than for Formosans. (Inequalities of this kind, of course, exist in every colonial country.)

artisans regularly receive higher pay than Formosans per-
forming the same work. Large Japanese concerns, with
the coöperation of Japanese banks, enjoy a definite advantage
in obtaining the lion's share of the island's business opportunities.

But, however justly it may be criticized on these and
similar counts, Japanese imperialism in Formosa has not been
of the decadent, parasitic type. It has been efficient and
hard-working. It has brought incidental benefits in the
shape of railways, roads, schools, hospitals, and assured
safety of life and property.

Formosa supplies almost all the sugar consumed in the
empire. In general its economy fits very smoothly into that
of Japan proper. Besides sugar the island is rich in rice,
bananas, pineapples, citrus fruits, and camphor. Japan
absorbs about half of its annual rice crop and provides a
ready market for its fruits.

With agricultural development approaching its limit, the
government is now promoting industrial enterprises on the
island. An aluminum plant using bauxite ore from the
Dutch East Indies has been put in operation in Takao, main
port of the south. An alloy steel plant is projected for
Keelung, the northern port of entry. There are a number
of fruit canneries, together with paper, cement, and chemical
plants. The centres of sugar-cane production are dotted
with mills. Formosa more than pays its own administrative
expenses; in 1936 it made a contribution of over five million
yen to the Japanese national budget.

There are several economic advantages which Japan
derives from this possession and which it would not enjoy,
at least in the same measure, if the island had remained under
Chinese rule or had passed under the sovereignty of another

power. Over a quarter of a million Japanese make a living here, mostly as officials and employees of the government and of Japanese firms. Only a small fraction of these could hope for work in Formosa if the island were under non-Japanese rule.

Some valuable items in the Japanese diet — sugar, bananas, pineapples, citrus fruits — are largely or entirely supplied from Formosa, without imposing any strain on Japan's limited reserves of foreign exchange. An advocate of free or freer trade might argue that Japan could buy these commodities elsewhere and point out that the production cost of Java sugar is lower than that of the Formosan product. But Japan has excellent reason to know, from practical experience, that this is not a free-trade world. Wherever her flag does not fly her goods are apt to encounter tariff and quota barriers. There are, of course, no such obstacles in Formosa. So Japanese textiles and other manufactures can be exchanged without limitation for the island's sugar and bananas.

Formosa is part of Japan, so far as tariffs are concerned. The existing free-trade arrangement with Japan, combined with the tariff levied on foreign goods, made it an economic appendage of Japan, just as the Philippines, for the same reason, became an economic appendage of the United States. During 1936 Japan received over 90 per cent of Formosa's exports and supplied over 80 per cent of the island's imports.

Its economic development has provided a good deal of direct and indirect employment for Japanese factories, firms, and shipping companies. If Chinese rule had remained, the scope of this development, in all probability, would have been much smaller. If Great Britain, France, or the Netherlands had added Formosa to their colonial empires,

Japan could have played but a minor rôle in exploiting its resources.

This process of development is still going on. A corporation capitalized at 30,000,000 yen was recently formed on the basis of partnership between the government and big business. It will endeavor, among other things, to promote Japanese agricultural settlement in Formosa (efforts in this direction have hitherto met with little success) and to bring marginal land in the mountainous parts of the island under cultivation. The Taiwan Electric Power Company, which floated a loan in America several years ago, has built a big hydroelectric power plant, of 100,000 kilowatts capacity, utilizing the power of Lake Candidius, in the central part of the island. This capacity will be increased by 60,000 kilowatts when three new generators which have been ordered in Germany arrive. This electrical power is expected to be the source of further industrialization.

Formosa, or, as the Japanese call it, Taiwan, is often referred to as the spearhead of Japan's southward advance. There is a naval base at Mako, in the Pescadores, a group of islands off the western coast, and foreign ships put in there at their peril. A wearisome period of detention, followed by a trial, a heavy fine, and possible confiscation of the ship, is likely to be the result of seeking refuge from a storm in Mako.

There is now no limitation on further naval fortification of Formosa, and the appointment of Admiral Seizo Kobayashi as Governor General after a number of civilians had filled this post indicates that the navy takes a special interest in the island. Governor Kobayashi, with whom I talked during my visit to Formosa, was noncommittal about future naval plans. No instructions, he said, had been received from

Tokyo; and he intimated that Japan's fortification policy would be influenced by that of other powers.

Formosa is a shipping and trade base as well as a naval outpost. The Bank of Taiwan and the China and South Seas Bank are financial agencies through which Japanese capital filters into trade and investment channels in South China, Malaya, Siam, the Philippines, and the Dutch East Indies. The two main ports, Keelung and Takao, are often visited by ships which are going to or coming from other ports of the South Pacific.

The secondary outpost which Japan has acquired in the south consists of the fourteen hundred widely scattered little islands of the Caroline, Marshall, and Marianas archipelagoes which Japan obtained as a mandate from the League of Nations after the War. The Equator was made the line of demarcation in dividing Germany's former Pacific possessions. Japan took the islands lying north of the Equator, while those to the south were assigned to Australia and New Zealand, also on a mandate basis.

The total area of the Mandated Islands, which extend over great distances (1300 miles from north to south and 2700 miles from east to west), is less than 1000 square miles; many of them are uninhabited coral reefs. But Japan has set about its task of governing these new possessions with its customary combination of administrative energy and business efficiency. There has been a considerable increase in the output of sugar cane, copra, pineapples, and other products which can be raised to advantage in the larger and more fertile islands, such as Palau, where the capital of the territory is located, Ponape, and Saipan. A special company has been organized to exploit the rock phosphate which constitutes the most important mineral deposit. Japan's indefatigable fishermen have considerably increased the annual catch in South Seas waters. Schools, hospitals, agricultural and marine experimental stations, have sprung up under Japanese rule; there is an effort to drill and regiment the easy-going Kanakas who make up the majority of the native population and to teach them habits of work.

Considering the limited area of the islands, there has been a remarkable increase in the number of Japanese inhabitants, of whom there are now about 54,000, as against 50,000 natives and a negligible handful of other foreigners. In view of the fact that the native stocks in many of the islands seem to be physically exhausted and show a tendency to decrease in numbers, or at best to remain stationary, there seems to be every prospect that the islands after another generation will be thoroughly Japanized. The success of Japanese colonization in the South Seas, especially when contrasted with the meagre results which have been achieved in Manchoukuo, affords strong evidence that the Japanese, when he quits his native country, prefers a warmer, rather than a colder climate. This is a serious argument for those who believe that Japan's course of empire must finally take the southern way.

Fortification of the islands is forbidden under the terms of the mandate. There have been occasional charges that this obligation has not been observed. No definite proof of these accusations has been submitted; and the testimony of two American visitors to the mandated region, Professor P. H. Clyde and Mr. Willard Price, supports the contentions of Japan's representatives at the sessions of the Mandates Commission of the League that no fortifications have been built.

The commission in one report observed that some of the

schemes for harbor enlargement seemed out of proportion
to the value of the islands' trade, and a German who visited
them complained of constant police surveillance.   Mr. Price
states that during most of his visit he was permitted to travel
about without official companions, but gives the following
humorous account of his impressions of the capital, Palau: —

The New Yorker who complains of the difficulty of finding a
policeman should delight in Palau.   There the procedure is simple.
Step out of your door, go ten paces in any direction, and you will
find a policeman behind you.   He will be courteous in the extreme,
cordially interested in knowing where the foreigner may wish to go
and eager to extend "every facility."   If certain destinations are
mentioned he may gravely shake his head and express the fear that
at those points full conveniences for the comfort of the visitor might
be lacking.

Some of the measures for the economic development of
the islands, the enlargement of the more favorable harbors,
the building of roads, the establishment of an air line between Tokyo and Palau, intersecting, but not communicating
with, the trans-Pacific air route from California to the Philippines and Hong Kong, are of indubitable potential naval
and military utility.   It may be taken for granted that the
Japanese Navy is thoroughly acquainted with the natural
features of the islands, which would be of distinct strategic
value as an outer line of defense against any hostile fleet
which might attempt to attack Japan from the south or from
the east.   It may also be taken for granted that Japan will
never voluntarily surrender its mandate or give back the
islands to Germany.   Mr. Hideo Mikami, a member of the
Japanese Diet who visited the South Seas Mandated Islands
with a commission of inspection, made the following vigorous

recommendations for their exploitation as a base for "southward advance": —

We must regard the Mandated Islands to the south and Manchoukuo to the north as two wheels of one vehicle in their importance to the well-being of our nation, instead of considering them as independent of each other. . . . It is imperative for Japan to equip the islands, along with Formosa, properly, with a view to making them a strategic base for the realization of this nation's policy in the South Seas regions. . . . The development of the South Seas regions is Japan's national policy. This great task cannot be accomplished without the united effort of the Japanese nation. It must rouse itself to energetic efforts, realizing that its mission is to open up this boundless storehouse of the South Seas for the benefit of humanity.[3]

When Japan looks south two large rich groups of islands lie squarely athwart its horizon. The first of these is the Philippines, an archipelago of over 7000 islands, of which the northernmost can be seen on a clear day from the southern tip of Formosa. South and southwest of the Philippines lies the vast Dutch East Indian Empire, one of the naturally richest and most thickly populated colonial regions in the world.

The Philippines at the present time, after almost four centuries of Spanish rule and four decades of American administration, are in a transitional stage of political development, the former ties with America being loosened without

[3] These are excerpts from Mr. Mikami's article in the magazine *Susumu Nippon* for January 1936. The concluding phrase about "the benefit of humanity" is characteristic and shows that Japanese imperialism does not for a moment yield to the Anglo-Saxon, French, Italian, and other brands in self-righteousness. Any Japanese forward step, such as the occupation of Manchoukuo or the extension of fishing to Alaskan waters, is likely to be described as incidentally, if not primarily, "benefiting humanity."

yet being absolutely severed. The Commonwealth régime which was established in 1935, after the American Congress had reached the conclusion that the Philippines were politically and economically a liability rather than an asset, is fully self-governing, so far as internal affairs are concerned. But there are important reservations of authority for the American Government.

The President of the United States, for instance, may suspend the taking effect of or the operation of any law which, in his judgment, will result in a failure of the Commonwealth Government to meet its financial obligations. Every amendment to the Philippine Constitution, which is closely, although not slavishly, modeled on the American, must be submitted for the American President's approval. The American representative in the Philippines, the High Commissioner, may, with the authorization of the President, take over the administration of the customs if there has been any failure on the part of the Island Government to meet its indebtedness or to fulfill its contracts. The United States may, in extreme cases, intervene for the restoration of law and order in the Philippines. The American Government retains the right to call into service "all military forces organized by the Philippine Government."

Moreover, until the date fixed for the expiration of the Commonwealth régime, which, at the time of writing, is July 4, 1946, American goods must be admitted into the Islands duty free. A reciprocal privilege is accorded to Philippine products, subject to certain quota restrictions for sugar and other products, until 1940. During the last five years of the period an export tax, beginning at 5 and rising to 25 per cent of the American tariff, must be imposed on exports to the United States, ostensibly for the double purpose of weaning the Islands from their dependence on the American market and of providing additional security for the complete settlement of Philippine bonded indebtedness.

The first President of the Philippine Commonwealth, Manuel Quezon, vigorously protested against the political and commercial restrictions on Philippine sovereignty and suggested, during a visit to the United States early in 1936, that the date of full independence be advanced to 1938 or 1939. Whether President Quezon was sincere in his expressed desire for earlier independence or whether he was merely bargaining for better economic terms of adjustment is difficult to say. Behind the façade of a democratic constitution he has already concentrated sweeping executive power in his own hands. The social and racial set-up in the Philippines is of the Hispano-American, not of the Anglo-Saxon type. At the top is a wealthy class, largely made up of descendants of the Spanish officials and landowners; at the bottom is a peasant population of various Malay tribes, Tagalogs, Visayans, Igorots, Moros, to mention only a few of the most important. The Filipino middle class is small, most of the retail trade of the Islands being in the hands of the Chinese, the universal storekeepers of Southeastern Asia. Such a background points to dictatorship rather than to democracy when the restraining American influence is withdrawn; and President Quezon may feel that he can consolidate his personal power more rapidly when there is no possibility of American interference.

On the other hand, the Philippines seem bound to face a major economic crisis if preferential access to the American market is entirely cut off. Practically all their sugar, except for a small amount consumed within the Islands, goes to America; it is apparently unable to compete on equal terms with the Javan and Cuban product; and the closing of the American market threatens the Islands with the severest kind of economic and social dislocation.   Sugar represents about 60 per cent of the value of Philippine export trade; about half the government revenue is derived from taxes on this one commodity.   The number of Filipinos who are directly or indirectly dependent on the sugar industry as large or small planters, laborers in the cane fields and in the sugar centrals where the cane is milled, as merchants and transportation workers, is estimated at several millions. There are, of course, alternative products which might be cultivated; but a swift cutting off of such an important source of employment and of revenue would almost certainly provoke a good deal of suffering and unrest.

There is also a political shadow over the future independence of the Philippines, the shadow of Japan.   The Islands unmistakably represent a promising field for Japanese investment, exploitation, and development, assuming that America voluntarily withdraws from its former predominant position in Philippine economy.   There is more arable land in the Philippines than in Japan, although the total area of the archipelago (114,400 square miles) is less than that of Japan (148,756 square miles).   Yet the latter is compelled to support five times as large a population.[4]   The Islands constitute one of the least densely populated regions in the Orient, with the second largest island, Mindanao, notably undeveloped.

The Philippines contain mineral wealth which Japan lacks. Besides gold, the production of which has been increasing at an accelerated pace since the devaluation of the

[4] The population of the Philippines is not known with absolute accuracy, but is estimated at about 14,000,000.

pound and the dollar gave the necessary stimulus to the profitable exploitation of medium-grade mines,[5] the islands are known to possess large quantities of iron, chromium, and manganese. Because of its proximity Japan is the natural market for Philippine iron and manganese; and Japanese buyers have been bidding for the chromium output of Masinloc, a district north of Manila. Chromium is very useful in the manufacture of stainless steel and armor plate.

Japanese economic penetration of the Philippines, so far as I could judge during a visit to the Islands in the latter part of 1936, has been cautious and circumspect. Although there is no legal limitation on Japanese immigration into the Islands, there is rigid self-limitation in Japan. No Japanese is permitted to set out for the Philippines until he has shown convincing proof that he will have an assured means of livelihood there. There does not seem to have been any recent noteworthy increase in the Japanese population of the Philippines, which is about 20,000.

The most striking signs of Japanese activity are to be found in Davao Province, in the southeastern corner of Mindinao, where about 14,000 Japanese have settled. Davao looks like a Japanese town, with Japanese signs on its main street, Japanese schools, hospitals, and social organizations, and Japanese vessels in the harbor outnumbering all others by two to one.

This colonization of Davao, which some sarcastic Filipinos already refer to as Davao-kuo,[6] has been mainly based on

[5] The value of Philippine gold production was $5,100,000 in 1932 and about $22,000,000 in 1936. Allowing for the depreciation of the dollar, there has been about a threefold increase in the amount of metal mined.

[6] This is a double play on words, referring both to Manchoukuo and to a Filipino dialect word which makes Davao-kuo mean "my Davao."

efficient cultivation of Manila hemp, one of the world's best forms of cordage, in plantations throughout the province. About 150,000 acres are under cultivation by Japanese, the majority of whom are small holders, although the large Furukawa and Ohta plantations contribute a considerable share of the production and carry on experimental stations with a view to discovering other crops which are suitable for the soil.

About half the Japanese holdings in Davao are in the form of sub-leases rented from Filipinos and Americans who have themselves leased national lands. The legality of this sub-leasing system has been a periodic subject of agitation. The policy on which the Philippine Government has apparently decided at the present time is not to disturb the present holders of the leases, but not to renew them as their terms run out. There are also projects for creating a permanent counterweight to Japanese penetration by organizing large-scale migration to Mindanao from overcrowded regions of Luzon, the largest northern island, and other parts of the archipelago. A penal farm has been established on the outer rim of the Japanese area of settlement. It is hoped that the convicts, after they serve their sentences, will settle down as pioneer settlers.

In the Philippines, as almost everywhere in East Asia, there has been a growing influx of cheap Japanese textiles. In the provincial towns there are many Japanese shops, with such names as Osaka Bazaar, Kyoto Bazaar, Nagoya Bazaar, where Japanese retail merchants sell their country's products. The figures of the United States Department of Commerce confirm the visual impression that Japan is capturing a large share of the textile trade of the Islands. In 1933 American mills supplied 67 per cent of the Philippine imports of cotton piece goods and Japan supplied 23 per cent. In 1934

Japan's sales rose to 52.7 per cent while America's share fell to 40 per cent.

One should not, to be sure, exaggerate the measure of Japanese commercial penetration in the Philippines. America's share of the Islands' import trade hardly varied between 1930 and 1935. It was 63.5 per cent in 1930; 63.6 per cent in 1935. Meanwhile Japan's share rose from 10.5 per cent to 14.2 per cent, evidently at the expense of other countries than America. But these figures would alter very rapidly if the Islands should lose their preferential access to the American market. In such an event the Filipinos would almost be pushed, economically at least, into the arms of Japan. Too impoverished to afford the higher priced American goods, the Filipinos, like other Orientals, would have to be satisfied with the cheaper and shoddier Japanese wares or go without.

The political position of the Islands in relation to Japan will become more delicate if and when the political ties with the United States are entirely severed. There is practically no danger of an aggressive Japanese move against the Philippines so long as the American flag is still flying there and American military and naval forces are still stationed in and around Manila.[7] The Islands have their element of economic attraction for Japan. But they are certainly not worth the risk and expense of war with America.

When the Philippines stand alone, this situation, of course,

[7] There are now about 4000 American troops and 6000 Philippine Scouts (Filipinos who have been recruited for the United States Army) in the Islands. The main force of the American Asiatic Squadron, consisting of the flagship cruiser *Augusta*, thirteen destroyers, and twelve submarines, is stationed during a large part of the year at Cavite, a small naval base in the Bay of Manila, and there is a small American air force in the Philippines.

will be greatly changed. It is unlikely even then that Japan would launch a direct campaign of conquest. But it may be expected that Japanese economic interests would be more forcefully asserted. The chances of civil disorder in which Japanese lives and property might be endangered would be greater. In a conversation with me in Manila, the former Philippine Commissioner in Washington, Mr. Pedro Guevara, an outspoken opponent of independence, outlined a frankly gloomy view of the possibility of Japanese intervention in the Islands after American withdrawal.

"Only a blind man," he declared, "can fail to see that Japan desires to dominate the Philippines, with their un-developed resources and strategic location. First will come Japanese economic investment, then immigration, finally political rule."

Many of the details of the termination of America's relationship with the Philippines are still obscure. It is not known, for instance, whether the absolute exclusion of the Islands from any preferential treatment in the American market will be modified by some form of supplementary trade agreement, and if so, to what extent. The question of whether America will maintain a naval base there after the coming of independence has also been left open for negotia-tion.

There is much to be said for a generous economic settle-ment between the United States and the Philippines which would ward off the danger of serious social disturbances, with their unpredictable political consequences. But there is little, if anything, to be said for an arrangement under which America would be saddled with any kind of responsibility for the defense of the Islands after the end of the Commonwealth régime.

There is much difference of opinion as to whether the decision to grant full independence to the Philippines was in the best interest of America and of the Filipinos. But this decision was overwhelmingly endorsed both by the American Congress and by a national plebiscite in the Islands. It seems unlikely that both America and the Philippines could be induced to reconsider the question and seek some new formula of adjustment of relations.

Responsibility without authority is always invidious, and it would be unfortunate if America were manœuvred into assumption of an obligation to defend the Philippines after the control of foreign and internal policy had passed entirely into Filipino hands. Withdrawal, if it is to take place, should be a clean-cut affair. America should have no more responsibility for maintaining the integrity of the future Philippine Republic than it has in relation to Siam or Czechoslovakia.

In the event of a complete American withdrawal, it is not improbable that Great Britain and France would take a lively interest in the future fate of the Islands, lying as they do on the flank of the sea route from Singapore to Hong Kong and Shanghai. Neither Great Britain nor France, the former with its vested interests in China and its possessions in Malaya, the latter with its near-by large colony of Indo-China, could regard the establishment of Japanese domination in the Philippines with unconcern.

After the Philippines, in Japan's southward line of expansion, comes the vast Dutch East Indies archipelago, which includes five times the area of Japan proper and is inhabited by about 65,000,000 people, mostly of Malay stock. Nowhere in southeastern Asia, not even in the Philippines, is there such keen apprehension about Japan's possible future designs as in this vast Dutch Asian empire.   Nowhere does one hear so many stories, true or apocryphal, of subtle Japanese espionage.   As a correspondent of the London *Times* recently wrote: —

Not for a hundred years have the Dutch in the Netherlands Indies been so worried as in the last five years. . . .   Strong measures have been needed to prevent undue economic penetration, and even the danger of armed invasion has had to be considered.

There are two understandable reasons for Dutch nervousness.   The Netherlands, a small country located many thousands of miles away from its Eastern empire, could scarcely hope to maintain its position there if it were compelled to face a Japanese attack single-handed.   And the archipelago, efficiently and scientifically exploited and developed (with the exception of some outlying islands, such as New Guinea and Celebes, which have been neglected up to the present time), is a tempting prize.   It is rich in many raw materials which Japan lacks, in tin, rubber, copra, pepper, palm oil, spices, and other tropical products.   Still more important, from the Japanese naval viewpoint, it is much the largest source of oil in the Orient.

But the Dutch are confident that they would not be left to shift for themselves in the event of an attack.   There is a strong British financial interest in the Royal Dutch Shell Company, which, with various subsidiaries, operates most of the oil wells in the colony.   Still more important is the consideration that the Japanese in the Dutch East Indies would be a most dangerous challenge to the British far-flung imperial interests in Australia, Malaya, and India.   The Dutch have watched with unconcealed satisfaction the progress of the Singapore base.

At the same time they have not been unmindful of their own defense. The air forces of the colony are being substantially strengthened, with special emphasis on flying boats and torpedo bombers. Submarine and seaplane bases have been established on the coast of New Guinea, which has been perhaps the least firmly held of the larger islands. The oil fields in Borneo and other islands are also well protected.

So far the differences with Japan have been of a purely commercial nature. A sweeping expansion of Japanese exports was checked through the institution of a quota system, although this was made flexible, so that Japan, with other exporters, will benefit when economic conditions permit larger imports. The Dutch authorities have been sensitive to the growth of the Japanese retail merchants and no Japanese firm is allowed more than 25 per cent of the import trade in any commodity. A shipping war which broke out between Dutch and Japanese lines engaged in the carrying trade ended unsuccessfully for Japan, partly because the Dutch merchants in Japan, who handle a considerable share of the export trade to the Dutch East Indies, persistently shipped goods in their own country's vessels.

By the spring of 1937 many of the sharper points of disagreement had been eliminated as a result of the conclusion of shipping and trade agreements. But an undercurrent of suspicion remains. This was plainly recognized by Mr. Kazue Kuwashima, Japanese Minister to the Netherlands, who remarked, after returning from a visit to the Indies: —

"The Netherlands Indies Government is nervous about Japan's so-called southward policy. This tends to give the Dutch authorities the impression that Japan will occupy the land at any moment. I have been led to the conclusion that this nervousness is very disadvantageous to Japan."

It is not only in the Dutch East Indies that loose talk in Japan about "southward advance," without specifying whether this advance is to be naval, political, or merely economic, has injured Japan's commercial interests. Malaya, the near neighbor of the Indies, feels increasingly safe under the protection of the giant Singapore naval base. But Japan's commercial progress is scrutinized more jealously because of the suspicion of ultimate political implications. Japanese espionage alone is feared in Singapore; the British authorities have not forgotten the espionage case which reached a spectacular climax when a well-known Japanese businessman, resident for a long time in Singapore, suddenly took poison and committed suicide when he feared damaging revelations as a result of the arrest of two Japanese secret agents with whom he had been in contact.

A leading Singapore newspaper, the *Straits Times*, in its issue of July 20, 1936, sounded the following warning against Japanese economic penetration of Malaya: —

Within a very few years the whole of the trade and banking of this colony will be dominated by the Japanese if effective preventive measures are not taken promptly. . . . Early drastic and discriminatory action is imperative. We have no hesitation whatever in urging this discrimination against Japan.

No special action followed this appeal; for several years Japanese sales of textiles in Malaya have been limited under the workings of a quota system which is so framed as to restrict Japan without injuring appreciably the trade of other countries.

Japan holds two iron concessions in Malaya which in 1935 had reached a combined production of a million and a half tones of the ore, most valuable in this age of intensive

competitive rearmament.   One of these is in the native state
of Johore, quite near the Singapore base, the other is in the
state of Tregannu, further north on the eastern coast of
Malaya.[8]

Japanese merchants and shipping companies play an important part in handling Malaya's two great staple commodities, tin and rubber.   The fast cargo boats of the Mitsui
Bussan Kaisha and the Kokusai Kisen Kaisha have competed
so successfully with British and American lines that, according to a reliable estimate, over 40 per cent of the rubber
shipped from Malaya to the United States in the latter part
of 1935 was carried in Japanese bottoms.   Japanese firms are
also active in purchasing and transporting tin, although on
a smaller scale than in the case of rubber.   Some suspicious
observers suggest that Japan's activities in the rubber and
tin trade are motivated by other than purely commercial
considerations, that its military and naval authorities are
aware of the advantage of keeping in Japanese physical
possession at all times considerable quantities of such strategic
raw materials as tin and rubber.

Boarding the comfortable express train from Singapore
to Bangkok, one travels northward through Malaya and
enters picturesque Siam, with its garish Buddhist temples
and saffron-gowned monks, its extensive paddy fields, where
little boys who look like Mowgli in the *Jungle Book* ride
naked astride water buffaloes, its carefree and habitually
insolvent peasants, and its almond-eyed Chinese traders and
money lenders.   As the only independent state in South-

[8] There are three main types of administrative authority in Malaya:
direct British administration in the large trade centres, such as Singapore
and Penang, supervised native rule in the so-called Federated Malay
States, and looser control over native potentates in the generally less developed Unfederated States.

eastern Asia, Siam occupies a pivotal position and is inevitably
a centre of international rivalry.

Great Britain has long been economically entrenched in
Siam, which borders on British possessions in three directions,
on Malaya in the south, on Burma in the west and northwest.   The financial adviser to the Siamese Government is an
Englishman, and the country's small foreign debt is held in
Great Britain.   British firms play an important part in exporting rubber, tin, and teakwood.

In recent years, and especially since the virtually bloodless revolution which led to the abdication of King Prajad-
hipok and the institution of the dictatorship of the People's
Party, a new Siamese political organization in which young
army and navy officers play an important part, Japan has
been challenging British ascendancy in the country.   The
most startling rumor in this connection, and also the one for
which there is the least positive evidence, is that Japan proposes to supply capital and technical assistance for the construction of a canal across the narrow Isthmus of Kra, which
is in Siamese territory.

The strategic and economic implications of such a canal
for the British Far Eastern defensive stronghold and commercial metropolis, Singapore, would be disconcerting, to say
the least.   As a British officer, Captain Cunningham-Reid,
remarked, in discussing the possibility of such a canal, in the
House of Commons: —

"Such a back door, enabling any battle fleet to sidetrack
Singapore, could not but have a profound effect on the local
strategical situation."

Economically also the proposed canal would be disastrous
to the interests of Singapore.   The present sea route to
Europe via Singapore would be shortened by about 600 miles,

and Bangkok and Saigon, main port of French Indo-China, would probably gain much of the trade that would be lost to Singapore. It is impossible to say with certainty how seriously this project of a Kra Canal has been mooted and how much secret pressure was brought by Great Britain in opposition. Actually, however, no work has been started on the canal. Inquiries which I made about it during a visit to Bangkok at the end of 1936 elicited a chorus of denials, in which both the Siamese Foreign Minister and the Japanese Minister to Siam participated.

Other signs of Japanese activity in Siam are less debatable. Japanese exports to Siam have risen rapidly, increasing from approximately 8,000,000 yen in 1932 to about 43,000,000 yen in 1936. Siamese naval cadets are being sent to Japan for instruction and orders for warships of the smaller types have been divided between Japan and Italy. Siam is the only country in the League of Nations which refused to condemn Japan's action in Manchoukuo. A Japanese cotton expert, Professor Mihara, is attached to the Siamese Ministry of Education and is endeavoring to select those parts of Siam where cotton may be grown most advantageously. If Siam could become a large producer of cotton it would serve a double purpose, from the Japanese standpoint. A supplementary source of this valuable raw material would be assured, and the balance of trade, now embarrassingly favorable to Japan,[9] could be adjusted more evenly.

On the other hand, there are developments which would

[9] The trade returns for 1936 indicate that Japan sold to Siam more than five times the value of the products bought in that country. Japanese businessmen, however, assert that the situation is not so one-sided as these figures would show, since some Siamese exports reach Japan indirectly.

indicate that Siam has by no means passed entirely within the Japanese orbit of influence. The tariff was recently readjusted on a basis unfavorable to Japan. Siam followed Great Britain's lead by associating itself with the international rubber and tin restriction schemes. A proposal by Japanese capitalists to build a sugar factory in Bangkok miscarried; and it is significant, incidentally, that there is no Japanese investment in Siam. Furthermore, the government has shown no haste to accede to Japan's desire to establish an airplane line between the two countries.

Siam to-day gives the impression of being acutely conscious of a nationalist spirit, which is fostered by the new régime. My guide in Bangkok, when I asked him why the government is spending so much money on new airplanes, warships, and military equipment, replied: "See what happened to Abyssinia. We must be prepared against any possible attack."

It is natural that, in view of this spirit, Siam should resent any suggestion of tutelage from Great Britain or any other foreign power. One may expect the country, in time, to get rid of its few remaining foreign advisers, to take all business enterprise more into its own hands. But its new nationalism will scarcely find satisfaction in exchanging Occidental predominant influence for Japanese. Siam will gladly accept technical aid from Japan, but without in any way committing itself to the rôle of a blind ally of the Island Empire in its South Seas policy.

The results, up to the present time, of Japan's southward advance may be briefly summarized as follows: —

(1) A substantial increase in export trade with all the South Seas countries except French Indo-China, where the

characteristically strong French protectionism has effectively dammed the inrush of Japanese goods.

(2) Scattered investments, of which the iron concessions in Malaya and the hemp production in the Philippines are most important.

(3) Intensive development and exploitation of Japan's own southern possessions, Formosa and the South Seas Mandated Islands.

At the same time the talk of southward advance has excited apprehension in the South Seas countries which has led to enlarged military preparations and has operated to Japan's disadvantage in the economic sphere.

The southward line of advance has its attractions. It leads to countries which are suitable, in parts, for Japanese migration and which are good natural markets for Japan's manufactured goods. But any expansion of Japanese activity beyond the economic sphere would expose the Island Empire to the danger of serious conflicts, almost certainly with Great Britain, probably with France, possibly with the United States. Moreover, Japan is not prepared for large-scale economic enterprises in the South Seas, calling for the investment of large sums of capital, because it is so heavily committed to the military-economic development of Manchoukuo.

So there is not likely to be any serious disturbance of the political *status quo* in Southern Asia and the South Pacific unless present conditions are disturbed by some unpredictable important new factor in the situation. One such possible factor would be the outbreak of a European war, which would greatly reduce, if it did not altogether paralyze, the striking power of Great Britain and France in the Far East. Another would be a radical change in Japanese for-

eign policy in the direction of an agreement with the Soviet
Union, a cessation of pressure on North China, and a concentration of effort on the tropical and semitropical lands
to the south.   Barring some such unpredictable contingencies,
the southward line of advance will remain important to
Japan commercially, but minor and secondary in a political
sense.

VIII

THE TRADE OFFENSIVE

JAPAN gave up the super-isolationist policy of seclusion from
the rest of the world seventy years ago, very largely under
the pressure of trade-hungry Western nations. To-day
these same Western nations are resorting to every known
kind of commercial restriction in an effort to stem the flow
of cheap manufactured goods from the factories and workshops of the Island Empire.

Japan's trade offensive, designed to conquer a larger
place in the markets of the world, was launched simultaneously with its political drive for empire on the continent in
1931. And of the two movements the trade offensive has
perhaps aroused the greater measure of concern. Few
Americans or Europeans have any intimate knowledge of
Manchoukuo or would be able to locate Chahar or Suiyuan
without reference to the map. But the growing influx of
Japanese wares is a subject of anxious discussion from London
to Los Angeles and from Boston to Batavia.

At the time when Commodore Perry's "black ships" put
into the Bay of Tokyo in 1853, the Japanese law prescribed
death as the penalty for any Japanese who should construct
a vessel large enough to undertake a long sea voyage. To-
day Japan's up-to-date passenger liners and merchant ships

are to be found in the ports of all six continents and are competing successfully with those of countries with centuries of unbroken navigating experience. Japan is now the third largest shipping power in the world. It has learned the industrial and commercial lessons of the West too well for the comfort of its teachers.

The Japanese trade figures for 1889 [1] are an amusing curiosity to-day. The total value of the international commerce of the empire in that year was 136,000,000 yen. This figure had increased almost exactly fiftyfold, to 5,725,875,-000 yen, in 1936. Equally significant is the change in the nature both of imports and of exports. The largest item of imported goods in 1889 consisted of textiles, while silk, tea, and rice, the typical products of a predominantly agricultural Oriental land, were the most valuable exports.

Now Japan has become the world's leading exporter of textile goods; rayon, canned foods, and a host of miscellaneous industrial products swell the list of exports, while almost two thirds of the imports consist of such raw materials as cotton, rubber, and wool, a large part of which are shipped abroad again after being turned into finished products in native factories.

Since 1931 exports have more than doubled, both in volume and in value, realizing 2,896,701,000 yen in 1938 as against 1,179,200,000 yen in 1931. To be sure, the yen lost about two thirds of its gold value between 1931 and 1936 as a result of drastic devaluation. But between 1931 and 1936 the prices of export goods rose less than 25 per cent from the low level of 1931. This is only 67.5 per cent of the level which prevailed in 1928, when the yen was at its

---

[1] Cited in *Things Japanese*, by Basil Hall Chamberlain, p. 357.

full gold value of between forty-eight and forty-nine American cents.[2]

Measured in terms of gold, Japan's share in world trade, even after the striking advance of the last years, has been only about 3.5 per cent; substantially less than that of Great Britain, the United States, France, and Germany, and little more than that of Canada. At first sight, therefore, the widespread agitation about the formidable increase of Japanese competition might seem unjustified, or at least grossly exaggerated. But there are several other considerations which must be taken into account.

Because of the consistently low prices which Japanese exporters have maintained, the volume of the empire's foreign trade, especially in exports, is out of proportion to its gold value. Two Japanese economic experts estimate that on a basis of volume Japan has reached 6.2 per cent of the world's export trade and 4.4 per cent of the world's import trade.[3] Its pre-depression export trade has doubled in volume.[4] Moreover, this export trade consists not of raw materials, in which the country is so poor, but almost entirely of manufactures and semi-manufactures where competition is most keen.

Finally, and this is perhaps the most disturbing of all factors to their foreign competitors, Japanese businessmen have displayed what seems an almost uncanny ability to undercut prevailing prices by extremely wide margins. Visits to factories and workshops in Osaka and other industrial centres, talks with foreign businessmen, travel in

[2] This calculation was made by the Yokohama Specie Bank.

[3] Cf. *Nippon: A Charted Survey of Japan, 1936*, by T. Yano and K. Shirasaki, pp. 66–69.

[4] According to the Yokohama Specie Bank the volume index of Japan's export trade in 1936 stood at 202.3, taking 1928 for 100.

other Eastern countries where Japan finds most of her large markets, have furnished a mass of concrete illustrations of Japan's undercutting capacity.

A visit to a typical medium-sized establishment, the Murakishi Hosiery Company in Osaka, where shirts, vests, and underwear were being made and packed for foreign destinations as rapidly as the nimble fingers of Japanese girl operatives could run sewing machines and sort and pack the finished garments, afforded a revealing view of one main factor in Japan's world-wide commercial penetration: the amazing cheapness with which goods of passable quality can be turned out.

Bright yellow undershirts, designed for the color-loving natives of India, the Philippines, and Africa, were priced at 6.50 yen (a little less than two dollars) per dozen. Other prices were 6.27 yen for sports shirts which were being sent to Northern Europe and 14.50 yen a dozen (about thirty-five cents apiece) for wool shirts which were being shipped to America.

It is estimated that the average price of Japan's textile exports in 1935 was 18 sen (about five cents) per square yard, as against 34 sen for British. Since 1928 Japan's textile exports have virtually doubled, while Great Britain's have been cut in half, with the result that Osaka has almost completely pushed out Lancashire in China and in many other Oriental markets.[5] Japanese rayon goods have been selling in Australia at ninepence a yard, as against two shillings a yard for British rayon. Between 1924 and 1933 the

[5] Japan's textile exports rose from 1,419,000,000 square yards in 1928 to 2,725,000,000 square yards in 1935. During the same period there was a decline in British textile exports from 3,867,000,000 to 1,949,-000,000 square yards.

sales of Japanese hosiery in Great Britain increased fourfold, from 381,000 to 1,620,000 dozens. Prices have been so low that the secretary of the British Hosiery Manufacturers' Association asserted the British manufacturer could not meet them, "even if he got his material for nothing." [6]

A Japanese ship which toured the ports of West Africa with samples offered automobiles for $275, bicycles for $5, typewriters for $12.50, and bicycle tubes for seven cents. To be sure, Japan has not as yet achieved any success in the mass production of automobiles and typewriters; the small internal market makes it difficult, if not impossible, to organize the large-scale manufacture of automobiles. But the cheap Japanese bicycle has made its way all over the world.

An American commercial authority with whom I talked in Hong Kong remarked that American apples and radio sets in South China were meeting severe competition from Japanese products, sold at about one third of the American prices. Incidentally, I had arrived in Hong Kong after a three-day voyage from Saigon on a French ship. I left Hong Kong for a trip of equal duration on a Japanese ship bound for Keelung, in Formosa. The cost of the first journey was more than three times that of the second.

Articles as varied as Swiss watches and garters are sent to Japan to be made up and subsequently sold as non-Japanese goods; the country's lower labor costs make it worth while to pay for the two extra shipments. A considerable number of Indian merchants in Kobe for some time made a living by chopping up Japanese cloth into "fents," or pieces small enough to escape the quota restrictions and the higher tariff imposed on Japanese cloth sent in larger units. This

[6] Cf. *Eastern Industrialization and Its Effect on the West,* by G. E. Hubbard, p. 56.

practice is to be sharply curtailed under the new Indo-Japanese trade agreement. An economics study association in Tokyo issues reprints of economic classics at prices far lower than those which prevail in the publishing trade in America and England.

These varied examples, taken at random, could be multiplied many times. Taken in conjunction with the special protective measures which many countries have enforced against the unrestricted entry of Japanese goods, they would seem to indicate that Japan possesses some magical power of turning out goods more cheaply than other industrial countries. Subjected to sober analysis, however, the magic resolves itself into several simple formulas of explanation: —

Japan is efficient.

Japan is hard-working.

And, most important of all, perhaps, Japan has developed the effective competitive combination of an Oriental living standard with an Occidental standard of productivity. This flat statement calls for a little qualification. The Japanese living standard is higher than that of China, India, and the Asiatic colonial countries. As regards quality and range of output, Japan's industries have not yet reached American or West European levels.

But all Japanese, from heads of business enterprises to girl apprentices fresh from work in the family rice fields, are accustomed to ways of living that are much simpler and more frugal than those of the West. And proofs of industrial efficiency, especially in the manufacture of consumers' goods of medium and low quality, are numerous. There can be no doubt that Japan has mastered the technique of the machine age far more quickly and successfully than any other Eastern country. Labor is cheaper in India and in China than it is in Japan. Both those countries have been longer in uninterrupted contact with the West. But one seldom if ever hears of special limitations on the importation of Chinese or Indian manufactured products. The general recognition of the Japanese competitive menace is a tribute to the skill with which the empire has acquired the tricks of industrial production and salesmanship.

There was a time, soon after the opening up of the country to foreign intercourse, when Japan imported industrial talent in the shape of foreign engineers. There was a later period when it imported most of its machinery. Now the Japanese not only are able to operate their own factories, but are able, in most cases, to use their own machines. In the textile mills which I visited in Osaka, the older machines, with manufacture dates of twenty years and more ago, are mostly from England and America. The newer machines are practically all of domestic make. In some cases, as with the Toyoda loom, foreign models have been improved on by native inventors.

Japanese industry reacted to the depression, which was most severely felt in 1930 and 1931, with intensive rationalization. Weak firms went to the wall; stronger ones were reorganized and consolidated. As a result Japan has come to enjoy several advantages over England in regard to the structure of its textile industry. The units of operation are fewer and larger. Typical of the concentration of production is the fact that in the cotton yarn-spinning industry more than 60 per cent of the spindles are owned by ten large companies. Moreover, a Japanese cotton mill is usually engaged not only in spinning, but also in weaving and finishing, whereas a division of functions is far more common in England. The financial position of the leading textile firms is strong; they are free from the heavy burden of debt and interest charges which clogs the progress of many British companies.

Individual productivity rose impressively during the depression in the Japanese textile industry. In 1929, on the average, it required 61.2 male and 218.9 female operatives to run 10,000 spindles. By 1934 the number of men workers required had fallen to 26.1, the number of women to 163.7. During the same period the daily wages paid per 10,000 spindles in operation declined from 362.93 yen to 174.29 yen. The reduction in labor costs, from the standpoint of the export trade, was even greater because of the severe decline in the gold value of the yen.

Some modern economists would regard such evidences of reduced employment and lower wages as cause for concern, rather than for exultation. These trends have certainly not helped directly to solve the population problem or to build up internal buying power. But in the field of international competition Japan's capacity has been formidably enhanced by the combined effect of lower labor costs and the depreciation in the external value of the yen.

The Japanese are a notably industrious people. In almost all trades and industries they work longer hours than are prevalent in Western countries without visible loss of efficiency. Holidays are few. A recent visitor to Japan from the international Labor Office estimated that the Japanese working week is about sixty hours and suggested that a reduction in hours would appeal to public opinion in other countries. While the working day in large factories averages between nine and ten hours, there is no limit, short of absolute physical exhaustion, to the length of labor in the small workshops which account for a surprisingly large amount of Japan's production, especially in the export trades. A well-known Japanese economist, Kamekichi Takahashi, estimates that about 65 per cent of Japan's exports come from small factories and workshops employing less than a hundred workers. About three quarters of the industrial working population of approximately six millions are employed in small enterprises with less than a hundred workers; about half of them are in the many tiny enterprises with five or less employees which do not come within the scope of Japanese factory legislation.

The most important small-scale industries are weaving of cotton, rayon, and woolen goods, manufacture of electric lights, bicycles, enameled ironware, rubber goods, preparing of food, woodworking, printing, bookbinding, and cement. As Mr. Takahashi says: —

Unlike the small-scale industries in Western countries, these small-scale establishments in Japan are not the beginnings of an industry which will grow into a large-scale industry. Rather are they units of industry which, though small in size, are fully matured, and not small units of a potentially large-scale industry. These small-scale industries are an indigenous growth resulting from the social and economic conditions prevailing in Japan. Their unique and lasting continuance may, therefore, be expected.[7]

The social and economic conditions to which Mr. Takahashi refers are overpopulation and its inevitable associate, poverty. Wages are low and hours are long in these Japanese sweatshops because there is an unfailing supply of surplus labor. In Kyoto, Japan's old capital and most beautiful large city, there is a quarter known as the Nishijin

[7] Kamekichi Takahashi, *Factors in Japan's Recent Industrial Development* (published by Japanese Council, Institute of Pacific Relations), pp. 8, 9.

SHIROKANE DAIMACHI — TYPICAL TOKYO STREET

TOY MAKING IN A SMALL JAPANESE TOY SHOP

or "western camp," a name which dates back to one of the obscure civil wars of mediæval Japan. Here the remote ancestors of the present-day weavers of Kyoto doubtless often worked on the magnificent costumes of the daimyos, or feudal lords, and on the richly embroidered kimonos and obis (Japanese sashes) of the court ladies. And here one finds a large number of the small weaving establishments which help to feed the stream of Japanese foreign trade.

A young weaver with whom I talked gave the following description of the conditions under which he worked, along with his father and brother: —

He started to work at six-thirty in the morning and continued until eight or nine at night, with intervals totaling about two hours for meals. He received two holidays a month and once every five days he could stop work after seven. On the other hand, he was obliged to remain at his loom until eleven-thirty at night in busy seasons. His earnings varied with the orders which he received, but averaged from 28 to 45 yen a month. Like most of the weavers whom I saw at work in Kyoto, this young man was unnaturally sallow. It is not surprising that ill health is common among these handicraft workers, in view of the long hours of indoor work, the darkness of the sheds and rooms where most of the work is done, and the dampness which is a necessary accompaniment of some of the processes.

A missionary whose work had brought him into close contact with the weavers for years estimated that their working day ordinarily amounted to about fifteen hours, although the labor is not so intense and standardized as it would be in a large factory. Forty yen a month represented good earnings. There are different classes among the weavers. I visited one shop where the owner possessed a capital of about 100,000 yen and employed some fifty workers. But this was exceptional. The ordinary shop has perhaps half a dozen regular workers, who are given ten or fifteen yen a month, plus food and lodging, and perhaps as many apprentices, who work for board and keep, with perhaps a yen or two of pocket money thrown in every month. Much of the weaving is farmed out to families at home.

Just as the permanent crisis of poverty in Japanese agriculture keeps the standard of living in these small workshops down pretty close to a subsistence minimum, so the long hours and low wages of the small shop make it easier for the big Japanese industrialist to obtain workers under a system which offers very small wages, although it does provide for the welfare of the worker in other ways.

This system may be described as the successful adaptation of the patriarchal Japanese family spirit to the management of large factories employing thousands of workers and equipped with the most modern machinery. There are no unions, not even company unions, in the Japanese textile mills. A personnel manager in the Kanegafuchi works at Osaka said to me: "We don't need any trade-union. We are just one big family, working for the good of the enterprise."

The lack of labor organization does not mean that the Japanese worker is deliberately exploited or ill treated. On the contrary, the typical Japanese factory manager is proud, often justly proud, of the arrangements for health, recreation, and education which are provided in his plant. Both the Kanegafuchi and the Toyo mills, which I was able to inspect personally in Osaka, were spick-and-span in outward appearance. Rows of trees were planted on the factory grounds

and there was a refreshing absence of the squalor that sometimes characterizes a poorly managed factory in other countries.

The dormitories in which the operatives live on the factory grounds would not have satisfied the requirements of
Western workers.   There is practically no furniture in the
large rooms which are shared by a number of girls, each of
whom rolls up the *futon,* or mattress, on which she sleeps
and puts it away during the daytime.   But they were quite
in line with Japanese living habits, where privacy is at a
minimum in most cases.   It it safe to say that the majority
of the peasant girls who work in Japanese large factories
have more comfortable living accommodations and better
food, provided in the company dining room, than they
would enjoy at home.

Classes in a number of subjects, including the favorite
Japanese woman's art of flower arrangement, are held in
free time.   The Kanegafuchi mill, where more men are
employed, has excellent athletic equipment, including a baseball field, tennis courts, and a swimming pool.   The Toyo
mill trains its girl workers not only in flower arrangement,
but in another well-known Japanese social grace — tea ceremony.

All this speaks for the effort of Japanese industrial pater-
nalism to be benevolent.   But there can never be any doubt
as to the paternalistic nature of the system.   The girls between the ages of fifteen and twenty-two, who tend most of
the looms and spindles, are recruited from peasant families,
as it is believed they will prove stronger and more docile.
An executive in one of the mills which I visited said that
the city flapper type was not desired.

In contrast to the small workshops, the large textile mills

maintain a fairly short working day, measured by Oriental standards. Hours of labor have been gradually reduced to eight and a half. But the work is intensive, and in matters where the trade-union in other countries often exerts a restraining influence on the employer, in questions of wages, speed-up methods, and general working conditions, the manager's word is law.

The money wage paid in Japanese mills is very low, even if one makes a very liberal allowance for the cash value of the food and lodging which are supplied free or at a nominal charge. In the entire textile industry the daily wage averages about seventy-five sen for women and girls and about 1.40 yen for men, who usually perform more skilled work. If one should reckon the value of the food and housing,[8] free medical and dental treatment and other incidental benefits, at another seventy-five sen (and this would be a generous estimate), the girl operative earns the equivalent of less than fifty cents for a day's work which is quite as productive as that of a girl in a Lancashire or New England mill town. The low wage is not peculiar to the textile industry; it is paid to all Japanese workers, except a small class of highly skilled mechanics, mainly in the metal and munitions industries. At the end of 1936 the average daily wage for male industrial workers in Japan was 2.15 yen, according to the estimates of the Bank of Japan; the wage for women was seventy-one sen. At prevalent rates of exchange these work out as roughly equivalent to sixty and twenty cents and give some idea of the enormous differential advantage which the Japanese employer who is producing for a foreign market enjoys over the American

[8] The charge for food and dormitory accommodation is usually about fifteen sen a day.

or West European competitor.   Earnings in the little work-shops are even smaller.

It is not only the manual worker who receives remuneration that seems very small by Western standards.   Salaries as well as wages in Japan are set at a very modest level. The stipend of a Cabinet Minister is 6800 yen (less than $2000) a year.   The governor of a prefecture receives about 5000 yen a year; the senior professor in a university about 4000.   The policeman, autocrat though he is in his relations with the people who are under his jurisdiction, is a proletarian in economic status, with a salary ranging from fifty to eighty yen a month.

I received an instructive object lesson in the frugality which is characteristic of the higher personnel as well as of the workers in a Japanese factory when I was invited to lunch with the director and several leading engineers of a large silk filature.   The simplest Japanese fare was served: rice and *soba* (a kind of macaroni), strongly flavored Japanese radishes, little slices of raw fish, and one or two diminutive cooked fish.   The sole item on the menu which even remotely suggested luxury was a slice of melon for dessert.

So it is the whole Japanese people, rather than the Japanese manual-working class,[9] that may fairly be regarded as sweated in its standard of living.   And this sweating is the result mainly of an impersonal natural factor: the over-population of the country.   A low wage and salary level must be regarded as one of Japan's most permanent weapons in its commercial offensive.

[9] The Japanese worker in a large factory is better off, materially, than the great majority of the peasants and handicraft workers and no worse off than a great many white-collar workers whose salaries are between fifty and seventy yen a month.

The drastic devaluation of the yen has also played its part, although rather a minor one, I believe, in promoting the sweep of Japanese goods throughout the markets of the world. Currency depreciation always serves as a temporary stimulus to the export trade of the nation which practises it because it makes exports cheaper and imports dearer. Suppose, for instance, that a Japanese businessman makes a shipment to America for which he receives $10,000. Before the devaluation of the Japanese currency this sum would have realized a little over 20,000 yen. Now, after the dollar itself has been lowered in value, the $10,000 could be exchanged for almost 35,000 yen. The advantages which the Japanese businessman gains in paying wages, taxes, and other internal costs of production are obvious.

But the cheapened currency has its drawbacks, as well as its benefits, for the Japanese exporter. If he receives more yen for his products, sold in foreign markets, he must pay out more yen, in much the same proportion, for his raw materials. And Japan is very dependent on imported raw materials. So the main advantage which Japan's export trade has derived from the fact that the yen has depreciated in gold value more than the dollar and the pound is a further paring down of already low labor costs.

While Japan's leading firms are keen competitors and guard their trade secrets jealously, they have demonstrated a good deal of capacity for joint action on behalf of common interests. For instance, the Japanese Cotton Spinners' Association, which controls about 97 per cent of the spindles in the country, exercises supervisory functions over production, dealings in raw materials, sales of manufactured goods, and employment. The existence of such a strong central body makes it easier to apply the quota systems which have been applied to Japanese textiles in many countries.

The Cotton Spinners' Association endeavors to adjust production to consumption by sealing up a proportionate number of the spindles belonging to its member firms when overproduction looms up as a danger. It also promotes the development of foreign trade by raising a special fund from a levy on the profits of its members in order to subsidize imports from lands which insist that Japan should take more of their wares if they are to admit more Japanese goods. While labor in the Japanese textile industry is unorganized, capital is highly organized. One regulation of the Cotton Spinners' Association is that "no worker may be taken on, while he or she is in the service of another employer, without the permission of that employer."

The high development of monopolistic capitalism in Japan affords certain unmistakable advantages in the field of foreign trade. The far-reaching interests of such great combinations of wealth as Mitsui, Mitsubishi, Yasuda, and Sumitomo facilitate close coöperation between manufacturer, banker, exporter, and shipper. Japan's exported products are almost invariably carried in Japanese ships and are not infrequently retailed by Japanese merchants in the countries where they are sold.

If production for export in Japan is largely carried out by tiny workshops, the marketing is largely in the hands of immensely powerful trading organizations. Over 40 per cent of Japan's exports and imports, for instance, are handled by the Mitsui Bussan Kaisha.

In the vanguard of Japan's trade offensive is its rapidly advancing merchant marine. Not only is the distribution of Japanese goods promoted by the existence of fast, efficient Japanese services to all parts of the world, but the receipts from the shipping industry help to keep the Island Empire's always precarious balance of international payments in order. "Income from shipping enterprises" figures as a favorable item in the balance sheet of international payments to the extent of 251,520,000 yen in 1934 and of 303,180,000 yen in 1935.

There is nothing more striking in Japan's remarkable record of material progress than its emergence as the third largest shipping power in the world. Its first steps in shipping after the country was opened up to foreign intercourse were slow and hesitating. Foreign captains and navigators were employed on many of the early Japanese ships. The first 6000-ton steamer was launched in 1898, thirty years after the policy of isolation had been abandoned.

To-day Japanese passenger liners, of which the largest run to 18,000 tons, fast cargo boats, freighters, and tramp steamers sail the trade routes in successful competition with those of the old established seafaring nations. No foreigner is now employed in an executive capacity on any Japanese ship. The best liners leave nothing to be desired in speed, comfort, and safety.

Shipping naturally experienced the full brunt of a world crisis that was especially destructive in the field of international trade. Here again the Japanese showing has been remarkable. Of 6,000,000 tons of world shipping that were tied up and out of service, Japan had only 16,000. At the end of August, 1936, Japan had 4,247,000 tons of registered shipping; in the spring of 1937 over a million tons of shipping were under construction at its humming dockyards. Shipbuilding has advanced hand in hand with shipping. There are large dockyards in the Tokyo-Yokohama district, in Yokosuka, one of the main naval bases, in Kobe, and in Nagasaki.   The time has passed when Japanese ships were laid down on the banks of the Clyde, although two ships which maintain a regular express service between Kobe and Shanghai still bear witness to the lasting seaworthiness of vessels turned out in the Scotch yard where they were constructed.

The N.Y.K. (Nippon Yusen Kaisha) celebrated in 1935 the fiftieth anniversary of its establishment.   When it came into existence in 1885 its assets consisted of fifty-eight small steamers and eleven sailing ships, with a total capacity of less than 70,000 tons; its capital was 11,000,000 yen.   Now these modest beginnings show a tenfold rate of increase, and the N.Y.K. tonnage is rated at 770,000, the capital at 116,000,000 yen.   In the beginning the N.Y.K. linked up Japan only with ports of China, Siberia, and other neighboring countries.   Now it operates one of the three main trans-Pacific services, together with lines to Europe, India, Australia, and the west coast of South America.

Behind the advance of the Japanese merchant marine lies a combination of hard work, natural aptitude for navigation, systematic government aid, and strong economic nationalism.   In connection with this last point it may be noted that it is far less common for a Japanese to travel on a foreign ship than for a foreigner to book passage on a Japanese vessel.

Shipping has been closely fitted in with the whole machinery for carrying on foreign trade.   The Mitsubishi interests control the N.Y.K. and several smaller lines.   The second largest line, the O.S.K. (Osaka Shosen Kaisha), belongs to the Sumitomo firm; and Mitsui, oldest and most powerful of the mammoth trusts, ships many of its export and import products in its own bottoms.

Reasonable coöperation, rather than cutthroat competition, has usually been practised by these steamship companies in dealing with each other. A conspicuous example of this was the agreement concluded between the N.Y.K. and the O.S.K. in 1931. The N.Y.K. withdrew from the South Atlantic route, leaving this to the O.S.K., which, in turn, discontinued its service to the West Coast of the United States and turned over the management of its European lines west of Suez to the N.Y.K.

Shipping and shipbuilding have long enjoyed the advantage of government subsidies. These amount to about 10,000,000 yen (a little less than $3,000,000) a year at the present time. Part of this money has been used to promote the modernization and competitive efficiency of the merchant marine. During the world crisis Japanese shipping firms realized that they were handicapped because they had too many old and slow ships in service. Legislation passed in 1932 placed a premium on the scrapping of obsolete craft and their replacement with modern vessels.

A replacement subsidy system was put into effect, with payments as the reward for simultaneously scrapping vessels which were more than twenty-five years old and building new steel ships, of not less than 4000 tons capacity and a speed of not less than thirteen knots an hour. The amount of the subsidy paid per ton of new shipping was progressively raised in accordance with the speed of the new vessels. Within a year and a half after this legislation had been enacted, 400,000 tons of obsolete shipping had been consigned to the scrap heap and 200,000 tons of new shipping had been built.

While there was at first some abuse of this subsidy arrangement (Japanese shipowners bought old vessels in other countries in order to scrap them and claim the benefit of the subsidy for new building), the speed of the Japanese cargo services has notably increased. Japan has the two fastest freight ships in the world, the *Canberra Maru* and the *Tokyo Maru,* which make the long run from Kobe to Sydney, Australia, in eleven days, whereas most cargo boats require twenty days for this trip. Fast freighters, used for carrying precious cargoes of silk, have cut down the time required for the sea voyage from Yokohama to New York, through the Panama Canal, from thirty-five to twenty-eight days; and one Japanese ship holds the world's record for speed on this run — slightly more than twenty-five days. As has already been pointed out, Japan has taken over a large share of the rubber-carrying trade between Malaya and America. Japanese freighters have been taking so large a share of the business in Indian ports that it is proposed to exclude them from coastal shipping there, unless an agreement reserving a share of business for British companies can be reached. The need for imported raw materials has promoted the progress of shipping companies, as Japanese vessels can usually reckon on two-way cargoes.

So the empire's trade offensive is sustained by a variety of favorable factors: labor that offers an unusual, if not a unique combination of cheapness and efficiency; a rising level of science, invention, and mechanical skill; close coördination in foreign trade methods; an efficient and far-flung shipping service. Most important of all, perhaps, foreign trade and the employment which it creates are what the Japanese like to call a life line, a necessity of national existence. With emigration an uncertain prospect and birth control unlikely to be widely adopted in any near future, with the rural areas crowded to the saturation point, industrialization is Japan's most hopeful means of providing work and food for its rapidly growing population. As two economists state the problem: —

> In Japan there is too great a mass of population, or an excessive surplus of labor, while there is too little of natural wealth or of capital resources to keep the people employed for their living. . . . Under these circumstances the Japanese people have no choice but to produce by their own exertions what they can sell abroad; otherwise they would be without means wherewith to obtain the necessaries of life. Hence the importance of their export trade. In other words, they have to export their surplus labor in the form of merchandise.[10]

A significant indication of the sacrifices which Japan finds it necessary to make in order to hold and improve its position in foreign markets is the marked deterioration in the terms of exchange between the country's manufactured goods and the raw materials which it purchases abroad. In 1931 the value of one hundred pounds of imported raw cotton was equivalent to that of 29.74 pounds of exported yarn and 143 square yards of cloth. By 1936 Japan was obliged to give, in return for the same hundred pounds of cotton, 47.68 pounds of yarn and 235 square yards of cloth.

So Japan had to give 60 per cent more cotton yarn or 64 per cent more of its cloth, whereas Great Britain in 1936 was giving only 27 per cent more in cotton yarn and 20 per cent more in cloth for its imported cotton. The same trend is to be found in other export trades. Japan was shipping abroad three and a half times as many rubber tires for a given quantity of crude rubber in 1936 as in 1931, whereas Great Britain had raised its exports of tires by two

[10] T. Yano and K. Shirasaki, *op. cit.*, p. 43.

and a half times.   Japan was exporting 65.3 per cent more leather boots and shoes, measured in terms of hides and skins, Great Britain 12 per cent more.   If one takes 1931 as 100, Japan's index of the volume of exports required to pay for a given volume of imports stood at 147 in 1936, Great Britain's at 104.[11]

This is the reverse side of the expansion of exports. While Japan's large industrial firms and trading organizations show profitable balance sheets, the competitive victories in the field of foreign trade have been dearly purchased by the long hours of labor and small remuneration of millions of laborers and handicraft workers.   Japan and England have consciously or unconsciously followed out contrasted economic philosophies.   Rather than depress its wage rates to the point where Japanese competition could be met, England has let go some of its Oriental trade.   Like America, England has assumed as a national burden the maintenance of large numbers of unemployed while maintaining a relatively high standard of living for those who are employed. In Japan, where there is no very strong public sentiment against long hours and low wages and where labor is very weakly organized, there is work for almost everyone.   In a nation of approximately 70,000,000, there are only about 360,000 registered unemployed.   But the wages of employed workers are often much lower than the American relief allotment or the British dole.[12]

---

[11] These figures are taken from an interesting article, "The 'Real Income' from Export Trade," by Guenther Stein, in the *Oriental Economist* for January 1937.

[12] Japan is not the only country in which absence of large-scale unemployment is offset by a generally low standard of living.   A similar situation prevails in the Soviet Union, Germany, and Italy.   Indeed, it is rather a distinctive feature of the modern dictatorship that it puts

A little over one fifth of Japan's industrial output is exported, but some industries are much more largely dependent than others on sales in foreign markets. The percentage of export is 75.3 for canned and bottled foodstuffs,[13] 78.5 for rayon yarn, 72.7 for rayon textiles, 57.1 for hosiery, 41.8 for pottery and porcelain, 29.1 for glassware.[14]

In a world governed by the Manchester free-trade economics of the last century, Japan's trade offensive would have gone much farther than is actually the case. But it is the bad fortune of the Island Empire that it has come of age industrially at a time when economic theory and, still more, economic practice have drifted far away from the ideals of Bright and Cobden. And just as Japan's political advance has provoked counter-arming from Vladivostok to Singapore, so the advance in export trade has been considerably retarded by a multitude of economic barbed-wire entanglements in the shape of quota restrictions, high tariffs, and other measures designed to check the world-wide sweep of "Made in Japan" products.

Japan's six chief markets are the United States, Manchoukuo, British India, Australia, China, and the Dutch East Indies. Access to Manchoukuo, of course, is not only free but highly preferential. In China, apart from the boycott sentiment that still exists in some parts of the country, there are no special barriers against Japanese goods, but in all the other four markets there are limiting regulations against them.

---

almost everyone to work, but very often at wages which would not compare favorably with what the unemployed receive in democratic countries.

[13] Japan's better grades of canned fish are almost exclusively exported.

[14] These percentages are for the year 1934.

Japan's foreign trade obstacles are of three main types. In countries like the United States and Great Britain there is the feeling that unrestricted admission of Japanese goods would break down existing standards of wages and profits. In colonial countries, such as the Dutch East Indies, French Indo-China, and Malaya, there is the tendency of the ruling power to protect the trade interests of its own nationals against Japanese competition. And in some of the new markets which Japan has found in South and Central America there are difficulties of exchange, because the Island Empire is unable to import large quantities of South American products.

More than sixty countries have imposed special restrictions on Japanese textiles; less than thirty have left the door open on equal terms. It is significant that, while Japanese textile exports to countries where no special restrictions are imposed increased by 17.2 per cent in 1935 over 1934, the gain in countries with high tariffs and exchange control systems was only 2.4 per cent. In lands with quota systems the position was virtually stationary, with an increase of .1 per cent. In 1936 there was an actual decline in cotton textile exports of 2.5 per cent in value and .6 per cent in volume.

The two most familiar forms of restriction on Japanese goods are especially high tariffs (sometimes based on the principle of alleged compensation for Japan's depreciated currency) and quota systems, under which Japan is allotted a quota of some commodity, usually based on the figures of imports in earlier years, before the export trade boom became so pronounced. The empire is sometimes able to surmount very high tariff walls because of the exceptional cheapness of its production, but quotas represent an almost impassable barrier. The difference in price between Japanese wares and the more expensive goods of other countries may sometimes encourage smuggling. But it is only in exceptional cases, as in North China, where the administrative power of the Chinese Government has been paralyzed, that this can appreciably augment the inflow of Japanese products.

During 1935 and 1936 Japan became engaged in two trade wars, the first with Canada, the second with Australia. The occasion for the conflict with Canada was a raising of already high duties on Japanese imports into Canada. Japan was in a strong position, because its purchases in Canada, in which wheat and pulpwood figured prominently, were considerably in excess of its sales to that country. In reprisal for the higher Canadian duties the empire stopped or greatly curtailed its imports of Canadian goods, until a change of government in Canada paved the way for a settlement along lines which were substantially satisfactory.

Japan again invoked as a weapon its power as an important buyer of raw materials when the Australian Government, in the spring of 1936, introduced a heightened scale of duties on non-British goods which especially affected Japanese textiles and rayon. Japan cut down as far as possible its purchases of Australia's staple export, wool, and introduced a licensing system for all purchases from Australia. The latter country applied further reprisals to Japanese goods. After dragging on for some months this trade war was settled by a sort of barter compromise. In return for a Japanese promise to buy not less than 800,000 bales of Australian wool, the Australian Government consented to lower the tariff for specified amounts of Japanese textile and rayon goods.

The way to this type of agreement was pointed by the Indo-Japanese convention of 1934. Both British and Indian textile manufacturers had been suffering from the greatly accelerated inflow of Japanese textiles. The Island Empire had a bargaining weapon as a large purchaser of Indian cotton. So an agreement was finally concluded on the basis that Japan might export annually 400,000,000 yards of cotton textiles on condition that it should at the same time buy not less than a million and a half bales of Indian cotton. This agreement was renewed, on terms somewhat less favorable to Japan, in the spring of 1937.

Much of the opposition to Japanese goods is attributable to the wide margins of undercutting which Japanese traders frequently employ. At first sight it may seem strange that the exporters should often quote prices much lower than would seem necessary for successful competition. There are, however, two reasons why low prices are likely to remain a weapon in the empire's trade offensive. One of these was explained to me by a Japanese economist in the following way: —

"Japanese exporters are following the example of Henry Ford, who placed the automobile within reach of many people who could never have afforded the purchase of an expensive motor car. Prices which seem low to the American or European are not low to the Indian peasant or the Chinese or Javanese coolie. Most of Japan's main markets are in Asiatic countries where the masses of the people are too poor to buy any but the cheapest manufactured goods. By quoting prices far below the American and European levels our exporters are reaching wide classes of people who would not be customers at all if they were offered only the comparatively high-priced American or European goods."

Another reason why it is difficult to conclude price-sustaining agreements with Japanese manufacturers is the intense competition in Japan itself, especially among smaller firms.

What of the future of Japanese commerce? A prominent industrialist, Mr. Ginjiro Fujihara, head of the Oji Paper Company, expressed himself very optimistically when I asked him what he thought of the prospects of the export trade over the next decade: —

"It is bound to expand and make further progress," was his prompt and unhesitating reply. "Our exports during the last five years have increased by approximately 1,200,-000,000 yen. The showing after another decade will be still more remarkable. Foreign economists are mistaken when they see the main reasons for Japanese expansion in a favorable exchange rate, inflation, and low wages. Of course these factors play their rôle. But the main thing, in my opinion, is the intense seriousness with which the Japanese people go about their work. They have been trained for centuries in habits of industry and no obstacles can hold them back."

Mr. Fujihara professes equal confidence in his book *The Spirit of Japanese Industry*, where he points to the notable progress of the Japanese machine-building industry as proof that, with further effort, Japan may take care of all the machine-building needs of the Orient, and suggests that, if checked in one place, it can expand in another.

Not all Japanese economic observers are as hopeful as Mr. Fujihara. Among the unfavorable elements in the foreign trade situation one may list the cumulative effect of the restrictions on Japanese goods which have been put in force in so many countries,[15] Japan's relative shortage of capital and poverty in raw materials, the possibility that rising living costs will bring about wage increases which will weaken the empire's competitive power. But there can be little doubt that Japan's traditional perseverance and frugality, combined with all the forces favoring export trade which have been enumerated, will enable the trade offensive to go on, although the pace will probably gradually slacken.

Japan has certainly established a firm place as a supplier of cheap consumers' goods to the poverty-stricken natives of Asia and Africa. Nothing short of a complete political debacle or economic collapse can take away the Island Empire's gains in these markets. The hope of many business-men that their country will soon supply Asia — if not other parts of the world — with most of its requirements in ma-chinery and products of heavy industry seems more uncer-tain as to realization, for here Japan's natural poverty is a severe handicap. In the spring of 1937 Japanese in-dustrialists were obliged to reject an order from Brazil for 10,000,000 yen worth of railway material because there was such a shortage of steel that this vital raw product was severely rationed, with preference for the needs of the army and navy.

The rising trade barriers all over the world have supplied

[15] The following typical excerpts from a report of the Japan Cotton Spinners' Association shows how sales of Japanese textiles are being checked: —

Egypt. The Egyptian Government, on July 18, 1935, suddenly abro-gated the Japan-Egypt trade convention and imposed an exchange in-demnity ad valorem duty of 40 per cent on September 20.

Union of South Africa. As a result of frequent tariff increases on Japanese goods, exports of cotton cloth have declined considerably.

Guatemala. Guatemala raised its tariff on Japanese goods by 100 per cent.

arguments to those advocates of nationalist economics who maintained that no market is altogether safe unless it is under Japanese political control.   However, it is impossible for Japan to go over to a purely self-centred nationalist economy, because the empire and the territories which it more or less directly controls, such as Manchoukuo and North China, are lacking in too many essential commodities.   It may be expected, therefore, that, without neglecting the possibilities of developing Manchoukuo and North China, Japan will endeavor to defend its international trade by concluding semi-barter commercial agreements when the free-trade conditions, which are now as advantageous to Japan as they were to England in the nineteenth century, are denied.

IX

THE STRUGGLE OF THE LIONS AND THE FOXES

THE salty and pungent Italian sociologist, Vilfredo Pareto, expressed the view that men are alternately governed by lions and by foxes. The former rule by force and direct action, the latter by the milder instruments of law, tradition, convention, and persuasion.

Pareto's parable is very applicable to contemporary Japan. For the constant struggle, now acute, now restrained, now open, now concealed, between the lions of militarism and the foxes of big business and civilian politics is a main clue to the understanding of the complex and confused pattern of Japanese political life. Militarism and big business are the two most powerful and articulate forces in Japan to-day. The power of the sword is counterbalanced by the power of gold.

The military and naval leaders of Japan, most of whom are descendants of the fighting samurai families of the Middle Ages, possess very great power and prestige. Besides receiving almost half of the national revenue for their needs, the army and the navy, especially the former, influence the foreign and domestic policy of the country to a degree that would be inconceivable in a country with a strong tradition of keeping armed forces out of politics.

The conciliatory efforts of the former Japanese Ambassador to China, Mr. Akira Ariyoshi, were repeatedly frustrated by the blunt words and blunter actions of Japanese military officers in North China, who paid scant regard to the civilian branches of the government. Japan's soldiers in Manchuria in 1931 more than once flouted the reassuring declarations of its diplomats. Still more recently the conclusion of the Japanese-German pact against Communism thwarted the patient efforts of the Foreign Office, which had been taking place over a period of several months, to promote friendlier relations between Japan and the Soviet Union.

A striking demonstration of the army's power in internal affairs was given early in 1937. The Hirota Cabinet had resigned because the War Minister, General Count Terauchi, violently resented criticism of the army in the Diet. The Emperor, on the advice of his first counselor, the venerable Prince Kimmochi Saionji, entrusted General Kazushige Ugaki with the formation of a new cabinet. General Ugaki's appointment was greeted by the two main political parties and received virtually unanimous endorsement in the press. But he could not become Premier because he could find no one to serve as War Minister.

Ugaki was disapproved by the army leaders on several grounds. He was considered too close to the Minseito, one of the main political parties. He had served as War Minister at a time when there was a reduction in Japan's military strength. He had made himself objectionable to the more extreme nationalist groups which had formed within the officers' corps during the tense years after the occupation of Manchuria. So Ugaki's appointment was effectively vetoed; another Premier had to be found in General Senjuro

Hayashi. This same veto right was exercised, although
in milder form, when the Hirota Cabinet was formed after
the February 26 outbreak in 1936. Several of Hirota's
original ministerial candidates were unacceptable to the army
and had to be dropped for this reason.

It is a regular practice for both the army and the navy,
through their Press Departments, to issue pamphlets which
not only discuss military and naval matters, but make the
broadest recommendations on questions of general policy.
Army pronouncements of this kind have been characterized
by a strong note of social radicalism and anticapitalism.

But great as is the influence of the army and navy in Japan,
it must reckon with the formidable power of organized
wealth, represented by the great industrial, commercial, and
financial dynasties which concentrate in their hands so large
a share of the country's wealth and productive power, the
Mitsuis and Mitsubishis, the Sumitomos and Yasudas.
There are no antitrust laws in Japan, and the country's rapid
economic development since the World War has been largely
along the lines of monopoly capitalism. The big aggregations of capital carry on an amazing variety of functions.
Everything they touch turns to profit, and there is very
little they do not touch. They operate banks and mines,
factories and shipping companies. Their ships carry the
products of their industrial enterprises to all parts of the
world; their commercial agents are in every large capital.

It is estimated that fifteen interests control altogether 70
per cent of Japanese trade and industry. Three of these,
Mitsui, Mitsubishi, and Sumitomo, control more than 25
per cent. Mitsui alone controls about 15 per cent. While
tiny industries and handicraft workshops survive because
of the remarkable capacity of Japan's artisans and small

producers to work long hours for very small remuneration, the large capitalist concerns usually swallow up any growing and prosperous new business. It is seldom that the small businessman can sustain prolonged competition with the huge aggregations of wealth. The result is that one can scarcely go into any corner of the Japanese Empire, however remote, without finding one of the big capitalist combines firmly entrenched and skimming the cream of whatever profits are to be made. In my own travels to the northern and southern ends of the empire I found Mitsubishi promoting experiments in extracting oil from coal in the mines of Naihoro, in Southern Sakhalin, and Mitsui systematically exploiting the sugar plantations of Formosa.

The House of Mitsui can look back on three centuries of money-making; it got its start in small trade and money-changing in the early days of the Tokugawa Shogunate. So it has accumulated long experience in dealing with strong-willed and habitually impecunious men of the sword and has survived many Japanese political and economic crises. There are now eleven main and branch lines of the House. Its leadership is determined not by strict primogeniture, but by ability, as weighed and appraised by a family council. There is a mediæval feudal element in the psychology of these Japanese Rothschilds which is reflected in the picturesque language of the oath which every member of the huge family must take on coming of age: —

In obedience to the precepts of our forefathers, and in order to strengthen the everlasting ancestral foundation of the families of our House and to expand the enterprises bequeathed by our forefathers, I solemnly vow in the presence of the August Spirits of our ancestors that, as a member of the House of Mitsui, I will observe and follow the regulations handed down in the Constitution of our House and that I will not wantonly seek to alter them. In witness whereof, I take the oath and affix my signature thereto in the presence of the August Spirits of our ancestors.

Mitsui's main rival, Mitsubishi, is of more modern origin. Its wealth dates not from the Shogunate but from the first decades of the Restoration period, when there were many opportunities for enterprising capitalists who could win government support.   The Mitsubishi house made its first large successful business *coup* by transporting troops to Formosa at a handsome profit in 1873.   It now controls the largest Japanese shipping company, the Nippon Yusen Kaisha, along with a miscellaneous assortment of mines, factories, banks, and trust companies.

These two great trusts for some time placed a distinct stamp on the two main Japanese political parties.   Mitsui was inclined to favor an aggressive foreign policy and expansive, not to say inflationary, finance; and this corresponded pretty closely with the programme of the Seiyukai Party. The Minseito, on the other hand, representing urban business and industrial interests, favored restraint in foreign policy and conservative finance, and this was closely in line with the views of the Mitsubishi house, which has been rather more modern and Western in outlook than the Mitsui.   At the present time, however, the political parties have so lost in significance that the big financial groups scarcely find them worth subsidizing, at least on anything like the former scale.   Moreover, the course of events during the last few years has definitely committed Japan both to a forward policy on the Asiatic continent and to highly expansionist financial methods, so that these issues have practically disappeared.

While the fighting services and big business do not appear openly in the political arena, the struggles and compromises between these two most potent forces in Japan are far more significant than the shadowboxing of the parties in the Diet. Parliamentary institutions, imported from abroad rather than created from within, have never struck very deep root in Japan. Even during the 'twenties, when liberalism reached its high point, the Diet possessed much less power than national representative bodies in the democratic countries of Europe and America.

Large powers were reserved for the throne. The army and navy remained to a large extent outside the scope of parliamentary control. The civil liberties which were theoretically assured to Japanese subjects never weighed very heavily in the scale against the wide powers exercised in practice by the police. The Japanese Constitution of 1889 was closely patterned on the Prussian model, which its architect, Prince Ito, regarded as most desirable for Japan because, among the parliamentary systems of the more advanced European countries, it left the largest measure of executive power in the hands of the government.

The Japanese national legislature is bicameral. The House of Representatives is elected on a basis of fairly complete manhood suffrage. The House of Peers consists partly of hereditary, partly of appointed, partly of elective members. The first group consists of representatives of the aristocracy; the second of men who are appointed to life membership for service to the state or for distinction in some cultural or scientific field. According to the late Dr. Inazo Nitobe, "Too frequently is nomination made of people who serve the party in power with funds, rather than the state by honorable service." [1]   Still a third group consists of elected representatives of the highest taxpayers.   Four members are selected by the Imperial Academy.

The House of Peers may reject any measure passed by the House of Representatives, and its composition marks it out for the function of a conservative brake on the course of legislation.   Moreover, the Diet lacks the full power of the purse which is the distinctive feature of full-fledged representative government.   If it should refuse to approve the budget, the government may approve the budget of the preceding year.   The cabinet is responsible to the Emperor, not to the Diet, and is not obliged to retire if the Diet passes a vote of non-confidence.   The sweeping veto power of the army and navy has already been pointed out.

Limited in power from the beginning, the Diet has receded still more into the background since the occupation of Manchuria and the accompanying upsurge of extreme nationalism.   The party cabinets which had become customary during the 'twenties disappeared after the famous "incident" of May 15, 1932, when a band of extremist young naval officers murdered the elderly Premier, Tsuyoshi Inukai, while a group of insurgent peasants made an abortive effort to cut off Tokyo's electric power supply as a demonstration against the suffering in the rural districts.   Nonparty cabinets have been organized since that time; and General Hayashi formed his cabinet without any representatives of the political parties, demanding that every minister should renounce any party affiliation he might have.

The two large parties, the Seiyukai and the Minseito, have been compromised by the notorious corruption and

[1] *Op. cit.*, p. 195.

identification with private business interests of some of their members;[2] a theme which Japanese conservatives are never tired of harping on and exaggerating. Moreover, while the two parties have fought each other lustily enough for the spoils of office and displayed an aptitude for adopting, along with other Western innovations, an effective technique of boss rule, they have practically run out of genuine political ideas. It is impossible to discern any important difference of viewpoint as between Seiyukai and Minseito. Some of their more independent members still lift up their voices in sessions of the Diet in sharp criticism of the army and the bureaucracy. But the criticism is negative; the party politicians seem to have lost all capacity for positive initiative.

A fresh element has been introduced into Japanese politics by the advance of the Shakai Taishuto (Social Mass Party), which rolled up an unexpectedly large popular vote and increased its representation in the Diet from three to eighteen in the election of 1936, obtaining thirty-six seats in the surprise election of April 30, 1937. The Shakai Taishuto is a moderate labor party, headed by professors, lawyers, and publicists. It has won support not only among the manual workers, but also among members of the white-collar classes who are disillusioned with the old parties.

But ballots have never decisively influenced the course of Japanese public life. Only in the event of a great national crisis, such as an unsuccessful war, could the Shakai Taishuto, or perhaps some labor group standing farther to

[2] A foreigner who had lived for many years in Japan told me a revealing story of a Japanese acquaintance who had remarked to him that the expenses of his campaign far exceeded his modest annual salary as a member of the Diet. On being asked how he expected to make both ends meet, the parliamentarian replied that one of the large Japanese capitalist concerns, anxious to see that properly patriotic men were in the Diet, was taking care of all his election expenses.

PRINCE KIMMOCHI SAIONJI (LEFT) AND THE LATE MR.
TSUYOSHI INUKAI

the Left, expect to play any leading part. Restrictions on freedom of propaganda and agitation in police-ruled Japan are severe, and the financial resources of the Social Mass Party are very meagre. So in normal times it could scarcely hope to win the wide popular support and the extensive political influence which have fallen to the lot of labor and socialist parties in Great Britain, France, and the Scandinavian countries.

What of the strength of Communism in Japan? This is difficult to gauge, because the movement is legally proscribed and any known or suspected Communist is sooner or later arrested by the ever-vigilant police. The Russian Revolution had its repercussions in Japan and for some time during the relatively liberal 'twenties the ideas of Marxism and Bolshevism were eagerly discussed by the Japanese educated classes. Communism made its converts not only among the better-read workers but also among professors, publicists, and other intellectuals. It was also a popular creed among the small group of Japanese women of the upper and middle classes who had received Western education and chafed against the subordinate rôle which is assigned to woman in the Japanese family system.

The police were naturally not indifferent to this spread of "dangerous thoughts." There was a wholesale round-up of Communist leaders in 1928, and repression became still more intense after 1931. A high Japanese police official, Mr. Motoi Mori, gives the following description of the vigorous action which was taken against suspected Reds: —

The highest number of arrests made in a year by the Metropolitan Police Board alone was 7609. The total number of arrests made in the country must have been very high. As Communism had penetrated educational institutions, wholesale arrests of Communist students were made from time to time.[3]

Japan is notably slow to inflict the death penalty[4] and there have been no recorded executions of Communists in the empire. The number of long-term political prisoners also seems very small in proportion to the huge number of arrests. Between 1933 and 1936, it is alleged,[5] 59,013 persons were arrested in Japan on the charge of harboring, preaching, or carrying into practice "dangerous thoughts." Of these only 4188 were indicted after examination, although 6056 were given the benefit of suspended indictment instead of outright discharge. About half of those indicted were sentenced to prison and most of these have completed their terms, so that there are now only 509 persons in Japanese penitentiaries who are classified as "thought criminals."

Official figures about numbers of political prisoners must always be accepted with some reserve. However, Japan, unlike the major European dictatorships, has never found its prisons so crowded that special concentration camps for political offenders were needed. In many cases no doubt a word of warning from the all-powerful and all-knowing police was sufficient to turn a student away from the forbidden study of Marxist literature. Communists who were regarded as active leaders have been severely handled, and

[3] An article by Mr. Mori, describing the police campaign against Communism, was published in the magazine *Gendai* for February 1937.

[4] Several Japanese in Manchoukuo who had been convicted of what to the Japanese mind must have seemed the supreme treasonable offense of selling arms to insurgent bandits were given long prison sentences instead of being executed.

[5] The following figures, which are presumably official, appeared in the *Japan Times* of August 15, 1936.

some have died or suffered permanent impairment of health as a result of their treatment by the police and in prison.

Police repression is not the sole cause of the decline of Communism in Japan since 1931. The fighting which accompanied the seizure of Manchuria aroused the nationalist spirit of the country. Hope was felt that the poverty and unemployment which were factors in promoting the spread of Communism might be overcome through a career of foreign conquest. The Japanese intellectuals, always responsive to new foreign ideas and influences, were impressed by the sweep of Fascism in Europe. A professor in one of the leading Tokyo universities listed as follows the influences which had been strongest among those students who take an interest in world affairs: "Nietzsche, Eucken, Bergson, Bertrand Russell, Marxism, Fascism." [6]

Soon after my arrival in Japan I visited the headquarters of the most radical trade-union organization which is permitted to maintain a legal existence in Japan. This is the Nihon Rodo Kumiai Zenkoku Hyogikai, or National Council of Japanese Labor Unions. At the entrance to the tiny Japanese house which was occupied by the Council I was surprised to see a typical Communist poster with the inscription, in German: "The Red Flag Shows You the Way Out of Misery." Red flags were stacked up in a corner. It was evident that this organization was just about as radical as the police would tolerate.

---

[6] My personal impression is that the number of such students in Japan is not particularly large. The young Japanese who has entered a university after severe competition, and often as a result of great sacrifice on the part of his family, is inclined to look neither to the Right nor to the Left, in a political sense, but to concentrate his attention on the prospects of obtaining a secure government post or a desired position in the employment of one of the big firms or banks.

A talk with its president, Mr. Kanju Kato, who sits farthest on the Left in the Japanese Diet, was, however, calculated to dispel any idea that Left-Wing labor represents
a powerful force in contemporary Japan. He claimed for
his National Council a membership of about 15,000, which
would represent only a small fraction of the approximately
380,000 organized workers in Japan. These, in turn, are
very few in relation to the 3,000,000 laborers now employed in factories and the additional 3,000,000 who work
in small handicraft shops. Mr. Kato admitted that, after
the Manchurian occupation, the workers, as he put it, had
lost spirit and had been affected by the prevalent nationalist
sentiment. Declaring that the employers' organizations are
very strong, by comparison with the trade-unions, he spoke
of the following causes of the weakness of the Japanese labor
movement: —

"Many workers are still bound by feudal ideas. The
women who make up a considerable part of Japanese labor
often do not regard themselves as independent individuals,
but simply as members of their families. Our overpopulation is constantly exerting an unfavorable influence on the
labor market, and the so-called rationalization of industry,
the introduction of labor-saving machinery and devices, is
steadily throwing people out of work."

With both liberalism and Marxism (both in its moderate
and in its extremist interpretation) distinctly in eclipse, the
Japanese political arena remains free for the struggle between the lions of militarism and the foxes of big business
and civilian bureaucracy. Of course this formula, like any
formula which might be used in summing up Japanese political life, is a necessary and deliberate oversimplification
of the contending forces. There are ardent militarists in

civilian clothes. There are military and naval officers who favor a cautious and discreet foreign policy and who take no special interest in schemes for social and economic reforms. As regards the "lions," a line of distinction must also be drawn between what may be called their conservative and their Fascist elements, between those who merely wish to keep the political parties in their place and to obtain a free hand in military and naval expenditure and those who wish to make far-reaching changes in the existing order. One must also recognize the difference between the capitalist opponents of the army and individual Japanese liberals and radicals, such as Yukio Ozaki and Professor Isoh Abe, head of the Social Mass Party, who are both antimilitarist and anticapitalist.

By and large, however, the antagonism between the two groupings which I have mentioned, with its alternation of clash and compromise, remains the best working hypothesis for interpreting the contemporary play of Japanese politics. The issues at stake have never been formally defined and laid down by either side. But they are clear enough from the attitude which the army and the business interests have adopted at certain critical periods.

Japan's lions would include, besides the leaders of the fighting services, the numerous small but active groups of extremists who have been advocating, in varied forms, a programme of super-nationalism and social radicalism. These groups have supplied many recruits for terrorist attempts on the lives of statesmen who were regarded as too moderate or too capitalistic. The army also enjoys close connections with two mass organizations, numbering millions of members, the Young Men's League and the Reservists' Association.

The former accepts as members youths between the ages of thirteen and twenty-five and has branches not only in all cities and towns, but also in every village of any size. It is especially important in the country districts, where it represents the main, if not the only, social organization of the young people. I saw something of the working of these leagues in villages around Niigata, on the west coast of Japan, and was impressed by the similarity of their activities to those of the Union of Communist Youth in Russia and to those of the young Fascist groups in Italy and Germany. They are supposed to take part in patriotic drives; to hold meetings, which are often addressed by retired military and naval officers; to promote local good works, sometimes helping out a local poor family with its sowing, taking up a collection for soldiers from their district in Manchoukuo, or doing some voluntary work in repairing roads and bridges.

The Reservists' Association, the membership of which, like that of the Young Men's League, is about three million, includes all the men who have served in the army and navy. Its fundamental object, as stated in its constitution, is "to develop the military spirit and to promote military efficiency, which in their turn will promote social welfare, encourage virtuous customs and habits and guarantee the stability of national defense." Its intellectual guiding staff is the Meirinkai, or Higher Ethics Society, a nationalist organization headed by General K. Tanaka.

The first item in the programme of the militarists and their allies is maintenance of the maximum amount of armament, an item motivated and justified by Japan's international responsibilities and vulnerability to attack. The army, with its primary interest in expansion on the mainland of Asia, habitually stressed in its public statements the alleged menace of Russia's increasing military preparations, as also the need for being able to cope with any emergency which might arise in Sino-Japanese relations. Cynical observers sometimes profess to see a connection between the sporadic outbursts of shooting along the Manchoukuo-Siberia frontier and the army's periodic demands for higher appropriations. Japan's exposed position, as regards air raids, is also emphasized in army propaganda.

The navy, less interested in the Soviet Union and Manchoukuo, places Japan's alleged need for southward expansion in the foreground of its propaganda publications. While designs of conquest are repudiated, it is suggested that only a strong navy can assure fair treatment to Japanese traders and colonists in that part of the world.

Another point on which military and nationalist organizations lay great stress is "clarification of national polity," to give the literal rendering of the characteristically ambiguous Japanese expression which is habitually used. This constitutes assertion in the strongest terms of the absolute power of the Emperor and condemnation and suppression of the theory associated with the name of Dr. Tatsekuchi Minobe, authority on constitutional law, who taught that the Emperor is an "organ of state" (a phrase that gave great offense to extreme nationalists) and therefore subject to constitutional limitations. In this theory military and naval leaders see an opening wedge for the institution of parliamentary control over their activities — something which they are not disposed to tolerate. The Japanese officer is inclined to insist, with emphasis, that his oath of allegiance is to the Emperor, not to the Diet.

The programme of Japan's lions calls for greater state control over industry (especially where strategic considerations are involved), more severe curbing of the great aggregations of wealth, and a better deal for the poverty-stricken, debt-ridden Japanese peasant. As the average Japanese officer is not well versed in economics, no inconsistency is seen in simultaneously demanding improvement of the lot of the peasant and fisherman and more money for military expenditures — money which is bound, in the long run, to come out of the national income, thereby adding, in one way or another, to the burdens of all classes.

Again and again the army and navy, urging considerations of national security, have sponsored legislative measures and policies which would scarcely have been adopted for purely economic reasons. The establishment of the obligation of all oil companies, Japanese and foreign, to maintain constantly on hand a reserve stock of oil equal to six months' average sales is one illustration of this tendency.[7] The law regulating the automobile industry, prohibiting the expansion of plants in which most of the stock is not owned by Japanese, is another.[8] The military and naval authorities are seriously concerned over Japan's lack of many essential raw materials. So they demand more investment in the extraction of oil from coal, regardless of the expense involved. The army took advantage of the trade

[7] The British and American oil companies carrying on business in Japan, while agreeing to maintain a three months' reserve, have flatly balked at the six months' requirement, contending that this would make necessary an unprofitable outlay for new storage equipment.

[8] This law mainly affected the Ford and General Motors plants in Japan, which supply a large part of the country's needs in automobiles and trucks. The army is very eager to build up a large-scale Japanese motor-car industry, but is handicapped by the limited internal market for automobiles.

dispute with Australia in 1936 to experiment with the use of staple fibre as a substitute for wool in uniforms.

A further example of the army's tendency to interfere in questions of economic policy on strategic grounds was the project for national control of the very important electrical power industry. This project, which had not received legislative sanction by the spring of 1937 because of the opposition of business interests, which resent any form of control, fell short of the army's demand for complete nationalization of the industry: this project was, however, enacted into law as a war measure early in 1938.

The army viewpoint, as usual, was based on military considerations. It was argued that, in the event of war, the need for electrical power for industrial use would enormously increase and that facilities would be required for shifting power from one part of the country to another. Inasmuch as private companies, impelled by incentives of profit, would not be inclined to expand reserve facilities for power production beyond immediate needs, the military spokesmen contend that the state should take over the industry and assume responsibility for operating it.

This military socialist outlook finds expression in more general terms in a pamphlet which was issued by the Press Bureau of the War Department in 1934. The following excerpts from this pamphlet reveal the strong leaven of social radicalism which has been at work in the Japanese Army, especially among the younger officers, in recent years:

The present economic system has been developed on the basis of individualism. For this reason economic activities tend to serve only individual interests and fancies, and do not always harmonize with the general interests of the state. The extreme emphasis on free competition may be a danger, arousing antagonism between the classes. Wealth accumulated by a minority causes misery among the masses, strikes, the failure of small industrial establishments, the ruin of agriculture; and all these factors upset the balance of our national life. . . .

It is desirable that the people should abandon their individualistic economic conceptions; instead they should recognize the importance of a collective economy; they should work towards the creation of an economic system which will rapidly realize the Empire's ideal. The state should rigidly control the entire national economy.

The agrarian crisis looms large on the horizon of Japan's army economists. Like the German National Socialists, the military leaders of Japan prize the peasant both as a sturdy and reliable soldier and as a human type which, as they believe, best embodies the old-fashioned national virtues and is most immune from the enervating and corrupting influences of the towns, from jazz music, American movies, and cafés, to "dangerous thoughts" on social and economic questions.

So there has always been an intimate connection between the agrarian distress and the ferment of social radicalism and terrorist inclinations among the younger officers. The latter are often sons of small landowners who have themselves felt the pinch of hard times. Moreover, the Japanese officer is supposed to be something of a father to the men under his command, and the junior officer is often moved to sympathy by the stories of distress which he hears from the peasant soldiers in his company. Although the peasants now constitute less than half of Japan's population, they still furnish the bulk of the nation's soldiers. This is partly because town life has a deteriorating effect on physique, partly because the officers in charge of selection (not all men of military age receive training) believe the peasant is morally the better type of recruit.

Opposed to Japan's military lions on many points are the foxes, the big business and financial interests, the mature statesmen and diplomats, most of the old-line politicians. Without questioning the necessity of adequate national defense and of social reform, these groups emphasize the perils of upsetting the country's financial balance through reckless increases in the military and naval appropriations and rash social and economic experiments. They are committed to the standpoint that Japan can find a way out of its difficulties without very seriously disturbing the *status quo*, internally and internationally. Bending to the occasional military storm, these men of propertied interests and moderate views rely on two powerful factors, inertia and money, to preserve existing economic and social relations, despite occasional assassinations of prominent statesmen and financiers.

Japan is among the many countries where post-War developments have destroyed or modified the conceptions which have formerly been associated with such words as "conservative, liberal, radical." Army officers, who are conservative, even mediæval, in their insistence on ultra-nationalism, the absolute power of the Emperor, and the rejection of all Western ideas of liberal constitutionalism, are often radical in their antipathy to wealth and their desire to place private enterprise under strict state control. (It should not be forgotten that the great majority of Japanese officers, to say nothing of the privates, are poor men, with little or no personal stake in the maintenance of the

capitalist order. Only fifteen generals and admirals receive the maximum salary of 6600 yen — less than $2000
— a year.)

On the other hand, the businessman or senior statesman,
often a man of Western education, who is a liberal in pre-
ferring a conciliatory foreign policy and in opposing arbitrary actions by the military and the police, is often a conservative in the sense of actively or passively opposing any
fundamental change in the existing economic order. Incidentally, the idea that old men, *per se*, are dyed-in-the-
wool reactionaries is singularly inapplicable to Japan. A
surprisingly large number of Japanese who have opposed
militarism and extreme nationalism have been in their seven-
ties or eighties. Among these one may mention the men
marked as victims of the February 26 outbreak: Viscount
Saito and Finance Minister Takahashi; the *Genro*, or last sur-
viving Elder Statesman,[9] Prince Saionji; the former Lord
Privy Seal and Court Chamberlain, Count Makino; the leader
of the Social Mass Party, Professor Isoh Abe; and the sturdy
veteran liberal who has sat in the Diet for fifty years, Mr.
Yukio Ozaki. The explanation for this liberalism of Japan's old men lies in the fact that, as a rule, they traveled
abroad in their formative years, when constitutional democracy in politics and *laissez-faire* theories in economics were
not so widely and so sharply challenged as they have been
during the last two decades.

It is significant that all the "alarums and excursions," the

[9] The *Genro* were originally a group of elder statesmen on whom the
Emperor traditionally called for advice on important questions. As the
group was diminished by death, no new members were appointed;
and the system, in name at least, will disappear with the person of the last
of the Genro, Prince Kimmochi Saionji.

individual assassinations and the larger conspiracies, which have marked the course of the last troubled years in Japan have not yet led to a decisive "showdown," to the definite replacement of an old by a new system of government. After the reverberating shock of a May 15 or February 26 "incident" the sequel is a groping for a new equilibrium, for a fresh compromise between the contending forces. It should be borne in mind that the antagonism between Japan's lions and foxes is not clear-cut, absolute, and uncompromising. It certainly exists; but there is also a secondary factor of interdependence between militarism and big business.

Japanese businessmen are by no means lacking in nationalist spirit. If they disagree with the generals and admirals it is more about method and degree than about ultimate objectives. Some influential Japanese industrial and commercial interests, if not Japanese economy as a whole, stand to gain from the policies which are sponsored by the fighting services, from the profitable war orders that are a natural accompaniment of armament expenditures, from the wide-open door for Japan in Manchoukuo. Japan's heavy industries, iron and steel, mining and metallurgy, shipbuilding and chemicals, are booming at the present time very largely as a direct and indirect result of the process of intensive armament on which the country has entered. Mr. Ginjiro Fujihara certainly does not speak for himself alone in the following frank exposition of the view that armaments are a useful means of opening trade doors: —

Diplomacy without force is of no value. No matter how diligent the Japanese may be, no matter how superior their technical development or industrial administration may be, there will be no hope for Japan's trade expansion if there is no adequate force to back it. Now the greatest of forces is military preparedness founded on the Army and Navy. We can safely expand abroad and engage in various enterprises, if we are confident of protection. In this sense, any outlay for armament is a form of investment.[10]

In the other camp, responsible senior military and naval officers, if not their impetuous juniors, are aware of the fact that Japan's military efficiency would be seriously and adversely affected by sudden and violent economic changes that would check the steady and striking advance in production and foreign trade. Anything that will dislocate the delicate mechanism of foreign trade and exchange, that will lower Japan's competitive power in outside markets, will interfere with the purchase of such vital military raw materials as cotton, rubber, tin, nickel, and oil and consequently handicap the armament programmes that are being pushed forward with great vigor by both the fighting services.

So, despite the strong antipathy to capitalism which is felt by many Japanese officers, — an antipathy that is compounded of traditional samurai contempt for trade and money-making and modern, half-assimilated ideas of Fascism,[11] — the sense of interdependence between Japan's lions and foxes has thus far prevented a fight to the finish. Sometimes the struggle between these forces is so insubstantial as to be perceptible only to keen observers. There will be a

[10] Cf. his *Spirit of Japanese Industry*, p. 134.

[11] Admiration for Hitler and Mussolini is widespread in Japanese military circles, but is often not accompanied by any very clear idea of Fascist and National Socialist philosophy. A certain Major I. Ishimoto, who participated in a round-table discussion of defense problems in the *Osaka Mainichi*, one of Japan's largest newspapers, finds in Germany confirmation of his own belief that "armaments preparation represents the very means to enhance the happiness of the nation and to decrease unemployment."

reshuffle in army appointments, a resignation allegedly motivated by ill health or need for rest.   On other occasions the subterranean struggle bursts forth with a violence that arrests the attention of the whole world.

Much the most spectacular of these violent explosions was the military revolt already mentioned, which broke out in Tokyo on February 26, 1936.   A group of unknown captains and lieutenants, carrying with them fourteen hundred soldiers of the First and Third Infantry Regiments of the First Division, murdered several leading statesmen and soldiers, made unsuccessful attempts on the lives of others, and for four days occupied part of the centre of Tokyo, including several important public buildings.

My first intimation of this outbreak came at about eight in the morning in the shape of a telephone call from the leading Japanese news agency.   The information, although brief and incomplete, was sufficiently startling.   Several high officials had been killed and the War Department and Metropolitan Police Board, among other buildings, were occupied by insurgents.   Hurrying downtown, I found an atmosphere of complete confusion, with a natural accompaniment of the wildest and most contradictory rumors. The Foreign Office was open (it was one of the buildings which the rebels did not think it worth while to occupy), but there was no one there to hold the customary press conference with foreign correspondents.   Troops were posted at the main street crossings in the central part of the city; but it was impossible to learn which were on the side of the government and which were insurgents.   Indeed during the early hours of the day it seemed doubtful whether any "government" was still in existence.   Early rumors were to the effect that every Cabinet Minister of any eminence, together with Prince Saionji and Count Makino, had been slaughtered by the rebels.

A number of journalists gathered in the office of the Japanese-owned English language newspaper, *Japan Times*, to exchange the latest reports. Fresh news was suddenly brought by an American-born Japanese journalist who burst in with the announcement: —

"The soldiers have wrecked the *Asahi* office. And there's a lieutenant riding around on a bike and handing out a proclamation about how this is a land of gods and everyone must be killed who's against the Showa restoration. The craziest stuff you ever heard."

This bit of news, so irreverently phrased by the Japanese, whose American education made him unsympathetic with the high-flown phrases and homicidal activities of his compatriots, was more accurate than most of the rumors that were flying about in Tokyo. One of the leaders of the revolt, Captain Shiro Nonaka, with his colleagues, had composed a manifesto [12] which is worth quoting in full as an indication of the motives and psychology of the insurgents: —

The essence of the nation of Japan, as a land of the Gods, exists in the fact that the Emperor reigns with undiminished power from time immemorial down to the remotest future in order that the natural beauty of the country may be propagated throughout the universe, so that all men under the sun may be able to enjoy their lives to the fullest extent. This fundamental constitution of Japan has been in existence from the remotest past down to the present time. The Meiji Restoration has greatly added to the national

[12] This manifesto was distributed to various Japanese newspapers and news agencies; but was promptly suppressed by the police and has never been published in Japan.

glory of Japan. The present time is a favorable moment for Japan
to bring about a greater expansion of national power and prestige.

In recent years, however, there have appeared many persons
whose chief aim and purpose have been to amass personal material
wealth, disregarding the general welfare and prosperity of the
Japanese population, with the result that the sovereignty of the
Emperor has been greatly violated. The people of Japan have
suffered deeply as a result of this tendency and many troublous
issues now confronting Japan are attributable to this fact.

The Genro, senior statesmen, military cliques, plutocrats, bureaucrats and political parties are all traitors who are destroying national
polity.[13] They infringed on the Imperial right of Supreme Command when they concluded the London Naval Treaty of 1930 and
changed the Inspector-General of Military Education in 1935.
No wonder many nationalists and military officers have on several
occasions attempted to make them reflect and repent by bloodshed
and warnings. But all attempts were fruitless.

Japan's relations with Russia, China, Great Britain and the
United States are so strained at present that a single misstep will
cast the Divine Land of Japan into ruin. The Imperial work
will fail unless we take proper steps to safeguard the Fatherland
by killing all those responsible for impeding the Showa Restoration [14]
and slurring Imperial prestige.

Under these circumstances the Imperial order to mobilize the
First Division for Manchoukuo was issued. We, who have been
in charge of peace maintenance in the capital, cannot but be deeply
concerned over the foreign and internal situation.

It is our duty to remove the evil retainers from around the

---

[13] "National polity" is a rather unsatisfactory rendering of the almost
untranslatable Japanese *kokutai*, which conveys a sense of the body and
spirit of the nation.

[14] Showa is the name of the era which coincides with the reign of
the present Emperor; and the term Showa Restoration is often employed
by military extremists to indicate a change of régime along the lines which
they desire.

Throne and to smash the group of senior statesmen. It is our duty as subjects of His Majesty the Emperor.

May the Gods bless and help us in our endeavor to save the Fatherland from the worst that confronts it.

February 26th,   CAPTAIN SHIRO NONAKA
ELEVENTH YEAR OF SHOWA   HIS COLLEAGUES

In this manifesto, strange as much of its phrasing may seem to a Western reader, one can recognize all the main ideas of Japanese Army radicalism of the last years: hatred of capitalists and moderate statesmen; boundless exaltation of the supposedly divine Emperor, combined with the suggestion that he is surrounded by bad counselors; concern for national defense.

Gradually during the breathless day of February 26 a fairly accurate picture of what had happened was pieced together. The soldiers concerned in the affair had been destined for service in Manchoukuo and had been served out extra supplies of ammunition. Obeying the orders of some fifteen or twenty junior officers (the colonels and majors seem to have stood aside), they had gone in detachments to the homes of Cabinet Ministers and others who were marked for death.

The aged Finance Minister, Korekiyo Takahashi,[15] whose rotund figure had won him the nickname of "Daikoku, the God of Wealth," thought snow was falling off the roof when soldiers were mounting the steps of his house. Within a few minutes he was shot and sabred to death. The gal-

---

[15] Takahashi, a man of humble origin, was one of Japan's outstanding politicians and financiers. Convinced that the country was being led to the brink of a dangerous economic crisis by excessive military expenditures, he stood up with uncommon courage for a pacific foreign policy and for limitation of army and navy appropriations.

lant wife of Viscount Saito sustained injury to herself when she tried to clap her hand over the mouth of the machine gun that poured a volley of bullets into the body of her husband. The Inspector General of Military Education, General Jotaro Watanabe, was shot down after a lively exchange of revolver bullets; the solitary soldier on guard at his home fired warning shots as a truck load of the rebels drove up. The Grand Chamberlain, Admiral Kentaro Suzuki, was wounded. Prince Saionji, whose death would have been the severest shock to the existing order, somehow received warning in time to make his escape from his residence at a villa near Shizuoka and remained under a heavy police guard, provided by the governor of the province, until the crisis had passed. Count Makino, another moderate senior statesman who was abhorred by the army extremists, had an extremely narrow escape when a band of assassins attacked the country inn where he was staying.

Most bizarre of all were the happenings at the official residence of the Premier, Admiral Keisuke Okada. There was a larger guard here and several policemen were shot down defending the entrance. The insurgents, after gaining admission to the large building, found and promptly shot a man whom they took for Okada. The Premier's death was announced in official communiqués. Only after the whole incident was settled was it revealed that Okada had achieved an almost miraculous escape. The man who was shot was his brother-in-law, Colonel Matsuo, who closely resembled him. As the insurgents remained in occupation of the residence, the Premier was obliged to remain in hiding, concealed in the servants' quarters, for two days, when he was smuggled out in the disguise of a mourner at his own funeral.

By the evening of February 26 two things were clear. A government still continued to function, with headquarters in the Imperial Palace, Home Minister Fumio Goto taking over the duties of acting Premier. And the insurgents, with no Lenin, Hitler, or Mussolini among them, had no concrete plan of action, no definite programme of seizing power and setting up an alternative government. It was characteristic of the psychology and mentality of the young radical Japanese officer that the outbreak, well planned and executed as a conspiracy, had no well-defined political objectives.

Under these circumstances the suppression of the revolt was only a question of time. Yet the government felt obliged to move warily. The rebels were most inconveniently located, from the standpoint of publicity. They were occupying the Diet Building, the War Department, the Metropolitan Police headquarters, and other public buildings in the very centre of the capital. Two large foreign embassies, the American and the German, were in the zone of disturbance and would have been in the direct line of fire if an effort had been made to clear the rebels out by force.[16]

Moreover the impressions produced by an armed clash between Japanese soldiers in the heart of Tokyo would have been disastrous at home and abroad. Another factor to be considered was that the navy was most indignant because three admirals, Okada, Saito, and Suzuki, had been the object of murderous attacks by soldiers, and a clash between the two services was something which the authorities were most anxious to avoid.

[16] The American Ambassador, Mr. Joseph Clark Grew, won general praise for coolness, presence of mind, and good judgment in not evacuating the Embassy.

In view of this situation, there was much to be said for the Fabian tactics of General Kashi, who was appointed military commander of the city. During two uncertain days, the twenty-seventh and twenty-eighth, he negotiated with the insurgents, endeavoring to persuade them to lay down their arms. There was wavering in the camp of the rebels; several times it was reported that an agreement to surrender had been reached, but more extreme counsels would then prevail and the insurgents remained stubbornly in occupation of the public buildings. Finally, on the morning of the twenty-ninth, General Kashi served an ultimatum on the mutinous troops, intimating that if they did not obey the imperial command, which had been issued on the previous day, to lay down their arms and return to their barracks, the strongest military action would be taken against them and they would be regarded as rebels and traitors. All traffic, except for military automobiles, was stopped; and Tokyo during the morning of the twenty-ninth looked like a city in the grip of a general strike. The insurgents decided not to push matters to extremities; they began to surrender in small groups. By mid-afternoon the rebellion was over; the streets were cleared of the barricades which had been erected; traffic was quickly resumed.

Two of the strongest impressions which I gained from living through these eventful days were the self-discipline of the Japanese masses and the absence of any visible signs of popular interest in the crisis that seemed to be rocking the edifice of government to its foundations. There was not a sign of looting and disorder. Shops remained open as usual, people went about their ordinary business as if nothing had happened. There was no demonstration of antiforeign feeling; the insurgents were notably polite to the few foreigners who were still in the Sanno Hotel when they took it over.

There was also no tendency to take sides. The rebels found no support outside their own ranks; but there was also no rush of volunteers to take up arms for the government. The average Tokyo small shopkeeper, handicraft artisan, laborer, seemed to view the whole conflict with as much indifference as the same classes might have shown when there was a sanguinary clash of the retainers of two rival clans in the Japanese Middle Ages. This popular indifference, incidentally, raises the question whether the rebels might not have succeeded if their enterprise had been more coherently organized — if, for instance, the Imperial Palace had been seized and orders issued in the name of the Emperor.

The storm that burst on February 26 was not without its preliminary rumblings. One of the most obvious danger signals, pointing to the likelihood of an ultimate explosion, was the accentuation of factionalism in the higher and middle ranks of the army. Cliques have existed among officers ever since Japan's modern army was formed. But they increased in number and bitterness during the tense years which followed the occupation of Manchuria.

For half a century after the Restoration of 1868 the powerful Choshu clan almost monopolized the high posts in the army, while the Satsuma clan, the other main factor in the Restoration, maintained a similar predominance in the navy. Since the War the significance of the clans has greatly diminished. The Choshu domination was broken during the 'twenties, when General Ugaki was War Minister.

Ugaki, however, as his recent unsuccessful effort to form a cabinet showed, became unpopular with the more extremist officers. He was regarded as too much of a politician and was accused of coquetting with the Minseito Party, with a view to becoming Premier.

The chief spokesman of this extremist group, which stood for the absolute authority of the Emperor, for Japanese nationalism of the strongest brand, for state control over the capitalists and financiers, and was contemptuous of Western parliamentarism, was General Sadao Araki, who occupied the post of War Minister from 1932 until 1934. A stronger personality than Araki in the same group was General Jinzaburo Mazaki, who was as silent as Araki was loquacious.

A more moderate atmosphere began to prevail at the War Department after the resignation of General Araki, ostensibly on grounds of ill-health, early in 1934. His successor was General Senjuro Hayashi (who became Premier early in 1937). Hayashi, although he was a firm champion of the army's professional interest in larger armaments, abstained from the bellicose public utterances of his predecessor and displayed more willingness to work in harmony with the moderate civilian statesmen.

But factionalism was not suppressed in the army. In July 1935, Hayashi took the bold step of dismissing Mazaki, idol of the younger fire eaters, from his influential post as Director General of Military Education.[17] A reprisal was not slow in coming. In the following month Lieutenant Colonel Saburo Aizawa, nationalist fanatic and expert swordsman, walked into the office of Hayashi's chief assistant, Major General Tetsuzan Nagata, and cut him down.

---

[17] Propaganda for building up morale is as much cherished in the Japanese Army as in those of the Communist and Fascist dictatorships. A Japanese friend who served in the Imperial Bodyguard once told me that he was surprised at the amount of time which was devoted to lectures on such subjects as Japan's national spirit, the unique rôle of the Emperor, and so on.

Hayashi then felt bound to resign, in view of the Japanese tradition that every civil or military official must assume responsibility for any accident which occurs during his tenure of office, even if the accident is attributable to causes quite beyond his control.

The spirit of Aizawa was undoubtedly shared by the men who led the February 26 outbreak. How far Mazaki was personally aware of the plot is one of many questions to which a satisfactory answer is impossible, on the basis of available information. But that Nonaka, Ando, and the other captains and lieutenants believed they were acting in accordance with Mazaki's ideas is not open to doubt.

The trial of Aizawa, which was in progress when it was interrupted by the rattle of machine guns on February 26,[18] throws much light on the mentality of Japan's military extremists. The extraordinarily light-hearted attitude toward political assassination was reflected in Aizawa's somewhat naïve statement that he expected to return to his post in Formosa after he had killed his superior officer. Aizawa did not show the slightest repentance for his action. He told how, on the eve of the assassination, he had prayed for divine guidance at two of the most sacred places in Japan, the Grand Shrine of Ise and the Meiji Shrine in Tokyo. Very typical of the spirit of February 26 were the following passages in Aizawa's testimony: —

The Emperor is the incarnation of the god who reigns over the universe. The aim of life is to develop according to His Majesty's

[18] The revolt was unfortunate for Aizawa personally. The trial had been dragging on in a leisurely way; he had been given full opportunity to state his views; and there was general expectation that he would get off with a mild sentence of imprisonment. His second trial (the original one was suspended by the revolt) was held behind closed doors and ended in a death sentence, which was promptly carried out.

wishes, which have not yet been fully understood by the whole world. The world is deadlocked because of capitalism, Communism, anarchism, atheism, and so forth. We should make it our objective as Japanese to bring happiness to the world in accordance with His Majesty's wishes.

I came to realize that the elder statesmen, those close to the Throne, powerful financiers and bureaucrats, were attempting gradually to corrupt the Government and the Army for the realization of their own interests; that the Imperial Army was gradually being changed into something of a private nature and that the Supreme Command was being violated in every respect.

Allow me to say something about the people, too. Young girls in the Tohoku district, where I was born, do not like to work on the farms and there is no opportunity to bring up serious young men. Mah-jong and cafés are becoming a fad in the country. Internal conditions are becoming deplorable. When I observed these conditions, the teachings on which I had been brought up — to give up everything for the Emperor in an emergency — burst out and encouraged me.

Here one has, in a nutshell, the characteristic feelings of the Japanese military fanatic: hatred of the wealthy classes, of financiers and bureaucrats; a strain of puritanism; an exalted conception of the position of the Emperor and of Japan's world mission. Aizawa's counsel, Lieutenant Colonel Mitsui, sounded an ominous note of warning, which was to be confirmed earlier, perhaps, than he expected: —

"If the court fails to understand the spirit which guided Lieutenant Colonel Aizawa, a second Aizawa, and even a third, will appear."

The dramatic assassinations were no new thing in Japanese history. Frequent political homicide may indeed be considered one of the characteristic features of the Island Empire. Not a few eminent statesmen were objects of attack

before the War. Okubo, one of the main architects of
the Meiji Restoration, was assassinated. Prince Ito fell at
the hands of a Korean terrorist. Marquis Okuma lost a leg
because an extreme nationalist who was impatient with the
slow course of negotiations for the abolition of extraterritoriality threw a bomb at him.

Ministerial insecurity of life has increased since the War.
There has been a tremendous toll of Premiers and ex-
Premiers — Hara, Hamaguchi, Inukai, Saito, Takahashi,
with Okada escaping only by the most amazing good fortune.
This extraordinary insecurity of life in the higher altitudes
of politics is in striking contrast with the placid orderliness
which is characteristic of Japanese life in town and country
in general. February 26 was typical in this respect: the
greatest political crisis in Japan since the War passing off
without a sign of rioting or disorder and without any loss
of life, except for the murdered officials and a few men especially engaged in guarding them.

A strict censorship was imposed on any discussion of the
underlying motives and causes of the outbreak in the press.
So it was to individual Japanese that I turned for enlighten-
ment on the singular toleration, in the Japanese mind,
toward assassination committed for professedly idealistic
motives. Again and again in Japanese history the assassin
has won more popular sympathy than his victim; a cynic
might suggest as a maxim of Japanese ethics: "The murderer
(assuming that he professes to be an enthusiastic patriot) is
always right." Three Japanese of the educated classes with
whom I discussed this phenomenon each had a different explanation. Probably each of the theories had some element
of validity.

"We are a severely regimented people," said one of my

informants. "Minute regulation of acts, of words, even of gestures and modes of behavior: this is the price we pay for internal order and stability and for such industrial and technical progress as we have made. Sometimes the regulation is from without, by the police or by other authorities. Quite often, though, it is an inner compulsion of inherited family and social tradition. We submit to this regimentation; sometimes it becomes almost second nature to us. But when someone kicks over the traces and commits not an ordinary crime but a political assassination that is invested, rightly or wrongly, with an atmosphere of idealism, there is an instinctive, silent sympathy with the rebel, regardless of the circumstances. It is a psychological reaction against extreme control."

The second Japanese with whom I talked, a university professor, mentioned the idea, which is as old as Confucius, that it is a reproach to a ruler if he is attacked, because there will be no bad subjects if the rulers are good.

"The average Japanese has a feeling that there must be something wrong, some lack of virtue in the man who is assassinated," he declared. "This feeling cannot be defended on grounds of reason or logic; but it is very strong nevertheless."

Recognition of this idea is implied in the statement of the Grand Chamberlain, Admiral Suzuki, who was wounded, that he desired to resign his office "because of his lack of virtue."

The third Japanese offered still another suggestion: —

"In spite of our carefully borrowed Western constitutional arrangements, the Japanese man in the street has little faith in parliamentary action as a means of righting his wrongs. When an assassination is committed for

professedly idealistic motives he is apt to believe that the murderer was defending the common people against the tyranny
of those in power.   The checks and balances in our political
system are so numerous and complicated that the majority
of the people have never acquired the habit of regarding
governmental power as something of their own which they
could influence and restrain by the ballot and by other
peaceful means."

The classical Japanese Kabuki drama has also made its
contribution to the psychology of sympathizing with the assassination that is not committed for selfish motives.   Take,
for instance, the tragedy of the forty-seven *ronin* (knightly
retainers), which is based on an actual historical occurrence
of the eighteenth century.   It was being played to crowded
houses immediately after February 26, when everything
that was calculated to excite popular passion was supposed
to be forbidden.

Now the forty-seven *ronin*, to whom a shrine has been
erected in Tokyo, might be regarded as the patron saints of
"idealistic" homicide.   They kill, and give their own lives
in obedience to the highest moral laws of Japanese chivalry.
In accordance with a familiar practice of mediæval Japan,
the feudal lord of the forty-seven had been condemned to
commit hara-kiri because he had drawn a sword in the court
of the Shogun, the *de facto* ruler of Japan, against a lord
who had insulted him.   The retainers bided their time; after
a lapse of years they struck down the man who was the cause
of their lord's death.   Their fate was the subject of long
and anxious deliberation on the part of the authorities.
Finally they were commanded to take their own lives.
Their memories are enshrined forever in the hearts of the
Japanese people as heroes and martyrs.

Another factor which made February 26 more possible was the extreme leniency with which crimes of violence committed by extreme nationalists had hitherto been treated. The band of naval officers who had killed the old Premier, Inukai, in the incident of May 15, 1932, had been permitted to use the courtroom in which they were being tried for murder as a platform from which to expound nationalist propaganda.[19] They were already free, the prison terms to which they had been sentenced having been shortened by an amnesty. Aizawa, who had committed what in any other army would have been regarded as the obvious capital offense of deliberately murdering a superior officer, was likely to be treated in the same way, judging from the course of his trial up to the outbreak.

Only one of the young officers who led the revolt, Captain Nonaka, followed classical precedent by committing hara-kiri. The others preferred to stand trial. But if they counted on lenient treatment they were disappointed. For the outbreak had been a disconcerting shock not only to the moderate statesmen, of whom so many were killed or narrowly escaped with their lives, and to the big capitalists, some of whom literally went into hiding until the revolt was suppressed,[20] but also to the higher army officers.

[19] It is significant that the main intellectual figure involved in the May 15 outbreak, K. Tachibana, received much more severe treatment and is still serving a prison sentence of twenty years. Tachibana was not involved in the murder of Inukai, but headed a band of peasants from his native Ibaraki Province in an effort to cut off Tokyo's electricity supply. He had once written: "The fruits of the Imperial Restoration were lost because Choshu and Satsuma rule handed over the Land of the Gods to capitalists who exploit the people and politicians who deceive them."

[20] I know personally of one well-known industrialist who not only left Tokyo but went about under an assumed name during the critical February days.

Two features of the revolt made it much more serious, to the Japanese military mind, than previous cases of actual and attempted assassination by self-styled patriotic officers. Troops had been drawn into the affair and an imperial command to lay down arms had not received instantaneous obedience. So the foundations of discipline were seriously undermined. The more thoughtful and farsighted military leaders could scarcely fail to be impressed by the dangerous prospects of social chaos that would open up if sergeants and privates were to follow the example set by captains and lieutenants in disregarding the orders of their superiors and killing any Cabinet Ministers of whom they disapproved.

So one important effect of the revolt was to drive a wedge between the old-fashioned conservative and the modern semi-Fascist groupings among Japan's lions and to strengthen the former at the expense of the latter. The ground was prepared for a new compromise with the foxes, who had been badly shaken and scared by the grim doings of the wintry morning of February 26. The essence of this unspoken and unwritten compromise was that the army leaders consented to purge their own ranks of extremists, while the civilian politicians and financiers agreed to find considerably larger sums for armament purposes and to give some satisfaction to the army's demand for an increasingly militarized economy.

The soldiers who took part in the uprising were pardoned on the ground that they had merely fulfilled their duty of obedience to their officers and were dispatched to Manchoukuo. The officers and a number of civilian nationalist extremists who were accused of complicity were tried by a court-martial which held its sessions in strict secrecy. Seventeen leading participants in the mutiny, thirteen officers and four civilians, were condemned to death; for some unexplained reason two of these sentences were apparently not carried into execution. Fifty-nine others received terms of imprisonment, of which six were for life and five for fifteen years.

At the same time there was a sweeping shake-up in the higher personnel of all military, naval, and civilian institutions. This was partly in response to the Japanese idea that any catastrophic untoward event demands the resignation of all those public officials who can be regarded as even remotely and indirectly responsible. At the same time the convenient opportunity was taken to demote and to remove from the capital those officers whose attitude was considered unreliable.

After February 26 there was a lull in the activities of the young officers. This is attributable partly to the firmer stand of the senior officers against breaches of discipline, partly to the effect of the severe punishment meted out to the participants in the revolt. It is not so much fear of death, against which the Japanese officer is steeled by centuries of ancestral fighting tradition, as the denial of any chance for public martyrdom, for delivering inflammatory speeches before a nation-wide audience, that tends to restrain new potential Aizawas and Nonakas. It would, of course, be dangerous to predict whether this restraint will prove permanently effective or whether military radicalism may not spring up with new vitality in the event of an unusually severe political or economic crisis.

The struggle between the lions and the foxes continued, but along more moderate lines. A new cabinet was formed by Koki Hirota, the former Foreign Minister. Hirota had succeeded to a remarkable degree in being all things to all men. Friends of peace in Japan prized his public assurance, as Foreign Minister, that there would be no war during his tenure of office. Foreign diplomats found him pleasant and conciliatory to deal with, in contrast to his predecessor, the stiff and unbending Count Uchida.

At the same time, unlike some of Japan's moderate diplomats, such as Baron Shidehara, who was Foreign Minister at the time of the Manchurian incident, Hirota has never been on the murder list of the extreme nationalists. An old friendship, never broken off, with the venerable Mitsuru Toyama, outstanding figure among Japan's superpatriots, has stood him in good stead.

Even such an adroit compromiser as Hirota, however, failed to keep his balance between the opposing demands of the lions and the foxes. From the first months of his Premiership differences of opinion began to crop up in his cabinet about the amount of money which could be allotted to the army and navy without endangering financial stability, about measures of industrial control and educational reform. The fiasco of Japan's "strong" policy in China, the conclusion of the mysterious and unpopular anti-Communism pact with Germany, and the sharp increase in the cost of living which set in toward the end of 1936 all weakened the cabinet's prestige.

The Diet met in January 1937, in a rebellious and critical mood. Sharp criticism of the army voiced by the veteran Seiyukai member, Kunimatsu Hamada, provoked an angry reaction and a demand for the dissolution of the Diet from the War Minister, General Count Hisaichi Terauchi. Hirota decided that the best way out of the situation was to proffer the resignation of the entire cabinet.

His successor, General Senjuro Hayashi, was a man of quite different stamp, a soldier, not a diplomat. It was said that after General Hayashi had received the foreign diplomatic corps he observed that this was more of an ordeal than reviewing an army. I had a long talk with General Hayashi before his accession to power and carried away the impression that the salient traits of his personality were 100 per cent loyalty to the traditional Japanese conception of a patriarchal Emperor, desire for a return to the simpler old Japanese ways of life, devotion to the interests of his service, combined with caution in speech and judgment and preference for gradual as against extreme methods in political life. Recognizing that German National Socialism, Italian Fascism, and Russian Communism had all influenced Japanese thought, General Hayashi expressed strong belief in the necessity of bringing Japan back to its old national spirit and ethics.

"If our capitalists are egotistical and inclined to oppress the rest of the population, such a situation, as opposed to the Japanese spirit, must be eliminated," he declared. "On the other hand, if a government of workers and peasants should oppress the bourgeoisie and other parts of the population, this would also be alien to the Japanese spirit. So Japan must follow Kodo, the Imperial Way, its old code of ethics."

Falling into the allegorical poetic strain which is not uncommon with Japanese soldiers, the general continued: —

"There is a place for every plant and animal. Flowers bloom and birds sing without interfering with each other. This is how people must live in the Japanese state. The whole Japanese people must understand the spirit of our sacred Imperial Regalia, the Sword, the Mirror, and the Treasure, and carry it out in life."

Despite his refusal to admit representatives of the political parties into his cabinet, General Hayashi, whose impressive walrus moustaches were the delight of every cartoonist in Tokyo, made a fairly good impression in Japanese liberal circles during the first months of his administration. He was mild and pacific in his replies to interpellations in the Diet and he appointed as Foreign Minister a conciliatory Westernized diplomat in the person of Mr. Naotake Sato, former Japanese Ambassador to France.

But Hayashi lost his credit with upholders of the parliamentary system when he abruptly dissolved the Diet, for no very convincing reason, on the last day of its session and precipitated a new election. What prompted him to take this step is doubtful; the ostensible reason was that the Diet had not acted quickly enough on certain bills. There was much resentment in military circles over some of the critical speeches which Yukio Ozaki and other independent deputies had made and the dissolution was regarded as a means of teaching the legislators a lesson.

The election, which was held on April 30, did not better Hayashi's position. No large party took the field in support of the cabinet; of the 466 seats in the Diet 381 were held by the two major parties and by the Social Mass Party, all of which had been outspoken in their opposition to the cabinet.

For several weeks after the election the doughty general fought a rear-guard action, intimating that he would face the new Diet and dissolve it again if it proved recalcitrant. But Hayashi, an essentially old-fashioned Japanese officer, was not the man to carry out a *coup d'état*. It was delicately intimated to him that he had lost the confidence not only of the political parties but of the group of senior states-

PRINCE FUMIMARO KONOYE

men close to the throne; and the deadlock which had arisen between the Hayashi Cabinet and the Diet was suddenly broken by the resignation of the former.

A new chapter in Japanese political history was opened by the appointment as Premier of Prince Fumimaro Konoye, President of the House of Peers. Konoye had long been regarded as a man with a brilliant political future and had declined appointment as Premier immediately after the February 26 affair. In forming a cabinet he enjoyed the advantage of not being committed definitely either to the lions or to the foxes; and his list of ministers bore the stamp of a national coalition, with all articulate forces in the country — the fighting services, big business, the permanent bureaucracy, and the political parties — receiving representation.

Descendant of a very old aristocratic family, Prince Konoye enjoys the reputation of being progressive and modernminded. He has already given some exemplifications of these qualities by outlining a scheme for reforming the House of Peers which would place more emphasis on service to the state than on birth or wealth, and by couching his first official statements in plain understandable language, avoiding the cumbersome classical phraseology, obscure and vague to the last degree, which former Premiers have been inclined to use.

At the outset it seemed probable that Konoye's main problem would be the familiar one of mediating between militarism and the business interests. Friction developed between his Home Minister, Eiichi Baba (who subsequently died), and the Ministers of Commerce and Industry, who represented the viewpoint of the businessmen and financiers. But within a few weeks everything was overshadowed by the outbreak of the war in China. There is reason to believe that Konoye regretted the development of hostilities and realized that in the beginning he had been misled by the army as to the danger which threatened the Japanese forces in North China. But he was powerless to arrest the march of events and almost automatically issued statements reflecting the ever-broadening scope of the conflict until his resignation as Premier early in 1939.

X

THE SEMI–FASCIST STATE

JAPAN is the sole large state which to-day defies ready classi-
fication as either a democracy or a dictatorship. The Island
Empire is obviously not a constitutional monarchy of the
type of Great Britain or Sweden or Belgium. The conception of the Emperor as the descendant of the Sun Goddess
Amaterasu and as himself partaking of the element of divinity is alone enough to mark off a sharp line of demarcation
from systems where the king is regarded as a being of purely
human clay.

Moreover, the liberties of speech, press, and assembly
which characterize genuinely democratic states are sharply
limited in Japan. Arrests on the suspicion of holding or
uttering "dangerous thoughts" are not uncommon. The
newspapers, besides practising a good deal of self-censor-
ship on delicate topics, are harassed by frequent police bans,
or prohibitions to report or discuss some event or subject.
There is just enough freedom of speech for some unusually
bold orator or publicist to say or write occasionally that there
is none. The police exercise strict supervision over public
meetings and demonstrations. When a political meeting is
authorized, a large number of officers of the law are always
present; and they do not hesitate to interrupt or silence altogether a speaker whose remarks they consider subversive.

When May Day labor demonstrations were permitted (they have been forbidden altogether during the last two years) there were almost as many policemen as demonstrators present.

Elections in Japan, while free in the sense that no overwhelming compulsion is brought on the voter to cast his ballot in a particular way, are almost meaningless. For the Diet, although free to denounce and criticize, is quite powerless to influence decisively the course of events. A phrase which is much in vogue is, "The constitutional politics peculiar to Japan."

And there can be no question that Japanese constitutional practices are peculiar. In 1936 a cabinet which had received endorsement by a popular election was almost immediately overthrown by a military insurrection — the famous February 26 incident.[1] In 1937, as has been noted, one prospective Premier who was approved by both the major political parties, General Ugaki, could not assume office, because the army vetoed his appointment. As a Japanese professor remarked to me: —

"In Japan it is not so important whether a Premier has the approval of the political parties. What really matters is whether he is endorsed by the Army."

So Japan by practically every test fails to qualify as a democracy. At the same time it deviates conspicuously from the modern pattern of dictatorship. This pattern,

[1] The fact that the outbreak occurred so soon after the election, which had strengthened the parliamentary position of the moderate Okada Cabinet, naturally inspired a belief abroad that there was some connection between the two events. This, however, does not seem to have been the case. The uprising was planned some time before the election and would doubtless have taken place regardless of how the voting turned out.

which may be seen, with minor variations, in Germany, Italy, and the Soviet Union, calls for a single, supposedly infallible leader, for a closely disciplined single party which possesses a monopoly of political power, for ruthless and absolute repression of even the mildest dissenting criticism, and for energetic propaganda for the ideas of the ruling group through press, schools, theatre, radio, and every other conceivable instrument of publicity.

No such régime exists in Japan. The army collectively wields great power. But there is no individual general, much less any civilian politician, who can be identified as a dictator. General Sadao Araki, War Minister from 1932 until 1934, for a time created a strong impression at home and abroad by his flamboyant pronouncements, characterized by a mixture of Japanese nationalist expansionism, Pan-Asianism, and social radicalism. But Araki disappeared from the War Ministry and is now almost forgotten.

One also looks in vain in Japan for that characteristic of Communism and Fascism, the omnipotent single party. Extreme nationalist groups whose views closely approximate those of the army are small in numbers and poll light votes in elections. One also misses the element of mass enthusiasm among the youth that is characteristic of the European Communist and Fascist régimes. There are periodic rumors of the emergence of a new party in the Diet with a programme which will satisfy the army. But if such a party ever is formed it will be of an artificial bureaucratic character; it will not be the result of any upsurge of mass sentiment.

There is also a substantial difference in the status of the press in Japan and in the European dictatorships. The

Soviet, German, and Italian newspapers of the present time are intensely propagandist in character. Strictly controlled by the ruling party, they are perpetually fighting for its ideas, trying to make their readers into good Communists, National Socialists, or Fascisti, as the case may be.

The Japanese press is also subject to control. But it is control of a negative, not of a positive, character. The Japanese editor is regulated on a basis of "Thou shalt not," not of "Thou shalt." As a result the government of the day is not infrequently criticized with a vigor that would be unthinkable in a European dictatorship. There is not even one newspaper in Japan that can be regarded as a consistent, unvarying supporter of the cabinet that may be in power. "The surest way for a newspaper in Japan to win subscribers is to attack the government," a prominent Japanese official once remarked to me.

A foreign diplomat on whom I called soon after my arrival in Japan observed that there was not a single newspaper which could be regarded as an authentic governmental organ. This is eminently true. Not only is no newspaper an official organ, but the whole Japanese press is distinguished by a happy irresponsibility in reporting and commenting on news. It is no easy task to pick one's way through the maze of inspired and semi-inspired items and the purely fictitious guesswork which one finds in even the more serious Japanese newspapers.

The Japanese press on the whole is inclined toward liberalism rather than toward ultra-nationalism; this tendency would be even more evident if it were not for the exigencies of police repression. It cannot for a moment be compared with the newspapers of the leading European dictatorships, which are mere gramophones, playing over and over the limited stock of records which are authorized by higher authority.

In one field, in that of personal scandal, the Japanese press, thanks to the absence of effective libel laws, is even freer than that of democratic lands. Coming to Tokyo from Moscow, where the only conceivable personal references to high officials are most complimentary ones, it was both amusing and surprising to find the lusty drinking bouts of the Premier of that time and the various foibles and idiosyncrasies of other ministers commented on habitually with the utmost license.

So Japan fails to conform to the regular specifications of dictatorship, just as it fails to meet the tests of democracy. A contributor to an American publication who characterized Japan as a dictatorship was challenged by a foreign resident of Japan to name the dictator. The truth of the matter is that while many features of Japanese administration are arbitrary and dictatorial there is no individual who could be accurately described as a dictator. More than that, there is not even any group that invariably realizes its will. The problem of where power actually resides in Japan is more baffling than in almost any other state, not only because there is the constant struggle, described in the preceding chapter, between the power of the sword and the power of gold, between the lions and the foxes, but also because of the Japanese instinct to avoid responsibility, to resort to collective rather than to individual action wherever possible.

There is a Japanese proverb, which would certainly not commend itself to Stalin, Mussolini, or Hitler, that anyone is a fool if he has power and shows it. For centuries in Japan divine honors were paid to an impoverished Emperor in Kyoto, while all real temporal power remained in the hands of the Shogun in Tokyo. A still more complicated system existed for a time in the thirteenth century, when an actual and a titular Emperor for a time coexisted with an actual and a titular Shogun.[2]   So in modern Japan it not infrequently happens that the army's candidate for the post of War Minister is by no means the strongest and most popular general, but is rather a man who is relied on to transmit to the cabinet the collective opinion of his colleagues.

It might seem that the divinity of the Emperor, a dogma that is impressed on every Japanese from his earliest school-days and that may never be publicly challenged in Japan,[3] would provide a ready explanation of the source of ultimate power in the empire.   Certainly the reverence which is accorded to the Emperor is of the most absolute and unreserved character.   Professor Chikao Fujisawa, a prominent figure in a movement to return to the *Kodo*, or Imperial Way, the traditional code of Japanese ethics, expounds the orthodox theory of Japanese monarchism in the following terms: —

"The moral basis of this country consists in the absolute unity between the Tenno (Son of Heaven, the customary

[2] Sir George Sansom, in *Japan: A Short Cultural History*, sums up this extremely complex situation in the following sentence (cf. p. 291): "We have thus, in Japan of the thirteenth century, the astonishing spectacle of a state at the head of which stands a titular emperor whose vestigial functions are usurped by an abdicated emperor and whose real power is nominally delegated to an hereditary military dictator but actually wielded by an hereditary adviser of that dictator."

[3] A noted scholar, Dr. Tetsujiro Inouye, was compelled to recant and apologize when he expressed doubt as to the reality of the sacred jewels, supposedly given by the Sun Goddess to Japan.   A history of the Nara period of the Japanese Empire was suppressed because of comments on the private life of the Empress Koken. (Cf. Harry Emerson Wildes, *Japan in Crisis*, p. 34.)   Any use of the sixteen-petaled chrysanthemum crest of the Imperial Family is a serious offense for a Japanese and is certain to cause the suppression of any book or magazine on which it may appear.

title of the Japanese Emperor) and his subjects. Far from being any organ of state, our Tenno governs the state as the supreme ruler in an unbroken line from ages eternal. . . . The sovereignty does not reside in the state, but in the august person of our Tenno, who is believed to be an actual living Deity. Dr. Minobe hurts our national feeling by thinking that our divine sovereign is a mere natural man acting as an organ of the state." [4]

A retired naval officer, writing in the magazine *Contemporary Japan*, characterizes the Emperor as "the personal incarnation of Divinity and therefore free from all evils and defects, representing all that is good and perfect."

The Japanese conception of the Emperor is deeply rooted in the mythology of Shinto, the original animistic religion of Japan, and in the family system which many conservative Japanese regard as second only to the throne itself as a stabilizing moral and social factor. The Imperial Family is believed to be directly descended from Amaterasu Omikami, the Sun Goddess, who is supposed to have given the following commandment to her grandson, Ninigi-no-Mikoto: —

"The Luxuriant Land of Reed Plains [Japan] is a land over which our descendants shall rule. Do thou, Imperial Grandson, go and rule over it; and the Imperial succession shall continue unbroken and prosperous, coeternal with Heaven and Earth." [5]

All other Japanese are supposed to be descendants of lesser gods in the capacious Shinto pantheon. So a paternalistic relation is established between the Emperor and the

[4] Cf. the magazine *Cultural Nippon* for June 1935.

[5] Japan's first human Emperor, Jimmu, is supposed to be fifth in line of descent from the Sun Goddess.

people; the ruler is conceived as the father, the head of the large family represented by the Japanese people. This cult of the Emperor who is at once a divinity and a benevolent father of his children-subjects is the backbone of the traditional conception of the Japanese state. It is deeper and more intense than the ideas of patriotism which are taught in every country, because it has a strong admixture of the supernatural and religious element.

The most impressive ceremony in every Japanese elementary school is the prescribed reading of the Imperial Rescript on Education which was promulgated by the Emperor Meiji. The whole student body stands at attention in the assembly hall, heels together, eyes cast down at the floor. A polished white wooden box is handed to the principal, who, with every token of deep respect, takes from it a document wrapped in the purest silk, unrolls it, and solemnly reads the famous Rescript, one sentence of which may be regarded as the Japanese equivalent of the Ten Commandments: —

Ye, our subjects, be filial to your parents, affectionate to your brothers and sisters, be harmonious as husbands and wives and true as friends; bear yourselves in modesty and moderation; extend your benevolence to all; pursue learning and cultivate the arts and thereby develop intellectual faculties and perfect moral powers; furthermore advance public good and promote common interests, always respect the Constitution and obey the law. Should emergency arise, offer yourselves courageous to the state, and thus guard and maintain the prosperity of our Imperial Throne, coeval with Heaven and earth.

The schoolboy who has listened to the reading of the Rescript may some day, if he has advanced far enough in the state service, attend one of the two annual large garden parties at which the Emperor personally appears. One of these is held in the spring, at the time when the soft, evanescent beauty of the pink and white cherry blossoms is at its best; the other in the fall, when the chrysanthemums are in bloom. Here, better than anywhere else, one has a close-up view of the men who rule Japan: generals and admirals whose breasts are covered with medals, Cabinet Ministers and diplomats in the stiff costume of frock coat and high silk hat which is prescribed for such ceremonies. Their wives on this day take out their most cherished heirloom kimonos, sober in hue but of finest texture.

The climax of the reception occurs when the Emperor, followed by the Princes of the Blood and high officials of the Imperial Household, and later by the Empress with her ladies in waiting, walks between the two lines of guests, who stand with bowed heads, for one is not supposed to let one's eyes rest on the Son of Heaven, while the military band plays the strains of Japan's rather mournful but impressive national hymn, "Kimigayo."

The cult of Emperor worship is strengthened by frequent pilgrimages to offer worship at Shinto shrines. The most sacred of these is the Grand Shrine of Ise, devoted to the spirits of the Imperial Ancestors. It is an obligation for every newly appointed Cabinet Minister to proceed to Ise and report his assumption of office before the shrine. Large excursions of school children and of high-school and university students are often taken to the shrines at Ise and elsewhere. With a view to avoiding any charge of religious persecution, the authorities draw a line of distinction between Shintoism as a belief and the performance of obeisance before historic shrines, which is regarded as an act of respect to the state and is obligatory for everyone, regardless of his religious convictions. Comparatively little difficulty has arisen in this connection in Japan, but in Korea missionaries have been dismissed from their posts as principals of schools because of unwillingness to bow before the Shinto shrines. The difference of psychology in the two countries tends to make the missionary in Korea more reluctant to perform the ceremony. What seems a natural act of patriotism to the Japanese Christian often impresses the Korean as a hateful recognition of the alien creed of a foreign ruler.

The cult of the divine Emperor is supported by all the watchfulness of a far-flung police system. Preparations for an imperial visit are carried out with the most meticulous care. I happened to visit the northernmost of Japan's large islands, Hokkaido, in August 1936, a few weeks before the Emperor was supposed to make a tour there at the time of the annual manœuvres. The local authorities and police were in a frenzy of activity. New roads were being laid, stations and public buildings painted and whitewashed, suspicious characters placed under preventive arrest. An unsightly slum quarter on the bank of the river in Sapporo, the capital, was being moved bodily some distance away.

A policeman is always on duty at the entrance to the Grand Shrine of Ise to see that no proper formality is omitted by the visitor. Nothing is more certain to bring about the prohibition of a foreign book or magazine than the publication of any material which is construed as disrespectful to the Emperor. There was a serious diplomatic flurry over a cartoon which appeared in the magazine *Vanity Fair* in the summer of 1935 showing the Emperor, heavily armed, as a candidate for the Nobel Peace Prize.

There is a pretty well authenticated story that when Vice President Garner visited Japan with a Congressional delegation, en route to the Philippines, in the latter part of 1935, he cherished the idea of introducing an unusual note into the imperial reception which was accorded to him. The genial Vice President had in his pocket a one-dollar Ingersoll watch, which he proposed to draw out with the remark that here was one object on which Japan could not undersell America. It was diplomatically fortunate, although perhaps journalistically regrettable, that Mr. Garner was induced to give up the idea.[6] The remark, which would probably have evoked a laughing retort if it had been made to a King of Belgium or Norway, would have produced consternation at the rigidly formal Japanese Court.

Nationalism, with its double assumption of the paternalistic Emperor, the very incarnation of the Japanese race, for whom it is a privilege to die, and of the divine origin of the Japanese themselves, is Japan's true religion. It has contributed more than any other factor to the making of the empire.

Soon after my arrival in Japan I visited the museum attached to the Yasukuni Shrine, which is sacred to the memory of men who have died in Japan's wars. Among specimens of mediæval Japanese swords, early cannon, trophies of the Russo-Japanese War, I paused for a time before the pictures of General Nogi and his wife. The faces were classical in their strength and in the beauty of a devoted idealism that recalled men and women who gave their lives under the inspiration of a very different philosophy — the pioneer Russian revolutionaries of the "People's Will" group in the last century.

Nogi, more perhaps than any other personality, embodied

<hr>

[6] Mr. Garner did pull out the watch and make the accompanying comment at a reception in China where no taboos were involved.

the chivalrous heroic ideal in modern Japanese life. He
was in command at the siege of Port Arthur, where both his
own sons perished along with tens of thousands of other
soldiers in the struggle to wrest this stronghold from Russia.
Hailed as a national hero after the capture of the town, the
general brooded over possible strategic mistakes he had
made. He desired to take his own life as an atonement for
those of the soldiers under his command. It was only at the
command of the Emperor Meiji, it is said, that he postponed
this resolution. But when his Emperor died the old general
committed hara-kiri in the customary samurai fashion; and,
as her husband had followed his Emperor, the wife followed
her husband. There was a classical Japanese drama in
modern life. The Nogi Shrine in Tokyo is one of the most
popular places of worship and pilgrimage in Japan.

Paradoxical as it may sound, it is just because the Emperor
is regarded as endowed with divine qualities [7] that he does not
govern in the direct personal fashion of a Louis XIV, a
Frederick the Great, or a Peter the Great. Routine temporal
affairs are not the primary sphere of activity for the Son of
Heaven, the spiritual head of the Japanese people. There
has always been a strong feeling among the wise elder statesmen who have unobtrusively guided Japan's destiny since
the Restoration that the name of the Emperor should not be
invoked in controversial matters.

At the time when the formation of a cabinet under General
Ugaki was blocked by the opposition of the army, some of
the more daring Japanese newspapers put forward the argument that the army, despite its alleged absolute devotion to

[7] A very well-informed veteran Japanese statesman once suggested to
a foreign visitor that the attitude of the Japanese people toward the
Emperor was comparable with that of Roman Catholics toward the Pope.

the throne, was actually disobeying the imperial will by refusing to coöperate with the man whom the Emperor had designated as Premier.   I asked a Japanese friend of long political experience what would happen if the Emperor should directly command some general to assume the post of War Minister in General Ugaki's cabinet.   My friend was a liberal who disapproved of the army's attitude, but his reaction to this question was prompt and negative.   "It is a cardinal principle of Japanese statecraft that the Emperor must not be drawn into any political dispute," he declared.

It is noteworthy that even at a time of greatest crisis, after the outbreak of February 26, the imperial command to the rebels to lay down their arms was only issued after some delay and after other efforts to reach a peaceable settlement had failed.   It was considered unusual when Emperor Hirohito, in his message at the opening of the Diet after the revolt, expressed regret at what had occurred.

So the source of power in Japan is not to be found in direct rule by the Emperor.   Neither is it to be sought in any all-powerful adviser.   The most eminent of these advisers is the eighty-eight-year-old Prince Kimmochi Saionji, who is always called on for counsel when a cabinet falls.   On such occasions his quiet villa on a sunny hillside at Okitsu, about a hundred miles southwest of Tokyo, is thronged with distinguished visitors from all walks of Japanese life.   The Prince, a striking personality, unusually tall for a Japanese, with large clear eyes, is quiet in manner, suave in speech. He listens to everyone and keeps his own counsel.   His final advice, based on a careful weighing of all the factors involved in the situation, is given to a high court official, who communicates it to the Emperor.

But Prince Saionji is in no sense a dictator.   He is rather a persuader, a compromiser who, during recent years, has undoubtedly seen many developments in foreign and domestic policy of which he disapproved. And he is not the only counselor who is close to the throne. The Emperor in certain matters is traditionally guided by the advice of the Privy Council. Ratification of treaties is submitted to this body and all acts of legislation proposed by the government are submitted to it before they are laid before the Diet. The present head of the Privy Council, Baron Kiichiro Hiranuma, is a thoroughgoing conservative, not to say reactionary, who is close to the army and whose influence undoubtedly runs at cross-purposes in some cases with that of Prince Saionji. On the other hand, two other officials whose functions bring them close to the Emperor, the Lord Privy Seal, Count Yuasa, and the Minister of the Imperial Household, Mr. Tsueno Matsudaira, father-in-law of the active and popular Prince Chichibu, brother of the Emperor, possess the reputation of being moderates and liberals.

In the last analysis, power in Japan is so diffused that a search for a dictator, for a man whose will can unmistakably determine the course of policy, is bound to end in the conclusion that there is no such person. The Japanese state, for want of a better term, may be characterized as semi-Fascist. Measured by any of the touchstones that distinguish dictatorships from democracies, it is more authoritarian than the United States, Great Britain, or France, less so than the Soviet Union, Germany, and Italy.

One such test, minor from the Japanese standpoint but not unimportant from that of residents of other countries, who desire to know how much the foreign news which they read in their newspapers is adulterated by censorship and other repressive measures, is the administrative attitude toward foreign journalists and writers. Japan's record in this field has changed for the worse during the last few years (a symptom of growing international tension and of the internal trend toward dictatorship), but is still notably better than that of the European dictatorships.

Japan does not, like the Soviet Union, hermetically isolate large numbers of its citizens against contact with foreigners by fear of arrest and administrative exile.[8] The censorship of outgoing cables, a permanent institution in the Soviet Union, is more rarely and sporadically applied in Japan.[9] In conspicuous contrast to all three major European dictatorships, Japan has never, so far as I have been able to ascertain, expelled the accredited representative of a foreign daily newspaper.

On the other hand, a well-known British journalist, Mr. A. Morgan Young, for many years editor of the *Japan Chronicle,* after retiring from this post was refused permission to return to Japan as correspondent for the *Manchester Guardian.* This was a clear case of penalizing a journalist for the expression of critical views. An English free-lance writer, Mr. Gerald Samson, was arrested and held in prison for about two weeks after the February 26 outbreak. The charges against him were never made public and he was finally expelled from the country. A traveling correspondent for the *Baltimore Sun,* Mr. Wilbur Burton, an

[8] One exception to this rule is contact with the Soviet Embassy, which is just about as dangerous for Japanese as frequenting of the Japanese Embassy in Moscow is for Russians. In general, however, the fear of associating with foreigners, so widespread in the Soviet Union, is not characteristic of Japan.

[9] During an experience of over two years of journalistic work in Japan I have noticed two instances of censorship: one at the time of the February 26 revolt, the other on the eve of the Japanese-German anti-Communism pact.

American, was refused admission to Japan after receiving a visa from the Japanese Consulate in Shanghai, apparently because the police, on the basis of some information in their voluminous dossiers, considered him a "dangerous thinker."

Police surveillance over the comings and goings and general activities of foreigners in Japan is close, but is not apt to be noticeable in Tokyo and other large cities and tourist centres. On the other hand, if one gets off the beaten track, the number of policemen who come up, present their cards, and launch out on a long list of relevant and irrelevant questions is amusing or irritating, according to one's temperament and state of mind at the moment of the inquisition. I made a trip in the northern provinces of Japan's Main Island and in Hokkaido on which the police record, at least in regard to my arrival and departure, is far more minute than my own.

Japanese police officials have a positive mania for suspecting dark designs of espionage in any innocent tourist who happens to carry a camera. The foreigner who wishes to avoid difficulties is well advised to be very sure, before taking a snapshot of a colorful kimono or a picturesque shrine, that he is not within the confines of one of the Island Empire's fortified zones, where photography of all kinds is strictly forbidden. One of the less pleasing sides of the irresponsibility of the Japanese press is the readiness with which accusations or insinuations of espionage are brought against a foreigner without the slightest attempt at serious proof. When I was in Formosa [10] I noted down the following

[10] Japanese police and military officials are generally more nervous and suspicious in colonial and semi-colonial countries, such as Formosa, Korea, and Manchoukuo, than in Japan proper. A friend who had visited a town in Korea told of an amusing and characteristic incident. A representative of the local police force called on him with a list of the

items from a file of translations from the local Japanese
press: —

A certain honorary consul in Taihoku was suspected for asking
questions of a professor in the Taihoku Imperial University regarding meteorology and air currents — subjects which are not connected with the questioner's own profession.

It is stated that it is not mistaken to regard foreigners as spies.

There was a certain foreigner who was shadowed because he
was friendly with a café dancer who could speak a little English.

In Japan, as in the European dictatorships, thought is the
most strictly regulated article of import.   Every visitor to
Japan must submit a list of the books in his possession for the
inspection of the police.   The tendency to exclude books
which are distasteful to the authorities and to place bans on
individual copies of magazines seemed to increase after the
revolt of February 26.[11]

Yet when everything is weighed in the balance and full
allowance is made for the insatiable curiosity of the police,
the pathological fears of officialdom about cameras and radios,
the national weakness for ludicrously overestimating both
the desire and the capacity of foreigners for military espionage, the journalist is still less harassed and less subject to

---

places he had visited and the persons with whom he had talked.   "We
should appreciate it," said the policeman, with all proper Japanese expressions of politeness, "if for the sake of our records you would fill
in anything we may have overlooked."   My friend, however, found
nothing to add.   The police supervision of his engagements had been
100 per cent perfect.

[11] An amusing and, I believe, unique feature of the Japanese censorship is that a magazine may be held for weeks or even months and then be
released and duly delivered to the surprised subscriber.   This has happened to me repeatedly with copies of the *China Weekly Review*, a publication which seems especially calculated to arouse the wrath of the Japanese censors.

administrative reprisals in Japan than he is in any of the leading European dictatorships. The real barrier to an adequate understanding and reporting of Japan seems to me to lie not so much in police pinpricks or direct and indirect censorship devices as in the extraordinary difficulty of acquiring an adequate knowledge of the spoken, and still more of the written, language. This barrier (which also exists in China) could only be surmounted if newspapers and news agencies should follow the example of governments and give their Far Eastern correspondents long assignments of language study, free from other work.[12]

What are the prospects that the present semi-Fascist régime will evolve into a full-blooded dictatorship on the German or Italian model? (A Communist dictatorship is not conceivable in Japan except as a result of an utterly disastrous war and a complete breakdown of the existing economic and social order.)

There has been no lack of thinking in Japan along lines which are suggestive of European Fascism. Ikki Kita, a Buddhist scholar who was arrested for alleged complicity in the February 26 revolt, was probably the most influential of Japan's Fascist theorists. He wrote a book which was quite widely known, although its circulation was forbidden, entitled *A Bill for the Reconstruction of Japan*. Here he outlined a scheme for limiting private wealth. No family was to possess more than 1,000,000 yen; private property in land was to be restricted to a value of 100,000 yen; the wealth of a corporation was not to exceed 10,000,000 yen.

---

[12] The staffs of the larger embassies in Tokyo regularly include diplomatic, consular, military, and naval attachés whose sole duty, for a period of from two to four years, is to master the treacherous intricacies of the language.

Acme

TOKYO VOTERS — MAY 1937

All wealth above these limits was to be confiscated and administered by the state for the general welfare. Kita advocated the creation of a number of state economic bodies to manage the nationalized wealth.

Along with this "share the wealth" programme Kita stood for the exalted conception of Japan's national mission which always finds an enthusiastic response in army circles. He envisaged "a great wave of Japanese civilization shaking Europe and America and illuminating the so-called civilized nations with Asiatic ideas," as a result of the fusion of Oriental and Western ideas which Japan was to consummate.

An associate of Kita's who was also arrested was Zei Nishida, a retired lieutenant. A man of lesser intellectual qualifications, Nishida was apparently an agitator of force and persuasiveness and a persistent fisher in troubled waters. In collaboration with Kita and others he created in 1924 the Hakurokai, or Society of the White Wolf, a secret organization which described as its aim: "To redetermine social problems by actual force on the basis of justice and a knightly spirit." Nishida later played an active part in several small secret extremist groups with flamboyant-sounding names, "The Federation of Samurai," "The Society of Starbeams," "The Society of the Celestial Sword."

A more moderate advocate of drastic reform was Nariaki Gondo, a scholar learned in the Chinese classics. A former schoolteacher in Mito, who had been dismissed for his supposedly subversive ideas, once praised Gondo to me very highly, declaring that Gondo alone understood the nature of Japan's agrarian crisis. Gondo summed up his views in a book entitled *A Model of Popular Self-Government*. He believes that ever since the Meiji Restoration agriculture has been exploited for the benefit of industry, with the result that the cities have become top-heavy and the countryside has become woefully impoverished. His remedy is state aid for agriculture, reversal of the taxation system which favors industry at the expense of agriculture, and more effort to settle the superfluous agricultural population in Manchoukuo, Brazil, and other foreign countries.

In considering Japan's possible future development it must be borne in mind that the Japanese may fairly be considered as the world's pioneer collectivists. Individualism has always been at a discount in this nation where clan loyalty and the family system are two of the strongest influences in moulding the national psychology. The masses of the people, very rare outbursts of indiscipline excepted, are docile in their attitude toward authority and are easily regimented. It is taken for granted that the police should have a finger in every pie, from telling the householder when he is to carry out the elaborate spring cleaning which every Japanese house must undergo to watching out for subversive literature.

There is, therefore, no such instinctive passionate opposition to the regimentation implied in Fascism as one would find in a more individualistic land. As additional factors promoting the Fascist trend one may note the strongly entrenched position of the army in public life and the big armament programme to which Japan, along with almost every other country, is committed.

This armament programme is making the state one of the largest purchasers, especially of the products of Japan's rapidly growing metal and chemical industries; and it is an easy step from extensive state purchases to some measure of state control over industry. Moreover, Japan's munitions and shipbuilding boom, while it tends to relieve population pressure, to keep employment at a high level, and to bring prosperity to certain favored industries, is revealing more clearly the country's poverty in most essential minerals and raw materials. An acute iron and steel famine, reflected in abnormally rapid price increases for these products, made itself felt early in 1937. The quantities of coal and copper (the two important minerals with which Japan is best supplied) which would have sufficed for industrial needs a few years ago are no longer adequate and must be supplemented with imports. This situation clearly points to ultimate rationing of raw materials, to the introduction of an import licensing system, to experimentation with the production of synthetic substitutes — in short, to various forms of the state intervention in economic life which is such a characteristic feature of Fascism.

Yet despite these considerations there are strong reasons for doubting whether Japan will witness any duplication of the European Fascist systems. Two prerequisites of a Fascist *coup*, a leader of exceptional popularity and a large organized following for this leader, are conspicuously absent. Moreover, many of the specific conditions which made for the rise of Italian Fascism and German National Socialism do not exist in Japan. There is no psychology of a lost war and a nationally resented peace treaty for a Japanese Hitler to exploit. Nor could a Japanese Mussolini offer any convincing proof of a "Red menace," finding expression in widespread paralysis of economic life through violent strikes.

The Japanese youth has not been caught by the Fascist idea. While the liberalism, verging Leftward into "parlor bolshevism," which was prevalent among Japanese students a few years ago has been decisively curbed, it has not been replaced by any general mass trend toward extreme national-ism.

Curiously enough, it is just the semi-Fascist character-istics of present-day Japan that place obstacles in the way of development of Fascism of the standardized European type. In super-policed Japan a Fascist leader would in all probability be checked before he could build up a huge personal following. The imperial tradition which is so cherished by the military and conservative classes militates against the emergence of an individual who would concen-trate the entire national spotlight on himself.

But while a precise imitation of the European Fascist pat-tern seems out of the question, there is an unmistakable gradual drift toward greater state control of everything, from ideas to import licenses. And the continuation of this trend seems inevitable unless the liberal forces in Japan display greater energy and vitality than they have mani-fested up to the present time, or unless the world situation takes a turn less favorable to military predominance in the shaping of national policies.

XI

THE SPLIT NATIONAL PERSONALITY

PSYCHOLOGICALLY modern Japan is a house divided against itself. Nowhere in the world can one find so many instances of coexistence of the very old and the very new; nowhere do the modern West and the ancient East jostle each other in such close proximity and create so many amazing contrasts and paradoxes. The personality of the Japanese to-day is at once a battleground and a compromise of instincts and influences, some of which originate in dim prehistoric times, while others are the products of the most modern inventions and intellectual trends.

"Tradition" and "innovation" are the two words which occur most readily to the foreign observer of Japanese life. By emphasizing one of these elements to the exclusion of the other it would be easy to convey a picture of Japan as either the most conservative or the most iconoclastic of countries. And indeed it is both. Amazing material progress in many fields since the Restoration of 1868 has gone hand in hand with the retention, unchanged, or in only slightly modified form, of many ancient folkways, beliefs, and habits.

It is a useful exercise, in this connection, to read Basil Hall Chamberlain's *Things Japanese,* one of the best surveys of Japanese life and culture which have ever been written.   Chamberlain's facts and figures about such things as industrial production and foreign trade are strikingly and completely outdated.   (His book was written in 1890.) But a surprisingly large number of the observations about food, dwellings, etiquette, customs, amusements, and arts are fully applicable to Japan of the present day.   A check-up of Chamberlain's observations in terms of Japan almost fifty years later would indicate that the Island Empire has changed more rapidly than the average country in some fields, while remaining more static in others.

The centre of Tokyo affords one of the most vivid object lessons in the contrast between Old and New Japan.   Here one sees the frowning gray walls which surround the Imperial Palace, long the military stronghold from which the Shogun dominated the tamed feudal lords of Japan.   The mediæval atmosphere is enhanced by a moat which runs around the walls; in its waters are reflected the curious outlines of the stunted pine trees which appear over the top of the wall.

The whole scene, one of the most beautiful in Tokyo or, indeed, in all Japan, conveys an impression of rocklike stability, of continuity "unbroken through ages eternal." And this impression is heightened if one stops to reflect that within these walls, sacred in the eyes of Japanese,[1] cere-

---

[1] A foreign-language newspaper in Japan once inadvertently published a photograph of one of the bridges over the moat upside down.   The next day the editor received a call from a formidable-looking person in a frock coat, who announced himself as a representative of Mitsuru Toyama, a well-known extreme nationalist, and demanded immediate satisfaction for the error, with an intimation that dire consequences would be the penalty of refusal.   The editor ordered the emissary out of his office and heard nothing more of the matter.   But a Japanese editor who had accidentally committed such a mistake would probably not have gotten off so easily.

monies of worship and formal court ritual are regularly carried out that were old when Europe was going off to the Crusades.

Yet directly opposite one side of the Palace rise the office buildings of the Marunouchi, Tokyo's main business and financial district, structures such as one might find in any medium-sized American city, modern in architectural design, in steel and concrete framework, in elevators, and in offices outfitted with swivel chairs, desks, typewriters, telephones and dictaphones. Here is concrete evidence of the emergence of a new Japan, a power in industry and trade.

Another striking contrast is between the office and the home life of many Japanese. The former is Western, the latter Oriental; the former up-to-date, the latter old-fashioned. Before I came to Japan a Japanese diplomat in Moscow had spoken to me of the dual lives led by most government employees, professional men and office workers. "It is a strain on us, both spiritually and financially," he said.

In Japan I could see how this dual life works out in practice. The businessman or clerk who is a Westerner in the office, where he sits on a chair, uses modern appliances, carries on much of his correspondence in English and other foreign languages, becomes an Easterner when he goes home. There he removes his shoes before he enters, sits on a cushion on the floor, which is covered with *tatami*, or matting, and eats the typical Japanese meals, with their predominance of rice, fish and other sea food, vegetables and pickles, and bean curd.

To go from the central part of Tokyo, with its hotels, foreign-style restaurants and cafés, large modern department stores and office buildings, into a residential quarter

of the capital, with the fragile-looking little houses built
of wood and bamboo, the sliding paper doors and windows,
is to span a distance between continents and a time period
of centuries.

The home life and social intercourse of the Japanese are
closely regulated by custom and convention. The atmosphere is one of leisure, of almost ceremonious politeness,
even among the poorest classes. A meeting of friends is
accompanied by what seems to the foreigner, accustomed to
a more rapid and nervous pace of life, an endless interchange
of deep, graceful bows. The Japanese are among the few
peoples who have no full-throated curses; their worst term
of abuse is *bakka hana*, which may be literally translated
"fool snake." One can live in Tokyo for years without
ever seeing a street fight or hearing a brawl. Behind all
this measured courtesy lie centuries of rigid discipline. The
first Tokugawa Shogun, Ieyasu, laid down the rule that any
samurai might cut down with impunity a commoner who
was guilty of disrespectful behavior.

In the household also Japanese conduct follows the old-
fashioned Oriental code. The *danna-san*, or head of the
family, is given every outward sign of the respect due to
the absolute master of the house. His wife must rise before he does, help him in dressing, and, with the servants,
if there are any, bow him out at the entrance to the house
as he departs for work and receive him with bows when he
returns.

The mores of the business world are, of course, quite
different. There is no chance for a display of elaborate
Japanese courtesy when one is struggling for a place on an
overcrowded local train or streetcar. And while Americans
usually find the Japanese slow in transacting business, the

day has long passed when the Japanese did not know what competition meant.[2] Manners, clothes, foods, even language, all change when the Japanese leaves the home for the office. The midday meal for the office worker of the higher grades is apt to consist of the Western-style fare which is now offered by many restaurants and lunchrooms all over Tokyo. The preparation of the food is apt to be pretty bad, by Western standards; but its attraction for Japanese is proved by the increasing number of eating places which discard the customary Japanese fare. On the Ginza, Tokyo's Broadway, one can buy efforts at imitation of almost any American dish, from griddle cakes to strawberry shortcake.

The Japanese girl, as well as the Japanese man, undergoes a metamorphosis when she goes out into the world to earn a living. And she is doing this in increasing numbers under the double stress of economic necessity and desire for a more varied and diverting life than she can hope to find in the home. Over 40 per cent of Japanese factory workers are women: girls are widely employed as restaurant and café waitresses, bus and elevator operators, clerks in offices and stores. Girls in employment, like girl students, forsake the graceful but inconvenient kimono, with its long sleeves, and put on some kind of simple uniform.

There is a noteworthy difference between the language used in city and in village and between the educated and uneducated classes. For the Japanese, with their usual facility for imitation and adaptation, have taken over thousands

[2] One of the pioneers of modern education in Japan, Mr. Yukichi Fukuzawa, notes that in the first years after the Restoration there was no word for competition in Japanese, because the very idea had no place in the classical ethical teachings.

of words and phrases from foreign languages, mostly English, and incorporated them into Japanese. These new words are mainly used in universities and high schools, in newspapers and magazines, and in business and engineering circles.

There are several reasons for this wholesale borrowing of foreign expressions. The Japanese language was lacking in equivalents for many contemporary political, economic, and philosophical terms, so that the simplest procedure has been to take over the proper foreign word, often in abbreviated form, and always with a specifically Japanese accent and inflection.

Alien words have been part of the general invasion of Japan by foreign ideas, foods, clothes, and customs. It is noteworthy that with words, as with more material inventions, the Japanese are seldom satisfied with mere imitation. The new words are often clipped to the first syllable and are so changed in pronunciation that few Japanese realize they are foreign. So they do not make the Japanese language appreciably easier to learn.

A good example of a foreign expression moulded to Japanese use is the cry *Awrai*, which is the signal from the girl conductor to the driver to proceed. *Awrai* is derived from "all right." It is not infrequently modified still further into "rice" or "ice." On the eve of the last American election a Japanese newspaper published pictures of the candidates, captioned, respectively, "Mr. Ru" and "Mr. Ra."

"Mr. Ru" could, with a little difficulty, be identified as President Roosevelt. "Mr. Ra," after still more thought, could be recognized as Mr. Landon. For the Japanese perceive no difference between *r* and *l* and frequently confuse the two consonants in writing and speaking foreign languages.[3] A *mobo* in Japan is a modern boy, a *moga* a modern girl. These last terms have distinctly critical connotations when pronounced by old-fashioned Japanese; they imply young persons who enjoy American romantic films, read disturbing books and magazines, dance to jazz music, and even wish to choose their own mates. A department store is a *departo;* an apartment house an *aparto; ero* stands for erotic; a *pamfu* is a pamphlet; *ajito* is agitation; a *dema* is a demagogue, and so on *ad infinitum.*

It is not only in Tokyo that one senses the remarkable blend of old and new which is at once the challenge and the enigma of Japan. From a height which commands a view of the seacoast around Yokohama one can see sleek cruisers and modern passenger liners mingled with the little sampans, or fishing boats, some of which have changed little in construction and appearance since the time when death was the penalty for leaving Japan or for building a boat of more than one hundred tons. From the windows of swift, punctual electric trains, which are operated with a minimum of accidents, one sees the oldest figure in Japan, the peasant, in his straw hat, supplemented by a straw coat in rainy weather, up to his knees in the watery muck of the paddy fields, sowing rice as his forefathers have done for generations.

The Japanese who own motor cars are sure to pass on their

---

[3] This inability to distinguish *r* from *l* leads to many amusing slips in the writing of English-language signs. Near my house, for instance, are a "restlant" (restaurant) and a "raundry"; and I once saw a postcard caption: "Gland (*sic*) view of the coast." An enterprising shop offered "Bicycles to rend." In general, foreign signs in Japan are a constant source of merriment; two of the best slips I have noticed personally were those of a barber who announced himself an expert in "headcutting" and of a tailor who put out the notice: "Foreign ladies has fits upstairs."

outings many little village shrines where little offerings of rice and other food are laid out to console the spirits of the departed, according to a custom that surely dates back for many centuries. Large modern trucks lumber past the many wayside images of the innumerable gods of the Shinto and Buddhist pantheons, gods who have their simple tokens of respect from peasants who, too poor to make any more expensive offering, have piled up little heaps of pebbles around their images.

No country, it seems safe to say, has advanced so far into the twentieth century while retaining so much that belongs to the fifteenth, or to the tenth, or to even earlier periods of human history. One of Japan's innumerable old festivals is the *Setsubun*, which is held in February. Then the people take parched beans, one for every year of their lives, and scatter them in the open rooms of their houses, crying, "Welcome, good luck. Out with you, devils." Groups of men in lions' masks go about the towns to perform this ceremony, accompanying it with sacred dances. And this ancient method of casting out devils, which originated in China in some forgotten epoch, is not only observed in modern Japan, but is communicated to the whole country with the aid of that ultramodern invention, the radio.

The Japanese Cabinet Minister, riding in a highly modern motor car, clothed in frock coat and silk hat, proceeds to the Grand Shrine of Ise and goes through a time-honored rite: the reporting to the Spirits of the Imperial Ancestors of his assumption of office. The Japanese Army is equally proud of its modern weapons and of its mediæval ideology. The Japanese military or naval officer does not yield to his colleagues in any country in the world in the keen interest

with which he studies every new invention, every development of such weapons as the airplane, the tank, the machine
gun, the torpedo. But what he really relies on for victory
is something intangible, the *Nippon Seishin,* or Japanese
spirit.

And this military spirit is the product of conceptions of
honor and chivalry which were formed in the Japanese
Middle Ages and which are surpassed by no code in the
world in the sacrifices which they demand from the warrior. It is an absolute point of honor, for instance, that no
Japanese officer shall ever be captured alive. During the
fighting at Shanghai in 1932 a Japanese officer, Major
Koga, was so badly wounded in both legs that he was ren-
dered completely helpless. In this state he was captured.
As soon as he was released he shot himself, leaving behind
a note of apology that his disability prevented him from committing hara-kiri in the classical fashion, squatting on his
legs and cutting open his stomach. His name became a
cherished memory to the Japanese Army, like that of the
three "human bombs" who rushed forward to certain death
with explosives tied around their bodies in order to blast
away some barbed-wire entanglements during the same
Shanghai fighting.

It is on this spiritual element of morale, embodied in such
stories of heroic self-sacrifice, of which Japanese military
history is full, that Japan's military leaders rely, rightly
or wrongly, to compensate for any material deficiencies of
armament.

Japanese businessmen are among the shrewdest and most
successful in the world. Many of them have traveled widely
abroad; they read foreign newspapers and technical journals
and plan their transactions in accordance with the best

available expert information.   Yet many of them are, to a Western mind, amazing in their trust in luck, in omens, in divination and astrology.   There is no unemployment among soothsayers in Japan.

Japan's leading soothsayer, "Professor" Donsho Kodama, every year attracts a distinguished audience, including generals and admirals, officials and businessmen, to listen to his New Year prophecies at the exclusive Peers' Club.   On the occasion of his last venture in prediction, Kodama, who employs old Chinese methods of divination, compared Sino-Japanese relations to a fire burning above a pan of water, with Japan representing the fire and China the water. With this arrangement the water would never boil no matter how hot the fire might become.   If Japan should tone down its policy and get under the water, according to the soothsayer, the water would boil and the delicacies in it would become tender.

Germany, according to Soothsayer Kodama, was facing the sunrise after passing through a dark night, while Italy could be likened to "a big man, cruising in a powerful ship, undisturbed by any thought of danger ahead."   England appeared to the seer as a man hiding on a mountain, which he interpreted as a sign that there would be no strong man for another five years, during which period Great Britain would be like an "ebbing tide."   France was revealed as a traveler suffering from cold on a snowbound mountain.   Its only course was to remain quiet for some time; and "Professor" Kodama extracted from this vision the belief that the Franco-Soviet pact would fail.

Just as the Supreme Court in America has sometimes shown itself not indifferent to election returns, so Soothsayer Kodama's prophecies seemed to tally rather closely with Japanese political preferences. But what was more interesting than these experiments in divination was the respectful attention which they aroused in an educated audience. In their attitude toward divination, the influence of the stars on human affairs, the significance of omens, even the most modern-minded, Westernized Japanese sometimes give the impression of living in the Middle Ages.

Closely allied with this belief in unseen forces which are shaping human affairs is the very pervasive rôle of symbolism in Japanese life. And here one is confronted with a new element of contrast and paradox. For Japan's contributions to Oriental civilization have been practical, rather than theoretical. The Japanese mind seems positively averse to metaphysics. Philosophic thought in Japan is both derivative and confused. The great Oriental systems of philosophy are associated with China and India. One instinctively thinks of the Japanese as the people who, far more than any other Asiatic race, have acquired the tricks of running railway trains, hotels, factories, and steamship companies more or less as Americans and Western Europeans are accustomed to having them run.

Yet it would be a grave omission to overlook the strong mystical and symbolic streak in the Japanese character. All Japanese life is shot through with it; but one sees it in most concentrated form, I think, at the New Year, which is far and away Japan's greatest national holiday. In other countries 1936 was just another year. In Japan it was the Year of the Rat, as the outgoing 1935 was the Year of the Wild Boar and 1937 is the Year of the Ox. Every year, according to Japanese calendar lore, is associated with one of the animals that mark the twelve signs of the zodiac. All sorts of omens, favorable and unfavorable, are associated with these signs; marriages are frequently concluded or rejected as a result of a soothsayer's recommendation as to the significance of the conjunction of the signs governing the years in which the prospective bride and groom were born.

Every Japanese house, whether it be a stately mansion with a spacious rock garden or a little shack with one or two little plants carefully tended in a tiny bit of soil (love of plants and gardens is one thing that is common to Japanese of all classes), is swept and garnished and decorated for the New Year. Cleanliness, in the Japanese view of life, is very closely associated with godliness, and every house is carefully cleaned, while the streets are swept and watered, on the eve of the holiday. Almost every house displays two sets of highly symbolic decorations, one at the outer gate, the other over the doorway.

Outside the gate one sees dark green little pines and bright green slender bamboos, with blossoms of plum mixed in. The pine stands for life and health, the bamboo for erectness, and the plum blossoms for purity and virtue. A smaller set of decorations hangs over the doorway. It consists of yellow rice straw, festooned with green leaves, seaweed, and an orange. The rice straw symbolizes purification and is supposed to ward off evil spirits, and the orange is associated with the continuity and prosperity of the family. Sometimes a lobster, which, like the crane and the tortoise, has the reputation in Japan of being a long-lived animal, is also hung up.

The childlike quality in the Japanese character, the ability to enjoy inexpensive amusements, is very much in evidence at the coming of the New Year. Everyone, rich and poor, eats the pink and white rice cakes which are a special New Year delicacy. Formal calls are paid on relatives and friends. At no other time can one see such an exhibition of women in brilliant, brightly colored kimonos and men in striped trousers and morning coats.

Children are very much to the fore during the celebration. There is scarcely a street or a lane in Tokyo where one does not see the tiny missile that is batted back and forth in battledore and shuttlecock flying through the air as children and maidservants join in the game. At the same time kites are flown all over the city.

New Year is only the most conspicuous example of the symbolism with which the Japanese instinctively invests his life. No poet could ever have written of a Japanese that "a primrose by a river's brim a yellow primrose was to him, and it was nothing more." The birth of a boy in a Japanese family is promptly announced by the flying of a paper carp from a pole; the carp is the symbol of a boy because it makes its way persistently against the stream.

The famous Japanese cherry blossoms, exquisite in their delicate pink and white beauty, are also surrounded with an atmosphere of poetic fancy. The cherry blossom has become the emblem of the loyal warrior, the knight without fear and without reproach, who is ready to lay down his life in the prime of manhood. Its swift disappearance, with its beauty still unspoiled, is contrasted with the tenacity which some flowers show in clinging to their stems, even after they have faded.

Japanese students in universities and higher schools are especially subjected to the strain of conflicting Eastern and Western influences. The uniforms which they wear are an outward sign of the severe regimentation of thought and conduct which the authorities endeavor to enforce. Yet in an environment that is essentially alien, from the old

Japanese viewpoint, they are exposed to a flood of Western scientific, literary, and moral conceptions which, on the more responsive minds, sometimes have all the intoxicating effect of a first draught of heady wine. Over and above this, the Japanese student is usually undernourished and overworked; from childhood he labors under the tremendous handicap of being obliged to learn reading and writing, without benefit of alphabet, by the long and painful method of memorizing thousands of complicated ideograms.

No wonder that, despite all the watchfulness of the police, "dangerous thoughts" make their appearance most often among the students; no wonder that those students who have interests apart from paving the way for a successful personal career fly with surprising volatility from one kind of extremist thought to another. The rootlessness which causes many Japanese student radicals to fluctuate uncertainly between Communism and Fascism is enhanced because the Japanese university, more, perhaps, than any other institution, still suggests a foreign importation. A well-known Japanese critic, Mr. Nyozekan Hasegawa, brings out this point forcibly in an article which he contributed to *Contemporary Japan*: —

So much that is foreign has been digested by the nation that once, while lecturing to an audience of students, I asked if there were anything about them which could be claimed as absolutely native to the country. There was nothing except the students themselves.

The auditorium and its furnishings, as well as the students' clothing and other personal belongings, were all of Western origin. Even the subjects under discussion were philosophy, law and other branches of Western learning. Brought up and educated amidst such surroundings, few Japanese find it easy to retain any culture which they can call their own.

Mount Fuji in Cherry-Blossom Season

The same dualism, the same tendency to adopt the new while retaining the old, is to be found in fields of Japanese life as far removed as sport and music. Many Western sports have taken a firm hold in the Island Empire. Japanese swimmers and track-and-field athletes have made excellent showings in Olympic Games, and the Japanese display a natural aptitude for tennis. Baseball is played more generally and better in Japan than in any other country except the United States and Canada. University baseball games are especially hotly contested.

At the same time Japan's native sports are not neglected. There is a large popular demand for tickets when the two annual *sumo* (Japanese wrestling) tournaments are held in Tokyo. The sport is not calculated to appeal to the amateur foreign onlooker, as the wrestlers, enormous mountains of men who deliberately eat large quantities of fattening foods, usually spend more time in making feints and false starts than in actual grappling.

On the contrary, *judo*, the Japanese art of self-defense, is a fascinating spectacle when it is practised by experts. The principle of *judo* is to let the opponent throw himself with his own weight; and a master of the art can reduce a much larger antagonist to helpless submission by means of moves which are so swift as to be almost imperceptible. Fencing is one of the classical Japanese sports and is enlivened by the ferocious war cries which the contestants emit, as a matter of course, with the idea of weakening the enemy's morale. Traditional Japanese sport lays more emphasis on perfection of form and on precise adherence to rules than on actual achievement.

The progress of Western music in Japan during the last decade has been amazing. Creditable performances of such a difficult work as Beethoven's Ninth Symphony are given in Tokyo, and even the humblest café usually entertains its customers with phonograph records of European songs and symphonies. A surprisingly large number of the Japanese who attend symphony concerts bring with them scores of the compositions. On a casual stroll through a residential quarter of Tokyo one hears the piano quite as often as the native Japanese instruments, the samisen, a kind of guitar, and the koto, which very distantly suggests the harp. Japanese music is not neglected, however; it is a regular accompaniment at the theatre and many of the Japanese folk songs are permanently preserved on the phonograph records which are characteristically produced more cheaply in Japan than in any other country.

The dualism that is so marked in Japanese daily life and in Japanese thought has also profoundly affected the economy of the country. For every large, well-equipped factory, with the most modern machinery and equipment, there are hundreds of tiny workshops which are only able to operate, in the face of the competition of the bigger plants, because of the intense labor and the mercilessly long hours. Two contrasted features of shopping in Tokyo are the few big *departos*, where one can buy anything that is available in Japan, and the long lines of little shops where the whole stock in trade would not be valued at a hundred yen.

The most dramatic contrast I have seen in the industrial field was at Tomakomai, in Hokkaido. After traveling a whole day through undeveloped country, much of it a frontier wilderness, I suddenly arrived at one of the largest, most productive, and best mechanized paper mills in Japan. It belonged to the Oji Paper Company, which controls about 90 per cent of Japan's paper output. To go through this plant was to be impressed again and again by the amount of labor which can now be performed by machine power. In all the processes of paper manufacturing, cutting up the logs, stripping off the bark, reducing it to the form of pulp with the aid of chemicals, until finally, in the last stage, paper is manufactured, the workers in this out-of-the-way Hokkaido plant seemed reduced to the status of very minor aides to the machine.

One huge combination machine in the mill, very important in the later stages of manufacturing paper, was a striking illustration of the tendency of the Japanese to discriminate in what is taken from other countries. The cylinder was made in Japan, but with an English frame. The electrical appliances had been purchased in Sweden, while some of the heavy parts bore a trademark of Beloit, Wisconsin.

It is little more than a step from this highly modern plant, which could challenge comparison with any paper mill in America or Canada, to a village inhabited by primitive aborigines, the Ainus. Visiting the two places in one day, as I did, gave me the sense of stepping across a wide social chasm. In Tomakomai a concert of Western music was advertised for the evening; the plant was saturated with the atmosphere of engineering, chemistry, modern invention.

In near-by Shiraoi are the memories of old days, gone never to return, when Hokkaido was a primeval wilderness and the Ainus roamed about its vast forests, hunting bears and other game with their spears and poisoned arrows and navigating the swift rivers in their narrow canoes, catching fish with spears and nets. Now all this is irrevocably changed. The bearded Ainu chief who had preserved his

cabin and his household as a sort of tourist museum said
to me: —

"Formerly we liked to eat only game and fish. Now
much of the forest land has been cleared and we can no
longer hunt and fish so freely. So now we are cultivating
patches of land and eating vegetables also."

The bear plays a large part in Ainu folklore and supersti-
tion. He is revered as a god; but this does not save him
from being killed and eaten with great ceremony when an
Ainu village is able to celebrate the so-called bear festival.
The chief had two fierce half-grown cubs in cages in his
yard; they were being fattened for the sacrifice.

Patriarchal beards, high cheekbones, and a generally
Mongolian cast of features, love of meat and aversion to
cleanliness, are among the things which distinguish the
Ainus from the Japanese. These picturesque aborigines
seem to belong among the disappearing races of the world.
They have not been able to adjust themselves to the absence of the wilderness to which they were accustomed. At
one time they battled with the Japanese for the mastery of
the Main Island; but they were gradually pushed northward until they are now practically all found in Hokkaido.
The Ainus are a very old race and their reproductive faculty
is declining. It is not uncommon for a childless Ainu
couple to adopt a Japanese foundling or poor child in order
to carry on the family name. It seems probable that in
time the 19,000 Ainus who are still in Hokkaido will become so merged with the Japanese that they will lose their
separate racial identity.

Perhaps the greatest of all the psychological conflicts in
Japan to-day rages around the tradition-hallowed family system, which conservative Japanese regard, along with rever-

ence for the Emperor, as one of the twin foundations of national life. One certainly cannot begin to understand Japan or the Japanese without understanding the main features and implications of this system. For, although it is yielding a little here and cracking a little there under the impact of such varied new influences as Christianity, capitalism, socialism, Hollywood movies, foreign dress, food, and ideas, it still retains a firm grip on the behavior and psychology of the average Japanese. In the country districts it is taken for granted; even in the large cities it is only a small class of Westernized Japanese who have broken away from it entirely, although a process of relaxation is visibly in progress.

The Japanese family idea is anti-individualist and anti-feminist. It causes the typical Japanese, whether he be official or clerk, farmer or businessman, to think of himself only secondarily as an individual and primarily as a mere link in a long chain of family descent that stretches both backward and forward over a period of uncounted centuries.

Authority in the family passes from father to eldest son; women occupy a definitely subordinate position. The head of the family has obligations as well as powers. He is morally bound to help his poorer relatives, to regard his property as a trust for the whole clan, rather than as his exclusive individual possession. The family system does much to keep unemployment at a low figure in Japan.[4] It is the Oriental substitute for the dole.

It is most unusual for a Japanese young man to take any step out of the ordinary without the advice and consent of his father. On matters of great importance a family

[4] There were 340,855 registered unemployed in Japan in 1937, as against about 500,000 in 1932.

council may be convened; and the opinion of brothers, uncles, cousins, and other relatives is taken and carefully weighed before a decision is made. The influence of the family system is clearly perceptible in the impersonal collectivism which marks so many transactions of Japanese public life. And the habit of thinking of the family as a closed unit tends to make Japanese men of wealth less liberal than Western millionaires in public benefactions. There are always so many poor and deserving offshoots of the family tree to be taken care off; and the number of potential dependents increases in proportion to the wealth and prestige of the man concerned.

The original Japanese family system presupposed a rigid and static economic order. It was assumed that the oldest son would carry on his father's trade or profession; and this is still very generally the rule among farmers, handicraftsmen, and actors. Very often the same first name was handed down from generation to generation, especially in trading families; this was supposed to generate a sense of confidence and stability. Migration from one place to another was discouraged. Now all this is breaking down with the growth of modern economic relations. The tranquil practice of the son automatically carrying on his father's trade or business does not harmonize with the age of the motor car, the airplane, and the Diesel engine. Since Japan has been more touched than any Eastern country by industrialism, the struggle between innovation and tradition, the old and the new, is especially strong.

The Japanese family is guided by the Confucian precept that woman owes three duties of obedience, first to her father, then to her husband, finally, after the death of her husband, to her eldest son. All the customs of everyday life tend to place the male members of the household in a privileged position. For instance, the wife is never supposed to leave the house while her husband is there. If he remains out late she sits up to await him. She must never retire before him and must always rise before him in the morning.

In very old-fashioned Japanese homes the father eats alone, or with his eldest son. The wife serves him and eats, along with other members of the family, after the father has finished. As a general rule the Japanese wife does not share the social life of her husband. When his friends visit him she bows to them, serves them at the table, but takes no part in the conversation. My eight-year-old daughter made an early discovery of the relative position of the sexes in Japan. She came running from play with Japanese children whom she had met on the liner on which we were crossing the Pacific and announced: —

"You know, in America girls go first; but in Japan it's the boys who are supposed to go ahead."

This order of precedence is almost universally observed in Japan when it is a question of getting on streetcars or buses and being served in public places. One of the hardest lessons to teach a Japanese maid is to serve ladies first. When a Japanese family goes out for a walk the husband is usually two or three paces ahead of his wife, who leads or carries the children. (Small children are habitually carried, papoose fashion, on the mother's back.) The boys in most Japanese families are given every preference over the girls, from the choicest tidbits at the table to better educational opportunities. Even a poor Japanese family will usually make every sacrifice in order to give at least one of the sons a good education.

But the Japanese girl who wants to qualify herself for a professional career has a hard row to hoe. There are almost no government colleges or universities for women; educational opportunity is mainly restricted to a few privately managed medical training and other higher schools and to missionary colleges. There is no coeducation in Japan; boys and girls are separated in schools at a very early age.

When a woman marries she usually goes to live in the house of her husband's family. She must obey her husband's parents, adjust herself to his family traditions, and bring up her children in this spirit. If she fails in any of these duties, or if she does not bear children, she may be divorced and sent back to her parents. A woman may apply for divorce only if her husband is *very* dissolute. When a woman has been divorced she receives no alimony and her husband has the legal right to keep all the children. As a general custom, all the wife's earnings and whatever she may own before marriage or inherit belong to the husband. Special legal provision must be made before marriage if a woman is to dispose of her own property.

Judged by Western standards, the position of woman in Japan is disadvantageous socially and politically, economically and legally. This is why the adjustments in marriages between Japanese and foreigners are much harder, as a rule, for the foreign wife than for the foreign husband. The Westernized type of Japanese girl who has been born or educated abroad often suffers cruelly when she is expected to conform to the rôle of the ever-obedient Japanese wife. In such cases the mother-in-law, steeped in old unbending traditions, is apt to prove more of a tyrant than the husband.

It is doubtful, however, whether there is a widespread feeling of revolt among the majority of Japanese women who have not been brought into contact with foreign influence. Custom and schooling alike have prepared them for many signs of outward subordination which would seem strange and distasteful to the American or Western European woman. Many features of the family system which seem harsh to Western eyes are softened in Japan by habit, affection, and the elaborate politeness which is ingrained in the Japanese character. Certainly many Japanese women, products of this system, give no impression of being crushed and browbeaten. On the contrary they display remarkably attractive qualities of restraint, gentleness, and self-sacrifice that give them a distinctive quiet charm of their own.

Moreover, the *okusan* or mistress of the Japanese household wields a good deal of real power behind the scenes. It is a samurai tradition that money is something discreditable, unworthy of a man's close attention. So the wife is the keeper of the purse. The husband usually brings her his earnings and she disposes of them, deciding how much can be spent for food after the rent is paid, how much for clothes, entertainment, and so on. She has the responsibility of saving for a rainy day, of buying the little presents for friends and relatives which play such a large part in Japanese life.

If the divorce scales are weighted against the woman, neither partner has much to say, as a rule, about the question of marriage. The go-between is an indispensable figure in the vast majority of Japanese matches, which are family rather than individual unions. When a boy or girl reaches marriageable age the parents look about for a suitable consort. The services of a go-between are enlisted. "Face" is a most important consideration in Japan, as in all Eastern countries; and a skillful intermediary can be relied on to steer the pre-marital negotiations along smooth channels, to soften or avert differences of opinion between the parents of the prospective bride and groom.

After a suitable candidate has been found the records of the family and of the boy or girl who is under consideration are most carefully scrutinized. The young people are only allowed to meet after both sets of parents have agreed as to the desirability of the match. The first formal meeting is then arranged at a theatre or some other public entertainment. After this, until the marriage, the couple see each other rarely and are never left alone together.

To be sure, this is a theoretical sketch of the system; in practice its stricter inhibitions are sometimes evaded. But the American idea of marriage by individual preference is still quite alien to Japan. An interesting sidelight on the psychology of the Japanese bride is to be found in a book by Mrs. Kiyooka, a Japanese woman who went to America as a girl and returned to Japan. Visiting a girlhood friend who was about to be married, Mrs. Kiyooka was surprised at the slight interest which the girl showed in the personality of her husband: —

She was showing me her handsome dresses and the hundred and one dainty little things that go to make up a Japanese bride's trousseau. . . . But about the wedding itself she seemed strangely indifferent. . . . As to the husband, he was her parents' choice. She had seen him once. He is "all right," she said. But evidently he was not considered of much importance, and no more was said about him. She did not seem to dislike him or object to him. She just did not take him into consideration at all.

Deep-rooted as it is, the Japanese family system is gradually relaxing and changing; and this silent, almost imperceptible revolution is one of the most important trends in the empire to-day. Several forces are undermining a régime that was best adapted to the static life of self-imposed isolation which the Japanese led before the Restoration and the opening up of contact with the outside world.

Modern education, which is universal in Japan, so far as elementary schools are concerned, tends in some ways to sap the foundations of the family system, despite the careful inculcation of textbook moral lessons on the duties of obedient wives and good mothers. In the schools foreign dress is worn, and habits of self-reliance and initiative which are scarcely compatible with the original Japanese patriarchal practices are cultivated. Farmers with whom I have talked in trips in the country districts have been almost unanimous in saying that the older generation no longer makes the extreme demands on the obedience of the younger which were customary one or two generations ago.

Foreign movies and, to a lesser extent, books and magazines have been a disintegrating influence, from the standpoint of old Japanese ideas. The romantic aura which surrounds the typical Hollywood film has instilled rebellious thoughts about the typical Japanese marriage of convenience into the minds of many of the younger people. The nervousness, frequently expressed in censorship cuts, which the police display in regard to foreign films is not without reason.

As feudalism gives way to capitalism, Japanese are no longer restricted in moving about the country or in changing occupations. The old stagnant security is gone; and the close-knit family system is inevitably suffering as a consequence. Every girl who enters a factory or office is an unconscious potential rebel against the severe restrictions which custom imposes on the Japanese wife and daughter.

Christian missionary activity has been an important factor in promoting a more individualistic outlook in Japan. It has been a counterbalance to the Confucian view of woman's predestined subordination. Mrs. Tsune Gauntlett, Japanese wife of an Englishman and a prominent leader of women's movements in Japan, attributes much of the credit for such modest improvement in the status of her countrywomen as has occurred to the influence of missionaries and mission schools.

The influence of the missionary effort cannot be measured by the small number of Japanese who have been converted to some form of Christianity.[5] The effect which mission schools, hospitals, and other institutions, individual missionaries, and such organizations as the Y.M.C.A. and Y.W.C.A., exercised on Japanese thought in a period of rapid transition is much wider. Almost all the leaders of the women's movement have been Christians or at least have been educated in mission schools. This is also true as regards a very large number of the pioneers in movements to organize workers and farmers.

Despite such strong and carefully cultivated influences for unity as Emperor worship, the family system, and the strong sense of racial solidarity, Japan's national personality remains split and divided in many ways. A people with more than the normal share of fixed unchanging institutions, habits, and taboos is at the same time being hurried on at a

---

[5] The number of Christians in Japan is a little over 400,000. Some 40,000 belong to the Russian Orthodox Church; the Orthodox Cathedral in Tokyo is a large and striking building, in typical Russian architectural style. The other Japanese converts are about evenly divided between the Roman Catholics and various Protestant denominations.

ASAKUSA

Tokyo's chief popular amusement quarter

feverish pace to changing ones by economic forces which are largely beyond its control. The closest student of Japanese life and character would hesitate to predict with assurance whether the mediæval or modern elements in the national psychology would take the upper hand in a moment of great emergency. In the synthesis and conflict of past and present, East and West, old and new, one finds both the fascination and the enigma of present-day Japan.

XII

THE DRIFT TOWARD WARTIME ECONOMY

Even before the guns began to go off in China, Japan was steadily drifting toward a wartime economy. What are the distinctive features of "wartime economy"? They are easy to identify. Every large nation experienced them to some degree during the World War. They were manifested in extreme form in Russia while the Soviet Government was carrying out its first Five-Year Plan, which was, incidentally, a high-speed programme of military preparedness. They have been clearly in evidence recently both in Germany and in Italy.

Under a wartime economy industry booms while orthodox finance is thrown overboard. Work is plentiful and money flows freely. While money becomes more abundant it also becomes less valuable; prices soar and acute shortages of essential commodities crop up from time to time. The scope of state control over industry, trade, and finance becomes more and more extensive. Labor disputes, in so far as they are not repressed by stern administrative measures, tend to occur more frequently because the wage which seems adequate to-day may fail to cover essential living costs within a few months in view of the rising prices. Persons dependent on fixed incomes and unorganized white-collar workers suffer especially from the fall in money value.

Households face a crisis with domestic help; girls prefer the higher wages and more regular hours in the munitions factories.

Japan's economic life is conforming more and more closely to the pattern which has just been outlined. Industrial jobs were never so numerous; the number of laborers in factories passed the three-million mark for the first time in Japanese history at the end of 1936.[1] Industrial output has been moving forward at a rapid pace. The output of Japan's industries almost doubled between 1931 and 1936; the increase in 1936, by comparison with 1935, was over 10 per cent.

It is noteworthy that all Japan's more striking gains have been in industries which directly or indirectly minister to military and naval needs.[2] Japan now leads the world in rayon output; this increased by four and a half times between 1931 and 1936. The plants which turn out rayon in time of peace can be turned to making explosives in the event of war. The output of the chemical industry as a whole has more than doubled, and Japan now ranks fourth among the world's producers of chemicals, being surpassed only by the United States, Germany, and the Soviet Union.

The value of the output of the machinery and tools industry was 1,458,000,000 yen in 1935, as against 410,-133,000 yen in 1931. A few years ago Japan was predominantly an importer of machinery and tools; now it is a heavy

---

[1] The number of factory workers at the end of 1936 was 3,067,417, representing an increase of 275,515 over the preceding year, according to the Social Affairs Bureau of the Home Ministry. The number of miners also increased by 45,677, reaching the figure of 320,481.

[2] A similar observation would hold good for other countries which have made strenuous war preparations during the last few years, namely the Soviet Union, Germany, and Italy.

exporter as well.[3]   There has been an even more spectacular reversal of rôles in the field of electrical machinery and apparatus.   Japan's exports of such products increased from 6,483,000 yen in 1925 to 33,852,000 in 1935, while imports simultaneously declined from 33,015,000 to 4,738,000 yen.   So a fairly complete measure of self-sufficiency has been achieved here.   This is not true as regards the chemical industry, where, despite Japan's great progress, the country is still an importer of chemical products to the amount of about 100,000,000 yen a year.

Japan has taken full advantage of the hydroelectric power possibilities offered by its many short and swift mountain streams.   Ninety per cent of its households are fitted with electric lamps and the country is second only to Switzerland in the utilization of electricity for lighting purposes.   More than nine tenths of the factories are operated with electric power, which is especially serviceable in the numerous cottage workshops.   Between 1921 and 1933 the amount of power generated in the empire increased from 4,249,000,000 to 16,962,000,000 kilowatt hours.   In the utilization of electrical power Japan stands third, after the United States and Canada.

Japan has been conspicuously successful in the manufacture of bicycles, which commenced on a large scale during the World War.   With one bicycle to every nine inhabitants, Japan is second in this respect only to the Netherlands.

Intensive armament has not been the sole factor in the

---

[3] Japan's exports of machinery and tools had grown from 5,922,000 yen in 1914 and 35,121,000 yen in 1931 to 159,409,000 yen in 1935, and almost equaled the imports in the latter year, which were valued at 164,088,000 yen.

country's industrial growth during the years 1931–1937. It is a general rule that the transition from an agricultural to an industrial economy passes through three stages. At first almost all manufactured goods are imported from abroad in exchange for agricultural products. Then the simpler kinds of consumption goods, such as textiles, are manufactured, while machinery and equipment are still purchased abroad. In the third and last stage of industrial coming of age, the heavy machine-building, chemical, metallurgical, and similar industries come into their own. Japan is now in this third stage of development.

Many of the factors which were outlined in Chapter VII as conducive to foreign trade expansion have also favored industrialization in general. The inexhaustible reserve of cheap labor has helped machine-building and chemical manufacturers, as well as textile producers. Japan is beginning to enjoy the fruits of a long and patient apprenticeship. One by one, foreign methods of production have been mastered, not always perfectly, but still well enough to permit Japanese companies to take over the business which formerly went to foreign firms. Kodaks, gramophones and gramophone records, electric fans — these are only a few of the newer items in the long list of "Made in Japan" products. It is significant of the shift which is taking place from light to heavy industrial production that between 1929 and 1933 the share of the textile, ceramics, and foodstuff industries in the total industrial production of the country should have fallen from 54 to 46 per cent, while the share of the four main branches of heavy industry, metals, chemicals, machine building and mining, should have risen from 35 to 46 per cent.

Japan's unmistakable and rapid progress in industry should

not create the impression that the Japanese are a race of industrial supermen or obscure the existence of some grave defects in the country's industrial structure. The most widespread of these defects is in quality and standardization. Except for a few lines where exceptional success has been realized, Japan, as regards quality of manufactured goods, stands somewhere between the Soviet Union and the more advanced countries of Western Europe and America. The foreign resident in Tokyo faces, in milder form, some of the shopping problems which would confront him in Moscow. The range of Japanese manufactures is wider than that of Russian, the quality better, but still, as a rule, inferior to that of America, Great Britain, or Germany.

Japan has also failed, as yet, to build up large-scale domestic automobile and aviation industries. The output of homemade automobiles in 1936 was only 9632,[4] as against about 30,000 cars which were assembled in the plants which Ford and General Motors maintain in Japan. Despite such individually brilliant exploits as the flight of the *Kamikaze* from Tokyo to London in less than four days at the time of the Coronation, Japan's civilian aviation is still slightly developed and the accidents to its military and naval airplanes are appallingly numerous.[5]

There are special reasons for the backwardness of automobile production and aviation by comparison with the swift and striking progress which has been achieved in such industries as shipbuilding, rayon, textiles, electrical equipment, and chemicals. The mountainous character of the

---

[4] To be sure, this figure represents a substantial increase over the 434 automobiles which were manufactured in 1931.

[5] Whereas only 20 army and navy fliers lost their lives in 1927, 93 were killed in air accidents in 1934, 77 in 1935, and about 100 in 1936.

country and the liability to floods, washouts, and landslides are serious obstacles to the building of a first-class network of roads. Moreover, in a country where over 90 per cent of the people earn less than a hundred yen a month, some type of car even cheaper than the Ford would be needed before the automobile could be placed within the reach of any large number of people.

Japan is physically very unsuited to flying. Swift changes of weather, treacherous air currents, frequent storms and clouds, all combine to harass the aviator; [6] and a forced landing is apt to take place on very inhospitable terrain, on a steep hillside or a patch of rice land oozing with mud. Both motor and airplane production are advancing as a result of large army and navy orders; but neither has achieved the progress which is possible only for industries which possess the constant support of a large mass market.

Precision and standardization of the finer and more delicate types of machinery suffer in Japan from the practice of farming out work to small producers. This practice commends itself to Japanese manufacturers on several grounds: it makes for cheapness; it limits the growth of a large and politically restless proletariat, concentrated in the large cities; and it spreads employment in the chronically impoverished villages. But some loss of the clockwork mechanical exactness which is associated with the conveyor method in the large factory seems inevitable.

The Japanese sometimes carries over into industry the temperamental qualities of the individual craftsman. One sometimes finds fountain pens or pairs of shoes of the same

[6] Two French flights from Paris to Tokyo, that of M. Japy in 1936 and that of MM. Doret and Micheletti in 1937, ended in crashes, with injuries to the fliers, on Japanese soil.

make which differ considerably in some details.   It is also a familiar foreign criticism that the Japanese is imitative, not creative; that he can make an excellent copy, but is helpless in the face of an unforeseen emergency that calls for improvisation.   It is undeniable that the Japanese system of education, with its emphasis on memorizing facts and dates and repeating without questioning whatever the teacher says, seems more fitted to develop industrious apprentices than creative geniuses.

Yet Japan has emerged from foreign tutelage in many important industries in a relatively short span of time.   Toward the end of 1933 there was an exposition of inventions by Japanese in Tokyo with seven hundred exhibits.   Many of these were relatively unimportant; but the exposition displayed Dr. T. Suhara's high-speed motion-picture camera and a micro-printing process discovered by Mr. J. Suzuki, which is of much practical value in the silk industry, where it greatly enlarges the usefulness of the microscope.   Japanese scientists have made valuable discoveries in bacteriology and chemistry; the latter science is especially significant in Japan, where it is hoped to overcome the natural poverty in raw materials and minerals by utilizing synthetic substitutes.   There seems to be convincing evidence that Japan's industrial coming of age is both genuine and permanent and that some of the early mistakes and defects which foreigners were inclined to attribute to fundamental incapacities of the Japanese temperament actually represented the sort of awkwardness which every country displays when it is first learning industrial ways.

If one should plot a graph showing the trend of Japan's industrial development during the last half century, the impression it would convey would be that of a gradual upward curve broken by four steep rises, each larger than its predecessor. The first of these bulges would coincide with the Sino-Japanese War of 1894–1895, the second with the Russo-Japanese War of 1904–1905. Both of these conflicts gave a fillip to the still infant Japanese industries.

Much more significant was the influence of the World War. Restricting its participation in the hostilities to minor operations which promised to serve its own interests, such as the seizure of the German South Seas Islands and the reduction of the German concession at Tsingtao, Japan was in an admirable position to profit from the diversion of almost all the industry and shipping of the large powers to war purposes. Japanese factories were swamped with orders; new markets all over the world lay open for Japanese commercial penetration.

Japanese economy experienced its full share of post-War deflationary bumps during the 'twenties and sunk into deep depression toward the end of the decade. It emerged from the slough of low production and unemployment and pointed sharply upward after 1931 under a triple stimulus. The drastic reduction in the gold value of the yen had the same quickening effect on export trade and on industry in general that was noticed in England and America after the pound and the dollar were allowed to slide to lower levels. The seizure of Manchoukuo opened up a large undeveloped colony for Japan's exploitation. Finally, and not least important, the army and the navy began to speak in much more commanding tones; and the annual increases in the budgets of the fighting services were reflected in ever-larger armament orders for the shipbuilding, engineering, metal, and chemical industries.

So Japan during the last five or six years has felt all the

invigorating effects of wartime economics: full employment, increasing production, utilization of all available plant and equipment. It has also experienced the familiar negative sides of wartime economy: straitened finances, rising prices, ominous shortages of essential commodities. The diversion of so much of the country's energy to unproductive war preparations has adversely affected the standard of living by causing higher prices and higher taxes. These disadvantageous aspects of an industrial boom that owed so much of its stimulus to munitions orders and to investments in Manchoukuo, many of which cannot yet yield any return, became more and more perceptible during the winter of 1936–1937 and the spring of 1937.

Japan's financial position may be compared to that of a man descending a mountain, who, after easily negotiating a gentle downward slope, begins to slide down a steeper incline at an accelerated pace. Whether this downward slide can be checked and moderated or whether it will go plunging on, gathering momentum, into an abyss of uncontrollable inflation is one of the most serious questions confronting Japanese statesmen at the present time. Wholesale and retail price-index figures, ordinarily regarded as the dull stuff of special economic reports, are reaching the status of first-page news in the Tokyo newspapers as it is more and more realized that the national financial equilibrium is in serious jeopardy.

Part of Japan's rising price trend is attributable to the world-wide increase in the prices of minerals, raw materials, and agricultural products, which, in turn, has been accelerated by the feverish competition in armaments in which all large countries are engaged. But another part is just as certainly due to the sharp growth in budgetary appropriations during the present year and to the ever-larger share of the national income which is earmarked for the needs of the army and navy.

Japan's budget for the fiscal year 1937–1938 (which runs from April to April), after several disputes, compromises, and changes, was fixed at the sum of 2,872,000,000 yen, an increase of about 560,000,000 yen over 1936–1937. By comparison with 1931–1932 the budget has almost doubled, while military and naval expenditures have increased more than threefold, from 454,600,000 yen to 1,411,000,000. The proportion of the budget which is assigned to defense purposes has increased from 31 per cent to 49 per cent. If one leaves out of account the new borrowing which will be necessary to balance the budget of the present year and considers only actual revenue, the fighting services are taking about 75 per cent of it.

Expenses connected with the military occupation of Manchoukuo (so far this has cost Japan almost 1,100,000,000 yen), improvements in army equipment and strengthening of the navy to meet the no-treaty situation which has arisen in the Pacific, are the main reasons for the steep rise in military and naval expenditures. Budgetary balance has been the price which Japan has paid for Manchoukuo and for the increased armaments which Japan considers essential to the maintenance of its self-asserted rôle as "the stabilizing force in East Asia."

Since 1931–1932 no Japanese Finance Minister has been in a position to make both ends meet without recourse to bond issues, which in some cases have provided about one third of the state revenue. The estimates for 1937–1938, for instance, call for the flotation of new loans to the amount of 965,400,000 yen. These so-called red-ink bonds are taken up by the Bank of Japan and,[7] to a lesser extent, by the Deposits Bureau of the Treasury, an institution which administers postal savings and thus has funds available for investment in government securities. The Bank of Japan, by means of open market operations, disposes of its bond holdings to commercial and savings banks, insurance companies and brokers.

For several years after Japan began to live above its national means no particularly disastrous financial consequences were visible. The absorption of new bonds proceeded quite smoothly. Crude monetary inflation was avoided. As late as April 1937, the specie reserve of 543,654,000 gold yen represented more than 100 per cent coverage for the note issue of 1,444,371,000 *paper* yen.[8] There was a gradual rise in the cost of living; but it was not so sharp as to inspire widespread demands for higher wages. Manufacturers who sold their products in foreign markets basked in the warm sun of profits which naturally shone on them when they received greatly increased prices, measured in yen, while the trend of wages was downward, rather than upward.

But in the latter part of 1936 the gentle downward slope of Japan's financial adjustment changed into a much steeper decline. The retail price index, which had only risen from

---

[7] The Bank of Japan was established as a central banking institution in 1882. It is a joint-stock bank in organization; but its governor and deputy-governor are appointed by the government. It has the exclusive right of issuing notes for the whole of Japan, except Formosa and Korea, where the Bank of Taiwan and the Bank of Chosen, respectively, have similar privileges as banks of issue. The national gold reserve is deposited in the Bank of Japan.

[8] There is an important distinction between the gold yen (which is reckoned at pre-devaluation rate of exchange and is now worth 84.4 cents) and the paper yen in everyday circulation, which is worth between 28 and 29 cents.

GAS MASKS FOR DOGS IN JAPAN

EN ROUTE TO THE JEHOL FRONT, 1931

129.6 to 157.6 between October 1931 and July 1936, leaped up to 171.9 in April 1937, an increase of 9 per cent over a period of nine months. The wholesale index in April 1937 was 27.2 per cent higher than it had been a year earlier.

The first upward swing in Japanese budget appropriations, in the two years after the occupation of Manchuria, was taken care of by means of loans. From 1933 until 1936 the budgets were held at a figure in the neighborhood of 2,200,000,000 yen, largely as a result of the restraining influence of the veteran financier and statesman, Korekiyo Takahashi, who was Minister of Finance. But Takahashi was murdered on the fateful morning of February 26, 1936, and his hope that the budget could be gradually brought into balance by preventing further increases in military expenditure and obtaining larger revenues as a result of growing business activity was frustrated. The record budget of 1937–1938 demanded both an unprecedented issue of bonds and new burdensome taxes. Increased excise taxes raised the price of tobacco, cotton goods, and other articles of general consumption; the income tax was pushed up; postal rates were raised.

One disquieting symptom after another appeared in Japan's body economic during the first months of 1937 and aggravated the prevalent mood of political restlessness and uncertainty. Labor began to show distinct signs of impatience when its wages, little above the subsistence level at best, were further decreased in buying power because of the abrupt rise in the cost of living. Spontaneous strikes swept over the country and affected the most varied classes: geisha, seamen, bus workers, factory laborers, shopgirls, waitresses, even prostitutes.

An acute shortage of iron, steel, and various building materials cropped up. Iron became so valuable that thefts of heavy chains were not uncommon. The government found itself compelled to forbid the use of steel in new buildings, while manufacturers were compelled to reject large orders for steel rails from abroad.

During the first five months of the year an adverse balance of 509,779,000 yen was rolled up, an increase of 223,700,000 yen over the corresponding period for the preceding year. This was attributable partly to the higher trend of raw-material prices, partly to the necessity for making extensive imports for the manufacture of munitions which yield no economic equivalent and are not reëxported.

The government experimented with a number of remedial measures. With a view to insuring the stability of the yen at the desired value of one shilling and twopence, several shipments of gold were sent abroad. A strict control over the purchase and sale of bills of exchange abroad was introduced, with a view to preventing flight of capital and speculation against the yen. The tariff on imported iron and steel was removed and the strictest economy in the use of these materials was prescribed. A commission was set up for the purpose of controlling prices.

But it remains a serious question whether the inflationary trend can be reversed after it has gone so far. Something like the spiral all-around rise in wages, costs, and prices which pessimists have been foreseeing for some years has actually started. The army and the navy, after obtaining record appropriations and an unprecedented share of the national budget, see their objectives balked by substantially higher bills for essential raw materials and for wages. This means that still higher appropriations will be demanded, in all probability, for 1938–1939; the budget in that year will almost certainly exceed three billion yen. But this will lead to still higher prices, with wages and salaries being raised in proportion, unless the spiral ascending movement is stopped by the enforcement of drastic measures of control.

The whole logic of the present situation points in the direction of an extension of the state control over industry and foreign trade which is such a necessary feature of the wartime economy and which is already so visible, in various forms, in the Soviet Union, Germany, and Italy. The government is considering a measure for the licensing of imports, with a view to excluding luxuries and all avoidable imports and giving priority to army and navy requirements and essential raw materials.

But when Japan's foreign trade balance is closely examined, economies are not easy to achieve. A large part of Japan's raw-material imports are shipped abroad in the form of exported manufactured goods, so that any reduction in imports would be offset by a decline in exports. Other items of import which might be classified as nonessential are accepted under barter agreements and therefore could not be excluded without injury to the export side of the balance of trade. One of Japan's leading business newspapers, *Chugai Shogyo,* in its issue of May 27, 1937, voiced the general opinion of business circles when it remarked, commenting on the import licensing proposal: —

The huge military budget and the necessary increase of military expenditures in the future are responsible for Japan's adverse trade balance. Larger productive capacity would effectively counteract the situation, but the rapid expansion of expenditures makes it difficult to do this in a brief period. All this suggests that the defense perfection programme, sponsored by the military, is too heavy for the Japanese economic strength to bear. It is incumbent upon the Government to reduce the defense expenditures.

The economic arguments for this conclusion are certainly cogent. But the political arguments against it have proved still stronger. No matter how much Japan's moderates kick against the pricks of the increasing burden of military and naval expenditures, the army, with its powerfully entrenched position in the state, has retorted that the burden can and must be borne, in view of the vast Russian military preparations, the uncertain outlook in the Pacific, and China's growing intransigence.

A natural accompaniment of wartime economy is a drive for maximum economic self-sufficiency; and Japan's thoughts have clearly been turning in this direction during recent years. The foremost champion of autarchy in the Hayashi Cabinet was the Minister of Commerce and Industry, Mr. Takuo Godo, a distinguished naval engineer. Minister Godo tersely summed up the programme of the army, the navy, and of Japanese economic nationalists generally when he declared: —

"If an emergency arises the country's industry and economy will be placed in a predicament, as they depend upon foreign countries. So defense cannot be perfected. Natural resources at home must be developed. Manufacture of substitute materials is also badly needed. For this reason the government is encouraging coal liquefaction, staple fibre and other industries. Larger production of low-content ores and utilization of sand iron are also encouraged."

One of the gravest concerns of the military and naval leaders is that Japan produces less than 10 per cent of its annual requirements in oil.[9] This is a powerful stimulus

[9] In 1934 Japan produced within the empire 58,700,000 gallons of oil products out of a total consumption of 686,900,000 gallons. The

BUS WORKERS IN A "GO SLOW" STRIKE

WAITRESSES OF THE MIMATSU RESTAURANT ON STRIKE

to the effort to produce oil from coal. Japan's two greatest business combinations, Mitsui and Mitsubishi, are both working on hydrogenation schemes, the former at Miike, in Kyushu, the latter at Naihoro, in Southern Sakhalin, where there are large undeveloped coal reserves.[10] Similar efforts in Manchoukuo were described in Chapter II.

Another oil-economy scheme is the compulsory dilution of gasoline, which is imported, with alcohol, of which Japan possesses an abundant domestic supply. Between 1937 and 1943 a sum of 95,000,000 yen is to be devoted to financing experiments in manufacturing oil.

The recent crisis in the supply of iron and steel vividly brought out Japan's weakness in this field. Japan does not possess within its borders enough good iron to keep its heavy industry supplied for a decade, at present rates of consumption. About 80 per cent of the iron ore and about 60 per cent of the pig iron and scrap iron which constitute the foundation of its munitions and other heavy industries must be imported from abroad, the iron ore mainly from China and the Straits Settlements.

Early in 1937 the government announced a plan for striking a balance between demand and supply of pig iron and steel without recourse to foreign imports, except for a negligible amount of pig iron, by 1941. It was anticipated that 6,200,000 tons of steel and 5,900,000 tons of pig iron

---

small deposits in the northern part of the Main Island are being worked intensively; but there seems to be no large source of oil in Japan or in Manchoukuo.

[10] During a visit to Sakhalin I was taken to the Naihoro mine in response to my request to see a coal mine. I was surprised at the nervousness and reticence of the engineer in charge and only later learned the explanation: that Naihoro was the place where secret experiments in coal liquefaction were being carried out.

would be required by this time. Self-sufficiency is to be attained by the application of the Krupp process for treating low-grade iron ore to the deposits at Anshan, in Manchoukuo, and Mozan in Korea, and by the utilization of sand iron, with which Japan is quite liberally supplied. Mr. Godo admits that the immediate commercial prospects for utilizing sand iron are not bright, but believes the state should subsidize efforts in this direction.

Advocates of autarchy in Japan see hope for at least partial emancipation from the present dependence on foreign wool and cotton in the development of the staple fibre industry. Five thousand tons of staple fibre, which is made out of wood pulp, were produced in 1935; by the end of 1936 output had mounted to almost 130 tons a day, or almost ten times the 1935 figure.

It is estimated that by mixing 20 per cent of staple fibre with cotton and wool fabrics Japan could cut down wool and cotton imports by 5 per cent and save about 45,000,000 yen in foreign currency. Optimists believe that much greater savings will be possible in the future as the production of staple fibre continues to increase. Wood pulp is priced at only twelve sen a pound in Japan, whereas cotton costs forty-seven sen and wool seventy-four. Because other production costs are higher, staple-fibre yarn is more expensive than cotton, although less costly than wool. But the champions of staple fibre maintain that larger output will mean lower unit costs.

How staple fibre will suit the consumer is a dubious question; but the interests of the consumer never receive much consideration in a state that is organized on a wartime basis. More serious, from the standpoint of nationalist economics, is the question whether a shift to staple fibre might not mean an exchange of one form of dependence on foreign raw material for another. For Japan at the present time is far from self-sufficient in its supply of wood pulp. Of the 1,010,000 tons of pulp which were consumed in the Island Empire in 1935, 280,000 tons were imported, mainly from the United States, Canada, Norway, and Sweden.

It is possible, however, that a more intensive development of the forests of Manchoukuo will solve this problem. Four Japanese timber companies are operating there. It is believed that their output of 60,000 tons can soon be doubled. Experiments are being made in utilizing the reeds in the river beds, as many of the best stands of timber are still inaccessible.[11] Besides encouraging the use of staple fibre Japan is endeavoring to develop cotton plantations in North China and a supply of wool by improving the breed of sheep in Manchoukuo. But Chinese political antagonism and the conservatism of the Mongols who are Manchoukuo's sheep breeders are formidable obstacles to the satisfactory realization of these schemes.

Inasmuch as many of Japan's plans for relieving by artificial means its poverty in raw materials depend on complicated scientific processes, some of which have not been fully worked out, it would be rash to pronounce a positive judgment as to prospective success or failure. It is, however,

---

[11] How far Japan's international balance of payments benefits by the relation of close economic dependency which exists between Manchoukuo and Japan is a delicate question in economics. At the present time Japan's balance of trade with Manchoukuo is heavily favorable, to the extent of about 250,000,000 yen a year. If Manchoukuo is considered part of the Japanese Empire, Japan's unfavorable balance of trade with the rest of the world must be reckoned as correspondingly greater.

highly probable that a good deal of time will be required before many of the projects which are now being considered yield large tangible results; and the costs of experimentation with synthetic substitutes will represent another burden on the hard-pressed finances of the country.

Wartime preparations in their broadest sense (including not only the increased manufacture of munitions and warships, but the development of Manchoukuo along strategic lines and the effort to build up industries which will make the country more self-sufficient) have been for Japan's economy both a powerful stimulus and a severe strain. The striking growth of the heavy industries could not have taken place without the stimulus. But in recent years the elements of strain have become more pronounced and more serious.

The diversion of an ever-larger part of the state revenue to essentially unproductive ends encounters more and more obvious obstacles: the lack of essential minerals and raw materials, the dependence on foreign imports for the export manufactures, the small reserves of gold and limited possibilities of additional production of the yellow metal.[12]

Japan's difficulties, although serious, should not be overestimated. The Japanese people have not as yet been compelled to endure an ordeal remotely comparable with what the Russians suffered between 1929 and 1933. In two re-

[12] In Japan, as in every other gold-producing country, output has leaped up in response to the higher prices which the metal has commanded in recent years. In 1934, 14,662 kilograms of gold were mined; 17,837 in 1935 and 21,077 in 1936. Yet even this higher figure represents only about $20,000,000, a sum which falls very far short of offsetting the prospective adverse foreign trade balance. (The output of gold in Korea is now in the neighborhood of 50,000,000 yen a year. There are rumored to be large gold deposits in Manchoukuo; but the output in 1936 was valued at only about 10,000,000 yen.)

spects, at least, Japan's position is still more favorable than that of Germany. There is no absolute shortage of the simple foodstuffs on which the Japanese masses live: rice, fish, bean products, Japanese vegetables. At a pinch, Japan, at least while sea communication was kept open with Korea and Formosa, could feed itself on a rationed basis, although individuals who were accustomed to a Western or semi-Western standard of living would suffer in the process. And the financial situation, while it has become steadily tighter, has not yet reached a point where it is a criminal offense to take small amounts in yen out of the country.

At the same time Japan's problems of adjustment to a wartime economy are sufficiently serious to call for a high degree of coördination between industry, finance, science, and foreign trade if plans are to be realized and more serious disasters avoided. Economic uncertainty has made for political restlessness and contributed in no small measure to the notably short lives of the Hirota and Hayashi Cabinets. And if Japan should take a sharp turn toward centralized control of production, trade, and natural resources, the relentless logic of its wartime economy, with the sacrifices and deprivations which such an economy always entails, would be largely responsible.

XIII

THE PERMANENT FARM CRISIS

AGRICULTURE is at once the social foundation of Japan and its greatest economic problem. Despite the fact that both the number of farm households and the amount of arable land have long been virtually stationary, more Japanese are engaged in farming than in any other single occupation. Although the cities and towns are absorbing the entire annual increase of population, more than 40 per cent of Japan's population still depends on the land for a living.

Conservative Japanese also regard the peasantry as the backbone of the country, the repository of its most sacred traditions. It is in the villages that the old customs and ways of life are most preserved. It is among the peasants that one finds most respect for the shrines and the gods; disturbing modern thoughts have made much less progress in the villages than in the cities. Army officers regard the peasant as the ideal soldier, morally and physically.

Yet it has proved impossible during recent years for the Japanese farmer to break even economically, in spite of his bare-subsistence standard of living. The villages have sunk deeper and deeper into debt; it is the official estimate of the Ministry of Agriculture and Forestry that the total peasant indebtedness amounts to a little over four billion yen. Private estimates place the total higher, at five or even six bil-

lion yen.[1]   Even the lower reckoning of the Ministry would
mean an average indebtedness of 700 yen for every rural
family; no small burden if one considers that the income of
the Japanese peasant averages about 300 yen a year.[2]

There is more social bitterness between town and country
than there is between capital and labor in Japan.   The heavy
fall in the prices of Japan's staple products, rice and silk,
which set in during 1930 and lasted several years not only
forced down the already low living standards of the peasants, but impoverished and bankrupted many of the small
landowning families which supply many officers for the
army.   A favorite theme of extreme Japanese nationalists
is the oppression of the peasantry by the banks, city merchants, and industrialists.   One of the participants in the
May 15 outbreak, Kawasaki, speaking in his defense, cried
out: —

"The future in store for the children of rural families is
nothing but slavish apprenticeship for the boys, and for the
girls lives as factory workers, maidservants, or abandoned
waitresses."

Among all the contrasts of paradoxical Japan none is more
striking than that between the cities, transformed by modern
industrialism in many respects, and the countryside, where
farming methods have remained essentially unchanged.
This is not because the Japanese farmer is slothful and

[1] Japanese statistics on agriculture are regrettably contradictory; one
often finds the widest discrepancies in estimates of farm income, rural indebtedness, and the value of agricultural production.   This fact, I think,
lends special value to the farmer's budgets which I sketchily compiled
from personal observation, incomplete and possibly unrepresentative though
these may be.

[2] This is the estimate of the economic magazine, *Diamond*.   In 1931,
the worst year of Japan's economic crisis, the average income was 143
yen.

unprogressive; rice yields have substantially improved over the last generation as a result of careful cultivation and the steady application of the latest discoveries in agricultural science. The production of wheat increased by 50 per cent between 1928 and 1934 and, where local conditions permit, considerable progress has been made in raising chickens and in producing fruit and vegetables. Old-time foreign residents of Japan often speak with surprise and appreciation of the increasing variety of home-grown fruits and vegetables which are now available.

But Japan's agriculture, in the main, is that of the small hand-cultivated rice field. It is the type of economy that one finds in China and India, in Siam and French Indo-China. And everywhere it implies, for the vast majority of the cultivators, a subsistence standard of living and a vicious circle of poverty and debt, each aggravating the other.

There are two reasons why the Japanese farmer, under the most favorable weather and market conditions, can expect only a meagre return for his hard labor, much of it up to the knees in the muddy water of the rice fields. These reasons are lack of land and lack of capital. There simply is not enough land in Japan to go around.[3] If one divides the amount of arable land by the number of farming families

[3] Critics of Japan (notably Miss Freda Utley, in her book *Japan's Feet of Clay*) are inclined to reject the theory that Japan is suffering from population pressure and to attribute the blame for poverty and malnutrition exclusively to mistaken economic and social policies. While it is undeniably true that the lot of the peasant could be alleviated by political and economic measures, there is, I am convinced, an absolute insufficiency of land in relation to Japan's present rural population. The best land in Hokkaido, sometimes pointed out as a population outlet, is already taken up and the quality of much of what remains is seriously impaired through the prevalence of ash in the soil.

Keystone View Co.

SARDINE FISHING AT BEPPU

Acme

A JAPANESE FARM LABORER

one finds that the average farm holding is a little over two and a half acres. Even if debt could be wiped out and taxes reduced it would be impossible to extract a comfortable living for the usually large Japanese rural family from two and a half acres of land. Lack of capital, combined with the small size of the holdings, explains the almost universal absence of machinery on the Japanese farm.

Even beasts of burden are rare. There are a little over a million and a half cattle, a little less than a million and a half horses, on the farms. Human hands and backs must do much of the work and carry many of the burdens that are assigned to animals and machines in richer countries. One is struck by the small number of customary farm animals, except chickens, in the countryside. There is extremely little spare land for pasturage; moreover, the hillsides are covered with an extremely troublesome weed known as bamboo grass, which cuts the tongues of grazing animals. Consequently the great majority of the Japanese farmers lack both the extra food and the extra income which farmers in America and Europe often receive from cows, sheep, and pigs.

Another factor that makes the lot of the Japanese farmer hard is his country's liability to natural disasters. It is estimated that flood and typhoon damage during 1934 and 1935 amounted to 440,000,000 yen, which was equivalent to a tax of 7 or 8 per cent on the farmer's income.

Floods, typhoons, and lack of an adequate supply of land are acts of nature, against which there is no appeal. The same observation would hold good as regards the evil times that have fallen on Japan's second most important agricultural product, silk. A variety of factors, among which the world depression and the rapid growth in the use of rayon are the most important, drove the price of silk to ruinously low depths. Approximately the same amount of silk that realized 661,442,000 yen in 1926 brought in only 203,871,000 yen in 1934. Since that year there has been some recovery; but the price of silk is still well below the pre-crisis level. In general the cash income of the agricultural population, according to the latest available figures, is still about 25 per cent lower than it was in 1925. On the other hand, taxes and interest charges are higher than ever; and the peasant, along with the Japanese of other classes, is bearing his share of the new indirect taxes which are helping to pay for the increased armament programme.

Moreover, the peasant, as a small producer, is economically face to face with big centralized industrial and trading and financial organizations, and naturally usually comes out second best in his dealings. During the worst years of the crisis the price of rice was lower than the cost of production. Even in better times the cream of the profits is skimmed by middlemen and rice speculators, who are better able than the peasant to buy rice when it is cheap and sell when it is dear.

The farmer is also unmercifully fleeced by the big capitalist combines that control the production and price of the artificial fertilizer necessary to reinvigorate Japan's old soil, which has produced rice crops over so many centuries. The amount the peasant must pay for fertilizer may run as high as 40 per cent of his earnings.[4]

---

[4] I found such a case, which is doubtless exceptional, with a group of very poor peasants in Chiba prefecture, near Tokyo. But the fertilizer bill is excessively heavy; it probably takes, as a rule, 15 or 20 per cent of the farmer's cash income. All efforts of farmers' coöperative organizations to break the monopoly which keeps up the price have thus far failed.

The distribution of taxes is another grievance of the country against the city. Direct and indirect government subsidies have been paid to industry and shipping while agriculture has been left to fend for itself, except when conditions became so bad that doles had to be paid to rural districts in order to avert actual famine. The average annual tax bill in the farm household is 58 yen,[5] which is heavy in relation to the low income of the peasant. Local taxes are especially high in rural areas because there are so few well-to-do residents to be taxed. The tax burden in the country districts is two or three times heavier, in relation to income, than in the towns.

Two outstanding social features of Japanese agriculture are the predominance of small holdings and the payment of rent in rice rather than in cash. Japan's approximately 5,600,000 farm households fall into three economic categories. The most prosperous, which includes 1,740,219 families, consists of those who own their land. Under this grouping there are some big landlords, especially in the northwestern provinces of the Main Island and in Hokkaido, where large land grants were parceled out when the island was opened up for settlement. But the majority are peasants who are only a little better off than their neighbors. The leading kulak of one country district which I visited proved to be a man who owned about twelve acres of land.

At the bottom of the rural economic scale are the 1,508,319 peasants who rent all their land, paying from a third to a half of the crop to the landlord. To this class of peasants even a year of good crops and high prices brings no relief, because they are usually obliged to buy rice for their own consumption before the next harvest is gathered. The largest intermediate class of Japanese farmers is made up of

[5] Cf. *Japan Year Book*, 1936, p. 469.

the households which own a little land and rent a little more. Into this category fall 2,368,948 families.

The heart of Japan's permanent rural crisis is to be found in the so-called Tohoku, or six northeastern prefectures of the Main Island. Whenever a natural disaster, to which the region is peculiarly susceptible, occurs, when unseasonably cold weather spoils the rice crop or the poorly regulated rivers overflow during periods of torrential rain, or a typhoon sweeps away fishing boats, as happened on a large scale in 1934, the government finds itself obliged to ward off actual starvation for the poorer peasants by doling out money for road building and other public works.

A pamphlet issued in 1935 by the Imperial Agricultural Society, the leading organization representing farmers' interests in Japan, gave an extremely gloomy picture of conditions in the Tohoku. As characteristic symptoms of the crisis prevailing in this part of Japan the pamphlet mentioned widespread hunger and disease, a growing mountainous burden of debt, inability of the local authorities to pay teachers' salaries, increased social unrest, and a marked increase in the sale of girls to the licensed quarters in the cities.

If Tohoku is the poorest part of Japan, Aomori is the poorest prefecture in that region. Some time ago an American magazine sought, with the aid of a mass of data on income and social welfare, roads and schools, to determine which is "the worst state in the Union." From the material standpoint Aomori may be considered the worst prefecture in Japan. It has the highest death rate and the lowest per capita income.

The town of Aomori superficially does not show any more distress than the ordinary Japanese provincial centre. But as soon as I left Aomori and visited a neighboring village I found concrete evidence of two things that make the life of the Tohoku agriculturist difficult, high taxes and widespread landlordism.   The first peasant I met was a small owner, a comparatively well-to-do man in a village where 90 per cent of the families rented all or part of their land.   Yet even he was facing a hard struggle to make both ends meet.

He owned a little less than four acres of rice land, from which he had harvested a crop of one hundred and fifty bushels.   Eighty bushels had gone for the consumption of himself and his large family.   For the seventy bushels which he sold he received 350 yen.   This had been by far the largest part of his cash income, which had been supplemented very slightly by some apples from a young orchard and by the sale of some straw sandals which he and his family made during the winter.   Out of an income of a little over 400 yen a year he had to pay 33.60 in national and 65.90 in local taxes.

A tenant farmer in the same village was in an even more difficult plight.   He had to hand over between a third and a half of his rice as rent to the owner of the land which he farmed.   In bad years (and in this northern region bad years for rice are not uncommon) this did not leave him enough to feed himself and his family, to say nothing of having any surplus for sale.   He received work relief on the roads at 80 sen (about 24 cents) a day.

The year 1934 was especially unfavorable in this north-eastern region and the term "famine" was sometimes used in Tokyo publications in describing the situation.   From talks with a number of long-time residents of the region, both Japanese and foreigners, I gained the impression that the more extreme and horrible forms of famine, such as recur periodically in China and such as large parts of Russia experienced in 1921–1922 and 1932–1933, had not occurred in the Tohoku. I could find no authenticated cases of death from outright starvation, with the familiar accompaniment of abnormal stomach swelling, much less of cannibalism.

But there was abundant evidence that the normal stark poverty of the district is aggravated by serious malnutrition in bad harvest years. The College of Agriculture and Forestry in Morioka, one of the larger towns in the Tohoku, displays specimens of the acorns and grasses to which the peasants resort when their ordinary diet runs low. Even now, when conditions have improved by comparison with 1934, the authorities find it necessary to feed in the schools some children whose parents are too hard-pressed to give them the customary simple *bento*, or lunch.

To some extent the present inhabitants of the Tohoku are paying the penalty for the bad judgment or bad luck of their forefathers, who sympathized with the Shogunate when the imperial power was established almost seventy years ago, mainly through the efforts of the great clans of Southern and Western Japan, Satsuma and Choshu. For many years the new government was a close corporation of prominent Satsuma and Choshu clansmen. Subsidies, necessary for the initial stages of Japan's industrial development, flowed into the Satsuma and Choshu regions.

Partly as a result of this historical accident the Tohoku has remained almost exclusively agricultural, with a few oil wells and copper mines in its richest prefecture, Akita, but with no big factories to increase the local wealth and to provide additional employment and earnings for a peasant population that can scarcely make a living from farming alone. For these northeastern prefectures have an unfavorable climate for the favorite form of Japanese agriculture, the lush rice paddy fields. Although the soil is not very rich, hardier crops, such as wheat, cabbage, potatoes, millet, and apples, can be successfully cultivated.

But the Japanese farmer likes to put his land into rice whenever there is any prospect of harvesting a crop. His wants are few and simple, but he is miserable if he cannot eat his fill of rice, which he calls "the king of grains." Moreover, because of the nation-wide demand for rice, it is a good cash crop when there is a satisfactory yield. The difficulty in the Tohoku is that the severe climate limits the amount which can be raised. Only one crop can be hoped for, as against two or even three in the warmer parts of the country. And there are certain to be periodic failures.

In visiting the Tohoku for the first time one has a keen sense of its regional peculiarities. The climate is markedly different from that of Tokyo, more temperate, less humid, with much heavier snowfall and prolonged cold in winter. The women wear *mompei*, or trousers, in the fields — a costume that is familiar in China, but not in other parts of Japan.

The Tohoku has a strong local dialect, which the Tokyo-bred Japanese understands with considerable difficulty. In character and temperament also there is a distinction between the inhabitants of the Tohoku and their fellow countrymen of the South and West. They are more placid and stolid, less fiery and quick-tempered. Women marry earlier here than in other sections. And, probably because of the absence of large towns, the Tohoku is socially more conservative, more attached to old customs, than other parts of the empire. Tohoku local patriotism is not without its element of bitterness. There is a feeling that the region has been improperly neglected; on one occasion I heard the opinion expressed: —

"They take our boys for the army in Manchoukuo and our girls for the geisha houses of Tokyo and Osaka, and give us nothing in return."

The government has made some effort to meet this criticism. Two companies, the Tohoku Development Corporation and the Tohoku Electric Power Corporation, have been organized with the authorization of the Diet. Each is capitalized at 30,000,000 yen, and may raise additional funds through bond issues. The government appoints the directors of the corporations and guarantees fixed dividends.

The Tohoku Development Corporation is to promote a variety of enterprises, concentrating its efforts on the production of cheap fertilizer. It will also engage in gold, silver, and sulphur mining. Tohoku local patriots believe the mineral resources of the region have been underestimated and will repay systematic exploitation. The electric power corporation expects ultimately to generate 150,000 kilowatts of hydroelectric power, utilizing Lake Tazawa, near Akita, and the Abukama River, near Sendai.

Besides this help from outside, some of the local officials, notably Governor Ishiguro of Iwate prefecture, advocate self-help through the inculcation of better farming methods and hygienic principles. An interesting example of this "self-help" was a training school for young farmers which has existed for five years at Rokuhara, in Iwate prefecture.

At the time of my visit there were about a hundred young men and women at the school, between the ages of sixteen and thirty. Some were taking the longer course of eight or ten months, others a shorter term of three weeks. A retired admiral had provided land for the project, about 2500 acres of arable fields and an equal amount of forest, and the school, with its dairy, incubators, sawmill, sewing and weaving courses for the girls, offered all-round training for farm life.

Hard work is a characteristic of the institution. The students rise at daybreak, perform setting-up exercises, and pay honor to the shrine of Amaterasu, patron goddess of Japan. Then, after the simple Japanese breakfast of rice, pickles, and bean-curd soup, they disperse to their tasks of clearing land, cultivating vegetable plots, taking care of the animals, and remain busily occupied until sunset, with time out for lunch and a little rest in the midday heat during the summer months. At sunset there is a second general muster before the shrine. The Japanese flag, which is raised every morning, is lowered with appropriate honors, and there is mass singing of patriotic and village songs. Both men and women wear simple uniforms and there is an atmosphere of intense nationalism and semi-military discipline which is suggestive of a German labor camp.

Altogether about 4000 young peasants have attended the school since it was established. The idea of giving practical agricultural training with an accompaniment of nationalist influence is being taken up and imitated in other prefectures. It is hoped that the returning students will be a progressive leaven in their villages, teaching better methods of farming and encouraging their fellow villagers to build separate quarters for their domestic animals, which are now housed along with human beings, and to construct houses with more light and better protection against cold.

One does not have to go as far away from Tokyo as the Tohoku to find very bad rural conditions. Indeed the worst place I found during travels in various parts of the country was the village of Yamachita, in Chiba prefecture, near Tokyo. Most of the peasants here were working on poor land under an oppressive landlord system. Several villagers with whom I talked complained that they could not earn more than twenty yen per *tan* (a *tan* is about a quarter of an acre) of land. Of this eight was spent on fertilizer, and seven was paid to the landlord as rent. A tenants' strike finally broke out. The landlord offered to reduce the rent to four yen; the peasants were holding out for three and a half.

The children were singularly dirty and afflicted with skin diseases; the chief food was a mixture of 40 per cent barley and 60 per cent rice. The local doctor spoke of prevalent malnutrition, one striking symptom of which was the incidence of "night blindness," people losing the use of their eyes after dusk and recovering it in the morning.

One cannot generalize about the Japanese rural districts; some are much more progressive and better off than others. The most prosperous district I have visited personally is in the neighborhood of the town of Anjo, near the big industrial centre Nagoya. This district is such a stronghold of coöperation that it has become known as the Denmark of Japan. About four fifths of the 20,000 farming households are enrolled in coöperative societies, which perform four separate services for their members. They market produce, purchase city goods in bulk, provide credit at more reasonable rates of interest out of loan deposits from their members, and perform various miscellaneous functions. The most important of the latter is medical aid; and a coöperative hospital is one of the most impressive buildings in the little town of Anjo.

There were several reasons for the sweep of the coöperative movement and the relative well-being in the Anjo district. A former teacher named Yamazaki had been an untiring missionary of the coöperative idea. There was substantial economic equality in the district; only three landlords owned as much as fifty acres. There were no old feudal ties or traditions. A large part of the land had been reclaimed through an irrigation project; and this made the peasants familiar with the idea of collective effort. The peasants were quicker than their fellows in many other parts of Japan to broaden and vary their farming methods. The staple rice crop was supplemented by poultry and eggs, fruit and vegetables.

An Anjo farmer named Hayashi, whom I interviewed in his cow barn during a torrential summer rain, gave me a sketch of the routine of life in a peasant household that was somewhat above the average without being in the landlord class. Hayashi cultivated five acres of rice land and half an acre of "dry land," on which he raised vegetables. For half of his rice land he paid rent in kind at the rate of 100 yen per acre annually. Unlike most Japanese farmers, he had gone in heavily for animal husbandry and possessed two hundred chickens, ten pigs, and a cow. His earnings, as he estimated, amounted to about 3000 yen a year. But 2000 yen had to go for fertilizer, fodder, rent, and taxes. Of the remainder he saved 500 or 600 yen, supporting himself and his family, which consisted of his wife, a younger brother, an old mother, and two small children, on 400 or 500 yen a year.

Breakfast at five-thirty in the morning consisted of rice, eggs, potatoes, and cabbage. There were two meals in the fields, at eleven and three, the fare including rice, boiled vegetables, pickles, and preserved fish. Rice, bean-curd soup, eggplant, and radishes made up the eight-o'clock supper. There was chicken, as a special luxury, about once a week; meat was almost never eaten. The Hayashi household was mainly self-sustained and self-supporting.

Producing the account book which every Japanese farmer keeps, Hayashi showed that expenditures at the coöperative store for *shoyu* (Japanese sauce), nails, socks, salt, oil, and a Japanese paper umbrella amounted to only 16 yen and 89 sen for a period of about five months. Clothes for the entire family cost about 50 yen a year.

Hayashi's recreations were few and simple; peasant dances at a few annual festivals, the game of Japanese chess, an occasional evening of reading poems at the headquarters of the local Young Men's Association. Like most Japanese farmers, he subscribed to a daily newspaper and also read several agricultural magazines. He was by no means without ideas on public questions. After dwelling on the familiar theme of the corruption of party politics, he spoke as follows on the questions of immigration and expansion: —

"We farmers can see that we are too crowded in our thickly settled villages. Some of our younger people must go somewhere, to Manchoukuo or to some other country. I believe that all races are equal and that people should be free to go to other countries and settle where they choose."

Hayashi was a devout Buddhist and remarked that religion is the sole true consolation amid the futility of most of life's undertakings.

From Hayashi's hospitable barn I went to the shop of Gentaro Itakura, Anjo's best-known citizen, whom I instinctively christened the Poor Richard of Japan. For it was by professing and practising the maxims of Benjamin Franklin's hero that Itakura, who had started out as a poor peasant with a minimum of education, had become the chief local celebrity. Thousands of people every year visit his farm. Imperial princes and governors have publicly commended him as a model Japanese subject. Farmers in remote parts of the country send him their sons as unpaid apprentices to be trained under his régime of hard work and relentless thrift.

With a plain cotton kimono wrapped about his body and his bare feet thrust into geta, he was a living exhibit for his philosophy of working as hard as possible and saving as much as possible. He needed little prompting to launch into the moral lecture with which he was evidently in the habit of edifying his guests: —

"All we need is more hard work and thrift. . . . I started out myself as a very poor man and now I have one of the best farms in the district. . . . I never read newspapers; it is a waste of time. . . . The governor of the prefecture once praised my industry; in response I decided to work still harder. . . . His Imperial Highness Prince Takamatsu once visited my farm and was graciously pleased to commend my humble labors; I was awe-struck by this mark of honor and decided I must redouble my efforts. My rules of conduct are as follows: Rise early. Work late. Raise everything you need yourself. Buy no city luxuries. Bow to the Imperial Palace twice a day. Attend services in the temples regularly."

Itakura proceeded triumphantly to cite examples of thrift in the conduct of his severely patriarchal household. His daughter-in-law, he said, nursed her children while she fed the chickens, "so as not to waste any time." He himself invariably replied to letters on the same paper, in order to avoid any expenditure on stationery. He produced a letter from a father of one of his former apprentices, in which the old peasant expressed his delight and gratitude when he found that his son, returned from Itakura's Spartan schooling, displayed the greatest concern when a little water leaked from the family pump and rushed with a basin to gather up the drops.

Itakura was a salty and picturesque character, such as one might find, in American overalls and shirt sleeves, in a New England village. But his ideas, while they naturally appeal to the conservative authorities, scarcely seem to meet the crisis of Japanese agriculture. The majority of the peasants are not willing to go back to the still more primitive, self-contained life of their fathers and grandfathers. And, even if they were, new economic difficulties would arise, because the industries which support the growing towns depend in some degree on peasant purchases.

Agrarian distress has called forth in Japan both revolutionary and reformist movements for relief. Near Mito, a picturesque old town in Ibaraki prefecture, northeast of Tokyo, is the large rambling thatched house where K. Tachibana, an intellectual with a burning conviction of the need for agrarian reform, once lived and wrote. Tachibana's philosophy was a mixture of Japanese nationalism and Tolstoyan rural Communism; he gathered around him a band of peasant disciples and created a farm community. Tachibana is no longer in the home of his family, who were country gentlefolk; he is serving a sentence of twenty years in prison for bringing up his peasant followers to Tokyo to participate in the demonstration against the "capitalist" government on May 15, 1932. But many visitors to Mito go to see the house, and a former schoolteacher, dismissed because of his participation in Tachibana's organization, told me that his name is still honored as that of a martyr by the more active-minded younger peasants.

Almost 400 persons, many of them peasants from Nagano prefecture, which has suffered especially because of the decline in silk prices, were arrested in 1935 for alleged participation in a "rural anarchist conspiracy." At the time of writing they have not been brought to public trial; but they are charged with creating insurgent organizations in various prefectures for the purpose of precipitating peasant revolts.

The most radical peasant organization which is operating legally is the National Farmers' Union, with 60,000 members, almost all recruited among tenants. The Union was established in 1922. In 1928 it was temporarily suppressed and permitted to function again after it had purged itself of suspected Communists. Even now it is a decidedly Left-Wing organization. It was surprising, in view of the strictness with which anything that savors of Communism is suppressed in Japan, to find a portrait of Lenin hanging in its Tokyo office and to find that its badge of membership is the Soviet hammer and sickle.

The ultimate programme of the Union, as its spokesman told me, calls for socialization of the land, with state ownership and cultivation under the direction of farmers' committees. Inasmuch as such revolutionary changes are outside the realm of immediate political possibilities, the Union concentrates its efforts on the realization of such reforms as reduction in farm rents, taxes, and prices of necessities consumed by farmers, cancellation of part of the rural indebtedness, free distribution of rice among the poorer peasants, enactment of laws which will give the tenants more security of tenure.

Tenancy disputes in Japan are often bitter and prolonged. In exceptional cases they lead to bloodshed and loss of life; the use of violence is more frequent than in urban labor disputes. The Farmers' Union frequently resorts to the typically Oriental methods of boycott and social pressure. Posters denouncing the landlord are pasted up; committees of protesting tenants gather around his house; the children of tenants in the local school declare a strike, with the idea of bringing pressure on the authorities to settle the dispute.

The spokesman for the National Farmers' Union admitted that the influence of his organization is limited. In this connection he spoke bitterly of the "unenlightenment" of the Japanese peasants, of their "undue respect for the authorities," of the persistence of feudal psychology, and of a filial attitude of some peasants toward the landowners, especially in the northern prefectures.

A much more influential agency in the reshaping of Japanese rural life is the coöperative movement. The Japanese coöperatives now number about 6,000,000 members, organized in 14,000 societies. About 70 per cent of these members are peasants; the movement is much stronger in the country districts than in the towns. I have already described the working of the coöperatives in Anjo. They endeavor to free the peasant from the clutches of that familiar Oriental figure, the village usurer, to get him higher prices for what he sells and lower prices for what he buys, to provide cheaper medical aid and other services. The Japanese coöperatives have now become large business organizations and carry on extensive merchandising and banking operations.

Mr. K. Sengoku, director of the coöperative central bank and a very influential figure in the movement, outlined a moderate programme of rural amelioration in a talk with me. The main points which he advocated were government control of the prices of rice, silk, and other staple agricultural commodities,[6] encouragement of the peasants to produce

---

[6] A form of control over rice and silk prices, based on the principal of maximum and minimum prices, is already in force. If the price rises above the maximum figure, the government throws reserve stocks on the market; if it sinks below the minimum, the government buys for storage.

HARVEST TIME IN JAPAN — THE WHOLE FAMILY HELPS

RESTING TIME IN THE FIELD WORK

what they can on their own farms, lowering of the cost of fertilizer, and creation of more peasant proprietors.

No doubt such measures, combined with the spread of coöperation, a shifting of some of the tax burden from the villages to the cities, and more equitable laws protecting tenants against arbitrary eviction [7] would relieve the more acute forms of agrarian distress in Japan.[8]   But it is doubtful whether any altogether satisfactory solution of Japan's permanent agrarian crisis is possible while the average farm family must make a living out of less than three acres of land.   The merciless pressure of population affects the standard of living adversely in many ways.   Not only is the quantity of foodstuffs which the farmer can hope to raise for his own use and for sale sharply limited; but the scarcity of land tends to keep both price and rental value of land abnormally high, with the result that those farmers who take advantage of state credit to acquire land of their own find themselves saddled from the outset with a crushing burden of interest charges.

Agrarian revolution is scarcely possible in Japan.   Most of the land is already parceled out in small allotments. There is no such clear-cut antagonism between a small class of big landlords and a large class of tenants as supplied fuel for the sweeping agrarian upheavals in Russia and Mexico.

[7] Hitherto the deputies who have represented rural areas in the Diet have generally represented landlord and mercantile, rather than tenant interests.

[8] It is only fair to remember that, hard as the lot of the Japanese farmer is by Western standards, it is doubtful whether any Oriental peasant is better off.   Japan is the only Eastern country which has placed a school in every large village.   The Japanese farmer has a somewhat higher income than the Indian peasant.   He is not plagued by bandits and is less likely to lose his life in famine, flood, or epidemic than is his Chinese neighbor.

But agrarian distress, in various degrees of severity, will most probably remain a problem for Japanese politicians and economists for an indefinite period.   The sole remedy that seems to promise fundamental relief is a drastic reduction in the number of farm households, and there is no ready answer to the question of where to place the superfluous ones. Emigration on a large scale has not proved feasible; rationalization has in many cases cut down, at least temporarily, the number of new jobs which are associated with industrial development; and there is the further problem of taking care of the half million people of working age who come on the labor market every year, because of the growing population.

The agrarian crisis is one of Japan's most permanent and serious handicaps.   Both from the military and from the industrial standpoint Japan will be at a distinct disadvantage while almost half of its population are living in such primitive conditions, with so little benefit of modern science and machinery, with grossly inadequate medical care, and, in some cases, without enough food to ward off physical deterioration.   It is one of the bitter contradictions of Japan's race for empire, justified by nationalist economists as the sole remedy for overpopulation and natural poverty, that the immense economic and financial sacrifices which it demands for military and naval armament seem to exclude any large-scale rehabilitation measures for the benefit of the peasants who, from the nationalist viewpoint, represent the best types of loyal Japanese subject.

XIV

THE INEVITABLE CONFLICT

THERE is an atmosphere of grim inevitability about the un-declared Sino-Japanese War, which is directly affecting the destinies of one quarter of the human race, which has already taken well over one million lives and driven many millions of Chinese into homeless exile. The two strongest forces in the contemporary Far East are revolutionary Japanese imperialism and revolutionary Chinese nationalism. They could not coexist forever without coming into conflict. One or the other had to prevail.

It becomes increasingly clear in retrospect that the seizure of Manchuria in 1931 was much more than an episode of annexation. It was a revolution, an assertion of the men of the sword, who had been pushed somewhat into the background during Japan's era of relative liberalism after the World War, against the monied interests and the political parties. It was a turning point in Japanese history com-parable with Mussolini's march on Rome or Hitler's acces-sion to power, even if the consequences were somewhat slower in unfolding.

The army at this time seized the effective leadership of the Japanese state and since then has more and more imposed its own ideas of how to emerge from the country's permanent crisis of poverty and overpopulation, which had assumed especially acute forms in connection with the world depression in 1931.   Its programme calls for unlimited expansion on the continent, under the banner of Pan-Asianism, and for rigid subordination of private enterprise to the needs of the state and national defense.

To the businessman the army offers prospects of wide markets and cheap raw material in China.   To the unemployed young engineer, technician, architect, it holds out the opportunity of building railways and factories and planning new towns in Manchoukuo and China.   To the peasant, more and more perplexed with the problem of maintaining his family on two or three acres of rice land, it proposes large-scale migration of the country-bred youth to the continent, the building up of a new Japan on the rolling plains of northern Manchuria.   As a retort to foreign restrictions on Japanese immigrants and goods it suggests a vast self-contained Asiatic empire, with Japan as the pivotal centre.

Now while the army has been developing its expansionist programme for Japan, Chinese national consciousness, under the impact of Japanese aggression, has been rapidly awakening.   Feeling against the protracted civil war with the Communists rose to a point where the Sianfu mutiny became possible.   Student demonstrations for a policy of active resistance to Japan could only be kept within bounds by severe police repression.   China had reached a psychological mood which made it more dangerous for Chiang Kai-shek to yield than to fight when confronted with new Japanese demands in the summer of 1937.

Here, in brief outline, is the uncompromising background against which the nocturnal skirmish on the Marco Polo Bridge developed by successive stages into a war which has spread all over China and brought millions of men into the field.

Both in Japan and in China there were moderate groups

which feared the destructive consequences of war and sought to avert it. But these moderates were helpless to arrest the drift toward conflict. There was only one conceivable basis on which Sino-Japanese understanding might have been reached during the uneasy years, full of crises and alarming rumors, that preceded the actual outbreak of hostilities. This would have been Chinese recognition of Manchoukuo in exchange for a binding Japanese engagement to refrain from further encroachments on Chinese territorial integrity, accompanied by a broad programme of economic coöperation between the two countries. But there was no Japanese cabinet that could effectively vouch for what restless army officers might do in North China, and there was no Chinese Government that could afford publicly to renounce Manchoukuo.

Several immediate causes hastened the beginning of a war that was fundamentally inevitable. The cessation of Chiang Kai-shek's anti-Communist campaigns after the Sianfu uprising produced a disturbing effect in Tokyo. It was anticipated that the Communist attitude of uncompromising hostility to Japan (the Chinese Communists on one occasion had formally declared war on Japan) would influence the councils of the Chinese Government. It is quite possible that Japan learned of or suspected the existence of the Soviet offer of a mutual-assistance pact to China in the spring of 1937.[1] An alliance between Russia and China, with its immense potentialities in man power and resources, has always been a nightmare of Japanese diplomacy.

Moreover, the international situation seemed singularly favorable for a bold stroke in China. The Soviet Union had just backed down under fire in a dispute over the owner-

[1] This offer was revealed early in 1939 by Mr. Sun Fo, President of the Chinese Legislative Yuan and an advocate of Sino-Soviet *rapprochement*.

ship of two islets in the Amur River. The decimation of the commanding staff of the Red Army by wholesale executions of leading generals in the spring of 1937 had diminished Japanese apprehensions regarding Soviet fighting capacity. The United States seemed firmly set on isolation. Great Britain was too much preoccupied in Europe to exert any strong influence in the Orient.

Even if Japan had been more conciliatory it is doubtful whether armed conflict could have been avoided. China was in a mood to take two forward steps for every backward step which Japan might take. Japanese failure to adopt any strong measures after several murders of Japanese by mobs and individuals in China during the last months of 1936 was too optimistically interpreted in China as a sign of weakness. The last wavering toward moderation of Japan's China policy coincided with the brief tenure of office of Mr. Naotake Sato, a diplomat of definitely liberal views, as Foreign Minister early in 1937. Mr. Sato made several conciliatory gestures, — unaccompanied, to be sure, by any concrete acts, — and Japanese businessmen and financiers visited China in an effort to find some basis for economic collaboration. But nothing permanent came of this short-lived phase. China, quite naturally unwilling to see a further growth of Japanese expansion in its territory, deliberately protracted and sabotaged negotiations with Japanese economic groups for railway and mining development in its northern provinces.

Under these circumstances only a spark was needed to set off an explosion. This was supplied when Japanese soldiers attached to the Peking Legation garrison,[2] engaged in

[2] After the Boxer Expedition of 1900, China was compelled to permit the stationing of foreign troops in Peking and Tientsin, and along the line of the Peking-Tientsin railway. This was a most valuable opening wedge

nocturnal military exercises, exchanged shots with a Chinese post stationed at the Lukowkiao Bridge, about twelve miles from Peking, on the night of July 7. Who fired the first shot will probably never be known with certainty, nor is the fact very important. Had the Lukowkiao clash never taken place, the irreconcilable conflict would have broken out on some other occasion.

The circumstantial evidence of premeditation, so strong in the case of the Mukden bomb incident which preceded the seizure of Manchuria, is absent in the Lukowkiao skirmish. Whereas the Japanese troops in Manchuria swung into action with a speed and precision that suggested long prearrangement, there was an interval of three weeks between the first exchange of shots and the attack in force on Peking which marked the abandonment of all hope of compromise. Once or twice during this interval the outlook for adjustment seemed fairly promising. But the forces that were pushing towards war were too strong. So intense was the feeling against surrender on the part of the Chinese junior officers and soldiers that some promises to withdraw from specified areas, given by General Sung Che-yuan, commander of the Chinese forces, could not be implemented. The Japanese began to pour in additional troops from Japan and Manchoukuo. The breaking point came toward the end of July, when minor clashes at Langfang, on the Peking-Tientsin railway, and at one of the gates of Peking, were followed by a large-scale Japanese offensive against the old capital, which drove all Chinese troops from its environs.

This was closely accompanied by two events which were suggestive, in different ways, as to the future course of the

---

for the Japanese conquest of North China, since Japan, in time of peace, could maintain substantial garrisons in the two largest cities of North China.

war. For some eighteen months before the beginning of hostilities a Japanese-sponsored state had existed in East Hopei, the former demilitarized zone where China was forbidden to maintain troops under the terms of the Tangku Truce of 1933. The Chinese armed police at Tungchow, capital of this state, after hearing false reports of Chinese victories, promptly rebelled, despite their period of training under Japanese officers and instructors, and massacred all Japanese and Koreans on whom they could lay their hands — men, women, and children. This incident was prophetic of Japan's inability to enlist any reliable Chinese support in the future years of the war.

About the same time the very small Japanese force in Tientsin (most of the Japanese troops had been sent inland to take part in the attack on Peking) was unexpectedly attacked by Chinese police in that city, where no resistance had been expected. With a little more effort the Chinese could have wiped out the small Japanese force, captured the airdrome, and destroyed a number of airplanes. But this last decisive effort was not made and the Japanese held out until reënforcements arrived. Subsequently the Japanese carried out a punitive bombing of the Chinese part of Tientsin and took special pains to bomb and burn down Nankai University, which they regarded as a stronghold of nationalism and anti-Japanese feeling. Almost two years later I found many of the professors and students of Nankai and of two former Peking universities established in Kunming, in the remote southwest of China, where they were carrying on their work as well as possible with scanty resources and technical equipment.

This Tientsin revolt was typical of a Chinese weakness which was to crop up again and again during the war: inability to press home an initial advantage decisively, to carry through an attack with irresistible dash.

As early as July 18, Chiang Kai-shek issued a statement declaring there could be no settlement which would "infringe upon the territorial integrity and sovereign rights of the nation. If Peking should become a second Mukden, what is to prevent Nanking from becoming a second Peking?"

This hypothetical question indicated the rejection of any "appeasement" theory and a conviction that Japanese appetite would simply grow with eating. This statement contained the following firm declaration, which has been frequently repeated, in various forms, by Chiang Kai-shek and by other Chinese leaders during the war: —

Let us realize that, once war has begun, there is no looking backward; we must fight to the bitter end. If we allow one more inch of our territory to be lost, we commit an unpardonable offense against our race. What would be left to us except to throw every resource of our nation into the struggle for final victory?

But war, like everything else, moves more slowly in China than in more closely knit and highly organized countries. Even after the occupation of Peking and Tientsin a period of two weeks elapsed without big military operations. Only after fighting began in the great international commercial metropolis of Shanghai was it clear that the war would be on an all-China, not on a local scale.

During the lull after the fighting at Peking and Tientsin, Japanese subjects were hastily evacuated from Hankow, Canton, and other cities where it was impossible to protect them. Tension increased rapidly in Shanghai after Chinese police killed a Japanese naval officer and sailor near the Hungjao airdrome. Chinese regular troops moved into the zone, which was supposed to have been demilitarized after the Shanghai fighting of 1932. Japan dispatched warships and reënforcements for the force of marines which maintained its headquarters in Hongkew, the predominantly Japanese quarter of Shanghai. The inevitable outbreak of hostilities took place on August 13.[3]

On the following day Shanghai experienced the full horrors of aerial warfare over a large city. Chinese airplanes, attempting to bomb the Japanese flagship *Idzumo*, which was lying in the Whangpoo River just off the Shanghai Bund, were driven off by strong antiaircraft fire. These airplanes accidentally loosened bombs on two of the most crowded sections of the city. One bomb fell on a refugee camp, killing almost a thousand people outright. Others crashed through the roofs of two of the city's leading hotels. Eight foreigners, including four Americans, were among the many victims of this holocaust.

This was the tragic prelude to a battle that lasted for three months, far exceeding in scope and destructiveness the previous fighting around Shanghai in 1932. During the first ten days the Japanese marines were so greatly outnumbered that they were in serious danger of being thrown back into the Whangpoo River, in which case very few civilian Japanese would have escaped alive. However, they stood their ground, supported by the fire of the warships in the river, and the Chinese constitutional inability to deliver the final knockout blow in an offensive was again evident.

Japanese troops landed on the lower bank of the Yangtze

[3] The weight of evidence, I think, indicates that the Chinese forced the fighting at Shanghai. Japan at this time was averse to an extension of the fighting to Central China; but was unwilling, for reasons of prestige, to evacuate its civilians from Shanghai.

River on August 23, threatening the left flank of the Chinese position. This relieved the pressure on Hongkew and from this time the Japanese were mostly on the offensive. The numbers of troops on both sides steadily increased during the fighting; soldiers from almost every province in China were to be found in the defense lines around the city. Japanese progress was slow, because of the superior Chinese numbers and because of the difficulties of the terrain in the environs of Shanghai, which is so cut up with creeks, canals, and gullies that mechanized weapons could scarcely be employed. The Japanese, however, took full advantage of their superiority in aircraft and heavy artillery.

The first serious break in the stubborn Chinese resistance occurred in mid-October, when the Japanese captured the much-bombed North Station and drove the defenders out of the industrial suburb of Chapei, which was burned down by the Chinese themselves before they evacuated it and years afterwards remained a desolate ruin. A decisive turn in the struggle for Shanghai came about in November, when the Japanese, as a result of negligence or treachery, were able to make an unopposed landing in Hangchow Bay, thereby threatening the Chinese right flank and rear.

Throughout the fighting the Chinese had displayed great courage in standing up to the hailstorm of Japanese bombs and shells, to which they could make only a feeble reply. But like all inexperienced troops they were apt to become panicky at any sign of being outflanked or surrounded. They were exhausted after three months of unequal fighting, in which the state of medical care, staff work, and service of supply left much to be desired. So it is not surprising that the retreat from Shanghai soon became a demoralized rout. There was no serious effort to defend the strong positions which had been constructed before the war, with the aid of German advisers,[4] in the neighborhood of Soochow.[5] The Japanese armies swept on to Nanking and captured the Chinese capital on December 13.

The behavior of the Japanese troops in Nanking was extremely bad. Large numbers of civilians, as well as almost all captured Chinese soldiers, were slaughtered. Thousands of women were violated. Looting and burning went on for weeks after the capture of the city. These outrages, of which there is abundant eyewitness and pictorial evidence, were in striking contrast to the very high standards of discipline which Japanese troops maintain at home and to their generally excellent conduct during the Russo-Japanese War. The reasons which are most commonly put forward in explanation are the imperfect control of the newly conscripted troops by their reserve officers, the lack of regular supplies, which stimulated looting, and the lack of inhibitions which the Japanese often experiences when he leaves his native country and sets foot in China. The Japanese record was also bad in some North China towns, such as Taiyuan-fu and Paoting-fu. On the other hand the conduct of the Japanese in Peking and Tsingtao, where no resistance was encountered, was excellent, and it was fairly good in Hankow and Canton.

The capture of Nanking was perhaps the occasion when

[4] A large German military mission, headed by General Alexander von Falkenhausen, had been in Nanking for several years before the outbreak of the war. It continued to assist Chiang Kai-shek until its members were recalled by the German Government in the spring of 1938, in line with Hitler's more outspokenly pro-Japanese policy.

[5] This Soochow, a town located between Shanghai and Nanking, should not be confused with Hsuchow-fu, a railway junction on the Tientsin-Pukow line which was the objective of Japanese attack in the following spring.

Japan was closest to the conclusion of a victorious peace with the Nationalist Government of China. Peace terms were proffered to China through the mediation of the German Ambassadors in Tokyo and Nanking. The main points were the payment of war reparations by China, the stationing of Japanese garrisons in some Chinese cities, the establishment of certain demilitarized zones, the formation of an independent government in Inner Mongolia, China's adherence to the anti-Comintern Pact, and the conclusion of an economic accord between the two countries. If one is to believe Mr. Wang Ching-wei, who quit China about a year later in order to make an abortive peace proposal of his own, Chiang Kai-shek was seriously inclined to accept the Japanese terms. However, there was apparently some stiffening of these terms during the interval between the retreat from Shanghai and the capture of Nanking. And Chiang's final decision was for continued resistance. The capital was shifted to remote Chungking, a thousand miles up the Yangtze River. But Hankow, on the middle Yangtze, became the chief Chinese military and administrative centre until it fell in October 1938.

The capture of Nanking coincided with the most serious incident of the war as regards Japanese-American relations. Japanese naval airplanes bombed and sank the American gunboat *Panay* as it lay in the Yangtze River between Nanking and Wuhu. Three Standard Oil tankers were sunk at the same time. Four lives were lost, one of the victims being an Italian journalist. At the same time British gunboats and merchant ships were shelled by Japanese shore batteries, with some casualties. The confusion attending the rapid Japanese advance, the reckless exuberance of victory, and the ignorance of many of the younger Japanese officers as to the serious consequences which might follow an incident with a foreign power were probably the main background factors in these attacks on foreign vessels.

The sinking of the *Panay* aroused genuine regret and concern in higher military, naval, and diplomatic quarters in Tokyo, because it has been a cardinal point of Japanese policy to try to keep America passive. The American demands for apology and indemnification were complied with, and a sum of about two and a quarter million dollars was paid as damages. The commander of the naval air force, Admiral Mitsunagi, was recalled. This is perhaps the only case in which disciplinary action has been taken against a Japanese officer for action directed against foreigners.

Meanwhile the Japanese forces had been overrunning North China, at least so far as the large towns and railway lines were concerned. The first military operation after the capture of Peking and Tientsin was against Nankow Pass, the key to the Chinese Northwest. The Japanese sustained some losses in forcing this very strong natural position; but the occupation of the remainder of the line of the Peking-Suiyuan railway (strategically important in the event of a war with the Soviet Union) proceeded with little difficulty. Some Mongolian cavalry units coöperated with the Japanese, who were able to exploit the traditional antagonism between these nomads and the Chinese agriculturists who had sometimes pushed them out of their grazing lands. A new Mongol state, with its capital at Kweihua, was set up under Japanese auspices. Its first head, the aged Prince Yun, soon died; his successor was Prince Teh, long a recognized leader of the Mongolian nationalist movement.

There were a few comparatively good Central Government units in North China, and the Communist Eighth

Route Army, which moved across the Yellow River from Shensi into Shansi to oppose the Japanese advance, maintained its tradition, acquired during a decade of campaigning all over China against Chiang Kai-shek, of a first-rate guerrilla force, able to fight hard and move quickly on minimum rations and supplies. But most of the troops in the northern provinces were the inefficient rabble that made up the old war-lord armies and were hopelessly inferior to the Japanese in arms, discipline, and morale. The Japanese encountered their stiffest resistance in the mountains of North Shansi; but finally pierced the hostile lines here and swept in to occupy the provincial capital, Taiyuan-fu, in November, with a converging movement from north and east.

By the end of the year the Japanese had crossed the Yellow River and captured Tsinan-fu, capital of Shantung Province, and Tsingtao, its chief port, which had been built up by the Germans as the centre of their pre-war leased territory. Before leaving Tsingtao the Chinese blew up and largely destroyed a group of Japanese textile mills in the city, valued at 250,000,000 yen.

Nominally the Japanese occupation of the five northern provinces, Hopei, Chahar, Suiyuan, Shantung, and Shansi, was pretty complete after six months of fighting. But between the railway lines which the Japanese utilized for their forward movements were large stretches of unoccupied territory. Here guerrilla bands, made up of fugitive soldiers and destitute peasants, began to appear. A self-styled Hopei-Shansi-Chahar Border Government was organized with the close participation of the leaders of the Eighth Route Army. The Nationalist Government appointed a new governor of Hopei, who established his headquarters in the southern part of the province.

Control of North China would have probably represented the maximum desire of the Japanese Army before the beginning of hostilities.   But China's refusal to accept peace on Japan's terms pushed Japan into more ambitious schemes. On January 16, 1938, the Japanese Government, after holding a council in the presence of the Emperor, decided to have no further dealings with the nationalist régime.   Japan was thus committed to the programme of reorganizing China with the aid of such dependent governments as it could bring into existence in the occupied territories.

The first of these, the Provisional Government of China, was organized in Peking in December 1937.   It was headed by Wang Keh-min, a veteran Chinese politician and financier who had formerly belonged to the Anfu Clique, a political grouping which had passed into oblivion after the Kuomintang became the ruling party in the country.   A second régime of the same type was the Reformed Government, set up at Nanking in March 1938.   Its leading members were mostly unemployed politicians.

A form of loose coördination between the two régimes was created by means of a coördinating committee.   Actual fusion, however, was delayed by personal jealousies between the leaders, by the Japanese desire to establish a more inclusive federal system for the whole of occupied China, and by efforts, abortive up to the spring of 1939, to induce Chinese of greater national prominence, such as Marshal Wu Pei-fu or the former Kuomintang leader, Wang Chingwei, to take part in the new governments.   This last development was delayed both by the aversion of educated Chinese to identification with the "carpetbag" administrations which obviously owed their existence to the will of the invader and by an effective campaign of individual terrorism against Chinese who coöperate with the Japanese. Thirty-nine of these had been killed in Shanghai alone up to February 1939.

Japanese military operations lagged during the first months of 1938. Chinese morale, which had slumped to a low point at the time of the loss of Nanking, had somewhat revived and the Japanese met stronger resistance north and south of the important railway junction of Hsuchow-fu, where the north-south Tientsin-Nanking and the east-west Lunghai lines cross. Moreover, there were differences of opinion in Tokyo as to how far the Japanese advance into China should be pressed. Some Japanese military leaders, concerned about the potential threat from the Soviet Union, were opposed to advancing beyond the line of the Yellow River.

However, more adventurous counsels prevailed. The Japanese forces sustained a reverse, the proportions of which were considerably exaggerated in the foreign press, at the town of Taierchwang, in Southern Shantung, early in April. A division which had rushed ahead too recklessly was cut off and forced to retreat with substantial losses. But in May a combined movement from north and south led to the capture of Hsuchow-fu. The appointment as War Minister of a fighting general, Seishiro Itagaki, signalized a determination to march on to Hankow.

The easiest way to realize this objective, by utilizing the Lunghai and Peking-Hankow railways, was blocked when the Chinese broke the Yellow River dikes near Chengchow and turned a large stretch of country into an impassable morass. The main Japanese advance was then directed up the mighty Yangtze River, a subsidiary force also making use of the Hwai River, farther to the north. Anking was taken on June 12, Kiukiang on July 26. As was often the case during the war, the Chinese resistance was spotty — steadfast at some points, weak and confused at others.

After the capture of Kiukiang, the last large town on the Yangtze below Hankow, the Japanese advance visibly slowed down. The typical diseases of the Central China summer, cholera, dysentery, malaria, took a heavy toll. The Chinese took advantage of the network of lakes south of the Yangtze and of the low mountains to the north of the river. They also put up a conspicuously stubborn fight along the railway which runs from Kiukiang to the important military and administrative centre of Nanchang. Indeed the latter town was only taken when Japan resumed active operations, after a winter lull, in March 1939.

October, however, proved to be Japan's month of victories. A surprise landing in Bias Bay on October 12 caught the Chinese completely off their guard. Canton, metropolis of South China and the cradle of the Kuomintang, fell practically without resistance on the twenty-first. The capture of Canton cost the Japanese only seventy-seven killed. Four days later Hankow was taken, the Chinese evacuating in fairly good order.

With the occupation of Canton and Hankow Japan achieved its chief military objectives. All China's main ports and its six largest cities (Peking, Tientsin, Shanghai, Nanking, Canton, and Hankow), 80 or 90 per cent of its railway network, and much the greatest part of its industrial plant were in the hands of the invaders. In a war between two highly organized European countries such a situation would mean the end of effective resistance.

But China's weakness, its very low level of economic development, is also a source of strength. Every province lives much on its own resources, with the masses of the people eating homegrown foodstuffs and wearing homemade clothing. So the loss of large centres and railways, while it disorganizes administrative activity and cripples the capacity for systematic military resistance, is not paralyzing to the whole life of the country, as it would be in Great Britain or Germany or Belgium. The course of the war has shown that Japan can take any place in China within geographical reason. But it has also shown that huge, loose, amorphous China has no positively vital centre, the capture of which would mean the end of the struggle.

After the loss of Canton and Hankow, Chiang Kai-shek continued to send out messages of defiance from Chungking. To the sympathetic British Ambassador to China, Sir Archibald Clark-Kerr, whom he met in the interior soon after the fall of Hankow, Chiang Kai-shek outlined his future strategy in approximately the following terms: —

We still possess a vast inland empire, where the Japanese cannot follow us, except at the price of ruinously extending their lines of communication in difficult mountainous country. These provinces in the interior have been neglected in the past but are rich in natural resources, in timber and in mineral ores. We now have the opportunity to develop these regions with refugee capital and refugee brains and labor from the occupied districts. We shall not abandon this occupied territory; our guerrillas will make it impossible for the Japanese to enjoy any peace or to extract any profit from their temporary conquests. And when we take back our lost territories, as we shall, we will have behind us a stronger, richer country.

Neither Chiang Kai-shek nor any intelligent Chinese with whom I have talked anticipates a speedy expulsion of the Japanese from the centres which they have occupied.

China's weakness in aircraft and artillery alone would pre-
clude such a possibility. The Chinese reckoning is on a war
of attrition which will wear down Japan and lead ultimately,
if not to a Japanese revolution, at least to a drastic change of
Japanese policy. China is also counting on the possibility of
a change of the international situation in its favor. T. V.
Soong, one of China's most prominent financiers and brother
of the three famous Soong sisters, Mme. Chiang Kai-shek,
Mme. Sun Yat-sen, and Mme. H. H. Kung, remarked to
me at a time when the Czechoslovak crisis was at its
height: —

What is worst for China is the present state of chronic alarm and
tension in Europe. In the event of an outright war between the
democracies and the dictatorships China would ultimately benefit, because the democracies, although slower moving, are vastly stronger
in natural resources; and China would share in their victory. China
would also gain from a genuine appeasement in Europe. But
China's natural friends, Great Britain and France, cannot pull their
full weight in the Orient when they are constantly confronted with
crises in Europe.

The Japanese are also thinking in terms of a prolonged
struggle. War Minister Itagaki has spoken of the likelihood of a ten years' or twenty years' war. One Japanese
officer has suggested the cheerful idea that the present conflict is the prelude to a century of warfare. And the Japanese, like the Chinese, offer arguments to show that time is
on their side. They maintain that their possession of the
ports and the rail and river arteries will paralyze any Chinese
efforts at military revival or economic reconstruction. They
point out that some of the largest normal sources of Chinese
revenue, the customs, the salt tax (largely derived from

coastal districts under Japanese occupation), and the consolidated tax (a levy on industrial property), have now passed into Japan's hands. They foresee a gradual crumbling of Chinese irregular resistance in the occupied territory and increasing dissension and impotence within the nationalist ranks.

By 1939 the Sino-Japanese conflict had become at once less and more than a war. It was less than a war because the scale of hostilities sharply decreased after the fall of Hankow. The fighting has become largely a matter of small Japanese drives for limited objectives, frequent "mopping-up" expeditions against guerrillas, and air raids on towns and routes of communication in the interior. On the Chinese side military initiative is largely restricted to partisan raids on Japanese outposts and lines of communication, together with well-organized terrorism against Chinese who cast in their lot with the invaders. This kind of warfare could go on for a long time without necessarily leading to the exhaustion or collapse of either side.

At the same time the struggle is more than a war. It is a supreme test of national endurance. The front is at once everywhere and nowhere. The Japanese are strung out over thousands of miles of thinly held lines of communication. They have occupied ten of China's provincial capitals. But there is not a single province which they have yet thoroughly reduced to order and submission.

With each country thinking in terms of a prolonged endurance contest the nonmilitary factors become increasingly important. When Japan is able to buy Chinese foodstuffs and raw materials for yen or for the Japanese-sponsored currency which has been introduced in North China, it is the equivalent of success on the battlefield. When China is able to route its exports away from Japanese-controlled territory, to reach foreign buyers through Burma or Indo-China or through some of the leaks in the Japanese blockade, it is a score for China. Bank notes are almost as important as bombs in the present struggle.

It is a question of capital importance whether Japan can, within a reasonably near future, restore sufficient order in the occupied territories to set about the profitable exploitation of the coal, iron, and cotton which are North China's main economic resources. And this, in turn, depends on the success or failure of the guerrilla warfare on which China is placing great reliance. Japanese military leaders profess contempt for this form of resistance.

"The guerrillas are like flies in summer," General Yamshita, Chief of Staff of the Japanese Army in North China, remarked to me early in 1939. "They are annoying, but we can easily brush them aside." And War Minister Itagaki about the same time told me that guerrilla activity had been reduced by 80 per cent during the year 1938. As proof of this statement he asserted that by the end of 1938 there were, on the average, fifty train wrecks, derailments, and other accidents a month as a result of guerrilla activity, whereas at the beginning of the year the number of such accidents averaged two hundred and fifty. Itagaki, who, as one of the active founders of Manchoukuo, had a good deal of experience in combating irregular warfare, went so far as to predict that it would be eliminated in North China by the end of 1939.

It is a frequent Japanese argument that the experience of Formosa, Korea, and Manchoukuo will be repeated in China. In all these countries the first years of Japanese administration were marked by a good deal of partisan activity, which gradually subsided with the passing of time. At present Korea and Formosa are entirely peaceful and the scope of semi-political banditry in Manchoukuo, by the testimony of well-informed foreign observers, had diminished very substantially between my first visit to that country in the autumn of 1935 and my last visit early in 1939.

To be sure the parallel with earlier Japanese conquests is not necessarily valid. Japan is dealing with an enormously larger territory and the national consciousness of some of the guerrillas is far higher than was the case in Formosa, Korea, and Manchoukuo. Moreover, so long as Chinese resistance is maintained in the interior, the partisans behind the Japanese lines will receive reënforcements and supplies.

However, it is difficult to cite an historical instance of such a serious military effort as Japan is making in China being frustrated by guerrilla warfare alone. Almost all foreign military observers in the Far East with whom I have talked are definitely skeptical as to the possibility of prolonged resistance in regions where the Japanese are able to maintain large forces. Moreover, the passive national temperament of the Chinese makes them less effective in partisan warfare than Lawrence's Arabs or the Irish Republican Army. The main burden of guerrilla resistance falls on the peasants in the regions which are affected, who are exposed to merciless reprisals (fairly indiscriminate shootings and burnings of their villages) when railway wrecks take place in which they are suspected of connivance. There have been cases when peasants paid the guerrillas not to attack the railways.

No uniform characterization of the guerrilla movement would be accurate, because its effectiveness varies a good deal in different provinces. The Communists and the peasants whom they have organized have caused a good deal of trouble for the Japanese in Shansi — more than Japanese generals like to admit.   On the other hand, the Reverend H. G. Romig, an American Presbyterian missionary (and American missionaries in China are very seldom pro-Japanese in sympathy), gave the following pessimistic appraisal of the guerrilla movement in Shantung in the *North China Daily News* of October 26, 1938: —

Many of the one-time guerrillas are turning into bandits and are harassing the honest and hard-working countryfolk who are getting tired of the unsettled conditions and have even expressed their preference for Japanese law and order. . . .   The guerrillas of Shantung are fighting a losing fight and this province seems to be doomed to complete Japanese domination.   The Japanese hold all lines of communication and control the coast, the people have had enough of war and disorder, and the will to resist appears to be waning fast.

Missionaries, because of their prolonged residence in the country, are usually reliable reporters of local conditions; and during a brief visit to Tsingtao early in 1939 I found that Mr. Romig's views were shared by some other foreigners.   There is always a rather thin dividing line between guerrilla warfare and banditry; and this line is very easily transgressed in China.

Japanese losses in men and material from partisan raids are not sufficiently serious to force Japanese evacuation of the occupied districts.   It is still an open question, I think, whether guerrilla activity will prevent profitable exploitation of these regions.   The situation in the first months of 1939 was that the Japanese were getting a good deal of industrial salt out of North China and were also able to operate on a small scale certain iron and coal mines which were located along railway lines within the protection of local garrisons. On the other hand, Japanese plans for replacing a considerable amount of American and Indian cotton with North China cotton are held up because so much of the territory away from the railways is held by guerrillas who forbid the planting of cotton and encourage the peasants to plant food crops as a substitute.

What of China's prospects of holding out in the deep interior? There is no decisive reason why this resistance may not go on for a long time, although it is most unlikely that the Chinese, without some strong outside military aid, will be able to launch any very serious counteroffensives. The output of arsenals in the interior, together with stocks of arms which were imported before the fall of Canton and new shipments which filter in through Burma and Indo-China, is sufficient for the needs of the small-scale fighting that is now going on.

China's primitive self-sufficiency has already been noted and the national currency has held up remarkably well when one considers the severe military blows which the Chinese have sustained. The free market rate of exchange for the Chinese dollar early in 1939 showed a depreciation of almost 50 per cent, compared with its pre-war value. But the internal purchasing power of the currency has not been affected to a similar extent, except in the case of foreign imports. Moreover the Chinese nationalist dollar has the advantage over the rigidly controlled Japanese yen or the Japanese-backed new bank notes in North China of being freely interchangeable for foreign currencies. In the free market of Shanghai the Japanese yen is at a premium of only 10 per cent over the Chinese dollar.

There is some defeatist sentiment in China, of which the most striking expression was the peace appeal of Wang Ching-wei, one of Sun Yat-sen's close associates and a former Premier and Foreign Minister in the Nationalist Government. Wang Ching-wei left Chungking in December and from the neutral territory of French Indo-China issued his appeal for peace negotiations on the basis of Prince Konoye's proposals of December 22.[6] He maintained that the continuation of the struggle was ruinous for China, that no effective foreign aid need be expected, and that Konoye's terms offered a way out for peace with honor.

A glamorous revolutionary in his youth, sentenced to life imprisonment for an attempt on the life of the Manchu Prince Regent, Wang Ching-wei in his later years became identified with the more conservative wing of the Kuomintang. Behind his peace appeal, behind the inarticulate peace sentiment which exists among some groups of the bureaucracy and of the well-to-do classes, lie several factors. There is a feeling of impotence in the face of Japanese military power. What perhaps weighed more strongly with Wang Ching-wei was the fear that prolonged war, with its accompanying widespread impoverishment, would lead to the triumph of Communism. To conservative Chinese, Soviet domination through social revolution is just as un-

[6] Konoye's terms were practically identical with those which were put forward by Japan toward the end of 1937 (see p. 369) except that the demand for a war indemnity was omitted. There was also a suggestion, designed as a bait for Chinese nationalist sentiment and as a blow at the foreign powers which have been supporting Chiang Kai-shek, that extraterritorial rights for foreigners should be abolished and foreign-administered concessions and settlements should be returned to China. Most Chinese nationalists were inclined to discount this offer on the ground that any such retrocession would be illusory if Japan established political and economic hegemony in China.

acceptable as Japanese domination through naked military force.

But Wang Ching-wei was promptly repudiated in Chungking and expelled from the Kuomintang. He retired to obscure private life in Indo-China, interrupted by an unsuccessful attempt on his life.[7] All Chiang Kai-shek's messages to the nation have expressed determination to continue the struggle until victory is achieved.

Behind the Generalissimo on this programme of resistance is an informal national coalition, including elements as diverse in outlook on other questions as the Communists, whose stronghold is in the northwest, and the conservative Kwangsi generals, Pai Chung-hsi and Li Tsung-yen, who had succeeded, before the beginning of the war, in giving their province an unusual measure of discipline, order, and regimentation. Kwangsi troops have made a good showing on several fronts in the war.

Chiang Kai-shek is, in one sense, a dictator who gives the final decision on every important question, military, political, diplomatic, financial. But he is also a skillful mediator, able to hold together individuals and groups which might otherwise become involved in irreconcilable feuds. There are potential elements of friction in China, although up to the spring of 1939 no serious rifts had appeared in the structure of national unity.

There is a good deal of distrust between the Kuomintang and the Communists, although the latter have been following a consistently moderate policy as regards internal politics, and have scrapped or at least shelved their former ideas of

---

[7] There are, however, occasional rumors that he will emerge as the head of a federal government for the Japanese-occupied parts of China.

sweeping social revolution. This is quite in line with the desires of the Soviet Government and the Communist International. (The latter is now an entirely subordinate agency of the former.) Stalin is far more interested in weakening Japan through prolongation of the war in China than in promoting a Chinese revolution.

In the western provinces into which the Nationalist Government has been pushed there are considerable Mohammedan and tribal minorities which have not always been on the best terms with the Chinese. One also encounters some antagonism between the old-fashioned semi-feudal "bosses" of the sleepy interior and the nationalist officials and refugees from the occupied areas who have been pouring into Szechuen, Kweichow, and Yunnan. The governor of remote Yunnan, in the extreme southwest, Lung Yun, is an old-fashioned war lord who concentrates in his own hands military, political, and financial power and has no Central Government troops in Yunnan to act as a restraining influence on him. Yunnan, incidentally, has assumed a position of unprecedented importance because it is the terminus of two of China's three chief routes of communication with the outside world. These are the Burma highroad and the narrow-gauge railway from Indo-China.[8]

While it would be unwise to overlook these possible forces of future disunion, the newly developed Chinese national spirit which made it imperative for the government to take a stand against further Japanese encroachment in 1937 is still

[8] The third is the long "Red route" from the Soviet Union across Chinese Turkestan to Lanchow and Sian. This is an old caravan trail which has been adapted for motor transport. Trucks which are sent over this long route of almost three thousand miles of very rough going are often left with the Chinese, because the return haul is considered to involve too much wear and tear.

strong. No military commander of any prominence has gone over to the Japanese. Even if Chiang Kai-shek should come to the conclusion that a compromise peace is inevitable (and of this there is still no sign) it is doubtful whether he could carry the country with him. The Communists certainly, the Kwangsi generals probably, would continue to fight.

Briefly summarized, the results and prospects of the Sino-Japanese War, as its second year draws to a close, are as follows. Despite Chinese progress during the years before the beginning of the war, Japan's margin of military superiority remains decisive. The Japanese have been able, with varying degrees of delay, to capture every military objective at which they have aimed. There has been no case when the Chinese have been able to retake an important city which has been lost. There is no reliable account of losses in the war. There is no record of Chinese casualties, and the periodic Japanese estimates of their own losses seem to err on the side of understatement. A Japanese War Department statement early in 1939 reported a little over fifty thousand killed. The actual figure, I suspect, is a little more than double this number — somewhere between one hundred and one hundred and fifty thousand killed. China's losses can only be a matter of guesswork; they may run as high as a million. The discrepancy between China's losses and Japan's is attributable partly to China's military inexperience and inferior weapons, partly to the appallingly inadequate provision for the wounded, great numbers of whom die for lack of proper medical care.

As against this preponderance of Japanese military strength, China has displayed unprecedented national unity and constancy in the face of a long series of defeats. If this spirit is maintained China may hold out indefinitely behind the mountain ranges that guard its interior, although the chances of driving the Japanese into the sea seem slight to an outside observer.[9]

Traveling in the interior of China, one finds improved roads, many new buildings in the towns, a number of new mines and factories starting up, partly with government funds, partly with private capital which has fled from the zones of Japanese occupation. In some cases machinery and equipment have been moved bodily into the interior. A movement for industrial coöperatives as a means of promoting the output of goods for everyday consumption has been launched and has made considerable progress, especially in the northwest. There has been a large influx of educated Chinese from Peking, Tientsin, Shanghai, Nanking, and Canton into the remote hinterland; Chengtu, in Szechuen, and Kunming, in Yunnan, are now perhaps China's two leading cultural centres, because so many "universities in exile" have established themselves in these reasonably safe towns of the interior. This influx of intelligentsia has brought about some reforms and a considerable quickening of the pace of intellectual life.

But the realization of Chiang Kai-shek's dream of build-

[9] Mao Tse-tung, outstanding Chinese Communist leader, published a rather schematic prophecy of the course of the war which is endorsed by many Chinese nationalists who do not share his social and economic views. The war is divided into three stages, one of swift Japanese advance (now ended), one of stalemate, then one of triumphant Chinese recovery. The first stage has worked out in practice and this may well be true as regards the second; but only the eye of nationalist faith can envisage China, land-locked, without substantial heavy industries and cut off from regular sources of foreign supply, launching a successful large-scale offensive, except on the possibility that some stronger power might divert the major share of Japan's attention and military resources.

ing up a strong industrialized China faces several formidable obstacles.   The provinces in which the new industries are to be established (Szechuen, Yunnan, Kweichow) are lacking in skilled labor and inhabited mainly by illiterates.   Essential materials can only be imported through expensive and round-about routes of limited carrying capacity.[10]   Finally, every new industrial centre is within range of Japanese air bombing.

Progress under such conditions is certain to be slow, although two important results of the war are likely to be a more even spread of the educated class over China and the opening up of communication with the outside world through China's neglected back door in the southwest.   Far more important than the Burma highway is the railway which is being constructed from Kunming to Lashio, in Burma. While this cannot be completed before the end of 1941 it will open up a new trade route which may well be of great importance, especially if the division of China into Japanese and nationalist spheres endures for a long time.

Dogmatic certainty either that Japan will conquer all China or that China will wear Japan down to the point of exhaustion, collapse, and revolution is usually the product of wish-

[10] I was able personally to collect some data on the French Indo-China railway (from Hanoi to Kunming) and on the Burma highway during a visit to Kunming in February 1939.   The railway, a remarkable piece of mountain engineering, is only operated in the daytime on the Chinese side of the border because of the danger of accidents.   Its carrying capacity is about 90,000 tons a month, and the French authorities in Indo-China, worried about possible Japanese designs on the colony, have not permitted shipments of munitions.   The director of military transportation in Kunming informed me that about one hundred trucks had arrived in Kunming over the Burma highway in January.   This is scarcely the equivalent of a single freight train.   There are ambitious plans for a daily service of forty trucks at each end of the road; but the liability of the highway to wash-outs, the inadequate surfacing, and the imperfect strength of some of the bridges are serious obstacles to the dispatching of large regular shipments of munitions and supplies by this route.

ful thinking.   The issue of the war, I think, still hangs in the balance.   It depends in no small measure on such imponderables as the national stamina of the two peoples and such unpredictable factors as the course of events in Europe.

Even if Chinese resistance should crumble and subside, preparing the way for an "undeclared peace" as the sequel to the undeclared war, the struggle would not be over.   As a shrewd foreign observer in Manchoukuo once remarked to me: —

"I never knew a Chinese here who privately did not hate the Japanese.   But the Chinese temperament is such that his hatred might go on festering for three hundred years, provided there were no convenient opportunity for an explosion."

XV

JAPAN AT WAR

THE war has been a searching test of Japan's national strength. It has revealed some of the weaknesses and limitations of the Island Empire. It has also disposed of the fallacy that Japan is so weak, politically and internally, as to be foredoomed to collapse under the strain of protracted hostilities. Japan approached the end of the second year of the war somewhat winded, but far from exhaustion or collapse. The ever-expanding machinery of national mobilization, human and material, has functioned smoothly and without open opposition. There have been no serious strikes, no riots or mutinies, no recognizable signs of acute war-weariness.

Outside Japan one often hears the question: What do the Japanese people think of the war? The correct answer, I believe, as regards the majority of the peasants, laborers, handicraftsmen, small shopkeepers, who make up the bulk of the population, is that they do not think at all, in the sense of analyzing, questioning, and reflecting. To them the war is the dispensation of a mysterious higher power, something like an earthquake, a fire, a flood, which they are powerless to avert or check.

No people in the world, not even the subjects of the European totalitarian states, are so trained to act automatically, without doubt or questioning, in a moment of

national emergency. Not only does the Japanese reservist
know where and how he must report for service; etiquette
and custom prescribe how he must be seen off at the station,
and even the ceremonial bows which his friends and neighbors must exchange with his parents when they congratulate
the latter on the glorious destiny which has befallen their
son in being called to arms.

I once asked a student in one of Japan's best preparatory
schools, himself the son of a highly educated family, how
much discussion of the war went on in the school, whether
the students argued about the rightness of the war and about
Japan's prospects of victory. His answer was illuminating
in its simplicity: —

"The students really don't discuss the war very much.
They know Japan is right. They know Japan will win."

A minority of the Japanese, mostly of the younger generation, share the army leaders' dreams of imperial grandeur
and destiny. This minority is very articulate. Another
minority, necessarily very inarticulate and largely composed of Westernized Japanese who are still affected by the
trends of the liberal twenties, are opposed to the war and
pessimistic about its ultimate results.[1] These suppressed
critics foresee a Japan that will be weakened and isolated after
the war, unable to realize economic benefits from its military
success, perhaps drawn into a fatal conflict with some stronger
power or combination of powers.

[1] There have been many hundreds if not thousands of arrests of suspected
"Reds" or antiwar liberals in Japan since the beginning of the war,
Mr. Kanju Kato, Left-Wing labor leader, and many of his associates in
political and trade-union activity were arrested in sweeping police raids in
December 1937. I do not know, however, of any executions for antiwar
activity. Japan at war, on its "home front," is still less ferocious than
the Soviet Union and Germany at peace.

But the predominant mood in Japan, so far as I could judge, has been neither enthusiasm nor protest, but rather resigned, stoical acceptance. One factor that militates against enthusiasm is the general feeling that no glory is to be won from defeating the Chinese. In this respect Japanese sentiment is comparable with what most Americans would probably feel in the event of a war with Mexico.

It has been a significant feature of Japanese war propaganda to exaggerate the amount of help which China has been receiving from the Soviet Union, Great Britain, and France. The purpose of this exaggeration is to convince the people that they are fighting, not China, but stronger powers which are standing behind China and trying to thwart Japan's legitimate demands for expansion. Censorship also keeps from the Japanese people any knowledge of the outrages which have been committed in many captured cities, any conception of the scope of Chinese resistance in the areas which are partially occupied, and any information about occasional Japanese setbacks.

On the military side Japan has not suffered enough to impair seriously the national morale. A great asset in this connection has been Japan's ability to keep the war outside its own territory. There is a vivid contrast between the Japanese city, where life in school, shop, and factory goes on much as before, and the many Chinese towns where normal activities are largely suspended or curtailed because of the constant menace of air bombing.

The war has thrown into clear relief the strong side of Japan's economy, self-sufficiency in food, and its weak side, the shortage of many essential raw materials, of gold and foreign currency. The Japanese Empire, with the addition of Manchoukuo, can feed its population virtually without foreign imports. Korea and Formosa can make up for any deficiency in the rice production of Japan Proper. The waters of the Pacific supply an abundance of fish. Manchoukuo provides soya beans and Formosa furnishes its contribution of sugar and fruits. The normal diet of the Japanese can be assured from these sources. Given reasonable efficiency in distribution, there would seem to be no danger of the food shortage which is the most demoralizing factor in war, short of outright defeat in the field.

On the other hand the hostilities in China, far less exacting as regards wastage of men and materials than would be a war with the Soviet Union or with one of the Western powers, have brought out the weak spots in Japan's economic balance sheet. Not only has it been necessary to stint to the limit civilian domestic consumption of cotton, wool, rubber, and metals; it has also proved impossible to maintain export trade at the previous level. Economically unproductive orders for war materials receive priority in allotments of the limited stocks of foreign exchange. Consequently even firms which propose to export their goods, thereby realizing valuable foreign currency, often experience difficulty and delay in receiving permits for purchase of imported raw materials.

By extremely drastic reductions in imports (a system of elaborate state control of foreign trade has grown up since the beginning of the war) Japan achieved a nominally favorable trade balance of about 60,000,000 yen in 1938. The precise figures were 2,896,701,000 yen (a decline of 12.7 per cent) in exports and 2,836,209,000 yen (a decline of 28.3 per cent) in imports. But the real situation is much less reassuring for Japan's balance of international payments than these figures, by themselves, would show, because Japan ran up a huge favorable balance (over 600,000,000 yen) in its trade with the countries of the so-called yen bloc, mainly with Manchoukuo and North China. Now the currencies of these countries are quite worthless in international exchange, so that Japan's real adverse balance of international trade amounted to about 550,000,000 yen.

Two years of war have eaten heavily into Japan's gold reserves. Figures on the exportation of the yellow metal have been treated as a secret since the beginning of the war. But it is known from foreign sources that these exports were 862,000,000 yen in 1937 and about 620,000,000 yen in 1938. At the beginning of 1938 the empire possessed a gold reserve of 801,000,000 yen. A sum of 300,000,000 yen from this fund has been earmarked as an export-promotion fund and most of this has apparently leaked away, leaving Japan with little visible gold, apart from the remaining 501,000,000 yen, which is supplemented by an annual output of newly mined metal to the value of some 200,000,000 yen.

The war, which has been costing Japan approximately 10,000,000 yen (2,800,000 American dollars) a day, has been financed almost entirely through new issues of state bonds.[2] The Japanese national debt has been growing rapidly. Between 1931 and 1936 (mainly because of ex-

---

[2] Japan has probably spent four or five times as much as China on the war. This reckoning is not so favorable to China's prospects of ultimate victory as it might seem, however, because China has sustained vast losses in sources of revenue, productive plants, and so on, whereas Japan's factories and shipping have been entirely untouched by war devastation. The yen for many years has been pegged at about one shilling twopence and has fluctuated in line with the movements of the British pound. Since the beginning of the war the yen, like the mark, the lira, the Soviet ruble, has been held at an artificial value by state control measures. While its nominal value is about twenty-eight cents its free market value outside of Japan is about eighteen cents, about 10 per cent higher than that of the depreciated Chinese dollar.

penses connected with the occupation of Manchuria) it rose from six billion to ten billion yen. By the end of 1938 it had reached the figure of sixteen billions and it is likely to pass the twenty-billions mark by the spring of 1940.

The total emission of "China Incident bonds" up to the beginning of 1939 was 5,630,500,000 yen. While there has been a strenuous effort to pass on these bonds to banks, insurance companies, and the general public, the quantity of unsold bonds in the possession of the Bank of Japan, the central bank of issue, has steadily increased, with the result that the currency in circulation has expanded. The precise figures in this connection are as follows: —

	Bonds held by Bank of Japan	Note issue
End of 1936	829,073,000 yen	1,865,703,000 yen
End of 1937	1,387,229,000 yen	2,305,071,000 yen
End of 1938	1,841,407,000 yen	2,754,923,000 yen

A currency increase of almost 50 per cent within two years indicates a tendency toward inflation, especially if one considers that goods for everyday consumption have decreased in quantity and deteriorated in quality. Japan is not rich enough simultaneously to carry on a war and to keep up its normal peacetime production. The people have been compelled, for the sake of airplanes, guns, and shells, to forgo, not butter, which few of them eat anyway, but leather shoes, cotton and wool clothing, and many little comforts and conveniences.

Accurate economic reporting has become impossible in Japan because many important statistics have been withheld from publication since the beginning of the war. But the general index of Japanese industrial production showed a negligible increase (from 167.3 to 171.2) between the first

half of 1937 and the first half of 1938. As war output unmistakably increased very substantially during this period
there was clearly a decline in production for civilian consumption.

Many substitutes are being introduced, with a view to cutting down imports. For example, charcoal is recommended
instead of gasoline. There is a compulsory mixture of staple
fibre with wool and cotton. People are urged to wear the
old-fashioned geta, or clogs, instead of leather shoes. There
have been more fanciful suggestions about the extensive use
of whaleskin and sharkskin. The building of new schools
and the installation of new telephones have been forbidden
and practically all nonmilitary construction that requires the
use of steel has been suspended. The gains in the Japanese
standard of living since the World War (mainly expressed
in terms of a wider range of homemade cheap manufactured
goods and an extension of transportation facilities) have been
largely eaten up by the present war.

Japan at war faces two main economic problems. The
first is that of keeping its international balance of payments
in order, despite the stress and strain of unproductive war
imports. The second is to ward off what Japanese sometimes refer to as "malignant inflation," to distinguish it from
the moderate type, the existence of which is already admitted.[3] Of these two problems the former is, I think, the
more serious.

Inflation can always be held in check under totalitarian
wartime economics through the introduction of a widespread

[3] The *Oriental Economist*, a leading Japanese publication in the
economic field, observes in its issue of February 1939: "The changes in
the accounts of the Bank of Japan signify that an inflationary movement
of certain proportions has been under way in Japan since the outbreak of
the China hostilities."

system of state control and rationing. So far this has not been necessary as regards foodstuffs. But Japan's industries are more and more operating under a complicated system of licenses and permits which applies to raw materials, to capital, and to distribution of labor. A legal basis for this wartime state control has been provided by the omnibus National Mobilization Act, passed by the Diet under strong pressure from the army in the spring of 1938. This act gives the government power to do almost anything in the industrial field, from conscripting labor for essential enterprises to expropriating property and limiting dividends.

Moreover, it must be remembered that the funds which are raised through the flotations of bonds revolve within a comparatively narrow circle. After the bonds are sold the money, for the most part, is paid to the industries and enterprises which are contributing to the prosecution of the war. The industrialists then deposit the money in the banks, which are thus enabled to purchase more bonds.[4]

The question of obtaining an adequate supply of gold and foreign exchange is more serious because its successful solution depends on factors which are largely outside of Japan's control. Japan's export trade with countries outside the yen bloc declined by about 35 per cent during 1938 because of a combination of causes: higher production costs due to the rising price level in Japan; diversion of some factories from export production to war manufactures; the business setback in the United States; boycotts in various parts of the world. The consensus of opinion in Japanese economic circles is that 1939 can be weathered without acute difficulty as regards foreign payments, but that 1940 and 1941 will be difficult

---

[4] During 1938 Japanese bank deposits increased by 3,370,000,000 yen and reached the figure of 19,117,000,000 yen.

years. It is hoped that by this time Japan will be able to extract from China enough coal, iron, cotton, and other mineral and agricultural products to lessen dependence on America and Europe. Whether this reckoning of conquest will be justified remains to be seen. The high-speed industrial and mining development which is being pushed ahead energetically in Manchoukuo, despite shortages of labor and materials, is another effort to find additional resources within Japan's own currency frontiers.

While the war, which has lasted far beyond Japan's original calculations of a few weeks or a few months, has thus imposed some fairly severe economic and financial strains, the Island Empire shows no signs of impending collapse. Theoretical economists who work out elaborate calculations to show that at some given time Japan must quit because its gold or its oil or some other vital material will be exhausted overlook the immense element of elasticity which war imparts to a nation's economy. It is quite fallacious to forecast a nation's wartime industrial effort by compiling figures of peacetime production. For ever since the ancient wars when women donated their hair to be used as bowstrings war has stimulated the use of substitutes, has brought into play unsuspected resources. Japan's cupboard has not been scraped entirely bare. Foreign securities held by Japanese firms and subjects could still be mobilized as a last resort. More gold could be brought out of private hoards if the government should carry out a severe drive. The economy screw could be turned in many places without producing unendurable hardship. With the period of big campaigns in China apparently ended, the use of expensive imported foreign war material may taper off.

This same consideration of elasticity applies to the much

discussed question of applying sanctions against Japan. Sympathizers with China often suggest that if America alone, or America in coöperation with the European democratic powers, would stop shipments of essential raw materials to Japan and cease purchasing Japanese goods, the forward thrust in China would soon come to an inglorious end. However, estimates of the effect of withholding oil or other materials from Japan are not of convincing value when no one knows with certainty the extent of Japan's military and naval reserves of such materials. Most Japanese believe that the army and navy possess emergency stocks of oil sufficient for two or three years.

Moreover believers in sanctions as an alternative to war, as a bloodless means of checking an aggressive power, seem to be lacking in a sense of elementary psychology. For a government that has enforced the sacrifices and aroused the emotions that are a part of war to retreat under visible foreign pressure would be equivalent to committing suicide. There are certainly enough nationalist fanatics in Japan to machine-gun out of existence a cabinet which would yield to this kind of pressure. Weak sanctions can be disregarded, written off as part of the cost of the war. Strong sanctions would most probably provoke reprisals which would soon lead up to war. If Japan found itself really threatened by deprivation of oil and minerals it would be far more likely to aim swift strokes at the Dutch East Indies, Malaya, French Indo-China, the Philippines, and other possessions of the sanctionist powers than to surrender without a struggle.

The political effect of the war has been to strengthen the "lions" of the army and navy against the "foxes" of big business. To be sure, some firms have profited by the war-industries boom. But free economic enterprise has been placed in a strait jacket. The large section of Japanese industry which depends on unhampered foreign trade has suffered severely. The soldier has more and more called the tune for the businessman and the banker. Permits are required for almost every business activity, and war profits, while not altogether eliminated, are sternly controlled.

It is doubtful whether Japan's senior military leaders desire to nationalize the big combinations of capital, although some of the younger officers and bureaucrats would favor such a course. But the army certainly proposes, in the name of national defense, to exercise a substantial measure of control over the heavy industries. War Minister Itagaki outlined the future pattern of Japanese economy in a speech which he delivered toward the end of 1938.

Heavy industries are to be placed under close state supervision, while the consumption-goods enterprises are to be left more to their own devices. Itagaki endeavored to make this programme more palatable to businessmen by promising an unlimited market in China for the output of Japan's factories. He declared that there need be no fear of a post-war slump, since the industries which are now turning out munitions could turn to the production of machinery and equipment for factories and mines in China.

Prince Fumimaro Konoye, the Premier during the first eighteen months of the war, was not a leader of Japan's drive for expansion on the continent. He is a member of the very old hereditary aristocracy, and his outlook was largely shaped by his mentor, the venerable Genro, Prince Saionji. And Saionji, like several other elderly Japanese statesmen, acquired a lifelong predilection for liberalism because of his visits, during young impressionable years, to foreign countries at a time when liberalism was more generally accepted, politically and economically, than it is to-day.

The steady broadening of the scope of the war was not the result of Konoye's design or desire. Delicate in health and somewhat inclined to hypochondria, he chafed under the burdens of a war premiership and was only induced to remain at his post by the argument that a change of cabinet in the early stages of the war would be interpreted abroad as a sign of weakness and divided counsels.

Konoye's original cabinet, which he formed a few weeks before the beginning of the fighting in China, was rather undistinguished in character. He carried out a drastic reorganization in the spring of 1938, bringing into the new cabinet two distinguished moderates, General Kazushige Ugaki as Minister of Foreign Affairs and Mr. Seihin Ikeda, long associated with the merchant-prince house of Mitsui, as Minister of Finance. With a view to placating the "strong" groups in the army, Konoye assigned the portfolio of Education to General Sadao Araki, a former War Minister and spokesman for a cult of nationalism so abstruse that Japanese themselves profess inability to render it in understandable Western terms. At the same time General Itagaki, whose prestige among the young officers was a guaranty against restless extremist outbreaks, became Minister of War.

Konoye's two moderate ministers significantly failed to survive very long. Ugaki became a target of extremist criticism because of the conversations which he carried on with the British Ambassador, Sir Robert Craigie, even though these conversations led to no concrete results in the way of satisfying British grievances in connection with Japanese military action in China. It was feared that he might become the victim of an assassination plot and the number of his personal guards was increased. By the autumn of 1938 his position had become so undermined that he felt obliged to resign. There was some difficulty in finding a candidate for the post of Minister of Foreign Affairs — a thankless office because of the habitual indifference of the Japanese military and naval authorities in China to the assurances which the Ministry of Foreign Affairs periodically extended to foreign diplomats. The post was finally assigned to Mr. Hachiro Arita, a veteran diplomat who enjoyed some prestige in nationalist circles because the anti-Comintern Pact with Germany had been signed during his previous tenure of office.

Ikeda remained in the cabinet a little longer, but was subjected to increasing pressure from the army. His personality and his position were rather strikingly similar to those of Dr. Hjalmar Schacht in Germany, and his fate was the same. When Konoye resigned with the turn of the year Ikeda was one of the few ministers who were not reappointed to the succeeding cabinet. Behind Konoye's resignation was a rather complex chain of factors: genuine weariness with the physical burdens of office; impatience at army dictation; chagrin over the failure of his peace overtures to China; apprehension, perhaps, of the adventurous courses into which Japan might be drawn by the anti-Comintern Pact. There was also a personal difficulty in the cabinet. The Home Minister, Admiral Nobumasa Suetsugu, wished to force through an artificial one-party system. Konoye was opposed to this measure and believed that a resignation of the whole cabinet would be an easier way out of the impasse than an outright dismissal of Suetsugu. The latter, along with Ikeda, failed to reappear in the new cabinet — a typical illustration of the Japanese tendency to eliminate simultaneously strong representatives of opposed viewpoints.

Konoye's successor was Baron Kiichiro Hiranuma. His appointment aroused some concern in Japan and abroad because of his long identification with the extreme nationalist camp. He was one of the founders of a conservative organization called the Kokuhonsha (Society of State Foundations) and had even been labeled as a Fascist, although there is little in his personality to suggest Hitler or Mussolini. An elderly man, with a long career in the state service which had brought him up to the rank of President of the Privy Council, Hiranuma is an old-fashioned Japanese conservative, temperamentally averse to foreign ways and modern innovations and closely associated with army leaders of similar views. During his first few months as Prime Minister he showed no disposition to strike out on extremist courses in domestic or foreign policy. His public statements indicated little deviation from the policies which had been formulated by Konoye.

Although the war has pushed Japan along the road of totalitarian economics its outward political structure has experienced little change. Periodic rumors that a one-party system would be set up either through a more or less forced coalition of the two large parties, the Seiyukai and the Minseito, or through the emergence of a new party, were not borne out during the first two years of the conflict. The Diet continued to hold regular sessions, although it exercised no real influence on state policies. There was some ventilation of local grievances in the Diet and members showed a certain amount of freedom in asking questions, although ministers developed a technique of giving evasive and essentially meaningless replies.

There has been a noteworthy eclipse of such liberalism as existed in Japan before the war. This is partly, of course, the natural result of the arrests which were mentioned earlier, of the increasingly severe censorship of newspapers, and of the intellectual magazines in which harassed Left-Wing professors formerly contrived to insert occasional "dangerous thoughts."

There has also been a change of heart on the part of what might be called fair-weather liberals and socialists. Japanese intellectual grasp of European political ideas and movements often leaves much to be desired. But the Japanese mind is both intuitive and keenly imitative. The golden age of Japanese liberalism was in the twenties, when the democratic form of government enjoyed the aura of a victorious war against a powerful military monarchy.

Now the trend, as seen from Japan, is distinctly in the opposite direction, and every new success of Hitler is a blow to the faith, never too robust, of those Japanese who would have considered themselves liberals or radicals a few years ago. A Japanese of this type, an old personal acquaintance, recently observed in private conversation: —

Morally there is little to be said for our action in China. But if one thinks in terms of national self-interest, there are three advantages which I can recognize as a result of the war. First we have smashed the possibility of a future hostile China that was growing stronger before the war. Second, our heavy industries are increasing production by leaps and bounds. We shall be a far stronger, more independent industrial nation after the end of the war. Third, the world must now realize that we are a great power.

The external aspects of Japan have not strikingly changed. There is vastly less public propaganda in the form of meetings, parades, rallies, and posters than one would have seen in any belligerent country during the World War. It would not be difficult to go to some seaside or mountain village thirty or forty miles from Tokyo and fail to see any signs that a war is in progress. The distinctive Tokyo street life, with its mixture of West and East, its rushing motor vehicles and its innumerable small shops and itinerant peddlers, each of the latter crying his wares through a special call or whistle, goes on much as before.

Yet there are changes, all in the direction of greater stringency and sobriety; and these become more numerous as the pinch of war is increasingly felt. The night life of Tokyo, never brilliant, has been appreciably damped down by the police. Dancing, always regarded with aversion by old-fashioned Japanese who see no evil whatever in properly licensed prostitution, has been almost completely suppressed. Permanent waves, very popular among the younger generation of Japanese girls, are frowned on as incompatible with the spirit of the national emergency. The Ministry of Commerce and Industry has forbidden fashion shows on the ground that these "only excite feminine vanity and encourage customers to make unnecessary purchases."

Along with the compulsory deprivations which follow from the government's policy of reducing imports to the minimum there are numerous unofficial efforts to stimulate thrift and sacrifice. People are urged to eat "Rising Sun lunches," consisting of balls of rice with pickled plums in the centre. There has been a movement to dispense with New Year and other holiday decorations, with costly entertainment and with ceremonial clothing, and some enthusiasts have gone so far as to suggest that neckties should be discarded, although this proposal has made little visible progress. Motoring for pleasure has become almost impossible because private automobiles are singled out for especially severe cuts in allowances of gasoline. The whale has been described as "man's best friend" and there are eager reckonings as to how much leather and beef could be saved through the use of whaleskin and the eating of whale steaks.

The Japanese are as natural collectivists as the Chinese are natural individualists. They respond quickly to appeals for patriotic self-denial. The Japanese employees of a Japanese-American firm which manufactures air-conditioning apparatus insisted that their own office should dispense with air conditioning in consideration of the sufferings of the soldiers in the summer heat of China. This is characteristic of a widespread feeling that even deprivations which are of no direct benefit for the prosecution of the war should be endured for their moral value. There is little difficulty in persuading the average Japanese to tighten his belt when the appeal can be made on the ground of national spirit. Japan's difficulty lies rather in the fact that the country is too lean economically to gain very much from even the most drastic process of belt constriction.

The war has brought about vast social changes in Japan, the final consequences of which can be only dimly foreseen at the present time. There has been a draining off of the chronic overpopulation in the villages as a result of mobilization for the army and labor recruiting for the munitions industries. Despite the sumptuary regulations of the police, the customary wartime profiteering finds a reflection in the increased employment of geisha, the expensive professional Japanese entertainers, and in the crowding of expensive inns and restaurants. Certain classes of skilled laborers are earning wages which are quite high by Oriental standards.

Many Japanese girls are forsaking the kitchen for the bench in the munitions factory.

On the other hand, there has been a growth of unemployment in the small handicraft industries which existed on a shoestring basis in the best of times. These industries are deprived of normal supplies of cotton, rubber, and various metals. It has been estimated that 1,300,000 persons are threatened with unemployment because of the contraction of production for peacetime consumption. As against this must be set the fuller employment and higher wages in the trades which benefit from war activity. The family system is a buffer between unemployment and absolute destitution and the state is undertaking road building and some other public works with a view to helping victims of the wartime unemployment.

What has been going on in Japan since 1931 is a revolution, although not a revolution of the type which the Chinese and their foreign sympathizers hope for. The men of the sword, descendants of the old samurai families who supply the majority of the army and navy officers, have been regaining the power and prestige which slipped away from them to some extent after the opening up of Japan to Western ways and influences.

Japanese literature is full of memoirs and stories which depict the economic decline of the unbusinesslike samurai and the rise of parvenu commoners during the Meiji Era, when the old shut-in feudal economy of self-isolated Japan was crumbling before the assaults of modern capitalism. As the empire's economic system became freer there was a stronger demand for parliamentary institutions. These acquired most reality during the twenties, when the army establish-

ment was reduced and a civilian premier felt strong enough
to enforce a naval-limitation agreement against the expressed
opposition of some of the more influential admirals.

The year 1931 was a time of great change, internally as
well as externally. The army kicked over the traces.
Without any formal *coup d'état* the political groupings
which stood for moderation in international affairs, Western
parliamentarism, and orthodox finance were reduced to com-
parative impotence. In Manchoukuo, a country three times
the size of Japan Proper, the army commenced to wield not
only military, but also political and economic power. While
Japanese big-business firms have made profits out of Manchoukuo it is the army that has drawn up the blueprints of
that country's economic development. It is the army,
primarily interested in defense considerations, that has insisted on such financially unprofitable measures as the extraction of oil from coal and the extensive utilization of low-
grade iron ore. It is the army that has given Manchoukuo
its Five-Year Plan, which closely resembles its far vaster
Russian predecessor in endeavoring to achieve a swift maximum development of those industries and mineral resources
which are most serviceable for wartime needs.

Now the war has extended this military economic control
to the occupied areas of China and, to a lesser extent, to Japan
itself. The army and the navy are carrying out a good deal
of direct economic exploitation in China. The army is
operating the railways, putting the receipts into its pockets
without paying a penny of interest to the foreign, mostly
British, bondholders. It also has a hand in many of the
monopolies which have been set up in North and Central
China. The navy is playing a similar rôle in some of the

occupied ports, notably at Tsingtao, where it has been levying tribute, in the form of high lighterage charges, on all
foreign ships which enter the port.

Japanese business has received its share of the spoils of war
in China. The octopus Mitsubishi Company has taken over
the Kiangnan Dockyard, near Shanghai. The Onota
Cement Company has appropriated the Lunghua Cement
Works in Shanghai, and a large new chemical works which
was completed near Nanking shortly before the beginning
of the war has been taken over for Japanese operation. Chinese government property has been expropriated outright.
Chinese owners of factories in zones of Japanese occupation
have been informed in many cases that they must negotiate
with Japanese firms if they desire to continue operation of
their plants. The usual Japanese terms are a 51 per cent
interest in the business.

So the army lions have left some pickings for the capitalist
foxes. But it is the fighting services that are now definitely
the senior member in the uneasy partnership with big business. There is scant consideration for those business interests
which are suffering from wartime shortages of raw materials
or for conservative business fears as to the ultimate disastrous
consequences of the present trend toward inflationary finance.
The samurai, overshadowed for a time, are again in the
saddle; the business interests must adjust themselves to the
subordinate rôle which they played during the Japanese
Middle Ages. The men of the sword, for the present
period, have acquired a definite ascendancy over the men of
gold.

Whither is the war taking Japan? Toward world power
or toward downfall? Broadly speaking, I think there are
three possible outcomes of the present struggle. Each of

these would have a definite effect on Japan's internal political, social, and economic structure.

(1) Japan may win, subjugating the northern provinces and coastal regions of China, perhaps in time adding to its empire the Oriental colonial possessions of other powers. Such a victory might be expected to consolidate the grip of the army, giving it the prestige of success. Fascism on the European model would be unlikely. The flamboyant Führer or Duce is a type that does not appeal psychologically to the Japanese, with his instinct for anonymous collectivism. The practice of attributing every military victory or other national success to "the august virtue of the Emperor" is a useful aid to national unity, a means of eliminating individual jealousies.

Moreover, Japan is not inclined to admit the need for copying foreign political models. Mr. Toshio Shiratori, Japanese Ambassador to Italy, the most outspoken extreme nationalist in the diplomatic corps and a leading spirit in the conclusion of the anti-Comintern Pact, once retorted, when I asked him whether Japan might "go Fascist": —

Why should we imitate Germany and Italy? It is rather a question of their imitating us. They have just discovered that certain ideas and institutions which Japan has maintained for several centuries are essentially sound and healthy for the progress of the state.

But while a Japan under permanent army tutelage would not duplicate the entire German-Italian political scheme, many Fascist features would be incorporated in the military state-capitalism which would probably emerge as the sequel to victory on the continent. Private capitalism would not be abolished, but would be rigorously controlled, with the building up of armed strength as the primary consideration. The regimentation which one already finds in Japanese education and social life would be stiffened in some ways, although Japan might well take a leaf out of the European Fascist books by providing more opportunities for mass recreation, more national labor service devices which would tend to break down class lines. The army, together with the Young Men's League and Reservists' Association, would take over some of the functions of a European Fascist party as the focus of all national activities.

(2) Japan may be checked without being decisively beaten. Military conquest may not be followed by profitable economic exploitation. Japan's military resources may be depleted to a dangerously low level by years of harassing guerrilla warfare. Inasmuch as China has also been gravely weakened by a devastating war which has been entirely fought on its territory, the stage might be set, if not for an enduring peace, at least for a truce. Japan would evacuate its more advanced positions, but would receive substantial economic concessions and political guaranties in North China. The difficult problem of political sovereignty in North China might be solved through the creation of a régime which would be less obviously a Japanese manikin than the present one and yet would not be directly associated with Chiang Kai-shek and the Kuomintang. The periodic Japanese flirtations with the elderly Marshal Wu Pei-fu, a powerful war lord in China fifteen years ago, might suggest the possibility of such a régime, which would serve as a kind of bridge between Japan and the Chinese Nationalist Government.

Some such compromise solution would be especially welcome to Great Britain, because it would afford the best, if not the only chance of maintaining reasonably intact the shaky edifice of foreign economic interests in China. A completely victorious Japan would permit the foreigner to remain only on sufferance; a completely victorious China might be no easier to deal with. A China that was strong enough to beat Japan would sweep away extraterritoriality and all other foreign privileges overnight and would probably be as intransigent as Mexico on all issues in which its real or supposed national economic interests conflicted with those of foreign traders.

But at the present time any conceivable formula of compromise peace falls far short of the aspirations both of Japanese imperialism and of Chinese nationalism. Such an outcome of the war could only be realized if both countries at the same time reached a stage of exhaustion where they felt that more was to be lost than gained from prolonging the struggle.

This second alternative would probably bring to Japan the return of some measure of political and economic liberalism. But many of the state controls in such fields as foreign trade and foreign exchange transactions will necessarily remain for many years because the strain which the war has placed on Japan's balance of international payments cannot be removed overnight.

(3) Japan may be smashed. This alternative cannot be ruled out, although I consider it highly unlikely, so long as Japan is only engaged in China. But the Island Empire's reckless militarists and navalists may overplay their hand. They may plunge their country into one or more wars with far stronger powers than China — with the Soviet Union, with America or Great Britain. I believe that the Japanese, with their racial solidarity and their high sense of nationalism

and discipline, would fight well against any odds up to their last ounce of collective strength. But once that last ounce of strength had been used up collapse would inevitably be swift and spectacular. In compact, highly integrated Japan there would be no gradual crumbling; breakdown would come about immediately.

It is extremely hard to envisage Japan after such a collapse because at the present time there is no strong organized opposition which could step into the place of the present government. Would the Japanese laborers and peasants and shop apprentices go on a grand orgy of killing and despoiling the well-to-do classes, ending in the establishment of some form of Oriental Communism? Or would they follow the example of Germany in defeat, nurse their wounds and their sense of nationalist wrongs and take the first opportunity to strike again for the prizes of empire, perhaps under the leadership of some unsuspected Führer who may now be fighting as an obscure private or corporal somewhere in China after being mobilized from his paddy field or his little shop? No one could predict with certainty, just as no one can anticipate precisely how a man will react to an overwhelming mental or physical shock. But my own impression of the Japanese temperament, with its absence of mob-mindedness, its deep-rooted instinct for form and ceremony, its tendency to cling desperately to the ideal of gentility, even in poverty, makes me doubt whether Japan, even in a supreme crisis of national disaster, would go the Russian road.

Which of these three alternatives does the future hold for Japan? Here again there can be no glib, ready, or certain answer. If Japan had only China to deal with and were insured against serious foreign intervention on China's behalf I am inclined to believe that its dream of continental empire would be realized, at least in part, although at a heavy cost in sacrifices and deprivations for many years to come. But Japan is being tossed in the stormy waters of world politics. It may be called on, in no distant future, to face sacrifices far exceeding anything which the war in China has demanded. The question whether Japan can rule East Asia depends not only on its own strength, military, economic, and psychological, not only on the resistance which China may still be able to offer, but on the unfolding of the tragic international drama, from which Japan cannot stand aloof.

XVI

CAN JAPAN RULE EAST ASIA?

How strong is Japan? On the answer to this question largely depends the destiny of East Asia, if not of the entire Asiatic continent. The most varied guesses have been ventured. Japan is depicted now as a nation of military and industrial supermen, now as a bluffer, a giant with clay feet likely to collapse at the first serious pressure.

Between Japan and the foreign observer are several walls to be surmounted. There is first of all the jealous secrecy that is maintained in regard to all information which has even a remote bearing on military and naval matters. Sometimes this system is carried to ridiculous extremes. Names of Japanese units which took part in operations many years ago are carefully deleted from books and magazines. An unsuspecting foreign tourist is likely to be haled before the police if he photographs such an innocent-looking object as a bunch of radishes in a fortified zone. When the Japanese forces landed in Bias Bay in order to attack Canton last October, the precise location of the landing was concealed in Japan for some time after it was known to the entire world through dispatches from Hong Kong.

But exaggerated and even absurd as some features of this system of Japanese counterespionage may be, it serves to keep even the keenest foreign observers pretty much in the dark as to the details of armament and troop movements and as to many aspects of the industries and services which cater to war needs. This atmosphere of secrecy has naturally become much more pronounced since the outbreak of the war. A good deal of industrial information which was formerly published regularly has now been suppressed. Huge exhibitions have been held to expose the alleged cunning devices of foreign spies and to warn the Japanese to be most careful in any conversations with foreigners.

A second wall against thorough, intimate knowledge of things Japanese is the personality of the average Japanese, which is apt to be reserved and repressed, with only rare and occasional lapses into unexpected frankness. Wartime conditions have naturally not made the Japanese more communicative.

A third and most effective rampart is the infinite complexity of the written language, knowledge of which is restricted to a very small class of foreign specialists. These hieroglyphs shut off the majority of even serious foreign students of Japan from direct contact with its books and publications. And very few foreigners, even of long residence in Japan, are able to carry on a conversation in Japanese, except on the simplest subjects, unless they have received the two or three years of exclusive concentrated language study which is given to diplomatic and military attachés and to missionaries.

If the written language is a strain for the Japanese themselves (poring over the characters in childhood makes an unusually large proportion of the population shortsighted), it is an admirable smoke screen against an enemy. A captured Japanese dispatch in time of war would require a major deciphering operation.

Finally, even when the physical items in Japan's balance

sheet are reckoned up, — the quality of her fighting services, her industrial power, her geographical advantages, her problems of finance, and her deficiencies in raw materials, — there still remain the intangible factors which almost defy accurate analysis.   How solid are the traditional foundations of Japanese society, the worship of the patriarchal Emperor, the family system?   How much of the Japanese way of life is ingrained and deep-rooted, how much merely the result of tradition and police regimentation and hence likely to crack under the shock of a major crisis?   How perilous, from the standpoint of the existing order, are the "dangerous thoughts" which the police are always on the alert to detect and repress?

Yet no book on the subject "Japan over Asia" would be adequate without an effort to arrive at some conclusions as to Japan's relative strength in the Pacific area compared with that of its neighbors and rivals.   Many elements, military, economic, and moral, must enter into such a calculation.

What of Japan's striking weapons, the army and the navy? As regards equipment and modern weapons, the army, despite the recent intensive efforts at rearmament, reflects Japan's industrial inferiority to America and Western Europe.   The tanks are of old models; the cavalry is still inadequately supplemented with mechanized units.   Military aviation has been stimulated by the war; but the Japanese air force is certainly still inferior to the German and Soviet in numbers and probably also in quality.   Arriving in Honolulu from Japan, one is impressed by the far more modern types of airplanes which the American Army and Navy possess.

To say that Japan has not reached the military technical level of more advanced countries is not to condemn her Far

Eastern adventure to inevitable failure. For geography is very much in Japan's favor, so long as her expansionist effort is limited to East Asia. The question of how Japan's armed forces would show up against those of a Western power is likely to remain academic, except possibly in the case of the Soviet Union, because it would be extremely difficult, if not impossible, to transport any Western army to Japan's chosen theatre of action. And while the Red Army certainly has more tanks, airplanes, and other modern weapons than the Japanese Army, the Soviet Union would face several off-setting disadvantages in the event of a war with Japan. Geography is again on Japan's side; the Soviet Union would be compelled to fight many thousands of miles away from its main centres of industry and population with a transportation system that is far from efficient even in time of peace.[1] The decimation of the higher command of the Soviet military, naval, and air forces and the atmosphere of political suspicion and intrigue of which this is an unanswerable indication find no parallels in Japan. The idea of a Japanese officer's betraying his country to a foreign power is unthinkable; and the Japanese Army is not filled with spying political commissars.

The Japanese Army, in the judgment of most foreign military observers, is stronger in morale than in material equipment. A Japanese who had been a fellow student at college in America told me that he was amazed at the amount of political training which went on during his period of mili-

---

[1] Orderly transportation is one distinct advantage of Japan over the Soviet Union. I have had a fair amount of personal experience with railway stations in both countries, and the contrast between the Japanese station, where one can accurately gauge the time by the arrival of the trains, and the Soviet station, with its hordes of people waiting to board chronically overcrowded and frequently delayed trains, is one between order and chaos.

tary service. In the Young Men's League to which he belongs before he is called to the colors, in the army itself, and later in the Reservists' Association, the Japanese conscript receives a very thorough indoctrination in nationalist ideas. The army is perhaps the best propaganda agency in Japan, and the young peasant who is the preferred type of soldier probably absorbs more ideas during his period of service than at any other time in his life.

Discipline is of a curiously paternalistic type, which is only understandable if one remembers how deeply the family system dominates Japanese psychology. The new recruit is gravely told that the company commander is his father and the sergeant is his mother. This kind of appeal would not go very far with the American Marines; but it works well in Japan, so far as the maintenance of discipline is concerned. Court-martials are almost unheard of; cases of drunkenness and disorderly conduct, among the troops in Japan, are almost unknown. The severest punishment for the soldier is to have his officer write to his family and complain about his behavior. The officers take a keen interest in their men's affairs; the mail of the company commander is filled with letters from the families of the men under his command, asking advice on all kinds of problems, from how to meet debt charges to the choice of a bride for their son. The radicalism of some of the younger officers is partly the result of their intimate knowledge of the hardships in some of the country districts.

Morale is also sustained by an extremely high-flown standard of military ethics. It is an indelible disgrace for a Japanese soldier to be captured; an officer who falls into the hands of the enemy is obligated to commit suicide at the first opportunity. A Japanese officer once told a foreign colleague who inquired why there was never any practice in retreating operations that these were unnecessary because a Japanese army would never retreat. Some officers express fear that previous easy victories, combined with lack of experience in warfare on the World War scale, may lead to overconfidence and disastrous results; but the majority believe that this absolute assurance of victory is a valuable wartime asset.

A foreign observer at one of the annual manœuvres of the Japanese Army before the outbreak of the present war observed that, while the display of airplanes and other modern weapons was not impressive, by modern standards, the fighting spirit of the soldiers was incomparable. In bayonet practice the officers had to hold back the men from turning a sham fight into a real one.

A striking feature of the Japanese Army is its extreme simplicity. It is for use, not for ornament, and makes a better impression on the battlefield than on the parade ground. Officers and men often do not shave for days at a time. Soldiers do not march in step except on parade; the Western emphasis on smartness is notably absent.

Soon after my arrival in Japan I obtained an appointment with a high officer in the Ministry of War. I was surprised to find him sitting unshaved in a tiny room with the dingiest kind of furniture. But this officer, as I realized later, was living up to the code of *Bushido,* or mediæval knighthood, which prescribes self-denial and absence of ostentation as virtues of a warrior. This is also emphasized in the following excerpt from the precepts to soldiers and sailors drawn up by the Emperor Meiji: —

The soldier and the sailor should make simplicity their aim. If you do not make simplicity your aim you will become effeminate and frivolous and acquire fondness for luxurious and extravagant ways. You will finally grow selfish and sordid and sink to the last degree of baseness, so that neither loyalty nor valor will avail to save you from the contempt of the world.

Here, as not infrequently happens, moral virtue is extracted from economic necessity. With its finances in a state of chronic strain, Japan cannot afford to pamper its troops. Officers and men alike subsist on rations of austere frugality, although the food is still more plentiful and better balanced than the diet of the peasant recruit at home.

Indifferent to smartness and precision, the military authorities are advocates of deliberate hardening exercises. An especially hot day in summer or an especially cold day in winter will be chosen for an all-day march. Gloves and vests are forbidden in winter. At the end of a stiff march troops will be ordered to ford a stream with full equipment or will be put through vigorous setting-up exercises. Endurance, in the Japanese military decalogue, ranks with courage and sacrifice among the higher military virtues.

The Japanese Army has now been subjected to the test of two years of warfare in China. Its successes were generally expected, because of Japan's well-known superiority to China in training and equipment. One feature of Japanese strategy, which could scarcely be duplicated against a stronger enemy without leading to unfortunate consequences, has been a tendency to rush ahead, especially with mechanized units, along railway lines, with scant regard for forces which may be able to threaten flank and rear. Against the Chinese, however, it has usually proved possible to escape from encirclement, although sometimes with heavier losses than would otherwise have been incurred.

Two features of Japanese military action which have won

the praise of foreign military observers have been the extreme mobility of their infantry (thanks to their ability to subsist and fight on minimum simple rations) and their skill in utilizing flat-bottomed boats on small waterways to facilitate their advance. This also speaks for the effectiveness of their previous espionage in China and for the care with which plans for future invasion had been worked out.

The war has indicated that Japan is not so weak in the air as had previously been believed. The very conditions of air combat make for utter unreliability in reports of enemy aircraft destroyed; and it would certainly be unwise to accept at face value the Japanese claims of ten Chinese airplanes destroyed for every one of their own that has been lost. But Japan certainly has retained the mastery of the air, despite Chinese purchases of British and American aircraft and the five hundred airplanes which the Soviet Union, according to a reliable foreign observer, sent to China during the first eighteen months of the war. In the air, as in other fields, Japanese fighting dash and initiative, the traditional willingness of the Japanese aviator, if he can reach his objective in no other way, to crash into it at the sacrifice of his own life, have given them a certain advantage over the more passive Chinese.

One respect in which the Japanese Army has fallen below expectations is in its highly undisciplined conduct in many Chinese cities, towns, and villages. The outrages committed in Nanking and other towns were winked at by the officers, perhaps were even conceived as a kind of Genghis Khan warning of the consequences of resistance. They have not led to demoralization in the shape of any breakdown of fighting efficiency in the field.

The Japanese military command is sometimes criticized

for excessive rigidity in adhering to a prearranged plan, in failing to allow for the possibility that an enemy may not do what he is expected to do. Here again the real test would probably only come in the event of a Soviet-Japanese war, because Japanese military superiority to China makes possible a wide margin of errors without incurring the penalty of heavy losses.

An interesting, although inconclusive trial of strength between the Soviet Union and Japan occurred in the summer of 1938 around the heights of Changkufeng, near the point where Siberia, Korea, and Manchoukuo come together. In origin the Changkufeng fighting was similar to scores of previous "border incidents"; but it far exceeded any previous clash in the scope of fighting and the numbers of casualties on both sides.

The Japanese version of the conflict was that the Soviet forces commenced to fortify the hill of Changkufeng, which was claimed as Manchoukuo territory. The Soviet Government maintained that Changkufeng was inside the Soviet frontier. After some minor desultory skirmishing the Japanese drove the Soviet troops from the hill by a surprise attack on the night of July 30. Serious fighting followed, in which the Soviet forces used tanks and airplanes, while twenty or thirty thousand men were engaged on each side.

Although sometimes intense in character, the fighting was restricted in area, since the Soviet troops made no attempt to attack other points on the border and the Japanese confined themselves to defending the crest of the height. This they still held when an agreement was reached in Moscow and fighting ceased on August 11. Subsequently, however, the Japanese troops withdrew from Changkufeng, their position being made untenable by the flooding of the Tumen River in their rear.

The strategic value of Changkufeng from the Soviet standpoint became evident when Soviet artillery was able to shell the line of the North Korean Railway, a connecting link between the important new port of Rashin and the interior of Manchoukuo. Each side endeavored to represent this miniature war as a victory. The Japanese admitted losses of 900 killed and wounded and estimated the Soviet casualties at 4500. The Soviet military authorities stated their own losses at 236 killed and 631 wounded and estimated the Japanese at 600 killed and 2500 wounded. A pamphlet entitled *How We Beat the Japanese Samurai* was jubilantly published in Moscow. Japanese Army officers with whom I have talked insist that Changkufeng reduced their apprehensions in regard to the Red Army, since its tanks made a poor showing, its airplanes failed to coördinate their bombing with the infantry attacks, and the infantry showed little fighting spirit.

The one certain thing that emerges from this crossfire of propagandist claims is that neither side desired a major war at that time. The careful localization of the hostilities and the failure of the Japanese to bring into play their own airplanes and tanks make it impossible to judge the relative strength of the two armies on the basis of this engagement. There seems to be no doubt that the Japanese troops which dug in on the crest of the height held out with great constancy against heavy artillery and airplane bombardment. Probably the net result of this clash was to inspire in each side more respect for the fighting quality of the other. This miniature war may, therefore, have been an important factor in staving off a disposition on either side to resort to large-scale hostilities.

The Japanese Navy is more up-to-date than the Army, although it is inferior to the navies of the United States and Great Britain in capital ships, seaplanes, and guns. On sea as on land, however, Japan enjoys the advantage of proximity to the prospective war zone. Any conflict in which Japan might become involved with the United States or Great Britain would have to be fought out in the waters of the Western Pacific, close to Japan's home bases. And Japan's defensive position, with one important exception, is immensely strong.

Japan Proper faces a huge ocean, across which an attacking fleet would be compelled to voyage thousands of miles, and enjoys the further protective advantage of island outposts covering the three principal directions from which an attack might be expected. The Kuril Islands, stretching out in a northeastern direction from Hokkaido to Kamchatka, are a defensive barrier against an attack from Alaska and the Aleutian Islands. The approach from the south, from Singapore and the Philippines, is covered by Formosa and the Loochoo Islands, while the far-flung South Seas Mandated Islands (a part of the Japanese Empire in everything but name) are ideally located for defense against an American advance from Hawaii. Japan has strengthened its naval position during the war by occupying Hainan Island, located midway between Hong Kong and French Indo-China and squarely athwart the sea route from Hong Kong to Singapore, and the Spratly Islands, off the coast of Indo-China, a little group of coral reefs which may be useful as advanced submarine bases.

Behind Japan are the narrow Japan and Yellow seas;

communication with its continental dependencies, Korea and Manchoukuo, and with the occupied ports of China, is short and easy. As two American naval writers say: —

There is not a naval power in the world that possesses the strength of geographic position that is Japan's.[2]

The weak spot in Japan's scheme of sea and air defense may be summed up in one word: Vladivostok. This Soviet Far Eastern stronghold is only seven hundred miles from Tokyo, by direct airline, and the flotilla of submarines which are stationed in and around Vladivostok might inflict serious damage on Japan's shipping in the event of war. Moreover, the concentration of Japan's main industries in four areas (Tokyo-Yokohama, Osaka-Kobe, Nagoya, and North Kyushu) provides tempting targets for air bombardment, although Japanese air defenses and the uncertain winds and weather make it doubtful whether such raids could be carried out without heavy losses.

The navy, like the army, zealously cherishes and cultivates the spirit of exalted nationalism that is practically a religion in Japan. The idea that death is always to be preferred to surrender is inculcated by recalling the memory of the transport *Kinshu Maru,* which, when placed in a hopeless position during the Russo-Japanese War, refused all proposals to surrender and went down with all on board, officers and men giving three last *banzais* for the Emperor.[3]

The navy was originally modeled along British lines. The uniform resembles somewhat the British, and English is the foreign language most generally spoken by naval officers,

[2] Denlinger and Gary, *op. cit.,* p. 191.
[3] The word *banzai,* repeated three times, is the customary Japanese cheer.

whereas their colleagues in the army are more likely to know
German or Russian.   The navy has, however, passed out of
the stage of tutelage and has developed a number of original
features.   A Japanese warship carries an unusually large
complement of officers, with the idea of having plenty of
substitutes to step into the places of those who may be killed
in action.   The quarters of the sailors, while kept scrupu-
lously clean, are cramped, by Western standards, and this
saving on space makes it possible to use thicker armor plate
and to crowd in a maximum number of guns.

Although conscription prevails for the navy, as for the
army, a large proportion of the sailors are volunteers, many
of them recruited from the weather-beaten fishermen.
The Japanese naval officer takes his work with almost fanatical seriousness and often shows a certain pride in having no
interests outside of his profession.

Secrecy is cherished in the navy as in the army, and no
details of new warship construction have been available since
the termination of the Washington Naval Limitation Treaty
at the end of 1936.   A so-called Third Replenishment programme, however, was approved by the Diet in 1937.   It
provides for a total expenditure of 1,200,000,000 yen
(nominally about 340,000,000 dollars, although the purchasing power of the yen, except in the case of imported material,
is much higher than its cash equivalent in American money),
of which 800,000,000 yen are for new construction.   The
programme is believed to call for four battleships of approximately 40,000 tons, mounting sixteen-inch guns (Japan
in 1938 declined American, British, and French proposals
to exchange information about the size of projected battleships), two aircraft carriers, and a number of cruisers,
destroyers, submarines, and naval aircraft.

Probably the same judgment would hold good for the Japanese Navy as for the Army.   Japan's armed forces are not strong enough, nor will they be in any predictable future, to attack the United States or the American continent with any prospect of success.   But they are strong enough to make any attempt of America or Great Britain to stop Japan in China a difficult and uncertain enterprise.   Combined action by the British and American navies could probably defeat Japan by a process of long-range blockade and attrition; but this would almost certainly be a matter of several years. And it would demand a condition which is conspicuously not realized at the present time: absence of preoccupations in other parts of the globe.

This brings one to a consideration of the very important international aspects of Japan's drive for empire.   Europe's disunity has always been Japan's opportunity.   It was no accident that the famous Twenty-one Demands, one of Japan's first blueprints of hegemony in China, were drawn up in 1915, when the European powers were absorbed in the World War.   Japan was not strong enough at that time, especially when the World War ended with America relatively fresh and powerfully armed, to harvest the fruits of this ultimatum.   Still it extracted some grains from the World War: a share of the German island possessions, a reversion of Germany's economic position in Tsingtao, access to the markets of nonbelligerent countries that were starved for the goods which powers engaged in war production could not supply.

Japanese nationalists were never enthusiastic about the stabilization of the Pacific area which was established by the Washington agreements of 1922, the Nine-Power Treaty, the Naval Limitation Treaty, and the related documents.

Most Japanese, with the exception of a few Westernized liberals, had always looked on China as their own proper exclusive preserve. They resented both the obligation to consult with other powers regarding dealings with China and the naval limitation which, as they felt, placed them in a position of inferiority in relation to the United States and Great Britain.

The Washington order for East Asia became as objectionable to Japanese nationalists as the Versailles system for Europe was to German nationalists. And Japan, not being hampered by the military disabilities of Versailles, began to tear down the Washington structure even before Germany was in a position to attack Versailles. The seizure of Manchoukuo and the denunciation of the Naval Limitation Treaty were clear indications of Japan's intention to go its own way and play a predominant rôle in the Orient.

Japan would never have gone so fast or so far in China if it had not been for the growing threat to peace in Europe. The anti-Comintern Pact grew rapidly in significance and became the trademark for a profitable league of aggression, from which Japan has thus far derived the largest visible profits. It is doubtful whether Great Britain and France have been very much weakened in Europe by the Japanese menace to their remote Oriental possessions. But they have certainly been much weaker in the face of Japan because of the necessity for concentrating all their forces in order to meet some possible deadly spring of Hitler or Mussolini in Europe. The vast Singapore base has remained without warships. French Indo-China, so far as I could judge from a recent visit, is in no position to resist a serious Japanese attack.

There has been a very obvious timing of some of Japan's

more risky moves to coincide with the periods of greatest crisis and strain in Europe. During the first fifteen months of the war Japan sent no expeditionary force to South China, despite the fact that China's largest supply of munitions was flowing in by way of Hong Kong and Canton. There were repeated air bombings of Canton, some of them very merciless; but these failed to stop for any long period of time the operation of the Canton-Hankow Railway, China's most important artery of supply.

The September crisis over Czechoslovakia offered Japan its opportunity to challenge with impunity Great Britain's preferred position in South China. A picked expeditionary force, in which some of the best Guards regiments were included, was fitted out with Canton as the objective. The Munich settlement occurred before the expedition set out; but its terms and the general European atmosphere convinced Japan that no outside interference need be apprehended. So the Japanese troops landed in the old pirate hide-out of Bias Bay on October 12; a lightning campaign brought them to Canton within ten days. Hong Kong was cut off from its hinterland and China was obliged to get its munitions through more roundabout and less convenient routes.

There was a similar timing in connection with the seizure of Hainan Island in February 1939. One glance at the map shows why Japanese occupation of this large island, which is about the size of Formosa, is intensely distasteful to Great Britain and France. It brings Japan within an hour's bombing range of the northern ports of Indo-China. It places Japan athwart the sea route between Singapore and Hong Kong and greatly accentuates the isolation of the latter exposed outpost of empire. The bellicose Home Minister,

Admiral Nobumasa Suetsugu, had pressed for the occupation
of Hainan as far back as the winter of 1937–1938; but the
majority of the cabinet rejected the idea for fear of subsequent political complications.

But within a year circumstances had greatly changed.
The move against Hainan was planned when Franco was
advancing on Barcelona and France, fearing an imminent
crisis in the Mediterranean, could pay little attention to what
was happening in China seas. Japan reckoned correctly that
it had nothing to fear but feeble Chinese resistance in seizing
an island that was both a most valuable strategic asset and
an economic prize. Hainan has been neglected and undeveloped; but Japan, over a period of years, may make
of it a second Formosa, a storehouse of tropical and sub-
tropical products.

Japan remained relatively passive during the first weeks
of the new crisis generated by Hitler's eastward march and
the efforts of Great Britain to forge a wall of resistance among
the East European countries. The seizure of the Spratly
Islands, a small group of coral reefs off the southeastern
coast of Indo-China, was a minor operation, although this
would certainly not have taken place if France had not been
too much concerned in Europe to assert its right of ownership over the Spratly group. Although the prize is a small
one, this move gives Japan an advanced submarine base west
of the Philippines and pushes its naval frontier much closer
to Malaya and the Dutch East Indies.

A very important bit of unpublished Japanese history during the winter of 1938–1939 and the spring of 1939 revolves
around a struggle that has unquestionably been taking place
behind the scenes over the question of transforming the anti-
Comintern Pact into a full-fledged military alliance, directed

against Great Britain and France as well as the Soviet Union. On the last day of my stay in Japan, Foreign Minister Arita, in an individual interview, categorically assured me that Japan had no intention of entering into any such alliance. He subsequently repeated this denial before the Diet.

There seems to be little doubt that Germany has put out feelers, if not formal proposals, looking toward the conclusion of such an alliance. And to Japanese extremists, especially in the naval camp, the temptation of swooping down on the rich and weakly defended British, French, and Dutch possessions in Southeastern Asia is very great. The moderates, however (there still are moderates in Japan, although the word must be used in a relative sense), are opposed to committing the Island Empire to unconditional participation in a European war. One of their strongest arguments is Japan's economic dependence on the United States and the British Empire. There is still sufficient freedom of the press for a spokesman of this viewpoint, Mr. T. Watanabe, formerly president of the Tokyo Chamber of Commerce and Industry, to publish the following statement in a Japanese magazine: —

Germany and Italy take only 1.5 per cent of our exports; America and the British Empire 50 per cent. From a business standpoint it is necessary and beneficial for us to maintain friendship with the democratic countries. Although it is inevitable that some third powers should be opposed to our action on the continent, the utmost caution must be employed to avoid unnecessary conflicts with them, especially with those which maintain intimate economic relations with us.

The decisive trial of strength between Japan's superimperialists and relative moderates will perhaps only occur if and when a major war breaks out in Europe. The former may be expected to urge active participation on the side of Germany and Italy, a clean sweep of the foreign concessions in China and of the colonial possessions of the Western powers. The oil in the Dutch East Indies would be an especially attractive prize, although the Dutch are reported to have prepared to destroy the wells by dynamite and fire in the event of a Japanese attack. The moderates will advocate a policy of caution, of aloofness in a European war which in any case, and however it may turn out, may be expected to advance Japan's cause in the Orient by weakening and exhausting its rivals.

American action may conceivably play a considerable part in influencing the issue of this internal dispute in Japan. The desirability, from a military and economic standpoint, of mantaining normal trade relations with the United States is the trump card of the opponents of unreserved alliance with Germany and Italy.

This trump card would be invalidated if the advocates of sanctions against Japan in America should have their way in stopping American purchases of Japanese goods and placing an embargo on American sales of raw materials to Japan. The consequences of such action might well be much more explosive than the sponsors of what is rather euphemistically called "nonparticipation in Japanese aggression" seem to realize. Japan has staked so much on its continental campaign that it is most improbable that it could be forced to retreat by mere economic pressure. If the American sanctions were ineffective they would have no practical value, apart from irritating Japan and perhaps causing more unpleasant "incidents" affecting American lives and property in China. If the sanctions were effective in the sense of causing serious stringency of raw materials, the chances are, I think, overwhelming that Japan, rather than back down under foreign pressure, would strike out for the raw materials of the neighboring British, French, and Dutch colonies. The last restraining influence would be withdrawn.

It is perhaps unreasonable to expect the average American who is indignant about Japanese aggression in China and wants to do something about it to foresee these possible consequences of an American economic war against Japan. There is reason to believe, however, that experienced American diplomatic observers of the Far Eastern scene are not oblivious of these considerations. Uncertainty as to Japan's reaction to sanctions, combined with the absence of any indication of a desire on the part of the American people to become involved in a Far Eastern war, has prevented American policy from being as anti-Japanese as the emotional temper of the country might have dictated.

Not that American-Japanese relations have been untroubled by the undeclared war in China. The American Embassy in Tokyo has been very busily employed in presenting representations about damage to American property, mostly belonging to foreign missions, as a result of Japanese air raids; about occupation and looting of American-owned houses; about withholding of permits to Americans to return to their homes in zones of military occupation.

The strongest American representations to Japan (apart from the notes which followed the sinking of the *Panay*) were contained in a note on the open-door issue which was dispatched to Tokyo on October 6, 1938. This note listed a considerable number of alleged Japanese discriminations against American trade, shipping, and economic interests in Manchoukuo and the occupied parts of China, and ended with the presentation of the following three demands: —

1. The discontinuance of discriminatory exchange control and of other measures imposed in areas in China under Japanese control which operate either directly or indirectly to discriminate against American trade and enterprise.

2. The discontinuance of any monopoly or of any preference which would deprive American nationals of the right of undertaking any legitimate trade or industry in China or of any arrangement which might purport to establish in favor of Japanese interests any general superiority of rights with regard to commercial or economic development in any region of China.

3. The discontinuance of interference by Japanese authorities in China with American property and other rights, including such forms of interference as censorship of American mail and telegrams and restriction upon American trade and shipping.

The implications of this note were far-reaching. Some of its requests could be and probably will be met as military operations subside. But the demands about discontinuance of exchange control and monopoly strike at the bases of Japanese policy in Manchoukuo and in occupied China. It is conceivable that the note, dispatched a few days after the Munich settlement, was based on a mistakenly optimistic interpretation of that event and on the expectation that active coöperation in the Orient might be expected from other powers with interests similar to those of the United States.

The Japanese reply was delayed for several weeks. During this time the Japanese military position became stronger with the capture of Hankow and Canton. When it was delivered on November 18 the reply proved to be evasive without being positively truculent. Some statements of fact in the American note were contested; there were assurances of theoretical respect for American rights, but there was no intimation of any intention to retreat from the economic positions which had been conquered in China.   Perhaps the most significant passage in the Japanese note was worded as follows: —

Any attempt to apply to the conditions of to-day and to-morrow inapplicable ideas and principles of the past would neither contribute toward the establishment of a real peace in East Asia nor solve the immediate issues.

In December the Japanese position was further elaborated by Foreign Minister Arita, who declared that the economic activities of other powers in East Asia "should be subject to certain restrictions dictated by the requirements of the national defense and economic security of the countries grouped under the new order." (This phrase "new order," which a foreign critic once characterized as really "new disorder," is frequently used by Japanese to describe the political and economic bloc of Japan, Manchoukuo, and China.)

Mr. Arita tried to soften this intimation of at least a partial closing of the open door by adding that "even if these restrictions are put in force there will remain vast fields of commercial and economic activity open to the people of other powers."   Both he and other Japanese have made full use of the argument that in 1937 American sales to Manchuria, never very large, were almost twice as great as in 1930, the last year that Manchuria was under Chinese sovereignty. The American State Department recently issued a statement to the effect that these increased sales were the result of swollen war trade and that the case against Japanese restrictions and discrimination was as strong as ever.   Japan maintains that this war trade could easily be transformed into reconstruction trade if American credits could be obtained.

About the end of 1938 the American Government dispatched another note to Tokyo on the open-door question, rejecting a number of points in the Japanese reply, reserving all rights for the future, but significantly abstaining from any intimation of economic reprisals.   There the matter remained for some time, the increasing gravity of the situation in Europe diverting attention from the Far East for the time being.   While not taking any direct economic action against Japan, America inflicted an indirect reprisal by extending an essentially political credit of $25,000,000 to the Chinese Nationalist Government in December 1938.   This credit, it is understood, will be largely used for the purchase of trucks and gasoline.   As might have been expected, the credit was greeted with satisfaction in China and with repressed exasperation in Japan.

Eager to keep America passive, the Japanese Government has exercised a restraining influence on press comments about America which it has not cared to exercise in the case of Great Britain, France, and the Soviet Union.   So, while the latter countries are not infrequently roundly abused for thwarting what Japanese euphemistically call their country's "most fair and just purposes in East Asia," the average Japanese is scarcely conscious of the bitterness of anti-Japanese feeling in America.

One other means of bringing pressure on Japan, the proposal to build a huge naval base at Guam, American-owned island in the western Pacific located only 1353 miles from Yokohama, is hanging fire at the moment of writing.   The House of Representatives deleted an item of $5,000,000 for harbor improvements and airplane facilities at Guam from the naval air base bill, although this item may be passed as part of some rivers and harbors legislation.   This $5,000,000 would be only a very thin opening wedge for the building up of Guam as a huge naval base. The cost of such a project would run into hundreds of millions of dollars and would only be justified if America had made up its mind to play a vigorous aggressive rôle in the Orient. Even on this assumption the utility of sinking vast sums into Guam is questioned in some naval circles, as the island is surrounded by Japanese mandated islands and would be exposed to fierce air attack and invested by submarines from the moment when hostilities broke out.

Great Britain has suffered much more than America from the Japanese invasion of China. The prolonged closing of the Yangtze River to non-Japanese shipping has affected British rather than American interests, since two British coastal and river steamship lines had regularly operated freight and passenger service on the Yangtze, whereas there are no American shipping lines and very few American boats on the river. The Japanese military occupation of the Hongkew and Yangtzepoo sections of Shanghai affects primarily British mills, factories, and wharves. This is also true of the refusal to pay interest on the bonds of the Chinese railways, which are in the hands of the Japanese Army, because the great majority of the bondholders are British. It is again British shipping that sustains most injury from the discriminations which the Japanese have introduced at Tsingtao, Chefoo, and other North China ports.

Faced with far nearer and more imminent dangers in the North Sea and the Mediterranean, however, Great Britain has not gone beyond notes of protest to Japan, supplemented by a modest amount of economic aid to China. British capital is interested in the projected new railway between Burma and Yunnan Province; British traders hope to make up on the Irrawaddy some of their losses on the Yangtze and to open up a new outlet through which the exports of the Chinese interior can flow outside of Japanese-controlled territory. Although Great Britain has sustained more provocation and more material loss than the United States, it has been still less able to consider using the weapon of sanctions because it has far more hostages, in the shape of Oriental colonial possessions, which would be the first objective of a Japanese Navy released from inhibitions.

France, a minor power in China, has diplomatically followed the American and British lead as regards protests and representations. Its main concern has been the security of Indo-China. Especially after the fall of Hong Kong, the Japanese press often attacked France for permitting munitions to reach China through Indo-China. Actually the railway between Hanoi and Kunming seems to have been closed to munitions shipments; but small quantities of arms have filtered into China across the Kwangsi border. The French have not realized their hope that by closing the railway to munitions shipments Japan would be placated to the point of being willing to leave Hainan unoccupied.

The Soviet Union, the sole power which is able to threaten Japan on land, has caused the Island Empire more concern than any other foreign country during the war in China. As a prominent Japanese diplomat once remarked to me, "We have been fighting China with our left hand and holding off the Soviet Union with our right"; and it is no secret that Japan's best troops and best war material have been kept in Manchoukuo.

Relations between Japan and the Soviet Union reached the greatest point of strain during the Changkufeng fighting, which has already been described. A serious new deadlock was threatened because of the Soviet insistence on modifying to Japan's disadvantage the terms of the annual fisheries convention. A naval Changkufeng seemed to loom up on the horizon. But after long haggling and delay a fisheries convention was signed in the spring of 1939, each side withdrawing some of its demands.

It has never been likely that the annual fisheries squabble would be a cause of Soviet-Japanese war; the issues at stake are not sufficiently important. On the other hand, a dispute on this question, as on many others, might serve as a pretext for a war which one side had determined to precipitate.

Soviet policy since the summer of 1937 has been to help China as much as possible without running any real risk of war. Several hundred airplanes, accompanied by pilots and instructors, have been flown into China; and trucks with munitions and other supplies have rumbled over the rough Red route from Chinese Turkestan. But Soviet aid has not assumed such proportions as would provoke a Japanese attack on Siberia. It has been rather sporadic in character, cut down when some action of the Chinese Government has displeased Moscow, increased when China has made a new gesture of resistance. The Soviet reckoning is that any aid to China which prolongs the war and produces a further drain on Japan's military and economic resources is desirable cheap insurance.

In the present "smash and grab" age of international relations Japan's future moves on the checkerboard of East Asia cannot be forecast with absolute certainty. It seems almost certain, however, that its actions will be closely coordinated with those of the European dictators, although Tokyo will not renounce all freedom of action in favor of Berlin or Rome. If Hitler should come into collision with the Soviet Union there is a 90 per cent probability that

Japan would throw all its military weight into an offensive against Eastern Siberia, even at the price of temporarily relinquishing some of its acquisitions in China.

If the threatened war is between the Berlin-Rome axis and the Western democracies, with Stalin in the rôle of the *tertius gaudens*, it will be touch and go whether Japan will strike immediately against British, French, and Dutch possessions in Southeastern Asia, as its extremists would desire, or sit on the fence, consolidating its position in China and blackmailing the democracies for economic, if not territorial, concessions as the price of nonparticipation — the policy which would be favored by its moderates.

Is Japan strong enough, in every sense, to rule East Asia? I put the question in this way because I think East Asia, from Vladivostok to Singapore and Batavia, represents the maximum which Japan could hope to swallow in any predictable future, although there are anti-British Japanese nationalists who envisage the Rising Sun flag flying over India and Australia and Japan as the leader of the entire Asiatic continent.

In some respects Japan is handicapped by its late appearance on the imperial stage. Mr. Shiratori, one of the cleverest, frankest, and most indiscreet of its diplomats, once remarked that if Great Britain could hold India with seventy thousand British troops, Japan could certainly, after a reasonable lapse of time, hold China with two hundred thousand. This comparison, however, breaks down at several points. The British conquest of India was gradual and was facilitated by antagonisms of race, caste, and religion which do not exist, on anything like the same scale, in China. Moreover, and this is perhaps even more important, it was carried out at a time when the conception of nationality was very imperfectly developed. The world-wide sweep of nationalism which is shaking the old British and French empires is a very serious obstacle to the establishment of a new Japanese Empire.

On the other hand, modern imperialists have certain mechanical advantages — airplanes and tanks and armored cars and far more effective lethal weapons — which were denied to their predecessors of the eighteenth and nineteenth centuries. Had it been undertaken a century ago, the conquest of Ethiopia would have required many years, that of Albania, at the least, many months. Against China's enhanced nationalist spirit one must, if one wishes to view the situation in true perspective, weigh Japan's increased striking power.

It is sometimes assumed that Japan must fail in China for lack of resources with which to exploit its victory. Japan's financial and economic difficulties have been pointed out in the previous chapter. These are all the more serious because the country is poor in accumulated wealth, thanks to its late appearance on the capitalist stage and its poverty in natural resources. It is obvious that Japan is handicapped in exploiting China because such a large part of its limited reserves of capital must be earmarked for war purposes. And by all the standards of Victorian economics danger signals are flying at many points on Japan's financial horizon.

But Victorian economists never envisaged the possibilities of the totalitarian state. This is an age when the power of gold is being more and more defiantly challenged by the power of steel. Countries which are poor in financial reserves and natural resources are pursuing the policy of investing the greatest part of their slender capital in armaments and then taking what they want at the point of the airplane and the tank.

Many economists predicted that the first Soviet Five-Year Plan would end in a fiasco because of inability to attract foreign capital.   It ended in tragedy, but not in fiasco.   The economic reckoning that the scope and tempo of industrialization under the Plan exceeded Russia's capacity to bear was sound.   What was left out of account was the ability of the Soviet Government to break the resistance of recalcitrant peasants by leaving several millions of them to starve, and the amount of unpaid serf labor on big industrial projects which could be extracted from kulaks and other luckless victims of the political police.

There were similar prophecies of failure for Germany's industrial rearmament.   Here again there was an inability to appreciate how much labor for a given end can be exacted by a despotic government through a mixture of terrorism, propaganda, and organized regimentation.   So I should hesitate to write off Japan's adventure in China as an inevitable defeat because of shortage of capital.   This shortage of capital is real and it will delay and obstruct the realization of some of the grandiose electrical power and irrigation projects which would require a good deal of imported material.   But the combination of the Japanese organizing capacity, already manifested in Korea, Formosa, and Manchoukuo, with the cheap labor of the Chinese who live in the occupied areas and must somehow earn their bowls of rice may achieve more than is anticipated.[4]

If one rules out, for the moment, the element of international complications and assumes that Japan will have a

[4] Loose estimates of "tens of millions" of refugees from the Japanese occupied areas are, I think, exaggerated.   Even in the Nanking area, where the war devastation was great, there has been a remarkable maintenance of the planted area.   And there are many country districts where the Japanese soldiers have not even appeared.

free hand in China it seems quite possible that expansion on the continent may, in a sense, prove to be Japan's economic equivalent for the WPA. It will be expensive; deficits will mount up; deprivations will be imposed on the Japanese population. But labor and capital will remain fully employed and dividends may begin to come in unless the guerrilla warfare is more prolonged and more efficient than Japanese expect. And restless spirits among the young officers who would otherwise be engaging in "blood brotherhood" plots and periodically assassinating cabinet ministers will find their energies occupied on the new frontiers of the continental empire.

Insofar as the present struggle remains merely a Sino-Japanese war I am inclined to believe that it will end either in a compromise peace which will give Japan much, if not all, of what it wants, or in an undeclared peace of exhaustion, following the undeclared war and leading to the establishment of an unrecognized frontier between the parts of China which Japan can hold and the regions of the interior where the nationalist régime will carry on.

Probably the key to the question of whether Japan will win or lose in its drive for empire is to be found in the international situation. If there should be a miraculous clearing of the European skies or if the democracies should win a quick victory over the totalitarian powers, Japan would be isolated, exposed to strong pressure, and probably forced to choose between the alternatives of retreating or fighting under unfavorable conditions. Europe in a state of constant tension which never quite develops into a big war means that Japan will, for the immediate future, concentrate its energies on consolidation in China.

Japan's opportunity lies either in a swift victory of the

Fascist states, in which it would hasten to claim its share of the spoils, or in a European war comparable with the last one in duration and intensity, a war in which there would be no real victors, in which every country at the end would be in a state of moral and physical exhaustion. Assuming that Japan avoided active participation in such a war, as it would probably endeavor to do, it might be expected to emerge relatively fresher and stronger than any European power and able to vindicate its Far Eastern ambitions against countries which would probably be in little mood to undertake new martial adventures.

So Japan's prospects as a great imperial power depend very largely on its skill in exploiting Europe's feuds without allowing itself to be drawn into them so deeply that it might share the general process of post-war exhaustion and collapse. It is also most important for Japan to keep America passive, because the immense weight of American wealth and resources, even though it might not be possible to bring this to bear immediately in the Far East, would wear Japan down over a long period of years.

If Europe, as seems only too possible, has passed the zenith of its civilization and is doomed to enter by war into a state of darkness and decline, there are, I think, only two potential indirect beneficiaries of this development. These are Japan and the Soviet Union, one Asiatic, the other at least semi-Asiatic. Their opportunity to benefit is based on the assumption that both remain aloof from the more destructive phases of the war and allow the nations of Western and Central Europe to destroy each other. The sequel of the decline and fall of modern European civilization may be the emergence of the greatest Oriental empire since the days of Tamerlane and Kublai Khan.

INDEX

INDEX

INDEX

Shipping, remarkable advance of Japanese, 211–215

Shirasaki, K., 198*n.*, 216*n.*

Shiratori, Toshio, 440; quoted, 409

Shrines, Japanese, 277–280

Siam, armament race and, 25; its Japanese imports, 167; centre of international rivalry, 191; Britain's power in, 191, 192; Japanese activity in, 191–193; acutely nationalistic, 193

Siberia, Japanese withdrawal from, 64

Simon, Sir John, fails to support Stimson, 138, 140

Singapore, great British naval base, 26, 154–156, 170, 171, 187, 189, 428; and proposed Kra Canal, 191, 192

Sino-Japanese War, inevitability of, 359, 360; background of, 360–362; the Lukowkiao Bridge clash, 362, 363; Japanese drive against Peking, 363; massacre in East Hopei, 364; the Tientsin revolt, 364, 365; the war in Shanghai, 365–367; capture of Nanking, 368, 369; terms of peace offer, 369; fall of Hankow, 369, 373, 374; sinking of *Panay*, 369, 370; the war in North China, 370–372; likely to be prolonged struggle, 373–378; guerrillas a factor in, 378–381; summary of, 385–388; three possible outcomes of, 408–413; key to outcome in international situation, 443, 444

Smedley, Agnes, 123*n.*

Smuggling, orgy of, in China, 89–93

Snow, Edgar, 118*n.*

Soong, Meiling, 112

Soong, T. V., 127, 376

South Manchuria Railway, agent of Japanese economic penetration, 45, 46; employing mainly Japanese, 49

South Seas, Japan's advance on, 166, 167, 194, 195

Soviet Union. *See* Russia

Spirit of Japanese Industry (Fujihara), 245, 246

Sports, in Japan, 305

Spratly Islands, Japanese occupation of, 424, 430

Stalin, 440; his position on Mongolian situation, 63; dogmatism of, 109; his aims in Sino-Japanese War, 384

Steel, shortage of, in Japan, 330, 333

Stein, Guenther, 217*n.*

Stimson, Henry L., and Far Eastern crisis of 1932, 137, 138, 140

Straits Times, 189

Suetsugu, Admiral Nobumasa, as Home Minister, 401, 430

Sugar, Formosan trade in, 84, 172; Philippine trade in, 180, 181

Suhara, Dr. T., his high-speed camera, 324

Suiyuan, primitive region, 98*n.*

Sumitomo, House of, its great power, 211, 213, 227

Sun Fo, reveals Soviet offer of assistance to China, 361*n.*

Sun Yat-sen, Dr., leader of Chinese nationalism, 80

Sun Yat-sen, Mme., 376; believes war with Japan inevitable, 129

Sung Che-yuan, Gen., ruler in

Hopei, 96; unable to keep promises, 363

Surabaya, new air base at, 170

Susumu Nippon, 178 and *n.*

Suzuki, J., his micro-printing process, 324

Suzuki, Admiral Kentaro, wounded in Feb. 1936 revolt, 251, 252, 259

Symbolism, in Japanese life, 301–303

TACHIBANA, K., imprisoned for part in revolt, 261*n.*; philosophy of, 354

Taiping Rebellion, 119

Taiwan. *See* Formosa

Taiwan Electric Power Co., 174

Takahashi, Kamekichi, estimates Japan's exports, 204

Takahashi, Korekiyo, victim of Feb. 1936 outbreak, 244, 250, 258; his influence on budget, 329

Takahashi, Admiral Sankichi, and Japan's advance to south, 167, 168

Takeuchi, Tatsuji, quoted, 19

Tanaka, Gen. K., 238

Tangku Truce, 91

Taxes, a grievance of country versus city, 343

Teh, Prince, Mongol nationalist leader, 370

Terada, Lieut. Col., a specialist in Mongolian question, 61

Terauchi, Gen. Count Hisaichi, forces resignation of Hirota Cabinet, 226, 264

Textiles, American-Japanese trade in, 159; average price of Japanese, 199, 200; advantage to Japanese, 202, 203

Things Japanese (Chamberlain), 197*n.*, 291, 292

Tientsin, Japanese raid censorship office at, 89; revolt at, 364, 365

Times, London, 187

Ting, Dr. V. K., predicts course of war, 132

Tohoku, heart of rural crisis, 344–349

Tokyo, revolt of Feb. 1936 in, 247–263; contrast of old and new in, 292–294

Tokyo Maru, 215

Toyama, Mitsuru, 264

Toyo mill, Osaka, 206, 207

Trade, of Great Britain, 11, 12, 140, 199, 200, 202, 203; Japanese, 11, 12, 159, 166, 167, 197–201, 218–224, 319–326; German, 53, 54; Formosan, 84, 172; American, 141–145, 159, 432–436; of Dutch East Indies, 167, 218, 219; Philippine, 167, 180, 181

Trade-unionism, in Japan, 235, 236

Trans-Siberian Railway, double tracking of, 67, 70

Tseng Yang-fu, mayor of Canton, 111, 112

Twenty-one Demands, of Japan, 85–87; timing of, 427

Tydings-McDuffie Act, charter of Philippine independence, 152

UCHIDA, COUNT, 264

Ueda, Gen. Kenkichi, his power in Manchoukuo, 28

Ugaki, Gen. Kazushige, disapproved by army leaders, 226, 254,